T0301755

The Competitiveness of Nations 3

Emerging Technologies in the Fourth Industrial Revolution

The Competitiveness of Nations: Theory and Practice

(Print) ISSN: 2810-983X
(Online) ISSN: 2810-9848

Series Editors: Dong-sung Cho *(The Institute for Industrial Policy Studies, South Korea and Seoul National University, South Korea)* Hwy-chang Moon *(The Institute for Policy & Strategy on National Competitiveness, South Korea and Seoul National University, South Korea)*

Published:

The Competitiveness of Nations 3: Emerging Technologies in the Fourth Industrial Revolution
      by Dong-sung Cho and Hwy-chang Moon

The Competitiveness of Nations 2: Government Policies and Business Strategies for Environmental, Social, and Governance (ESG)
      by Dong-sung Cho and Hwy-chang Moon

The Competitiveness of Nations 1: Navigating the US–China Trade War and the COVID-19 Global Pandemic
      by Dong-sung Cho and Hwy-chang Moon

The Competitiveness of Nations: Theory and Practice

The Competitiveness of Nations 3

Emerging Technologies in the Fourth Industrial Revolution

Dong-sung Cho

The Institute for Industrial Policy Studies, South Korea
Seoul National University, South Korea

Hwy-chang Moon

The Institute for Policy & Strategy on National Competitiveness, South Korea
Seoul National University, South Korea

World Scientific

NEW JERSEY · LONDON · SINGAPORE · BEIJING · SHANGHAI · HONG KONG · TAIPEI · CHENNAI · TOKYO

Published by

World Scientific Publishing Co. Pte. Ltd.

5 Toh Tuck Link, Singapore 596224

USA office: 27 Warren Street, Suite 401-402, Hackensack, NJ 07601

UK office: 57 Shelton Street, Covent Garden, London WC2H 9HE

Library of Congress Cataloging-in-Publication Data

Names: Cho, Tong-sŏng, author. | Mun, Hwi-ch'ang, author.
Title: The competitiveness of nations 3 : emerging technologies in the fourth industrial revolution /
    Dong-sung Cho, The Institute for Industrial Policy Studies, South Korea,
    Seoul National University, South Korea, Hwy-chang Moon, The Institute for Policy &
    Strategy on National Competitiveness, South Korea, Seoul National University, South Korea.
Description: New Jersey : World Scientific [2024] | Series: The competitiveness of nations:
    theory and practice, 2810-983X | Includes bibliographical references and index.
Identifiers: LCCN 2023057833 | ISBN 9789811282225 (hardcover) |
    ISBN 9789811282232 (ebook) | ISBN 9789811282249 (ebook other)
Subjects: LCSH: Competition, International. | Industry 4.0.
Classification: LCC HF1414 .C56 2024 | DDC 338.6/048--dc23/eng/20240104
LC record available at https://lccn.loc.gov/2023057833

British Library Cataloguing-in-Publication Data
A catalogue record for this book is available from the British Library.

For any available supplementary material, please visit
https://www.worldscientific.com/worldscibooks/10.1142/13566#t=suppl

Desk Editors: Aanand Jayaraman/Yulin Jiang

Typeset by Stallion Press
Email: enquiries@stallionpress.com

Printed in Singapore

About the Authors

Dong-sung Cho is Professor Emeritus and former Dean of the College of Business Administration at Seoul National University. He additionally held the position of President at Incheon National University. After he received a doctoral degree from Harvard Business School (HBS) in 1977, he worked at Boston Consulting Group in Tokyo and Gulf Oil Corporation in Pittsburgh before joining Seoul National University. He has been a visiting professor at Harvard Business School, University of Michigan, Boston University, Duke University, INSEAD, Helsinki School of Economics (currently Aalto University), University of Sydney, the University of Tokyo, and Peking University. He has published 120+ research articles in major journals, and authored and coauthored 60+ monographs such as *The General Trading Company: Concept and Strategy* (1988, Lexington Books), *Tiger Technology: The Creation of a Semiconductor Industry in East Asia* (2000, Cambridge University Press), and *The Mechanism-Based View* (2014, SEBA). He is a frequent speaker at international conferences such as the World Economic Forum, the World Knowledge Forum, and the Quacquarelli Symonds (QS) Conference. He is Chairman of the Board of Inspection at the Supreme Prosecutors' Office in the Republic of Korea and Honorary Consul General of Finland in Korea. He served as the President of Incheon National University from 2016 to 2020. He is the Second President of the Hanseatic League of Universities, which is a society of 120 plus universities from around the world. He also tops the list of "Representative Management Gurus" in Korea.

Hwy-chang Moon (PhD from University of Washington) is Professor Emeritus and former Dean in the Graduate School of International Studies at Seoul National University. Professor Moon currently serves as the President of aSSIST University in Seoul, Korea, a consultant to the United Nations Conference on Trade and Development (UNCTAD), and an Honorary Ambassador of Foreign Investment Promotion for South Korea. He has been frequently invited to deliver lectures at various universities including Stockholm University and Helsinki School of Economics (currently Aalto University) in Europe, Keio University and Beijing Normal University in Asia, and The State University of New York at Stony Brook and Stanford University in the United States. Alongside this, he has conducted many consulting/research projects for multinational companies (e.g., Samsung Electronics), international organizations (e.g., UNCTAD), and governments (e.g., Korea, Malaysia, Dubai, Azerbaijan, Guangdong Province of China, and India). Professor Moon has also been invited by international newspapers and media for interviews and debates, including the *New York Times*, NHK World TV, and Reuters. He has published numerous articles and books, including *The Strategy for Korea's Economic Success* (2016, Oxford University Press) and *The Art of Strategy: Sun Tzu, Michael Porter, and Beyond* (2018, Cambridge University Press).

About the Contributors

Farzana Akter is currently working as an Assistant Professor in the Department of Business Administration at North Western University, Khulna, Bangladesh. She obtained her MBA in Small Enterprise Promotion and Training (SEPT) from Leipzig University, Germany. Her research interests include digital entrepreneurship, entrepreneurial intention, women entrepreneurship, and firm internationalization.

Gerardo del Cerro Santamaría is a Senior Research Fellow at the Future Earth Urban Knowledge-Action Network and Earth System Governance Project, a member of the European Union Expert Group in Regional Policy (Regio Program), and a recipient of a United States Fulbright Award in Urban Planning. He has served as a Program Director (Gateway Engineering) at the US National Science Foundation. Del Cerro has taught at MIT, and has been a Visiting Scholar at Columbia University, the London School of Economics, and University College London. He was Research Professor of Planning and Megaprojects at The Cooper Union for the Advancement of Science and Art in Manhattan for 23 years and is the author of over one hundred academic publications. His most recent book is *Contesting Megaprojects. Complex Impacts, Urban Disruption and the Quest for Sustainability* published by Columbia University Press in 2024.

María M. Feliciano-Cestero is a Ph.D. candidate set to graduate in May 2024, specializing in the International Commerce program at the Graduate School of Business Administration, University of Puerto Rico, Río

Piedras Campus. She holds a Master of Arts in Education (M.A. Ed.) with a concentration in Mathematics Education from the Inter-American University of Puerto Rico, Metropolitan Campus, and a Bachelor of Science (B.S.) with a focus on Pure Mathematics from the Inter-American University of Puerto Rico, San Germán Campus. With a rich academic background, she boasts over 15 years of teaching experience and a versatile professional portfolio. Her expertise extends beyond the classroom, encompassing roles as an information and data analyst, administrative assistant, teaching and research assistant, as well as a facilitator and coach for educational workshops. Furthermore, she serves as a peer reviewer for various esteemed journals, contributing her insights on topics such as the impact of emerging technologies and digital transformation on economic development, employment, and business.

Minji Hong is a researcher at the Institute for Policy and Strategy on National Competitiveness (IPSNC) based in Seoul, South Korea. Currently, she is working on global competitiveness research, with a focus on bridging Asian and Western perspectives. She has co-authored book chapters and research articles in the fields of international affairs and business strategies. Her research interests include policy studies, economic development, international relations, business strategy, and national competitiveness.

Mohammad Awal Hossen is currently working as an Assistant Professor in the Department of Management at Jashore University of Science and Technology, Bangladesh. He obtained his Master of Public Management (MPM) from the KDI School of Public Policy and Management, South Korea. His research interests include entrepreneurship in emerging countries, the entrepreneurial ecosystem, and the institutional framework for internationalization.

Dilong Huang serves as a researcher at the Institute for Policy and Strategy on National Competitiveness (IPSNC) situated in Seoul, South Korea. He has achieved a Master's degree in International Commerce from the Graduate School of International Studies (GSIS) at Seoul National University. He holds a Bachelor's degree in Korean Language and Literature from Nanjing University in China and has previously participated as an exchange student at Korea University under the auspices of the Korean Government Scholarship Program. At present, he is furthering his academic pursuits through a dual-degree PhD program, jointly administered by aSSIST University and Franklin University Switzerland, with a specialization in Business Administration. His primary research domains encompass National Competitiveness, Business Strategy, and Foreign Direct Investment.

John Jackson Iwata is a professional in teachers' education and librarianship. He possesses both a Bachelor of Education, and Master of Arts from the University of Dar es Salaam, Tanzania; as well as a PhD from the University of KwaZulu-Natal, South Africa. Besides lecturing and managing library collection, Mr. Iwata has since 2010 assumed a number of leadership roles including Periodicals Librarian, Chairperson of the Steering Committee for establishing Co-operative Archives, Deputy Director, and the Director of Co-operative Library and Archives at Moshi Co-operative University. Also, he has been involved as a team leader in preparing information sciences' training programs and some of the University's legal documents. During his postdoctoral studies at the University KwaZulu-Natal, Mr. Iwata participated in the University Curriculum Transformation Project (UCDP), specifically on the decolonization and transformation of university education in South Africa. His research areas focus on information literacy, curriculum development, and management of indigenous knowledge.

Ashish Kumar has been a Principal Research Scientist in the Health Services & Systems Research at Duke-NUS Medical School since January 2021. Prior to this, he was Principal Consultant, Economics and Operations at Bell Labs Consulting (part of Nokia Group, where he worked for a total of 21 years). He has led consulting projects in more than 10 countries and has served as research lead for two health systems' research projects. He has co-authored a book and several research publications. His first two degrees are in industrial engineering and his PhD in management is from IIT Delhi. He is interested in applying systems thinking in health.

Sean Shao Wei Lam has a PhD and a Master's in Industrial and Systems Engineering, Operations and Business Analytics, from the National University of Singapore. He is currently the Head of Data Science in the SingHealth Duke-NUS Academic Medical Centre, overseeing a team of data scientists for the enhancement of patient care and outcomes through health services research. Sean is also an Assistant Professor at the Signature Programme in Health Services and Systems Research, Duke-NUS. He has more than 20 international publications and has won numerous local and international awards.

Laurence Liew is the Director for AI Innovation at AI Singapore and a serial technopreneur with extensive experience in high performance computing (HPC), Cloud, and artificial intelligence (AI). He has built and operated several pioneering platforms and solutions in these domains and led teams that IBM and Microsoft acquired. He is also Singapore's representative at the Global Partnership in AI (GPAI) and the Co-Chair of the Innovation and Commercialization Working Group. He graduated from NUS with a First Class Honors in Engineering and a Master's in Knowledge Engineering.

Arkadiusz Mironko is an Associate Professor of Management and Entrepreneurship at Indiana University East. Previously, he worked at the Rotterdam School of Management Erasmus University in the Netherlands, and the Anderson Graduate School of Management at the University of California, Riverside. His research interests are in global business strategy, global competition, and knowledge creation and transfer through foreign direct investments (FDI) and research and development (R&D). Mironko is the author of the book *Determinants of FDI Flows within Emerging Economies* (2014), and several other publications. He teaches courses in global competition, business strategy, entrepreneurship, and leadership.

S. M. Misbauddin is currently working as an Assistant Professor in the Department of Management at Jashore University of Science and Technology, Bangladesh. He obtained his MBA in SEPT from Leipzig University, Germany. His research areas include business ecosystems, digital transformation of business, internationalization of business, effectuation, and social entrepreneurship.

Kirankumar S. Momaya is a Chair Professor, Competitiveness with SJMSOM, IIT Bombay. He has authored or co-authored more than 65 journal papers. He was elected President of the leading professional society the Global Institute of Flexible Systems Management (GIFT) for the period 2018–2019. He has undertaken visiting professor assignments in Japan, and published in leading Business, Management, and Accounting (BMA) journals from Asia such as *IIMB Management Review*, *Journal of Flexible Systems Management (JFSM)*, *Vikalpa*, and *Japan Society for Research Policy and Innovation Management* (Japan). Dr. Momaya is the Editor-in-Chief of the *International Journal of Global Business and Competitiveness (JGBC)*, co-published by Springer.

Md Noor Un Nabi received his PhD from Leipzig University in Germany in international business and entrepreneurship. He was a postdoctoral staff at the Centre for Area Studies (CAS) and the International SEPT Program at Leipzig University where his research area included analysis of global commodity chains. Since 2012, he has been working as a Professor in Business Administration Discipline at Khulna University in Bangladesh. He worked as a Visiting Professor at the International SEPT Competence Centre at Leipzig University in Germany. His research interests include digitalizing business models, international entrepreneurship, global value chain, upgrading Small and Medium Enterprises (SMEs), and internationalization of SMEs from developing and emerging market countries.

Mariusz Sagan is an Associate Professor at the SGH Warsaw School of Economics. He is the author and co-author of over 100 publications on regional and urban development, international business, and corporate strategies. He is an expert and practitioner in the field of economic development, especially peripheral regions, FDI, urban strategy, and entrepreneurship.

Maria Cecilia Salta-Macesar is a Consultant to the United Nations Conference on Trade and Development (UNCTAD). She has been a part of the Association of Southeast Asian Nations (ASEAN) Investment Report Team for the last 7 years. She was the Officer-in-charge of the Investment Policy Group at the ASEAN Secretariat for 1.5 years. Prior to that, she was the Senior Officer of the Group at the ASEAN Secretariat for 7 years.

Wenyan Yin is an Assistant Professor at Seoul School of Integrated Sciences and Technologies (aSSIST) and a Lecturer at the Graduate School of International Studies at Seoul National University. In addition, she serves as Consultant to UNCTAD. She has published a number of articles including those in the journals indexed by SSCI, A&HCI, and

SCOPUS. Her research areas include global value chain, foreign direct investment, international business strategy, and national competitiveness. She has also conducted many research projects related to international competitiveness and FDI for firms and governments.

Fatema Tuj Zohora earned her Master's in Business Administration (MBA) majoring in Marketing from Khulna University, Bangladesh, where she is currently working as an independent researcher. Her research interests lie within the intersection of digital entrepreneurship, marketing, and firm-level capabilities. She has published research papers regarding the application of digital technology in healthcare, and the influence of digital platform-based word-of-mouth marketing in the selection of healthcare service providers.

Acknowledgments

We would like to extend our thanks to Korea Trade-Investment Promotion Agency (KOTRA) for their continuous support for this project. With their extensive global network, we were able to reach out and gather valuable survey data from over 60 countries. We would especially like to thank our research team who spent countless hours gathering information and working on this manuscript. In particular, we express deep appreciation for Dr. Wenyan Yin, whose significant contributions, from project inception to completion, have been invaluable in guiding and improving the overall quality of this work. We would like to recognize Dilong Huang and Minji Hong for their crucial assistance in conducting extensive research, editing the manuscript, and contributing to the timely completion of this project. We would also like to further extend our thanks to Stephen Ranger for his editing with valuable comments and suggestions, which helped us improve the manuscript. Furthermore, we express our appreciation to all the authors of the invited chapters in Part III of this book. Their contributions have enriched the practical implications of this book with a focus on the special theme of emerging technologies in the Fourth Industrial Revolution. For the publication of this book, we are particularly grateful to John Stuart, Yulin Jiang, and other colleagues at World Scientific who recognized the value of this book and provided many insightful suggestions.

Contents

Introduction

Over the course of modern history, there have been three major industrial revolutions that have profoundly reshaped economies, societies, and cultures. The world is now faced with the Fourth Industrial Revolution, which is anticipated to bring about significant changes within a generation. As evidenced in the first three revolutions, *technological* innovation has consistently been at the heart of change, serving as the driving force behind industrial transformation. In the late eighteenth century, the first industrial revolution was characterized by the adoption of water and steam-powered technologies. This helped to pave the way for the transition from hand production to more mechanized-based manufacturing. The second industrial revolution, which came in the late nineteenth century, occurred with the adoption of electric power, which led to mass production. The third industrial revolution, emerging in the second half of the twentieth century, ushered in the digital age. This phase was dominated by the advancement of information and communications technologies such as electronics, telecommunications, computers, and the Internet, which drastically changed communication, commerce, and the dissemination of information.

The Fourth Industrial Revolution, which commenced in the 21st century, gained prominence after the World Economic Forum's chairman, Klaus Schwab, discussed it in his book titled *The Fourth Industrial Revolution*. What distinguishes this revolution from its predecessors is its fusion of technologies, blurring the boundaries between physical, digital, and biological realms. Consequently, unlike the past industrial revolutions, there is no singular or universally accepted definition of the technologies characterizing the Fourth Industrial Revolution. Instead, discussions often highlight a range of exemplary technologies, such as artificial intelligence (AI), robotics, the Internet of Things (IoT), three-dimensional (3D) printing, nanotechnology, and biotechnology. These are either broadly applicable or industry-specific technologies.

Despite the complexity of the technologies associated with the Fourth Industrial Revolution, there are four common characteristics shared by these emerging technologies. First, technology evolves in a nonlinear manner, undergoing significant changes at an unparalleled pace. Second, multiple technology standards can be observed in nearly every industry, as exemplified by the varied energy sources in the automotive sector. Third, these nascent technologies are increasingly interwoven across an expansive range of industries and disciplines. Lastly, they hold immense potential for success, given their relative ease of scalability both within industries and across borders.

Due to the four defining characteristics of the Fourth Industrial Revolution technologies, they may present even greater opportunities and challenges for both companies and policymakers. Much like the two sides of a coin, the innovation and integration of these groundbreaking technologies will inevitably lead to beneficial and detrimental consequences. A prime example of this dichotomy is the introduction of the artificial intelligence chatbot platform ChatGPT. While this state-of-the-art model has been hailed for its vast applicability across industries, enhancing labor efficiency and offering innovative solutions, it is not without its pitfalls. Concerns regarding the transparency of its feedback, potential biases in information processing, and ethical dilemmas surrounding privacy breaches and the displacement of the work force loom large. This has led to an increasing and urgent demand for firms to develop and integrate technologies more responsibly, and for policymakers to introduce more effective laws and policies for regulation.

The dual impacts of emerging technologies, encompassing both opportunities and threats, will not be experienced uniformly among individual firms and countries. The effects of these influences will differ based on their unique perceptions, response strategies, and capabilities. There can be two extremes of perceptions on the adoption of breakthrough technologies. The view that perceives emerging technologies as fundamentally flawed can be a perilous one, as it might deter individuals from harnessing the technological advantages. Conversely, an overly optimistic view that only focuses on the benefits can be equally hazardous, potentially paving the way for technology to replace the role of humans. We advocate for a more balanced viewpoint: to see emerging technologies as complementary to human abilities. This approach allows countries to maximize the potential of technological advancements while mitigating associated risks. Rather than allowing technologies like AI to dominate, it is crucial to recognize their strengths and limitations, and strategically allocate roles between humans and technology.

As economists such as Erik Brynjolfsson and Andrew McAfee have emphasized, industrial revolutions could yield larger inequalities. Likewise, the rapid change in technologies in the Fourth Industrial Revolution will lead to a widening technological and economic divide between developed and developing countries, as well as between firms that readily adopt new technologies and those that do not. Consequently, firms and countries that are better prepared will reap greater benefits from technological breakthroughs and are less likely to face disruption. As seen during the COVID-19 pandemic, the varying levels of digital technology adoption and infrastructure highlighted disparities. Developing countries suffered more due to lockdowns, while developed countries and their enterprises experienced less damage and even identified new growth opportunities.

While we cannot foresee what technologies will likely emerge in the future, it is essential to conduct a thorough and systematic investigation of emerging technologies, their potential impacts, and appropriate response strategies by firms, thereby becoming better prepared for the future. In this respect, following the previous two editions of Institute for Policy and Strategy (IPS) National Competitiveness Research (Cho and Moon, 2022, 2023), we chose emerging technologies in the Fourth Industrial Revolution as an underlying theme for this third edition.

As we conclude this comprehensive exploration into the emerging technologies of the Fourth Industrial Revolution and their implications for national competitiveness, we recognize the essential interplay between technology, policy, and strategy in shaping the future landscape. When technological advancements are paired with sound policy frameworks and strategic implementation by firms, they coalesce into greater value creation for both the market and society, which supports enhanced national competitiveness. The third edition delves into both the conceptual frameworks of emerging technologies in the Fourth Industrial Revolution (like ABCD technology) and diverse case studies that span national competitiveness from the micro to the macro levels. Each industrial revolution has typically given rise to a leading nation, showcasing excellence in areas like technology, economy, and society: the UK during the First Industrial Revolution and the United States in the subsequent Second and Third Revolutions. Our aspiration is for this edition to assist policymakers to achieve a linkage between technology and societal progress. In doing so, they can be better poised to navigate the challenges and opportunities of the Fourth Industrial Revolution.

Part I

IPS National Competitiveness Research (NCR) 2023

The first part of the book is composed of five chapters: "Literature on National Competitiveness and A Case Study of ChatGPT," "Conceptual Framework and Analytical Methodologies," "Highlights," "Application of MASI: The Cases of the US and China," and "Snapshot of Top 30 Economies." These chapters serve as an introduction to the analytical framework and methodology of the Institute for Policy and Strategy (IPS) National Competitiveness Research (NCR), while also evaluating the robustness and reliability of the findings.

The first chapter, titled "Literature on National Competitiveness and a Case Study of ChatGPT," lays out a foundation for the research on national competitiveness by addressing the limitations of previous studies on national competitiveness. In doing so, it addresses the necessity to introduce a new comprehensive model that can more effectively evaluate and analyze national competitiveness. In this regard, the IPS model is introduced, which accounts for the development levels and the size of nations in assessing and comparing the national competitiveness. Furthermore, this chapter verifies the usefulness of the IPS model in analyzing national competitiveness by exploring the recent literature and presenting the case study of the online chatbot platform ChatGPT. Through a comprehensive review of scholarly works and the use of a timely case study, the chapter demonstrates the practicality and effectiveness of the IPS model, thereby laying the groundwork for subsequent chapters on this research.

Chapter 2, titled "Conceptual Framework and Analytical Methodologies," presents the comprehensive methodology employed in evaluating and analyzing national competitiveness. The next chapter titled "Highlights" (Chapter 3), is a pivotal part as it unveils the results of the IPS National Competitiveness Research 2023. It summarizes the rankings of cost and differentiation strategies, presenting valuable insights to countries seeking to bolster their competitive positions. In Chapter 4, "Application of MASI: The Cases of the US and China," we conduct a comparative analysis of the two largest economies in the world: the US and China. By examining their structures of competitiveness, this chapter highlights the unique features that contribute to the strength of each economy. Furthermore, it underscores potential areas of collaboration between these economic giants, demonstrating how they can bolster their competitiveness despite their rivalry. The last chapter of Part I, titled "Snapshot of Top 30 Economies" (Chapter 5), presents a brief analysis of the key issues that have influenced the economies ranked in the top 30 of the National Competitiveness Research 2023, and thus verifies the validity of their rankings.

Chapter 1

Literature on National Competitiveness and a Case Study of ChatGPT

National competitiveness has long been a source of focus in economics with traditional scholars such as Adam Smith and David Ricardo having laid down important bases in this regard. There was though little change until 1990 when the field experienced a significant breakthrough with Michael Porter's introduction of a novel competitive theory: the Diamond Model. This model has since been adapted and expanded by subsequent scholars to construct various extended models and conduct empirical studies. This chapter evaluates how the eight determinants of the most recently extended model or the IPS model — a framework for analyzing national competitiveness — have evolved in the current era by examining the recent literature on each determinant. Furthermore, this chapter presents a case study of technological disruption brought about by ChatGPT, which is perceived as a "chance event" within the IPS model's framework. The study explores how this technology could substantially influence national competitiveness, as conceptualized by the eight factors of the IPS model. While acknowledging the potential adverse effects of technology development, this chapter primarily emphasizes the positive impact of ChatGPT. Nonetheless, to take advantage of such developments, concerted efforts from various stakeholders, including individuals, firms, and governments, are necessary.

The subsequent section begins with an outline of the historical context and the effectiveness of the IPS model in assessing national competitiveness due to its comprehensive nature. This chapter explains how the

IPS model has evolved by integrating the extensions of Porter's original Diamond Model. The IPS model serves as a fundamental framework for evaluating and measuring national competitiveness in the context of the IPS National Competitiveness Research. Later in this chapter, we elucidate how each determinant of the IPS model can contribute to the augmentation of national competitiveness, drawing upon recent studies. Finally, this chapter employs the IPS model to systematically scrutinize the impact of ChatGPT, specifically focusing on its positive implications for national competitiveness. This approach underscores the practicality of the model when it comes to systematically and comprehensively analyzing real-world cases.

Theoretical Evolution on National Competitiveness[1]

Competitiveness is, in fact, an intricate term. In an age of globalization, national competitiveness has been conceptualized and measured in many different ways (Berger, 2008; Fainshmidt *et al.*, 2016). For instance, preceding studies have utilized national export performance (Grein and Craig, 1996), national productivity (Moon *et al.*, 1998; Porter, 1990; Scott, 1985), firm-level foreign sales (Rugman *et al.*, 2012), and industry-level performance (Pajunen and Airo, 2013; Sakakibara and Porter, 2001) to measure national competitiveness. However, despite these diverse approaches, many studies on national competitiveness tend to solely focus on productivity as the primary indicator of national competitiveness (Fainshmidt *et al.*, 2016).

Porter (1990: 6) indicated that the only meaningful concept of competitiveness at the national level is national productivity. Productivity refers to the internal capability of an organization, while competitiveness refers to the relative position of an organization against its competitors. These two important concepts are often confused and used interchangeably. The relative competitive position in the international market, not just the absolute amount of productivity, is the critical element for a nation's competitiveness. Another important point in defining a nation's competitiveness is that it is more meaningful to assess a nation's competitiveness in comparison to other nations with similar comparativeness structures (Cho and Moon, 1998). In this respect, a nation's

---

[1]This section is an abstract and summary of Chapter 1 from Cho and Moon (2022).

competitiveness can be defined as a nation's relative competitive position in the international market among nations in a similar situation. In this regard, our study — IPS National Competitiveness Research — releases intra-group rankings for comparative evaluation among economies of similar levels of competitiveness and size as well as overall rankings among all countries.

Research on national competitiveness began in the early 1980s, but the theoretical background is based on many important concepts of works from traditional economists, which includes trade theories such as mercantilism, Adam Smith's absolute advantage, David Ricardo's comparative advantage, HO model by Heckscher and Ohlin, Leontief's paradox, and Vernon's product cycle. Traditional trade theorists argued that national competitiveness is a function of capital, labor, and natural resources. However, many developed countries, such as those in Western Europe and Japan, have prospered without abundant natural resources, and many resource-rich countries like those in Latin America have not experienced such a comparative level of development.

Porter (1990) argued that the traditional model, whose origins date back to Adam Smith and David Ricardo and are embedded in classical economics, is at best incomplete and at worst incorrect. He then introduced the Diamond Model in his book titled *The Competitive Advantage of Nations*, to capture the fundamental sources of national competitiveness and address the problems of traditional theories.

There are two prerequisites for a good competitiveness theory. One is that it should be comprehensive enough to capture more than one variable, such as natural resources or labor, to explain the ever-increasing complexity of the real world. The other is that the theory should be dynamic enough to properly grasp the changing nature of national competitiveness; this condition has not been effectively fulfilled by the classical theories such as absolute advantage and comparative advantage. Porter's Diamond Model satisfies both of these conditions. It consists of four comprehensive variables — factor conditions, demand conditions, related and supporting industries, and firm strategy, structure, and rivalry. In addition, Porter demonstrated that it is dynamic by arguing that national prosperity is created, not inherited. This implies that national competitiveness does not grow out of resource endowments or currency value, as traditional models suggest, but it can be created by strategic choices based on the four determinants of the Diamond Model.

Since the introduction of the Diamond Model, it has been widely used to analyze the strength of a single or a few countries to suggest ways to pursue further development (Fainshmidt *et al.*, 2016). Results from many of the studies have confirmed the validity of Porter's idea on the competitive advantage of nations and the strengths of major industries (Kharub and Sharma, 2017). Nonetheless, Porter's Diamond Model is not free from criticism.

Grant (1991) argued that most of the existing studies adopted a case approach, much in line with Porter's original approach, which may lack accuracy and generalizability. However, such criticism mainly points at the limitations of the quantification and operational problems of the Diamond Model, rather than a problem with the model itself. Regarding the criticism on the conceptual framework, many scholars have argued that although Porter's single diamond includes several important variables, it is not comprehensive enough to be used in explaining the increasingly complex economies of today.

Moreover, some international business scholars have criticized that the Diamond Model only identifies home country factors as the source of national competitiveness while ignoring the role of multinational activities and their influence upon competitiveness enhancement. Hence, the single diamond is not effective when analyzing small economies because their domestic variables are very limited (Rugman, 1991) while their geographical constituency must be established using very different criteria (Dunning, 1993). In the era of globalization, international factors cannot be ignored given the extent to which they influence a nation's competitiveness. To address these issues, the Double Diamond Model (Rugman and D'Cruz, 1993) and the Generalized Double Diamond Model (Moon *et al.*, 1998) were proposed.

The Double Diamond Model, developed by Rugman and D'Cruz (1993), recommends that managers build upon both domestic and foreign diamonds to become globally competitive in terms of survival, profitability, and growth. While Rugman and D'Cruz's North American diamond framework fits well for countries like Canada and New Zealand, it does not carry over to other small nations relying on integration with other (foreign) countries for access to international resources, such as Korea and Singapore. Thus, Moon *et al.* (1995, 1998) adapted the double diamond framework to a generalized double diamond that works better for analyzing smaller economies.

Another limitation of the Single Diamond Model is the lack of distinction between human factors and physical factors. Porter duly explains the sources of national competitiveness possessed by the economies of advanced nations, but the model is limited in its applicability especially when explaining the levels and dynamic changes of economies in less developed or developing countries. To address this, Cho (1994) proposed the nine-factor model by incorporating the role of human factors, which was not included in Porter's Diamond Model. In this model, the human factors include workers, politicians and bureaucrats, entrepreneurs, and professionals, and the physical factors include endowed resources, domestic demand, related and supporting industries, and other business environments. An external factor, chance event, was added to these eight internal factors, making a new paradigm titled the nine-factor model. The human factors in the nine-factor model drive the national economy forward by creating, motivating, and controlling the four physical factors in Porter's Diamond Model. Human factors mobilize the physical factors, and the countries combine and arrange the physical factors to obtain international competitiveness. The role of human factors is particularly important in developing countries because physical factors are not sufficiently developed at this stage.

These two models (double diamond and nine-factor) are meaningful as they extend the scope and sources of national competitiveness. At the same time, they need to be incorporated into a single framework to analyze and explain national competitiveness more thoroughly. The IPS report incorporates both extensions into a single framework referred to as the IPS model (see Figure 1), which analyzes national competitiveness by physical factors and human factors in terms of the domestic and international contexts. This model is an effective way to explain the development pattern and sources of competitiveness for large and small countries as well as both developed and developing economies. Cho *et al.* (2009) have empirically tested the explanatory power of the IPS model. The results showed that the IPS model is more comprehensive than the Generalized Double Diamond and nine-factor models when it comes to explaining the country-specific advantage of nations with heterogeneous attributes.

In addition to the above-mentioned extended models, theoretical extensions have been largely absent to date, as Porter's original model continues to be criticized for being overly orientated toward the home country and the crucial influences of national institutions

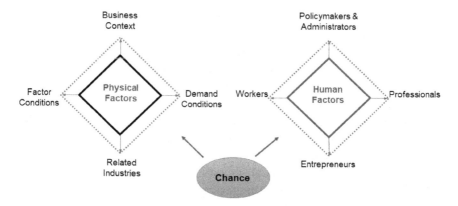

Figure 1.   IPS model.

(Fainshmidt *et al.*, 2016). In this respect, Fainshmidt *et al.* (2016) suggested two additional variables including multinational firms and governance quality, to enhance the explaining power of Porter's Diamond Model. Such an attempt though overlaps with the above-mentioned extended models, such as by Moon *et al.* (1998) and Cho (1994), and the IPS model (Cho and Moon, 2013). Therefore, to the best of our knowledge, the IPS model is the most comprehensive approach among the extended models of Porter's single diamond framework, which further provides the justification for adopting the IPS model for the analysis and evaluation of national competitiveness for our research. The following section delves into the evolution of the impacts of the eight components of the IPS model, as informed by recent academic literature.

The Literature on the Eight Factors of the IPS Model

Factor conditions

The factor conditions component of the IPS model evaluates the abundance of natural resources and their exploitation through their processing. Although natural reserves have a positive influence on a nation's overall economic performance, their mere possession does not guarantee superior national competitiveness. Such a trend has been demonstrated clearly by the phenomenon known as the "resource curse" (James and

Aadland, 2011). There are other crucial factors required to fully leverage natural resources for economic benefits. For example, Ambriško *et al.* (2015) emphasized the need to lower transportation costs within the mining industry, which make up 20–30% of total production costs. More specifically, Andrejiová *et al.* (2015) underscored the role of belt conveyors in improving operational efficiency within mining industries. This example showcases the importance of refining transportation systems and reducing operational costs tied to the processing of raw materials. Similarly, Madzík *et al.* (2016) identified a significant correlation between natural resources and national competitiveness. However, they also stressed the necessity for strategic resource management, which includes efficient resource transportation.

Demand conditions

Demand conditions include two aspects of a country's market: size and quality. Both elements play a crucial role in economic growth and development. Arai (2022) found that construction companies involved in a bidding process across larger geographical areas (i.e., spanning multiple market areas) tend to bid at lower prices than those operating within smaller geographical areas (i.e., a single market area). This validates the concept of economies of scale and implies that a larger market size can enhance cost competitiveness. In another study, Gabaix and Laibson (2006) analyzed consumer behavior and concluded that helping consumers circumvent myopic behavior boosts their welfare. As consumers become more educated and sophisticated, thereby exhibiting less biased behavior, companies may risk losing clients who previously demonstrated myopic tendencies. This shift highlights the need for companies to improve their efficiency. In the same vein, Lee *et al.* (2021) found that consumer sophistication fosters innovative purchasing behavior, which is characterized by the consumption of a wider variety of products and an increased interest in newly introduced items. Such evolving consumer behavior induces firms to innovate and meet the escalating demand for diverse goods.

Related industries

The component of related industries refers to both industrial and residential infrastructure, which collectively underpins business development.

Palei (2015) underscored the positive influence of infrastructure on businesses, suggesting that it reduces input costs by facilitating transportation and boosting worker productivity. Górniak (2022) elaborated on the crucial role of the logistics sector in preserving business competitiveness by ensuring an efficient supply chain. This observation accentuates the vital role of industrial infrastructure in enhancing national competitiveness by bolstering business competitiveness. Lau *et al.* (2009) highlighted the importance of the cluster effect in strengthening industry competitiveness, as it offers access to specialized suppliers and a wealth of information, thereby enhancing overall efficiency. Conversely, Verner (2011) emphasized the need to develop residential infrastructure, such as the education sector. This development reinforces the positive relationship observed between education expenditure, research and development (R&D) expenditure, and national competitiveness.

Business context

The business context assesses the international business environment and its impact on a firm's strategy, structure, and competitive conditions. Dang and Nguyen (2021) discussed the benefits of market openness through foreign direct investment (FDI), acknowledging its role in capital inflows and associated spillover effects, such as technology transfers and the enhancement of managerial skills. Consequently, FDI enhances the competitiveness of the domestic economy while creating additional job opportunities. In a similar vein, Aurangzeb and Stengos (2014) corroborated the positive influence of FDI inflow on a country's economic growth. They elaborated on the immediate effects of FDI on the domestic economy, such as increasing the productivity of the export sector. They also discussed secondary effects, which include the establishment of globally competitive industries, investment in research and development, and the promotion of specialization.

Workers

Worker productivity and working conditions are pivotal factors in determining national competitiveness. Dong *et al.* (2020) pinpointed labor productivity as a vital element for enhancing national competitiveness, as it sets the stage for generating more income from given resources.

Interestingly, when labor productivity is improved, for instance, through digitalization, it can more effectively meet labor market demands, thereby reducing the gap between worker supply and demand (Novoskoltseva *et al.*, 2021). Despite the clear importance of labor efficiency in driving national competitiveness, Harmider *et al.* (2019) emphasized the significance of labor resource management in boosting regional competitiveness as it reduces labor costs. This highlights the importance of not only worker productivity but also the improvement of working conditions.

Politicians and administrators

The stability of institutions, including political entities, is often recognized as a key factor in national competitiveness. For instance, Novoskoltseva *et al.* (2021) highlighted the importance of overcoming institutional erosion and ensuring transparency in public services as essential conditions for economic growth. Similarly, Mushibah (2017) pinpointed the level of political stability as a crucial moderating factor in shaping the business environment, which can be measured by the inflow of FDI. Additionally, Ulman (2013) found a significant positive correlation between a country's competitiveness index and its corruption rate, asserting that highly competitive countries tend to have lower corruption rates. These findings suggest that a lower rate of corruption in the government or public sectors is a strong determinant in creating a favorable business environment, which subsequently influences national competitiveness.

Entrepreneurs

The extent to which a country provides conducive conditions for entrepreneurs to establish businesses is another vital factor in determining national competitiveness. For instance, Milanović (2020) highlighted the role of Small and Medium Enterprises (SMEs) in enhancing national competitiveness, attributing this to their innovative nature and agility to adapt swiftly to changes. In line with other studies emphasizing the significant role entrepreneurs play in driving national competitiveness, Nicolae *et al.* (2016) observed that the environmental conditions of a region impact an entrepreneur's inclination to initiate new business there. Barriers to entrepreneurship include regional or national characteristics such as a preference for routine or a value placed on financial stability (i.e., job security).

Moreover, Kane (2010) pointed out the job creation that arises from start-up businesses each year, thus stressing the importance of entrepreneurs in fueling a country's economic growth. In this context, Kane (2010) concluded that policymakers should formulate more policies aimed at attracting start-up businesses rather than traditional, large, and mature businesses to expand a nation's job market.

Professionals

Professional competence is a critical aspect of an economy, particularly in those driven by knowledge. Morozova and Mashentseva (2018) argued for professional standards to ensure that employee training aligns with employer expectations, spotlighting the role of professional managers and the necessity to establish training standards to boost competitiveness. In the same vein, Suntharasaj and Kocaoglu (2008) addressed the issue of brain drain, a situation where talented professionals migrate to other countries, thereby negatively affecting national competitiveness. As an example, they discussed the US National Competitiveness Investment Act, a policy crafted to attract global talent in science, technology, engineering, and mathematics (STEM). Harvey (2014) proposed several conditions necessary to create a favorable institutional context to attract foreign talent, citing China as an example. The study emphasized factors such as the quality of life in the recipient country (including air quality), the openness of local communities, and the presence of institutional challenges and risks in retaining talented employees. Hence, implementing policies to meet these conditions is a significant strategy for attracting talent and constitutes a crucial step toward enhancing national competitiveness.

A Case Study of ChatGPT and Its Impacts on the National Competitiveness

Compared to previous artificial intelligence (AI) models, ChatGPT has garnered significant attention from the public and multiple industries (McKinsey & Company, 2023). Within just five days of its launch in November 2022, the number of its users soared to 1 million, expanding exponentially to a staggering 100 million within two months. This growth rate made it the fastest-growing application in history (*Reuters*, 2023a).

ChatGPT, having been trained on extensive, high-quality textual data, can generate more complex and accurate responses than other existing language models (*The Economist*, 2023b). The popularity of ChatGPT can be attributed to its versatility — it can automate a range of tasks from simple administrative ones such as drafting emails to more complex tasks like identifying programming errors in codes. Moreover, its wide applicability across various industries further enhances its appeal.

While ChatGPT holds potential for significant contributions across various industries, its initial success has sparked controversy over its potential to replace human labor, particularly with knowledge-intensive tasks like coding, which have never been under threat before (*The Economist*, 2023a). Moreover, the rapid advancement of recent AI technologies has amplified fears of the most extreme risks, such as losing control of the technology or having it become clever enough to outsmart humanity (*The Economist*, 2023c). In response, hundreds of technologists and researchers have highlighted the potential dangers of AI in multiple open letters, advocating for a six-month "pause" to allow for the development of safer technology (*Reuters*, 2023b). Such an action though may prove to be too drastic, rather a collective effort should be made to establish constructive regulations that prohibit the misuse of AI.

In light of these considerations, this chapter specifically focuses on discussing the potential positive impacts of using ChatGPT, or AI technology more broadly, for enhancing national competitiveness. Specifically, we employ the IPS model to systematically investigate the influence and usefulness of such technologies with regard to the eight components of the IPS model. Table 1 provides a summary of how the IPS model can be applied to explore an external factor such as the release of ChatGPT.

Factor conditions

Although the application of AI technology like ChatGPT might not seem so clear when it comes to the realm of natural resources, its vast potential is actually evident across various stages of oil production, ranging from data analysis and exploration, to maintenance, safety management, and operations during production. For instance, AI technology is being deployed to analyze geographic information, and assist with tasks such as classification, segmentation, and prediction (*Geo Week News*, 2023). By harnessing AI's analytical prowess, firms can identify prospective

Table 1.   The application of the IPS model on the impacts of ChatGPT.

Eight Factors	Impact of ChatGPT/or Generative AI Technology
Factor conditions	• Improving oil production process and enabling automation of tasks: example of Devon Energy • Development of alternative resources: sustainable energy
Demand conditions	• Improving products and services' quality: examples of Netflix and Buzzfeed • Use of generative AI in expanding existing markets
Related industries	• Improving industrial infrastructure: implication on the logistics sector • Improving living infrastructure: example of education
Business context	• AI facilitates market trend analysis • Use of AI in the recruitment process
Workers	• Demands for new jobs amid the emergence of generative AI • Improvement in the productivity of workers: example of client services roles
Policymakers and administrators	• Data analysis capability of AI facilitates the legislation • AI enables the strategic movement of policymakers
Entrepreneurs	• AI helps business decisions: identifying investment opportunities and risk factors • Starting a business using ChatGPT
Professionals	• Use of AI in the medical industry: diagnosis of the patients • Use of AI in the customer accounting profession

exploration sites to augment their natural resource reserves. Furthermore, AI technology plays a pivotal role in supporting maintenance work during the phases of oil production. Devon Energy, an oil production company, has used AI technology integration for system automation, leading to enhanced efficiency and reduced operational costs. ChatGPT's capabilities could also be harnessed to expand the scope of resource development, particularly in driving innovation in sustainable resources. AI technology, given its capacity to process vast data sets, emerges as a potent tool for business analysis, thereby enabling a more efficient identification and evaluation of green investment opportunities (GreenBiz, 2023). By doing so, companies can elevate their efficacy in spearheading sustainable energy solutions. This, in turn, assists nations in diversifying their natural resource base, thereby fortifying the competitiveness of factor conditions.

Demand conditions

Generative AI technology can profoundly enhance business operations by augmenting the quality of products and services. Specifically, AI has the potential to uplift customer support services by delivering accurate, timely responses and personalized product recommendations. For instance, Poshmark, a second-hand retail platform, showcased AI's effectiveness in suggesting products to customers and streamlining order fulfillment processes (*NYT*, 2023b). Through the integration of AI technology, companies can more adeptly address customer needs and widen their customer base. The implementation of ChatGPT can further intensify personalization for each consumer. It utilizes individual customer data, such as previous purchases and interactions, to better predict consumer needs and preferences (Mollick, 2022). Moreover, ChatGPT aids firms in identifying opportunities for new businesses by accurately targeting the needs of customers and addressing the gaps in the market (LinkedIn, 2023). Demonstrated as an efficient market research tool, ChatGPT simplifies the market research process, assisting companies in identifying competitors and defining target audiences (GapScout, 2023). With its capacity to process vast amounts of textual information online, ChatGPT emerges as a robust market research tool that aids firms in concentrating on vital information and discerning market trends (Jain *et al.*, 2023).

Related industries

The utilization of ChatGPT is anticipated to significantly enhance the efficiency of logistical tasks, a critical aspect of business operations and supply chain management. The benefits of incorporating ChatGPT in the logistics sector are expansive. This AI tool streamlines communication among customers, logistics providers, and warehouses, while simultaneously automating administrative tasks such as shipment monitoring and management (ShipLilly, 2023). Furthermore, ChatGPT can be leveraged to suggest optimized routes by analyzing shipping data, including shipping patterns and demands, thereby augmenting efficiency and reducing operational costs (Medium, 2023; Shj, 2023). As an illustration, DHL utilizes AI technology to monitor real-time shipment data, enabling them to determine the optimal route and maintain a vigilant watch over their supply chains (Freight Connections, 2023). When it comes to the realm of education, despite the initial resistance toward integrating ChatGPT into the classroom, teachers and instructors are now beginning to acknowledge the opportunities it presents as an effective teaching tool, fostering greater interactivity within the classroom (*MIT Technology Review*, 2023). ChatGPT has proven its efficacy in assisting with class preparation and planning. For instance, it can be employed to generate multiple-choice questions for students, serving as a valuable resource for both teachers and learners (*NYT*, 2023d).

Business context

Employing generative AI to enhance business capabilities among firms has many advantages as it can streamline processes and provide diverse strategy options across borders. The use of generative AI is found to be effective in innovating existing business processes and promoting firm strategy for internationalizing existing businesses. This is made possible due to the core competence of ChatGPT to search and extract information from a vast pool of data. With such a function, companies can expand their business scope without the need to hire and educate new employees in every business area. Unlike AI tools with specific functions, such as Google Translate, ChatGPT is a general-purpose AI technology that can be applied to multiple tasks, including translation, logistics processes, and market research (as discussed in the previous paragraph). By overcoming language barriers in information search and advertising, firms can gain better knowledge of foreign markets and broaden their business scope to the international market.

Workers

While there are concerns that ChatGPT may automate certain jobs — stirring anxieties about potential job displacement — it also generates demand for new roles and enhances overall workforce efficiency. Historically, the advent of new technologies has often been accompanied by apprehension over job displacement, particularly among low-skilled workers who are most susceptible to being replaced by automation. AI, however, has shown itself to be instrumental in enhancing workforce productivity. By harnessing AI technologies, businesses can streamline administrative processes, thereby allowing employees to concentrate on more strategic and complex tasks. The automation and assistance that AI tools provide free up valuable time and resources, enabling the workforce to focus their efforts on higher-value activities, ultimately boosting productivity and fueling growth. The use of ChatGPT not only enhances work performance but also improves the quality of services provided by the human labor force. This collaboration between AI technology and human workers serves as a potent tool to boost efficiency in the current and future labor market, laying a solid foundation for enhancing national competitiveness. Importantly, improved worker efficiency positively impacts the quality of their work, leading to superior services provided to customers.

Policymakers and administrators

The incorporation of AI technology into the regulatory framework streamlines the process of data analysis, empowering policymakers to identify areas requiring specific regulations. By leveraging AI's analytical prowess, policymakers can identify crucial areas to prioritize, leading to the design of more effective interventions. Pham *et al.* (2020) underscored the effectiveness of AI technology across various stages in combating COVID-19, including diagnosis, tracking, and patient number prediction. This facilitates timely and appropriate policy implementation. Consequently, a data-driven approach enhances the ability of policymakers to make informed decisions and efficiently allocate resources, leading to more effective and targeted regulations. AI further ensures that the appropriate message reaches each audience at the optimal time (*NYT*, 2023c). ChatGPT plays a pivotal role in facilitating effective communication between administrators and the public. By leveraging the accelerated text generation capabilities of ChatGPT, policymakers can produce a significantly larger volume of comments. In fact, the usage of AI tools for comment generation predate the development of ChatGPT itself. For instance, in 2018 it was revealed that at least a million comments submitted to the Federal Communications Commission were auto-generated (*NYT*, 2023c). This demonstrates the government's potential to successfully integrate this technology into its systems, enabling more active and effective public engagement.

Entrepreneurs

ChatGPT offers a prime example of how AI technology can be utilized to process vast amounts of data with exceptional precision and in significantly less time compared to human labor. This capability can be harnessed to identify and develop business opportunities for firms that require extensive information about existing industries and companies. Furthermore, ChatGPT can play a crucial role in identifying potential risk factors associated with investments, thereby facilitating investors' decision-making (Despallieres, 2023). Specifically, ChatGPT can be used to analyze information from audit reports or incident reports to identify risk factors relevant to a particular business domain (Security Intelligence, 2023). Moreover, it can be employed to detect customer complaints posted on social media platforms, which can pose a risk to a company's reputation, and identify patterns for effective mitigation strategies (Security Intelligence, 2023). The utilization of ChatGPT proves particularly beneficial in supporting the operations of start-ups, which often face limitations in terms of information and resources. This application of ChatGPT saves valuable time for start-up companies and enables them to function with a smaller workforce. Additionally, ChatGPT can be employed for branding purposes, including tasks such as designing company logos, crafting slogans, writing content for advertisements on blogs, and even creating websites from scratch (Fast Company, 2023). These functionalities offered by ChatGPT empower start-ups to streamline their operations and enhance their brand presence while optimizing resource allocation.

Professionals

In various industries, ChatGPT has emerged as a valuable tool for professionals who require extensive qualifications, rigorous training, and informed judgment. ChatGPT facilitates the automation of routine administrative tasks for professionals, while also enhancing their knowledge in their respective fields. A prominent example of this is the utilization of AI technology in the medical industry, where AI algorithms are employed to improve the identification of patients with potential diseases like heart failure. This can be done with the AI detecting abnormal symptoms such as irregular heart rhythms (*Wall Street Journal*, 2023). While qualified doctors can perform this task as well, medical professionals can still benefit from the adoption of generative AI technology by enhancing efficiency and accuracy in carrying out these tasks. Despite ChatGPT's ability to process vast amounts of information quickly, it is important to acknowledge the limitations of AI technology when making moral judgments or self-correcting biases on its responses. Technology industry experts further emphasize that companies require individuals who possess the expertise to effectively utilize powerful data-centric tools, interpret raw data, and make informed decisions — tasks that can only be accomplished by experienced human professionals (*NYT*, 2023a). In other words, the management and decision-making responsibilities in many areas still rest with humans. Instead, ChatGPT serves as a complementary tool to enhance the capabilities of workers.

Implications and Conclusion

After analyzing the impact of emerging technologies like ChatGPT across eight different factors, this chapter concludes that the enhancement of national competitiveness stems not only from the inherent benefits of these new technologies but also from their spillover effects on existing businesses and their potential to stimulate the growth of related industries. Yet, despite its impressive performance in generating sophisticated and coherent responses, it is crucial to recognize that ChatGPT is still a work in progress. For instance, it cannot be considered entirely reliable due to potential biases in the information it draws from, and its inability to make moral judgments. Consequently, a consensus on how to regulate such technologies is yet to be reached, underscoring the need for more attention from policymakers.

Nevertheless, it is indisputable that the advent of ChatGPT, and generative AI technology in general, represents a significant milestone in the business realm. When applied thoughtfully across industries, the advantages — such as amplified productivity and efficiency — tend to surpass the limitations inherent in the technology. Companies must then adopt nimble strategies and prudent management skills to effectively assimilate these technologies into their operations. Balancing the risks associated with adopting potentially unfinished technology, as some argue, while maximizing the benefits of these innovative advancements for businesses, calls for the implementation of regulations. In this case, a collaborative discourse among government bodies, corporations, and educational institutions should be established. Evaluating the pros and cons of adopting such technology from a range of perspectives is crucial. Through these consultations, a holistic framework can be devised to steer the responsible and advantageous use of AI tools while alleviating potential risks.

In conclusion, the adoption of generative AI technologies such as ChatGPT represents a significant shift in the business landscape, offering immense potential while posing various challenges. Drawing upon the literature review of the IPS model, these AI technologies have demonstrated profound implications for the eight factors that influence national competitiveness, ranging from natural resources to business context, professional competencies, and institutional stability. These applications have shown substantial potential in enhancing productivity, efficiency, and innovation, thus bolstering national competitiveness. However, concerns over labor displacement, data biases, and the lack of moral judgment call for a more comprehensive regulatory framework. The importance of achieving a delicate balance between harnessing the benefits of these new technologies and mitigating associated risks underscores the need for collaborative efforts among all stakeholders, including governments, businesses, and educational institutions. Moving forward, these discussions will aid in establishing an inclusive framework that promotes responsible and beneficial use of AI technologies, thereby fostering sustainable growth and enhanced national competitiveness. A thoughtful, multi-faceted approach to AI integration can ensure that the transformative power of these technologies is harnessed responsibly and effectively for the benefit of all.

References

Ambriško, L, Grendel, D, and Lukáč, S. 2015. Application of logistics principles when designing the process of transportation of raw materials. *Acta Montanistica Slovaca*, 20(2): 141–147.

Andrejiová, M., Grincova, A., Marasová, D., and Grendel, P. 2015. Multicriterial assessment of the raw material transport. *Acta Montanistica Slovaca*, 20(1): 26–32.

Arai, K. 2022. Geographic market size and low bid competitiveness in construction companies. *Competitiveness Review*, 32(1): 85–102. ISSN: 1059-5422.

Aurangzeb, Z. and Stengos, T. 2014. The role of Foreign Direct Investment (FDI) in a dualistic growth framework: A smooth coefficient semi-parametric approach. *Borsa Istanbul Review*, 14(3): 133–144.

Berger, T. 2008. Concepts on national competitiveness. *Journal of International Business and Economy*, 9(1): 3–17.

Cho, D. S. 1994. A dynamic approach to international competitiveness: The case of Korea. *Journal of Far Eastern Business*, 1(1): 17–36.

Cho, D. S. and Moon, H. C. 1998. A nation's international competitiveness in different stages of economic development. *Advances in Competitiveness Research*, 6(1): 5–19.

Cho, D. S. and Moon, H. C. 2013. *From Adam Smith to Michael Porter: Evolution of Competitiveness Theory* (extended edition). Singapore: World Scientific Publishing.

Cho, D. S. and Moon, H. C. 2022. *The Competitiveness of Nations 2: Government Policies and Business Strategies for Environmental, Social, and Governance (ESG)*. Singapore: World Scientific Publishing.

Cho, D. S., Moon, H. C., and Kim, M. Y. 2009. Does one size fit all? A dual double diamond approach to country-specific advantages. *Asian Business & Management*, 8(1): 83–102.

Dang, V. C. and Nguyen, Q. K. 2021. Determinants of FDI attractiveness: Evidence from ASEAN-7 countries. *Cogent Social Sciences*, 7(1): 2004676.

Despallieres, M. 2023. Chat GPT and trading: Revolutionary or ridiculous? https://financefeeds.com/chat-gpt-and-trading-revolutionary-or-ridiculous/. Accessed July 1, 2023.

Dong, N. T., Diem, T. T. A., Chinh, B. T. H., and Hiem, N. T. D. 2020. The interaction between labor productivity and competitiveness in Vietnam. *The Journal of Asian Finance, Economics and Business (JAFEB)*, 7(11): 619–627.

Dunning, J. H. 1993. Internationalizing Porter's diamond. *Management International Review*, 33(2): 7–15.

Fainshmidt, S., Smith, A., and Judge, W. Q. 2016. National competitiveness and Porter's diamond model: The role of MNE penetration and governance quality. *Global Strategy Journal*, 6: 81–104.

Fast Company. 2023. 15 useful ChatGPT prompts for startups. https://www.fastcompany.com/90875084/chatgpt-prompts-for-startups. Accessed July 1, 2023.

Freight Connections. 2023. ChatGPT and the like: Artificial intelligence in logistics. https://dhl-freight-connections.com/en/trends/chatgpt-and-the-like-artificial-intelligence-in-logistics/. Accessed July 1, 2023.

Gabaix, X. and Laibson, D. 2006. Shrouded attributes, consumer myopia, and information suppression in competitive markets. *The Quarterly Journal of Economics*, 121(2): 505–540.

GapScout. 2023. How to use ChatGPT for market research. https://gapscout.com/blog/how-to-use-chatgpt-for-market-research/. Accessed July 1, 2023.

Geo Week News. 2023. Is the geospatial industry going to be affected by the current AI boom? https://www.geoweeknews.com/blogs/chatgpt-artificial-intelligence-is-the-geospatial-industry-going-to-be-affected-by-the-current-ai-boom. Accessed July 1, 2023.

Górniak, J. 2022. Selected logistics development level indicators: A review and comparative analysis in European Union countries. *Comparative Economic Research. Central and Eastern Europe*, 25(1): 127–144.

Grant, R. M. 1991. Porter's competitive advantage of nations: An assessment. *Strategic Management Journal*, 12(7): 535–548.

GreenBiz. 2023. My exclusive interview with ChatGPT about AI, climate tech and sustainability. https://www.greenbiz.com/article/my-exclusive-interview-chatgpt-about-ai-climate-tech-and-sustainability. Accessed July 1, 2023.

Grein, A. F. and Craig, C. S. 1996. Economic performance over time: Does Porter's diamond hold at the national level? *International Executive*, 38(3): 303–322.

Harmider, L., Taranenko, I., Honchar, L., Ovcharenko, O., and Dotsenko, G. 2019. Modeling of labor potential as a factor of influence on the region competitiveness. *Montenegrin Journal of Economics*, 15(2): 111–125.

Harvey, W. S. 2014. Winning the global talent war. *Journal of Chinese Human Resource Management*, 5(1): 62–74.

Jain, V., Rai, H., Parvathy, E., and Mogaji, E. 2023. The prospects and challenges of ChatGPT on marketing research and practices. http://dx.doi.org/10.2139/ssrn.4398033. Accessed June 15, 2023.

James, A. and Aadland, D. 2011. The curse of natural resources: An empirical investigation of U.S. counties. *Resource and Energy Economics*, 33(2): 440–453.

Kane, T. J. 2010. The importance of startups in job creation and job destruction. Hoover Institution. https://ssrn.com/abstract=1646934. Accessed July 1, 2023.

Kharub, M. and Sharma, R. 2017. Comparative analyses of competitive advantage using Porter diamond model: The case of MSMEs in Himachal Pradesh. *Competitiveness Review*, 27(2): 132–160.

Lau, M. C. K., To, K., Zhang, Z., and Chen, J. 2009. Determinants of competitiveness: Observations in China's textile and apparel industries. *China & World Economy*, 17(2): 45–64.

Lee, D., Moon, J., and Jeong, J. 2021. Consumer sophistication as an enhancer of innovation in the food industry: Measurement development and validation. *British Food Journal*, 124(11): 3803–3820. ISSN: 0007-070X.

LinkedIn. 2023. Delving into the applications of ChatGPT in market research and competitive analysis. https://www.linkedin.com/pulse/delving-applications-chatgpt-market-research-analysis-daniel-cromwell. Accessed July 1, 2023.

Madzík, P., Dankova, A., Pitekova, J., and Ferencz, V. 2016. Effects of the energy and mining industry on management of national competitiveness. *Acta Montanistica Slovaca*, 21(1): 67–75.

McKinsey & Company. 2023. What is generative AI? https://www.mckinsey. com/featured-insights/mckinsey-explainers/what-is-generative-ai. Accessed July 1, 2023.

Medium. 2023. How can logistics companies benefit with the usage of ChatGPT? https://anolytics.medium.com/how-can-logistics-companies-benefit-with-the-usage-of-chatgpt-c38e85d4c4cb. Accessed July 1, 2023.

Milanović, J. 2020. Analysis of the competitiveness of the sector of small and medium enterprises and entrepreneurs in the Republic of Serbia. *International Review*, (1–2): 128–135.

MIT Technology Review. 2023. ChatGPT is going to change education, not destroy it. https://www.technologyreview.com/2023/04/06/1071059/chatgpt-change-not-destroy-education-openai/. Accessed July 1, 2023.

Mollick, E. 2022. ChatGPT is a tipping point for AI. *Harvard Business Review.* https://hbr.org/2022/12/chatgpt-is-a-tipping-point-for-ai. Accessed July 1, 2023.

Moon, H. C., Rugman, A. M., and Verbeke, A. 1995. The generalized double diamond approach to international competitiveness. In A. M. Rugman, J. V. den Broeck, and A. Verbeke (Eds.), *Research in Global Strategic Management* (pp. 97–114). Greenwich, CT: JAI Press.

Moon, H. C., Rugman, A. M., and Verbeke, A. 1998. A generalized double diamond approach to the global competitiveness of Korea and Singapore. *International Business Review*, 7(2): 135–150.

Morozova, E. V. and Mashentseva, G. A. 2018. Professional standards in the system of personnel training. *2018 XVII Russian Scientific and Practical Conference on Planning and Teaching Engineering Staff for the Industrial and Economic Complex of the Region (PTES)*. IEEE.

Nicolae, M., Ion, I., and Nicolae, E. 2016. Regional differences in entrepreneurial perceptions and implications for the Romanian competitiveness policy. *Management & Marketing. Challenges for the Knowledge Society*, 11(1): 394–409.

Novoskoltseva, L., Ignatyuk, H., Fyliuk, L., Chubuk, N. K., and Hevchuk. A. 2021. The global competitiveness of national economies. *Journal of Interdisciplinary Research*, 11(2): 101–106.

NYT. 2023a. Four experts on tech hiring talk about where the jobs are. https://www.nytimes.com/2023/03/01/opinion/chatgpt-artificial-intelligence-tech.html?searchResultPosition=15. Accessed July 5, 2023.

NYT. 2023b. The chatbots are here, and the internet industry is in a tizzy. https://www.nytimes.com/2023/03/08/technology/chatbots-disrupt-internet-indus-try.html?searchResultPosition=4. Accessed July 5, 2023.

NYT. 2023c. How ChatGPT hijacks democracy. https://www.nytimes.com/2023/01/15/opinion/ai-chatgpt-lobbying-democracy.html?searchResult Position=37. Accessed July 5, 2023.

NYT. 2023d. Don't ban ChatGPT in schools. Teach with it. https://www.nytimes. com/2023/01/12/technology/chatgpt-schools-teachers.html. Accessed July 5, 2023.

Pajunen, K. and Airo, V. 2013. Country-specificity and industry performance: A configurational analysis of the European generic medicines industry. *Research in the Sociology of Organizations*, 38: 255–278.

Palei, T. 2015. Assessing the impact of infrastructure on economic growth and global competitiveness. *Procedia Economics and Finance*, 23: 168–175.

Pham, Q., Nguyen, D. C., Huynh-The, T., Hwang, W., and Pathirana, T. N. 2020. Artificial intelligence (AI) and big data for coronavirus (COVID-19) pandemic: A survey on the state-of-the-arts. *IEEE*, 8: 130820–130839.

Porter, M. E. 1990. *Competitive Advantage of Nations*. New York: Free Press.

Reuters. 2023a. ChatGPT sets record for fastest-growing user base — Analyst note. https://www.reuters.com/technology/chatgpt-sets-record-fastest-growing-user-base-analyst-note-2023-02-01/. Accessed July 5, 2023.

Reuters. 2023b. Elon Musk and others urge AI pause, citing 'risks to society.' https://www.reuters.com/technology/musk-experts-urge-pause-training-ai-systems-that-can-outperform-gpt-4-2023-03-29/. Accessed July 5, 2023.

Rugman, A. M. 1991. Diamond in the rough. *Business Quarterly*, 55(3): 61–64.

Rugman, A. M. and D'Cruz, J. R. 1993. The double diamond model of international competitiveness: The Canadian Experience. Management International Review, 33(2): 17–39.

Rugman, A. M., Oh, C. H., and Lim, D. S. K. 2012. The regional and global competitiveness of multinational firms. *Journal of the Academy of Marketing Science*, 40(2): 218–235.

Scott, B. R. 1985. U.S. competitiveness: Concepts, performance, and implications. In B. R. Scott and G. Lodge (Eds.), *U.S. Competitiveness in the World Economy* (pp. 13–69). Boston, MA: Harvard Business School Press.

Security Intelligence. 2023. Using a private version of ChatGPT as an enabler for risk and compliance. https://securityintelligence.com/posts/using-chatgpt-as-an-enabler-for-risk-and-compliance/. Accessed July 5, 2023.

Sakakibara, M. and Porter, M. E. 2001. Competing at home to win abroad: Evidence from Japanese industry. *Review of Economics and Statistics*, 83(2): 310–322.

ShipLilly. 2023. How Chat GPT thinks it can revolutionize the logistics industry? https://www.shiplilly.com/blog/how-chat-gpt-thinks-it-can-revolutionize-the-logistics-industry/. Accessed July 5, 2023.

Shj. 2023. What are the implications of Chat GPT on the transportation & logistics industry? https://shjintl.com/2023/04/14/what-are-the-implications-of-chat-gpt-on-the-transportation-logistics-industry/. Accessed July 5, 2023.

Suntharasaj, P. and Kocaoglu, D. F. 2008. Enhancing a country's competitiveness through "National Talent Management Framework". *PICMET'08-2008*

Portland International Conference on Management of Engineering & Technology, IEEE. 10.1109/PICMET.2008.4599637.

The Economist. 2023a. How to worry wisely about artificial intelligence. https://www.economist.com/leaders/2023/04/20/how-to-worry-wisely-about-artificial-intelligence. Accessed July 5, 2023.

The Economist. 2023b. Large, creative AI models will transform lives and labour markets. https://www.economist.com/interactive/science-and-technology/2023/04/22/large-creative-ai-models-will-transform-how-we-live-and-work. Accessed July 5, 2023.

The Economist. 2023c. How generative models could go wrong. https://www.economist.com/science-and-technology/2023/04/19/how-generative-models-could-go-wrong. Accessed July 5, 2023.

Ulman, S. R. 2013. Corruption and national competitiveness in different stages of country development. *Procedia Economics and Finance*, 6: 150–160.

Wall Street Journal. 2023. How doctors use AI to help diagnose patients. https://www.wsj.com/articles/how-doctors-use-ai-to-help-diagnose-patients-ce4ad025?mod=Searchresults_pos2&page=3. Accessed July 11, 2023.

Verner, T. 2011. National competitiveness and expenditure on education, research and development. *Journal of Competitiveness*, 3(2): 690–699.

Chapter 2

Conceptual Framework and Analytical Methodologies[*]

In Chapter 1, we examined existing studies related to each factor comprising the eight elements of the IPS model and illustrated their significance in boosting national competitiveness. Additionally, we validated the usefulness and applicability of the IPS model through real-world cases, such as evaluating the impact of ChatGPT on national competitiveness. This chapter presents the theoretical background of IPS National Competitiveness Research and the Measure-Analyze-Simulate-Implement (MASI) methodology that is used in our research, and discusses how it differs from other national competitiveness reports published by the International Institute for Management Development (IMD) and the World Economic Forum (WEF).

The Theoretical Evolution of National Competitiveness

Porter (1990) developed a comprehensive approach to analyzing national competitiveness titled the Diamond Model. It was then extended by other scholars through two extended models: the Double Diamond Model (Moon et al., 1998; Rugman, 1991) and the Nine-Factor Model (Cho, 1994). Later, a new comprehensive model was introduced by integrating

---

[*]This chapter is abstracted and extended from IPSNC (2022).

these two models into one framework (Cho *et al.*, 2008, 2009; IPS, 2006), which was labeled as the IPS Model and became the underlying analytical framework for IPS National Competitiveness Research.

It is very important to note that the reliability of national competitiveness rankings should be based on rigorous models and methodologies. Policymakers, who often become sensitive to the results of national competitiveness reports, may then pursue distorted policies based on misleading research results. However, despite the extensive history and the two renewed reports on national competitiveness, there are several limitations to the national competitiveness research methodologies and findings of IMD and WEF.[1] To solve this problem, we address the theoretical and methodological problems of the existing reports. Hopefully, policymakers and business leaders will derive useful implications from our research.

Critical Review of Existing Reports

The IMD and WEF are world-renowned institutions that publish national competitiveness reports annually. This section will present a careful examination of their methodologies that reveals some notable limitations.

Theoretical background

These two reports provide different perspectives on defining competitiveness. IMD describes competitiveness as "the ability of a nation to create and maintain an environment that sustains more value creation for its enterprises and more prosperity for its people" (IMD, 2014: 502). By contrast, the WEF labels competitiveness as "the set of institutions, policies, and factors that determine the level of productivity of a country" (WEF, 2019: 13). While their definitions of competitiveness contrast, both institutes adopted very similar factors when assessing competitiveness in their earlier reports (see Cho and Moon, 2013 for details). Regarding the evaluation model, IMD added "location attractiveness" to its original model in 1999 and introduced a completely new category in 2001, which consisted of four variables: economic performance, government efficiency, business efficiency, and infrastructure. Moreover, IMD formerly

---

[1] Please refer to Cho and Moon (2000, 2013) for the discussion on these limitations.

used a single index until 2002 but introduced customized rankings according to population size in 2003, and in the following year, it released two more rankings based on GDP per capita and geographic region.

Conversely, WEF measured competitiveness using eight variables, but since 2000 it has changed the number of variables frequently. Up until 2007, WEF showed frequent changes in the indices from the Current Competitiveness Index (CCI) to Microeconomic Competitiveness Index (MICI) and Business Competitiveness Index (BCI). It also launched a new index, the Global Competitiveness Index (GCI) in 2005 as part of an attempt to integrate the two separate indices (Growth Competitiveness Index and BCI) into a single index. More recently, the WEF introduced the GCI 4.0 in 2018, which provides a series of factors and attributes that drive productivity growth and human development to address the Fourth Industrial Revolution (WEF, 2019: 7). However, careful observation will reveal that these evaluation models and indices are not as rigorous as Porter's Diamond Model.

Table 1 summarizes the major differences among the three national competitiveness reports in measuring national competitiveness.

Methodology

Although both IMD and WEF reports employed eight variables that are almost identical in their earlier publications, they produced

Table 1. Comparison of the three competitiveness reports.

Report	IMD World Competitiveness Yearbook (2023)	WEF Global Competitiveness Report (2019)	IPS National Competitiveness Research (2023)
Sponsoring institute	International Institute for Management Development	World Economic Forum	IPSNC
Location	Lausanne (Switzerland)	Geneva (Switzerland)	Seoul (Korea, Republic of)/Geneva (Switzerland)
First publication year	1989	1996	2001
Theoretical base	No particular theory	No particular theory	IPS model

(Continued)

Table 1.   (*Continued*)

Report	IMD World Competitiveness Yearbook (2023)	WEF Global Competitiveness Report (2019)	IPS National Competitiveness Research (2023)
Main factors	A collection of four factors – Economic performance – Government efficiency – Business efficiency – Infrastructure	A collection of 12 factors – Institutions – Infrastructure – ICT adoption – Macroeconomic stability – Health – Skills – Product market – Labor market – Financial system – Market size – Business dynamism – Innovation capability	A collection of eight factors Four physical factors – Factor conditions – Demand conditions – Related industries – Business context Four human factors – Workers – Policymakers and administrators – Entrepreneurs – Professionals
Criteria	256 (computed in the rankings)	103	98
Database	Hard data: 164 Soft data: 92	Hard data: 56 Soft data: 47	Hard data: 57 Soft data: 41
Weights	Hard data: 64.1% Soft data: 35.9 %	The same weight for factors, sub-factors, and criteria	Different weights for different strategies
Partner institutes	A global network of 57 partner institutes	Local partner institutes	KOTRA offices abroad Partner scholars
Number of Economies	64 economies	141 economies	62 economies
Strengths	– The first and largest survey on national competitiveness – A collection of multiple variables for competitiveness	– Like IMD, but more effective in elaborating the variables – Ongoing efforts to improve the study	– Strong theoretical basis with minimum multicollinearity – Useful information of intra-group rankings – A series of analytical tools for policy implementation

Table 1. (*Continued*)

Report	IMD World Competitiveness Yearbook (2023)	WEF Global Competitiveness Report (2019)	IPS National Competitiveness Research (2023)
Weaknesses	– Weak theoretical basis – Lack of consistency among partner institutions conducting the surveys	– In general, like IMD, but more emphasis on soft data – Lack of consistency among partner institutions conducting the surveys	– Improved weighting method, but still controversial

Note: As WEF published "Global Competitiveness Report Special Edition 2020," GCI and its rankings release have been suspended since 2020. Instead, the report suggests priorities for policymakers to consider in their decision-making process and overcome the COVID-19 pandemic.

Table 2. **Weights of the three main pillars at each development stage.**

Sub-index	Factor-Driven Stage (%)	Efficiency-Driven Stage (%)	Innovation-Driven Stage (%)
Basic requirements	60	40	20
Efficiency enhancers	35	50	50
Innovation and sophistication factors	5	10	30

Source: Global Competitiveness Report 2017–2018 (WEF, 2017).

contrasting results. This was because they applied different weights to similar variables. For the IMD report, hard data accounts for two-thirds of the factors in determining the overall ranking, while survey data accounts for one-third of the overall ranking. The WEF report, conversely, applies different weights to the variables considering a country's development stage (see Table 2). In the 2006–2007 Report, the WEF classified countries by the level of GDP per capita. Following this classification, countries with a GDP per capita smaller than US$2,000 are in the factor-driven stage (Stage 1); countries with a GDP per capita between US$3,000 and US$8,999 are in the efficiency-driven stage (Stage 2); countries with a GDP per capita larger than US$17,000 are in the innovation-driven stage (Stage 3); countries between two of the three stages are regarded as in transition stage (WEF, 2006: 12). However, in the 2007–2008 Report, the WEF added another criterion in classifying the development stage, the share of exports of mineral goods in total exports (goods and services). As a result, the countries whose exports of mineral products exceeded 70% of total exports are categorized in the factor-driven group, regardless of other criteria that determine the development stage of the country.

Policy implications

In addition to presenting the competitiveness rankings, it is important to provide the implications of these findings. For example, in the WEF Global Competitiveness Report 2019, Singapore ranked first, while the Philippines ranked 64th among 141 countries measured. This raises questions such as: Will such a result help the Philippines change its policy to enhance its competitiveness? Does this mean that the country has to invest more capital and effort in developing technologies in the hope that someday it might catch up with Singapore?

In our research, we argue that a nation's competitiveness is more relevant when it is compared with nations holding similar comparative advantages. For example, the comparison between Singapore and Switzerland would be a better comparison than the comparison between Singapore and the US. Therefore, to derive useful policy implications, we also need to consider rankings in groups of similar countries (Intra-Group Ranking), along with the overall national competitiveness rankings. Hence, the IPS National Competitiveness Research (the IPS research) reports suggest both intra-group rankings and overall rankings based on cost and differentiation strategies.

IPS National Competitiveness Research

By addressing the problems of existing studies, the IPS research introduces a four-step framework for the analysis. First, the competitiveness of 62 countries is measured by using the IPS model. Next, the competitiveness of these countries is analyzed within the country group. The structure of national competitiveness is demonstrated through strategy simulation, followed by the Term-Priority (TP) Matrix. Figure 1 illustrates the MASI methodology of the IPS research.

Figure 1. The MASI methodology

Measuring national competitiveness based on cost and differentiation strategies

There are two conditions that can support a solid analytical framework. One is whether it is comprehensive enough to explain the complexity of the real world through key variables. Another is to assess whether such a framework is dynamic enough to outline the changing nature of national competitiveness. Porter's (1990) Diamond Model satisfies both conditions; it incorporates four competitiveness variables: "Factor Conditions," "Demand Conditions," "Related and Supporting Industries," and "Firm Strategy, Structure, and Rivalry." Hence, Porter argues national competitiveness is not only dependent on resource endowments — as traditional economic theories suggest — but can be created by a combination of strategic choices along with the four determinants of the Diamond Model.

Despite its advantages, Porter's Diamond Model is not free from criticism. Specifically, it is limited to be applied in the international business context. As a result, the model demonstrated weaknesses in analyzing small economies whose domestic resources are very limited (Rugman, 1991). Especially, in the current era of globalization, international factors must be considered in assessing a nation's competitiveness. To address this problem, the Double Diamond Model (Rugman and D'Cruz, 1993) and the Generalized Double Diamond Model (Moon *et al.*, 1998) were introduced.

Another issue is that the Single Diamond Model does not distinguish human factors from physical factors and includes labor in Factor Conditions. Still, the roles of different groups of human factors are important for countries at different levels of economic development. Human factors can mobilize, combine, and arrange physical factors with the aim of obtaining international competitiveness. In this regard, Cho (1994) proposed the Nine-Factor Model by adding four human factors — workers, policymakers & administrators, entrepreneurs, and professionals — which are not well reflected in Porter's Diamond Model.

These two models, the Double Diamond and Nine-Factor, are significant as they extend the scope and source of national competitiveness. The IPS research incorporates both of these extensions into the IPS model, which analyzes national competitiveness by assessing the roles of both physical and human factors in domestic and international contexts (see Figure 1 in Chapter 1).

We used 98 criteria in measuring the national competitiveness of 62 countries in the 2023 IPS NCR research. Among these, 57 criteria are hard data and the other 41 criteria are soft data. The hard data were collected from various statistical figures published by international and government organizations. We collected the soft data with the assistance of our partner institution, the Korea Trade-Investment Promotion Agency (KOTRA), which operates more than a hundred offices internationally. Additionally, for 2023 we employed ChatGPT as a supplementary tool for measuring the 41 survey data. Please refer to the relevant section in the Highlights (Chapter 3) for more details.

Analyzing national competitiveness

Table 3 illustrates a 3×3 matrix of country groups. By considering both the size and competitive structure under both cost and differentiation strategies, we can now more realistically compare the relative positions of each country. Depending upon which strategic choice is made, the rankings of competitiveness among countries/regions would change. For instance, Kuwait ranks 13th when utilizing the cost strategy. However, it would drop to 24th under the differentiation strategy.

Simulation with two scenarios

To enhance their competitiveness for a higher standard of living and a better business environment, two generic strategies of cost and differentiation can be applied at the national level (Porter *et al.*, 2000). The cost

Table 3. Typology of country groups under cost and differentiation strategies.

CSI/DSI \ Size	Small	Medium	Large
Strong	Small-strong countries	Medium-strong countries	Large-strong countries
Intermediate	Small-intermediate countries	Medium-intermediate countries	Large-intermediate countries
Weak	Small-weak countries	Medium-weak countries	Large-weak countries

Note: CSI: cost strategy index, DSI: differentiation strategy index.

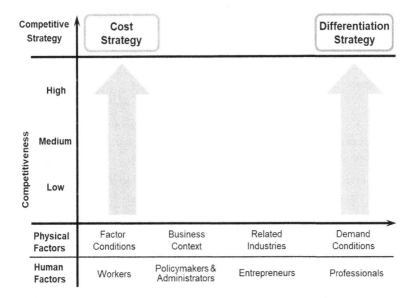

Figure 2. Competitive strategies of nations

strategy strives to achieve a "lower cost and higher efficiency," mainly utilizing cheap workers and naturally endowed resources. By contrast, the differentiation strategy emphasizes "higher cost but higher value-added," focusing more on Demand Conditions and Professionals. The differences are illustrated in Figure 2.

We impose different weights on the competitiveness variables for cost and differentiation strategies (see Table 4). To derive appropriate weights for the competitiveness variables in our research, we use the Analytic Hierarchy Process (AHP), which is a popular multi-criteria decision-making tool in the related literature (Sureshchandar and Leisten, 2006).

Table 4.   **Weights for cost strategy and differentiation strategy.**

Main Factors	Weights CS	DS	Sub-Factors	Weights CS	DS
Physical factors					
Factor conditions	32/120	4/120	Energy resources	3/4	1/4
			Other resources	1/4	3/4
Business context	16/120	8/120	Structure	3/4	1/4
			Strategy	1/4	3/4
Related industries	8/120	16/120	Industrial infrastructure	3/4	1/4
			Coordination and synergy	1/4	3/4
Demand conditions	4/120	32/120	Demand size	3/4	1/4
			Demand quality	1/4	3/4
Human factors					
Workers	32/120	4/120	Quantity of labor force	3/4	1/4
			Quality of labor force	1/1	3/1
Policymakers and administrators	16/120	8/120	Policymakers	3/4	1/4
			Administrators	1/4	3/4
Entrepreneurs	8/120	16/120	Personal competence	3/4	1/4
			Social context	1/4	3/4
Professionals	4/120	32/120	Personal competence	3/4	1/4
			Social context	1/4	3/4

Note: CS: cost strategy, DS: differentiation strategy.

For both cost and differentiation strategies, equal weight (50%) is imposed on physical and human factors. However, factors and sub-factors are given different weights. For the differentiation strategy, more weight is given to Demand Conditions and Professionals, whereas for the cost strategy more weight is given to Factor Conditions and Workers.

We can derive the following two simulations based on the cost and differentiation strategies. This simulation shows the changes in the score of the competitiveness index when the cost and differentiation strategies are applied. Specifically, the two strategies — cost and differentiation strategies — are applied to all countries. The indices of the two strategies are calculated to determine the relationship of the changes in the competitiveness index (CSI–BD, DSI–BD) with the size of a country or its

Table 5.   Multiple linear regression model for the changes in variables.

	CSI-BD (Model 1)	DSI-BD (Model 2)
Size	0.044	−0.022
(*p*-value)	(0. 000)	(0.006)
Competitiveness (BD)	−0.313	0.143
(*p*-value)	(0.000)	(0.000)
Constant	7.141	0.540
(*p*-value)	(0.000)	(0.559)
N (observations)	62	62
R^2	0.659	0.463
Adjust R^2	0.647	0.444
F-statistic	57.019 (df = 2; 59)	25.400 (df = 2; 59)
(*p*-value)	(0.000)	(0.000)

Notes: (1) CSI: cost strategy index, DSI: differentiation strategy index, BD: base data, CSI-BD: cost strategy index-base data, DSI-BD: differentiation strategy index-base data. (2) If the *p*-value of an independent variable is smaller than 0.01, the variable is significant in these models.

competitiveness (BD). The results are summarized in Table 5. Some important implications are derived from this analysis. First, the cost strategy is more suitable for countries of larger size (e.g., Australia, China) or with lower competitiveness (e.g., Pakistan) (Model 1). Second, regardless of a country's size, the differentiation strategy is more appropriate for countries that have higher competitiveness (Model 2). This highlights that a country should choose carefully between cost and differentiation strategies to enhance its competitiveness through an accurate assessment of its current position.

Based on the previous illustration, an economy has two scenarios, either cost or differentiation strategy, to choose from. As Figure 3 illustrates, the Base Data (BD) is the starting point. The rankings that result from the choice of a Cost Strategy (CS) are shown on the left, and the rankings as a result of choosing a Differentiation Strategy (DS) are listed on the right. Table 6 demonstrates the indices of the cost strategy and differentiation strategy. For example, the Philippines ranks 33rd with a cost strategy, while falling to 37th position with a differentiation strategy. The difference in France's case is even larger. It ranks 20th with a

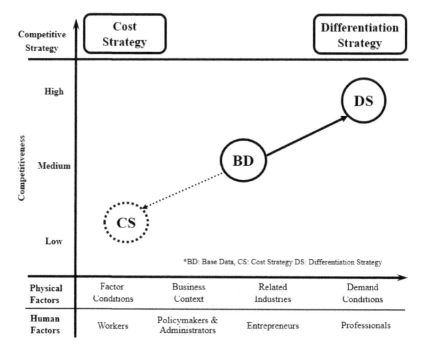

Figure 3.   Changing rankings with different strategy simulation

Note: BD: base data, CS: cost strategy, DS: differentiation strategy.

differentiation strategy but falls to 34th with a cost strategy. Therefore, choosing the appropriate strategy is more crucial for France than for the Philippines, given the significant difference between the two extreme choices.

Implementation using term-priority matrix

The Term-Priority Matrix is a policy tool to improve weak criteria. First, the 98 criteria are classified into strong (criteria in which a country displays relative strengths) and weak categories (criteria in which a country shows relative weaknesses). The strong and weak criteria are classified according to their relative performance against the sub-factor ranking that they belong to. If the criterion ranking is higher than the sub-factor ranking, the criterion is classified as a strong one, and vice versa. Second, the

Table 6.   Base data and the two strategies' rankings.

Country/Region	BDR	BDI	CSR	CSI	DSR	DSI	Country/Region	BDR	BDI	CSR	CSI	DSR	DSI
Singapore	1	61.31	5	48.65	3	69.26	Indonesia	32	39.88	31	35.87	29	47.26
Denmark	2	60.76	7	47.38	1	71.86	Panama	33	39.36	26	37.15	34	44.34
Canada	3	59.72	1	54.51	8	65.30	Slovenia	34	39.32	40	33.03	32	45.35
Netherlands	4	59.61	10	45.80	4	69.02	Greece	35	38.46	36	33.81	38	43.43
United States	5	58.83	8	46.58	5	67.50	Colombia	36	38.32	39	33.33	33	44.60
Switzerland	6	58.36	12	44.96	2	69.29	Spain	37	38.31	47	31.21	36	43.95
Sweden	7	57.99	9	46.43	6	66.92	Thailand	38	37.73	35	35.32	35	44.07
UAE	8	56.91	3	50.29	9	64.64	Philippines	39	37.55	33	35.49	37	43.69
Australia	9	56.49	2	52.03	11	61.95	Dominican Republic	40	35.38	45	31.81	40	42.81
Finland	10	56.40	11	45.67	7	66.44	Mexico	41	34.99	37	33.81	44	39.24
New Zealand	11	53.91	4	48.91	17	58.10	Peru	42	34.89	41	33.00	41	42.04
Belgium	12	53.18	14	42.04	10	62.41	Jordan	43	34.00	44	31.97	47	37.53
Hong Kong	13	52.99	17	40.56	12	61.57	Hungary	44	33.83	53	28.61	46	38.43
Austria	14	51.05	16	40.62	15	58.71	Croatia	45	33.44	55	27.73	42	40.25
United Kingdom	15	50.99	20	39.77	13	60.88	Argentina	46	33.26	43	32.05	45	38.66
Germany	16	50.56	18	40.55	16	58.16	Oman	47	32.75	42	32.42	54	32.10
Taiwan	17	50.30	19	40.38	14	59.87	Turkey	48	32.48	56	26.04	43	39.93
China	18	48.81	6	47.44	19	53.68	Nigeria	49	31.74	52	28.66	48	37.44

(*Continued*)

Table 6. (*Continued*)

Country/Region	BDR	BDI	CSR	CSI	DSR	DSI	Country/Region	BDR	BDI	CSR	CSI	DSR	DSI
Korea	19	47.70	21	39.30	18	56.80	Brazil	50	31.32	48	30.92	50	35.02
Kuwait	20	44.59	13	43.51	24	48.54	Egypt	51	31.24	46	31.23	49	36.34
France	21	44.27	34	35.48	20	51.30	Russia	52	29.72	38	33.49	60	28.86
Czech Republic	22	43.83	27	36.23	23	48.87	Cambodia	53	28.29	49	30.33	55	32.00
Saudi Arabia	23	43.29	15	40.88	27	47.95	Ukraine	54	28.14	54	27.75	52	33.47
Italy	24	43.22	28	36.14	21	50.79	Guatemala	55	28.10	50	30.14	59	29.85
Israel	25	42.82	30	35.92	28	47.90	Slovak Republic	56	28.00	59	22.86	53	32.55
Japan	26	42.78	32	35.69	22	50.01	South Africa	57	26.54	62	17.65	51	34.89
Poland	27	41.18	29	35.95	26	48.14	Bangladesh	58	26.39	57	25.69	56	31.68
Chile	28	41.08	23	38.47	31	46.01	Kenya	59	26.29	58	24.56	57	30.72
Vietnam	29	40.96	25	37.34	25	48.19	Pakistan	60	26.18	51	29.15	61	27.88
India	30	40.65	22	39.09	30	46.03	Sri Lanka	61	24.54	60	22.50	58	29.94
Malaysia	31	39.90	24	38.18	39	43.41	Morocco	62	22.54	61	19.70	62	27.12

Note: BDR: base data ranking, BDI: base data index, CSR: cost strategy ranking, CSI: cost strategy index, DSR: differentiation strategy ranking, DSI: differentiation strategy index

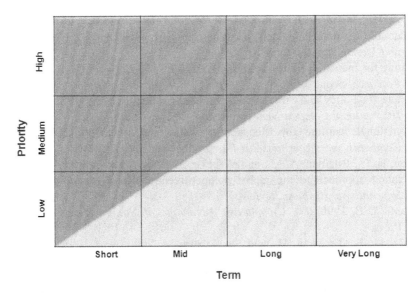

Figure 4.   The term-priority matrix

sub-factors with weak criteria are categorized into 12 groups by terms (or time span) and priorities of policies. The degree of priority (y-axis) is determined by the degree of the correlation coefficient between the sub-factors and GDP per capita. The upper-left triangle represents the more important and effective policies while the lower-right triangle shows the less important ones (see Figure 4).

References

Cho, D. S. 1994. A dynamic approach to international competitiveness: The case of Korea. *Journal of Far Eastern Business*, 1(1): 17–36.

Cho, D. S. and Moon, H. C. 2000. *From Adam Smith to Michael Porter: Evolution of Competitiveness Theory*. Singapore: World Scientific.

Cho, D. S. and Moon, H. C. 2013. *International Review of National Competitiveness: A Detailed Analysis of Sources and Rankings*. Cheltenham, UK and Northampton, MA: Edward Elgar Publishing Limited.

Cho, D. S., Moon, H. C., and Kim, M. Y. 2008. Characterizing international competitiveness in international business research: A MASI approach to national competitiveness. *Research in International Business and Finance*, 22(2): 175–192.

Cho, D. S., Moon, H. C., and Kim, M. Y. 2009. Does one size fit all? A dual double diamond approach to country-specific advantages. *Asian Business and Management*, 8(1): 83–102.

Institute for Industrial Policy Studies (IPS). 2006. *IPS National Competitiveness Research*. Seoul: IPS.

Institute for Policy and Strategy and National Competitiveness (IPSNC). 2022. *IPS National Competitiveness Research 2022*. Seoul: IPSNC.

International Institute for Management Development (IMD). 2014. *World Competitiveness Yearbook 2014*. Lausanne, Switzerland: IMD.

Moon, H. C., Rugman, A. M., and Verbeke, A. 1998. A generalized double diamond approach to the global competitiveness of Korea and Singapore. *International Business Review*, 7: 135–150.

Porter, M. E. 1990. *The Competitive Advantage of Nations*. New York: Free Press.

Porter, M. E., Takeuchi, H., and Sakakibara, M. 2000. *Can Japan Compete?* Cambridge, MA: Perseus Publishing.

Rugman, A. M. 1991. Diamond in the rough. *Business Quarterly*, 55(3): 61–64.

Rugman, A. M. and D'Cruz, R. J. 1993. The "double diamond" model of international competitiveness: The Canadian experience. *Management International Review*, 33(2): 17–39.

Sureshchandar, G. S. and Leisten, R. 2006. A framework for evaluating the criticality of software metrics: An analytic hierarchy process (AHP) approach. *Measuring Business Excellence*, 10(4): 22–33.

World Economic Forum (WEF). 2006. *Global Competitiveness Report 2017*. Geneva, Switzerland: WEF.

World Economic Forum (WEF). 2019. *Global Competitiveness Report 2019*. Geneva, Switzerland: WEF.

Chapter 3

Highlights*

Overall Rankings

Three key global institutions release national competitiveness ranking reports annually: the International Institute for Management Development (IMD), the World Economic Forum (WEF), and IPS Switzerland. Both the IMD and WEF each release a single overall competitiveness ranking, while IPS Switzerland differs by releasing two distinct strategy rankings — one based on cost leadership and another grounded in differentiation strategies. These fluctuations in rankings, influenced by strategic choices, underscore the dynamic nature of national competitiveness. Instead of perceiving competitiveness as static, based solely on the existing stock of resources, economies can adopt a more proactive stance. They can leverage both domestic and international resources more effectively to bolster their overall rankings.

Tables 1 and 2 show the results of the two strategy rankings. In fact, the rankings based on cost strategy (CS) and differentiation strategy (DS) offer markedly different outcomes. Under CS, the top four economies are Canada (1), Australia (2), United Arab Emirates (UAE) (3), and New Zealand (4), which are all featured with relatively rich resources. By contrast, in DS ranking, developed economies such as Denmark (1), Switzerland (2), Singapore (3), and the Netherlands (4) tend to dominate

---

*This chapter presents the highlights of IPS National Competitiveness Research 2023. To see more information about the rankings of economies by factor and sub-factor, please visit the IPSNC website (https://www.ipsncr.org/).

Table 1.   The rankings for the two strategies.

Country/Region	CSR	CSI	Country/Region	DSR	DSI
Canada	1	54.51	Denmark	1	71.86
Australia	2	52.03	Switzerland	2	69.29
UAE	3	50.29	Singapore	3	69.26
New Zealand	4	48.91	Netherlands	4	69.02
Singapore	5	48.65	United States	5	67.50
China	6	47.44	Sweden	6	66.92
Denmark	7	47.38	Finland	7	66.44
United States	8	46.58	Canada	8	65.30
Sweden	9	46.43	UAE	9	64.64
Netherlands	10	45.80	Belgium	10	62.41
Finland	11	45.67	Australia	11	61.95
Switzerland	12	44.96	Hong Kong SAR	12	61.57
Kuwait	13	43.51	United Kingdom	13	60.88
Belgium	14	42.04	Taiwan, China	14	59.87
Saudi Arabia	15	40.88	Austria	15	58.71
Austria	16	40.62	Germany	16	58.16
Hong Kong SAR	17	40.56	New Zealand	17	58.10
Germany	18	40.55	Korea	18	56.80
Taiwan, China	19	40.38	China	19	53.68
United Kingdom	20	39.77	France	20	51.30
Korea	21	39.30	Italy	21	50.79
India	22	39.09	Japan	22	50.01
Chile	23	38.47	Czechia	23	48.87
Malaysia	24	38.18	Kuwait	24	48.54
Vietnam	25	37.34	Vietnam	25	48.19
Panama	26	37.15	Poland	26	48.14
Czechia	27	36.23	Saudi Arabia	27	47.95
Italy	28	36.14	Israel	28	47.90
Poland	29	35.95	Indonesia	29	47.26
Israel	30	35.92	India	30	46.03
Indonesia	31	35.87	Chile	31	46.01
Japan	32	35.69	Slovenia	32	45.35

Table 1. (*Continued*)

Country/Region	CSR	CSI	Country/Region	DSR	DSI
Philippines	33	35.49	Colombia	33	44.60
France	34	35.48	Panama	34	44.34
Thailand	35	35.32	Thailand	35	44.07
Greece	36	33.81	Spain	36	43.95
Mexico	37	33.81	Philippines	37	43.69
Russia	38	33.49	Greece	38	43.43
Colombia	39	33.33	Malaysia	39	43.41
Slovenia	40	33.03	Dominican Republic	40	42.81
Peru	41	33.00	Peru	41	42.04
Oman	42	32.42	Croatia	42	40.25
Argentina	43	32.05	Turkey	43	39.93
Jordan	44	31.97	Mexico	44	39.24
Dominican Republic	45	31.81	Argentina	45	38.66
Egypt	46	31.23	Hungary	46	38.43
Spain	47	31.21	Jordan	47	37.53
Brazil	48	30.92	Nigeria	48	37.44
Cambodia	49	30.33	Egypt	49	36.34
Guatemala	50	30.14	Brazil	50	35.02
Pakistan	51	29.15	South Africa	51	34.89
Nigeria	52	28.66	Ukraine	52	33.47
Hungary	53	28.61	Slovak Republic	53	32.55
Ukraine	54	27.75	Oman	54	32.10
Croatia	55	27.73	Cambodia	55	32.00
Turkey	56	26.04	Bangladesh	56	31.68
Bangladesh	57	25.69	Kenya	57	30.72
Kenya	58	24.56	Sri Lanka	58	29.94
Slovak Republic	59	22.86	Guatemala	59	29.85
Sri Lanka	60	22.50	Russia	60	28.86
Morocco	61	19.70	Pakistan	61	27.88
South Africa	62	17.65	Morocco	62	27.12

Note: CSR: cost strategy ranking, DSR: differentiation strategy ranking.

Table 2.   Matching the rankings for the two strategies.

Country/Region	CSR	DSR	Country/Region	DSR	CSR
Canada	1	8	Denmark	1	7
Australia	2	11	Switzerland	2	12
UAE	3	9	Singapore	3	5
New Zealand	4	17	Netherlands	4	10
Singapore	5	3	United States	5	8
China	6	19	Sweden	6	9
Denmark	7	1	Finland	7	11
United States	8	5	Canada	8	1
Sweden	9	6	UAE	9	3
Netherlands	10	4	Belgium	10	14
Finland	11	7	Australia	11	2
Switzerland	12	2	Hong Kong SAR	12	17
Kuwait	13	24	United Kingdom	13	20
Belgium	14	10	Taiwan, China	14	19
Saudi Arabia	15	27	Austria	15	16
Austria	16	15	Germany	16	18
Hong Kong SAR	17	12	New Zealand	17	4
Germany	18	16	Korea	18	21
Taiwan, China	19	14	China	19	6
United Kingdom	20	13	France	20	34
Korea	21	18	Italy	21	28
India	22	30	Japan	22	32
Chile	23	31	Czechia	23	27
Malaysia	24	39	Kuwait	24	13
Vietnam	25	25	Vietnam	25	25
Panama	26	34	Poland	26	29
Czechia	27	23	Saudi Arabia	27	15
Italy	28	21	Israel	28	30
Poland	29	26	Indonesia	29	31
Israel	30	28	India	30	22
Indonesia	31	29	Chile	31	23
Japan	32	22	Slovenia	32	40

Table 2. (*Continued*)

Country/Region	CSR	DSR	Country/Region	DSR	CSR
Philippines	33	37	Colombia	33	39
France	34	20	Panama	34	26
Thailand	35	35	Thailand	35	35
Greece	36	38	Spain	36	47
Mexico	37	44	Philippines	37	33
Russia	38	60	Greece	38	36
Colombia	39	33	Malaysia	39	24
Slovenia	40	32	Dominican Republic	40	45
Peru	41	41	Peru	41	41
Oman	42	54	Croatia	42	55
Argentina	43	45	Turkey	43	56
Jordan	44	47	Mexico	44	37
Dominican Republic	45	40	Argentina	45	43
Egypt	46	49	Hungary	46	53
Spain	47	36	Jordan	47	44
Brazil	48	50	Nigeria	48	52
Cambodia	49	55	Egypt	49	46
Guatemala	50	59	Brazil	50	48
Pakistan	51	61	South Africa	51	62
Nigeria	52	48	Ukraine	52	54
Hungary	53	46	Slovak Republic	53	59
Ukraine	54	52	Oman	54	42
Croatia	55	42	Cambodia	55	49
Turkey	56	43	Bangladesh	56	57
Bangladesh	57	56	Kenya	57	58
Kenya	58	57	Sri Lanka	58	60
Slovak Republic	59	53	Guatemala	59	50
Sri Lanka	60	58	Russia	60	38
Morocco	61	62	Pakistan	61	51
South Africa	62	51	Morocco	62	61

Note: CSR: cost strategy ranking, DSR: differentiation strategy ranking.

the top rankings. Conversely, the United States (US) and China show a stark difference depending on their strategic choice. The US ranked eighth in the CS ranking, but it rose to fifth in the DS ranking. For its part, China ranks sixth in the CS ranking, yet falls to nineteenth in the DS ranking.

Among the 62 economies, Russia exhibited the most significant difference between cost and differentiation rankings, a gap of 22 places. Seven other countries — Malaysia, New Zealand, China, Saudi Arabia, Oman, Kuwait, and Pakistan — also showed considerable differences of 10 places or more. These eight nations all achieved higher rankings with CS. In total, 24 countries, including the aforementioned eight, displayed improved rankings when adopting CS. In contrast, 35 countries registered higher rankings when pursuing DS. Three countries — Vietnam, Thailand, and Peru — demonstrated identical rankings for both strategies.

2023 IPS Competitiveness Ranking Changes by Cost and Differentiation Strategies

This section divides the 62 economies into four categories based on the shifts in ranking under cost and differentiation strategies relative to the base data rankings. As outlined in Chapter 2, the IPS model comprises eight factors: four physical ones (Factor Conditions, Demand Conditions, Related Industries, and Business Context) and four human-centric ones (Workers, Policymakers and administrators, Entrepreneurs, and Professionals). The base data ranking assigns uniform weights to all eight factors, while cost and differentiation strategies use distinct weights for these factors. For instance, when a cost strategy is employed, greater weights are inherently given to cost-driven ones such as factor conditions. In contrast, if a country utilizes a differentiation strategy, varied weights are allocated to each of the eight factors, and more weights are given to demand conditions and professionals.[1] As illustrated in Figure 1, the two strategies' rankings could ascend or descend relative to their base data rankings, contingent on whether the cost or differentiation strategy is selected.

Figure 1 presents four potential scenarios, with the 62 economies categorized into four groups: Groups 1, 2, 3, and 4. It is apparent

---

[1] Please refer to Chapter 2 for more details about the weights.

Figure 1.   Ranking changes by cost and differentiation strategies

Note: CS: cost strategy, DS: differentiation strategy.

that Group 1 should implement both cost and differentiation strategies. The economies in Group 1 have lower national competitiveness rankings, irrespective of whether cost or differentiation strategies are adopted. Instead, their competitiveness and sustainable development largely depend on external factors such as resources from other economies, given their relatively small size. As such, promoting either CS or DS solely by leveraging their own resources presents a significant challenge. Group 1 countries should then encourage internationalization or regional clustering, fostering collaborations to improve either CS or DS, which in turn would enhance their competitiveness depending on the specific areas. For instance, since it might be difficult for Group 1 countries to promote CS independently, they could form partnerships with neighboring countries that excel in CS.

Countries classified under Group 2 should adopt DS to enhance their competitiveness ranking, given that their DSR is higher than their BSR. Conversely, as the CS would reduce their competitiveness ranking, it is crucial for Group 2 countries to adjust their resources toward a differentiation strategy, aiding them in advancing from their current developmental level. Examining the performance of Group 2 countries in various sub-factors, they demonstrate strengths in the areas of Demand Conditions and Professionals, factors associated with DS. Consequently, these economies, typically characterized as developed or innovation-based, rely on continuous innovation for sustainable growth. It is recommended that these economies pursue a differentiation strategy that will help consolidate their leading positions.

For Group 3 countries, CS plays a more significant role than the DS. Predominantly composed of developing countries rich in resources, along with a few resource-based developed countries, Group 3 economies heavily rely on their abundant natural resources to pursue higher rankings. As a result, they are advised to favor a cost strategy over a differentiation strategy. Evaluating the performance of Group 3 countries in different sub-factors, these nations show strength in the criteria of Factor Conditions and Workers, factors that are typically associated with CS.

Lastly, the economies in Group 4 are characterized by their significant potential for future development. Most of these are developing economies, classified as either weak or intermediate in our group ranking. Both strategies could boost their competitiveness, due to the vast potential for improvement available on adopting either one. However, despite the considerable potential for advancement through either CS or DS, our analysis indicates that initiating with CS before transitioning to DS could accelerate development. This is because DS tends to be more effective for advanced countries that already have a strong economic development foundation.

Intra-group Rankings

In Figure 2, the 62 economies are categorized into nine groups according to their size (large, medium, and small) and competitiveness levels (strong, intermediate, and weak). Under the cost strategy simulation, 20 countries are classified in the strong group, while 15 and 27 countries are classified in the intermediate group and the weak group, respectively. Similarly, under CS, 21 countries are classified in the large group; 23 countries in the medium group; the rest (18 countries) in the small group.

By contrast, under DS, 19 countries are classified in the strong group. While 20 and 22 countries are classified in the intermediate and weak groups, respectively. According to the classification based on size,

CSI & DSI \ Size	Small		Medium		Large	
Strong	**CS Ranking** 1. U.A.E. 2. Singapore 3. Denmark 4. Netherlands 5. Switzerland 6. Kuwait 7. Belgium 8. Austria 9. Hong Kong SAR	**DS Ranking** 1. Denmark 2. Switzerland 3. Singapore 4. Netherlands 5. U.A.E. 6. Belgium 7. Austria 8. Hong Kong SAR	**CS Ranking** 1. New Zealand 2. Sweden 3. Finland 4. Germany 5. Taiwan, China 6. United Kingdom	**DS Ranking** 1. Sweden 2. Finland 3. United Kingdom 4. Taiwan, China 5. Germany 6. New Zealand 7. Korea	**CS Ranking** 1. Canada 2. Australia 3. China 4. United States 5. Saudi Arabia	**DS Ranking** 1. United States 2. Canada 3. Australia 4. China
Intermediate	**CS Ranking** 1. Panama 2. Czech Republic 3. Israel	**DS Ranking** 1. Czech Republic 2. Kuwait 3. Israel 4. Slovenia 5. Panama 6. Greece	**CS Ranking** 1. Korea 2. Chile 3. Malaysia 4. Vietnam 5. Italy 6. Poland 7. France 8. Thailand	**DS Ranking** 1. France 2. Italy 3. Vietnam 4. Poland 5. Chile 6. Thailand 7. Spain 8. Malaysia	**CS Ranking** 1. India 2. Indonesia 3. Japan 4. Philippines	**DS Ranking** 1. Japan 2. Saudi Arabia 3. Indonesia 4. India 5. Colombia 6. Phillipines
Weak	**CS Ranking** 1. Greece 2. Slovenia 3. Dominican Republic 4. Hungary 5. Croatia 6. Slovak Republic	**DS Ranking** 1. Dominican Republic 2. Croatia 3. Hungary 4. Slovak Republic	**CS Ranking** 1. Oman 2. Jordan 3. Spain 4. Cambodia 5. Guatemala 6. Ukraine 7. Kenya 8. Sri Lanka 9. Morocco	**DS Ranking** 1. Jordan 2. Ukraine 3. Oman 4. Cambodia 5. Kenya 6. Sri Lanka 7. Guatemala 8. Morocco	**CS Ranking** 1. Mexico 2. Russia 3. Colombia 4. Peru 5. Argentina 6. Egypt 7. Brazil 8. Pakistan 9. Nigeria 10. Türkiye 11. Bangladesh 12. South Africa	**DS Ranking** 1. Peru 2. Türkiye 3. Mexico 4. Argentina 5. Nigeria 6. Egypt 7. Brazil 8. South Africa 9. Bangladesh 10. Russia 11. Pakistan

Figure 2. Intra-group rankings based on cost and differentiation strategy

Note: CS: cost strategy, DS: differentiation strategy, CSI: Cost Strategy Index, DSI: differentiation strategy index.

21 countries belong to the large group; 23 countries, to the medium group; and 18 countries, to the small group under DS. Moreover, it is important to note that the classifications ultimately depend upon the strategies the countries adopt. For example, the classification of Kuwait would change from a small–strong group to a small–intermediate group were it to adopt CS instead of DS. By contrast, the group classification of Korea would change from a medium–intermediate group to a medium–strong group were the country to choose DS over CS.

Large group

Although the overall competitiveness rankings change, the list of the top four countries belonging to the large–strong group remains the same: Canada, Australia, China, and the US, regardless of which strategy they adopt. Contrarily, if Saudi Arabia adopts the differentiation strategy, it drops to the large–intermediate group from the large–strong group. Similarly, Russia belongs to the weak cluster under both CS and DS simulation.

Medium group

In the case of CS, only six countries/regions, including New Zealand, Sweden, Finland, Germany, Taiwan, China, and the United Kingdom are classified in the medium–strong group. However, under DS, Korea would be added to the medium–strong group. This shows that the employment of the different strategies affects the overall national competitiveness ranking and the classification of most countries/regions. For example, Ukraine ranks sixth place in the medium–weak group under CS but would move up to second place if the country adopts DS.

Small group

Considering the CSR, UAE, Singapore, Denmark, Netherlands, Switzerland, Kuwait, Belgium, Austria, and Hong Kong SAR take the top positions as strong countries/regions. However, under DSR, Kuwait would be classified in the small–intermediate group instead of the small–strong group. Moreover, Israel belongs to the intermediate cluster under both strategies. Yet, Greece would rise to the small–intermediate group from the small–weak group when the economy chooses DS.

Simulation

In this simulation, economies are given one of two choices: cost or differentiation. The results from choosing the two strategies are summarized in Table 3. For example, the Netherlands' ranking will fall from fourth to

Table 3. Base data and the rankings for the two strategies.

Country/Region	Base Data	Cost Strategy	Differentiation Strategy
Singapore	1	5	3
Denmark	2	7	1
Canada	3	1	8
Netherlands	4	10	4
United States	5	8	5
Switzerland	6	12	2
Sweden	7	9	6
UAE	8	3	9
Australia	9	2	11
Finland	10	11	7
New Zealand	11	4	17
Belgium	12	14	10
Hong Kong SAR	13	17	12
Austria	14	16	15
United Kingdom	15	20	13
Germany	16	18	16
Taiwan, China	17	19	14
China	18	6	19
Korea	19	21	18
Kuwait	20	13	24
France	21	34	20
Czechia	22	27	23
Saudi Arabia	23	15	27
Italy	24	28	21
Israel	25	30	28
Japan	26	32	22
Poland	27	29	26
Chile	28	23	31
Vietnam	29	25	25

(Continued)

Table 3.   (*Continued*)

Country/Region	Base Data	Cost Strategy	Differentiation Strategy
India	30	22	30
Malaysia	31	24	39
Indonesia	32	31	29
Panama	33	26	34
Slovenia	34	40	32
Greece	35	36	38
Colombia	36	39	33
Spain	37	47	36
Thailand	38	35	35
Philippines	39	33	37
Dominican Republic	40	45	40
Mexico	41	37	44
Peru	42	41	41
Jordan	43	44	47
Hungary	44	53	46
Croatia	45	55	42
Argentina	46	43	45
Oman	47	42	54
Turkey	48	56	43
Nigeria	49	52	48
Brazil	50	48	50
Egypt	51	46	49
Russia	52	38	60
Cambodia	53	49	55
Ukraine	54	54	52
Guatemala	55	50	59
Slovak Republic	56	59	53
South Africa	57	62	51
Bangladesh	58	57	56
Kenya	59	58	57
Pakistan	60	51	61
Sri Lanka	61	60	58
Morocco	62	61	62

10th if it adopts CS. Yet, its ranking will rise back to the fourth when it adopts DS. By contrast, Canada shows a slightly higher rank when adopting CS, but drops to the eighth if it pursues DS.

Quantification of qualitative data through ChatGPT

For 2023, we made a strategic addition to our approach by incorporating ChatGPT to delve deeper into and measure the competitiveness across the 41 survey criteria. ChatGPT has been instrumental in enhancing the quality of our data, thanks to its comprehensive database and advanced linguistic modeling abilities. It has been particularly beneficial in circumstances where data collection through conventional means is hampered, as in the case of our overseas offices in Russia and Ukraine. With geopolitical tensions, such as the Russia–Ukraine War, affecting the operations of our on-ground teams, the capacity of ChatGPT to independently conduct surveys has proven invaluable.

To efficiently quantify qualitative data, we devised specific prompts for 41 survey questions across 62 countries. For example, consider a survey question aimed at understanding the sensitivity of Argentine consumers toward product quality. We posed the question to ChatGPT as follows:

Please evaluate the sensitivity of Argentine consumers to product quality. Provide a score on a scale up to 10, where a higher score indicates greater sensitivity to product quality. Please provide the score only.

This type of questioning was used to interrogate ChatGPT about all 62 countries, covering the 41 survey items. The results obtained from ChatGPT were combined with the KOTRA survey data by calculating an average score from both sources for each survey question for every country.

The adoption of this method has brought about significant improvement in the precision of our findings. It has allowed us to extract insightful data while overcoming obstacles such as military conflicts that could otherwise impede comprehensive research. This hybrid approach, blending human intelligence with artificial intelligence, symbolizes the potential of technology in aiding in-depth, large-scale studies and contributing to more accurate and reliable outcomes.

Chapter 4

Application of MASI: The Cases of the US and China

This chapter examines the cases of the US and China to assess the application of the MASI framework (Cho and Moon, 2013) that was introduced in Chapter 3 and its implications for the dynamic relationship between these two countries. Despite their differences and conflicts over sensitive issues, such as political systems, culture, and ideology (Center for Strategic & International Studies [CSIS], 2019; Mitter and Johnson, 2021), both countries can explore common ground and areas of shared interests to foster cooperation. By doing so, they can establish a mutually beneficial relationship that leads to a win–win outcome. This chapter seeks to analyze the competitiveness of the two countries, investigating their strengths and weaknesses to explore the potential for enhanced partnership. The comprehensive study of these countries provides a valuable blueprint for other economies, inspiring them to assess their competitive areas and establish cooperative relationships with each other.

The Case of the US

Measurement

In 2023, the US is fifth place in the overall competitiveness ranking with regards to the base data. Out of the eight factors of the IPS model, the US shows higher competitiveness, particularly in the four factors — Demand Conditions (1), Related Industries (10), Entrepreneurs (1), and

Table 1.   Structure of the US national competitiveness.

Factors	Rank
Factor conditions	11
Demand conditions	**1**
Related industries	**10**
Business context	18
Workers	25
Policymakers & administrators	14
Entrepreneurs	**1**
Professionals	**6**

Professionals (6) (see Table 1). Conversely, the US has a relatively lower ranking in Business Context (18) and Workers (25).

Analysis at the sub-factor level[1]

As the US is categorized in the large–strong group, its strengths and weaknesses should be compared with the other large-strong economies (Australia, Canada, and China) rather than with every other country from the overall competitiveness ranking. Figure 1 shows that the US performed weaker than the average large–strong economies in the two sub-factors under Factor Conditions. In addition, for Quantity of Labor Force, the US was 80% of the average level of the other large–strong economies, thus its performance was relatively weaker in this sub-factor as well. However, for other sub-factors (Demand Size, Industrial Infrastructure, and the Personal Competence and Social Context of both Entrepreneurs and Professionals), the US demonstrated a very strong performance with higher competitiveness when compared to the average of the remaining three large–strong economies.

---

[1]The comparative analysis is at the sub-factor level using the base data that give the same weights for the eight factors of the IPS model.

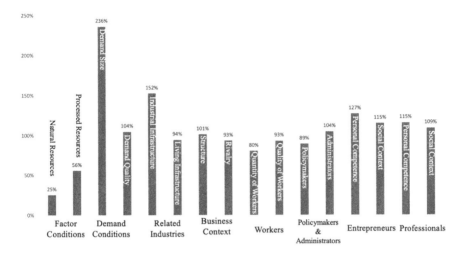

Figure 1.   Relative position of the US (sub-factor level)

Simulation

The US ranked fifth in the overall national competitiveness ranking (Base Data). Yet, if it pursues a cost strategy (CS), its overall ranking will drop to eighth place. By contrast, under a differentiation strategy (DS), the US rank will stay the same at fifth place. As Table 1 shows, the US has a competitive structure with relative strength in criteria from the factors of Demand Conditions, Related Industries, and Entrepreneurs, which are improved by DS and therefore help to strengthen its national competitiveness.

Implementation

Identification of weak criteria

The weak criteria of the US are summarized in Table 2. If the rank of a certain criterion (e.g., wood production) is lower than that of the sub-factors (e.g., processed resources) it belongs to, we identify it as a weak area for the US. Fifteen out of 16 sub-factors under the eight factors are categorized as weak criteria and will be included in the term-priority matrix. The sub-factor of energy resources is excluded given its nature of uncontrollability, meaning that it will be less likely to be influenced by the

Table 2. Weak criteria for US public policy formulation.

Factor Conditions	Demand Conditions	Related Industries
Processed Resources (12) – Wood production (13) – Livestock (18)	**Demand Quality (9)** – Consumer sophistication: quality (10) – Consumer sophistication: health and environment (11) – Consumer sophistication: international standard of IPR (26)	**Industrial Infrastructure (1)** – Vehicles (2) – Total expenditure on R&D (6) – Civil aviation (8) – Internet users (18) – International travel (22) – Capital accessibility (24) – Maritime transport (26) – Capital value (28) – Mobile phone subscriber (47) **Living Infrastructure (29)** – Gini index (34) – Secondary enrollment rate (36) – Student international mobility (38) – Personal security (45) – CO_2 emissions (56)

Business Context

Structure (10)
- Firm's decision structure (11)
- Ethical practices (13)
- Equal treatment (18)
- Firm's decision structure (22)

Rivalry (43)
- Goods imports as % of GDP (59)
- Goods exports as % of GDP (61)
- Services imports as % of GDP (62)

Entrepreneurs

Personal Competence (1)
- The process of decision-making (3)
- Entrepreneurs' core competence (14)
- Entrepreneurs' education level (14)

Social Context (3)
- New business (6)
- Social status of entrepreneurs (9)

Workers

Quantity of Workers (38)
- Monthly compensation for manufacturing workers (42)

Quality of Workers (18)
- Management business relationship (19)

Professionals

Personal Competence (6)
- The ability to manage opportunities (8)
- Decision-making (9)
- Processionals' education level (9)
- Professionals' international experience (22)

Social Context (7)
- Professionals' compensation (12)
- Openness to foreign professionals (14)
- Social status of professionals (16)

Policymakers & Administrators

Policymakers (15)
- Ethics (28)

Administrators (13)
- The result of policy implementation (14)
- The process of policy implementation (16)
- Ethics (19)

strategic operations of policymakers. Out of 98 criteria, 43 criteria under 14 sub-factors are classified as weak areas for the US, which demands improvement through the support of relevant policies (see Table 2). The following illustrates the strengths and weaknesses of the US with regard to the 16 sub-factors.

- Factor Conditions

Natural Resources (15): The US ranked 15th in this sub-factor, achieving high competitiveness in most criteria such as coal reserves (6), natural gas reserves (8), land area (13), and freshwater resources (15).

Processed Resources (12): The US ranked 12th in this sub-factor, showing high competitiveness in the criteria including oil production (7), natural gas production (7), coal production (8), and wood production (13), despite its relative weakness in livestock (18).

- Demand Conditions

Demand Size (1): The US holds exceptionally high competitiveness in all criteria of this sub-factor such as GDP (1), goods and services: import (1), goods and services: export (2), and GDP per capita (3).

Demand Quality (9): The US showed high performance in most criteria of consumer sophistication on design (7), new technology (7), quality (10), and health and environmental issues (11). However, the US revealed relative weakness in the criterion of consumer sophistication on international standards of Intellectual Property Rights (IPR) (26).

- Related Industries

Industrial Infrastructure (1): In this sub-factor, the US outperformed in the criteria that are related to scientific technology such as total scientific research institutions (1), international patents granted (1), and total expenditure on R&D (6). By contrast, it displayed a relatively lower competitiveness in criteria indicating communication and transportation such as maritime transport (26), and mobile phone subscribers (47).

Living Infrastructure (29): The US ranked 29th in this sub-factor, achieving medium-level competitiveness. Among the 12 criteria, the criteria in which the US demonstrated its relative strength include leisure, sports, and cultural facilities (1), tertiary enrollment rate (9), Human Development

Index (HDI) (16), and social safety net (19). Conversely, the Gini index (34), secondary enrollment rate (36), student international mobility (38), personal security (45), and CO_2 emission (56) are classified as weak criteria of the US.

- Business Context

Structure (10): The US recorded high-level competitiveness in most criteria, including unique brands (4), social value (4), health, safety, and environmental concerns (8), and global standards (9). Comparatively, the US performed slightly weaker in criteria such as firm's decision process (11), ethical practices (13), equal treatment (18), and firm's decision structure (22). Still, the overall performance of the US in this factor remained strong.

Rivalry (43): The US showed low-level competitiveness in both goods (59) and services openness of imports (62). In addition, the US performance in a criterion of goods openness of exports (61) was particularly low. Still, the US revealed a slightly stronger performance in criteria such as portfolio openness with regards to outflows (10) and inflows (19) and FDI openness in terms of outflow (21).

- Workers

Quantity of Workers (38): In most criteria, the US demonstrated medium-level competitiveness including criteria of working hours (23), employment rate (35), and monthly compensation for manufacturing workers (42). However, the US achieved higher competitiveness in the criterion size of labor force (3).

Quality of Workers (18): The US exhibited high-level competitiveness in most criteria of this sub-factor including literacy rate (7) and attitude and motivation (7), education (13), and the openness of labor market (13). Yet, the US showed a slightly weaker performance on the criterion of management business relationship (19).

- Policymakers & Administrators

Policymakers (15): The US displayed high competitiveness in most criteria of this sub-factor, such as the process of legislature (2), the result of legislation (7), education level (7), and international experience (8). Compared to this, the US showed a slightly lower competitiveness in ethics (e.g., bribery and corruption) (28).

Administrators (13): The US possessed high-level competitiveness in areas including educational level (7) and international experience (9), but recorded slightly lower rankings in policy implementation (14), the process of policy implementation (16), and ethics (e.g., bribery and corruption) (19).

- Entrepreneurs

Personal Competence (1): The US demonstrated an exceptionally strong standing in this sub-factor, indicating strong performance in most criteria including the result of decision-making (1), entrepreneurs' international experience (1), the process of decision-making (3), and lower rankings in entrepreneurs' core competence (14) and entrepreneurs' education level (14).

Social Context (3): The US recorded a very high-level competitiveness in all of the following criteria, availability of entrepreneurs (1), support of the social system (2), openness to foreign entrepreneurs (2), new business (6), and social status of entrepreneurs (9).

- Professionals

Personal Competence (6): The US showed strong performance in this sub-factor, achieving strong performance in most criteria including professionals' core competences (3), the ability to manage opportunities (8), decision-making (9), professionals' education level (9), although its performance in a criterion, professionals' international experience (22), was only moderate.

Social Context (7): The US exhibited high competitiveness in all criteria of this sub-factor, including the mobility of professionals (4), availability of professionals (6), professionals' compensation (12), openness to foreign professionals (14), and social status of professionals (16).

Constructing a term-priority matrix

The 14 sub-factors listed in Table 3 are organized into a 4 × 3 matrix to provide an overview of policy recommendations. The sub-factors for the short term (Term 1) are listed in the order of correlation with GDP per capita and in priority of importance, which includes Administrators,

Table 3.   Correlation with GDP per capita (2022).

Priority	Term 1 Sub-factor	r.	Term 2 Sub-factor	r.	Term 3 Sub-factor	r.	Term 4 Sub-factor	r.
High	Administrators	0.901 (0.000)	Living infrastructure	0.809 (0.000)	Social context of entrepreneurs	0.836 (0.000)	Demand quality	0.719 (0.000)
	Industrial infrastructure	0.875 (0.000)						
Medium	Policymakers	0.780 (0.000)	Structure	0.761 (0.000)	Personal Competence of Entrepreneurs	0.791 (0.000)	Demand Size	0.655 (0.000)
			Social Context of Professionals	0.736 (0.000)	Personal Competence of Professionals	0.650 (0.000)		
Low	Rivalry	0.572 (0.000)	Processed resources	0.400 (0.002)	Quality of workers	0.602 (0.000)	Quantity of workers	−0.427 (0.000)

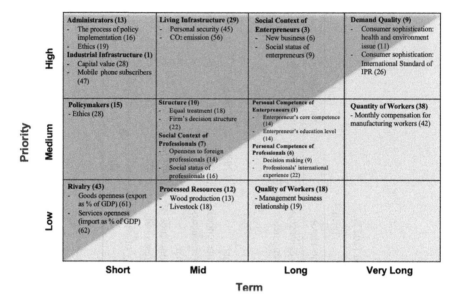

Figure 2.　Term-priority matrix: The case of the US

Industrial Infrastructure, Policymakers, and Rivalry. Hence, the higher correlation represents the areas that could have a stronger influence on the competitiveness of the country. The sub-factors under the midterm (Term 2) include Living Structure, Structure and Social Context of Professionals, and Processed Resources. The sub-factors in the long term (Term 3) include the Social Context of Entrepreneurs, Personal Competence of Entrepreneurs, Personal Competence of Professionals, and Quality of Workers. The sub-factors in the very long term (Term 4) are Demand Quality and Size, and Quantity of Workers. As shown in Figure 2, sub-factors covered by the upper-left-hand corner represent the areas that can be improved relatively easily and quickly by the government or the public sector and have higher influences on economic development. Therefore, it would be more effective for the US government to pay more attention to the areas in the upper-left-hand corner of Figure 2.

The Case of China

Measurement

Out of the 62 economies, China ranked 18th in the overall competitiveness ranking with regard to base data. Looking at its performance in each

Table 4. **Structure of China's national competitiveness under cost and differentiation strategies.**

Factors	Rank
Factor conditions	30
Demand conditions	**2**
Related industries	33
Business context	38
Workers	**1**
Policymakers & administrators	22
Entrepreneurs	21
Professionals	22

factor, it can be noted that China performed exceptionally strong in factors such as Workers (1) and Demand Conditions (2), while performing moderately in the other six factors (see Table 4).

Analysis at the sub-factor level[2]

China was categorized in the large–strong group. Hence, it would be more relevant to compare it with the other large–strong economies (Australia, Canada, and the US) when analyzing the relative strengths and weaknesses. Figure 3 shows that China's performance was weaker than the average of the other large–strong economies in many sub-factors. It was particularly weaker in the sub-factors of Natural Resources and Processed Resources under Factor Conditions, where it was less than 20% of the average level of all the other large–strong economies. However, for some sub-factors such as Demand Size and Quantity of Workers, China recorded stronger performance than the average of the other large–strong economies.

Simulation

Although China ranked 18th in the overall national competitiveness rankings (Base Data), its ranking will rise to sixth place if it pursues CS.

---

[2]The comparative analysis at the sub-factor level using the base data that give the same weights for the eight factors of the IPS model.

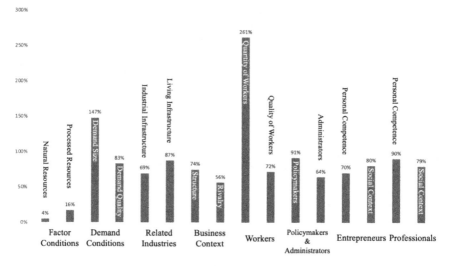

Figure 3.   Relative position of China (sub-factor level).

In addition, under DS, its ranking will move down to 19th place, which is slightly lower than its current ranking (18). China has a competitive structure with relatively high scores in criteria from factors of Demand Conditions and Related Industries in the physical factors and Workers and Policymakers & Administrators in the human factors. Therefore, China should pursue a cost strategy for further enhancement of its national competitiveness.

Implementation

Identification of weak criteria

The weak criteria that China needs to improve are summarized in Table 5. If a rank of a certain criterion is lower than that of the sub-factors it belongs to, we categorize it as a weak area. Fifteen sub-factors under all eight Factors (Factor Conditions, Demand Conditions, Related Industries, Business Context, Workers, Policymakers & Administrators, Entrepreneurs, and Professionals) have weak criteria and will be included in the term-priority matrix. In doing so, we excluded uncontrollable variables such as natural resources under Factor Conditions. Accordingly, 46 criteria under 15 sub-factors — or about 47% of the total 98 criteria — are classified as China's weak area.

Table 5. Weak criteria for public policy formulation of China.

Factor Conditions	Demand Conditions	Related Industries
Natural Resources (38)	**Demand Quality (24)**	**Industrial Infrastructure (33)**
– Land area (39)	– Consumer sophistication: quality (35)	– Capital value (36)
Processed Resources (23)i	– Consumer sophistication: health and	– Scientific research institutions (38)
– Wood production (24)	environment issues (36)	– Vehicles (40)
– Natural gas production (27)	– Consumer sophistication: international	– Mobile phone subscribers (40)
– Livestock (52)	standard of IPR (43)	– International travel (44)
	– Consumer sophistication: new	– Internet users (47)
	technology (43)	**Living Infrastructure (34)**
	– Consumer sophistication: design (49)	– CO_2 emission (40)
		– HDI (42)
		– Student international mobility (47)

(Continued)

Table 5. (*Continued*)

Business Context	Workers	Policymakers & Administrators
Structure (24)	**Quantity of Workers (1)**	**Policymakers (14)**
– Unique brands (27)	– Monthly compensation for	– Ethics (15)
– Social value (28)	manufacturing workers (25)	– International experience (17)
– Equal treatment (30)	– Employment rate (26)	– The process of legislature (22)
– Ethical practices (31)	**Quality of Workers (41)**	**Administrators (30)**
– Firms' decision structure (38)	– Management business relationship (51)	– Ethics (34)
– Global standards (39)		– The result of policy implementation (51)
– Firms' decision process (41)		
– Health, safety, and environmental		
concerns (44)		
Rivalry (59)		
– Services openness (import as % of		
GDP) (60)		

Entrepreneurs	Professionals
Personal Competence (24)	**Personal Competence (19)**
– The process of decision-making (29)	– Decision-making (20)
– Entrepreneurs' international	– Professionals' education level (29)
experience (30)	– The ability to manage opportunities (29)
– The result of decision-making (46)	– Professionals' education level (30)
Social Context (17)	**Social Context (23)**
– New business (21)	– The mobility of professionals (30)
– Social status of entrepreneurs (31)	– Social status of professionals (31)

- Factor Conditions

Natural Resources (38): China ranked 38th in this sub-factor, showing medium-level performance in most criteria such as natural gas reserves (23), freshwater resources (36), and land area (39). Compared to this, China showed a relatively stronger performance in the other two criteria, coal reserves (15) and crude oil reserves (19).

Processed Resources (23): China holds a moderate level of competitiveness in this sub-factor. Specifically, China showed moderate to high performance in all criteria such as coal production (5), oil production (22), wood production (24), and natural gas production. (27). However, as an exception, China was very weak in the criterion of livestock (52).

- Demand Conditions

Demand Size (2): China performed exceptionally strong in this sub-factor, recording a high performance in most criteria including goods and services: export (1), goods and services: import (2), and GDP (2), although China was weaker in terms of GDP per capita (35).

Demand Quality (24): China's performance in Demand Quality was moderate, which was highlighted by its moderate or weak performance in most criteria such as consumer sophistication on quality (35), health and environmental concerns (36), international standard of IPR (43), and new technology (43).

- Related Industries

Industrial Infrastructure (33): China exhibited moderate performance in all criteria for transportation and communication. For example, China recorded average in maritime transport (24), civil aviation (33), vehicles (40), and mobile phone subscribers (40). It was slightly stronger in the criteria for technological development such as international patents granted (3) and total expenditure on R&D (12).

Living Infrastructure (34): China ranked 34th in this sub-factor. Among all criteria, China showed moderate performance in most such as student per teacher (elementary) (27), social safety net (28), tertiary enrollment rate (29), leisure, sports, and cultural facilities (30), medical service (32), and Gini index (32).

- Business Context

Structure (24): China revealed medium or relatively weak performance in most criteria of this sub-factor measuring business strategy and governance among firms, such as unique brands (27), social value (28), equal treatment (30), ethical practices (31), and firm's decision structure (38).

Rivalry (59): China showed low-level competitiveness in this sub-factor. Particularly, China's performance on most of the criteria was weak, and particularly weak performance is captured in the criteria such as services openness exports (54), goods openness imports (57), and services openness imports (60).

- Workers

Quantity of Workers (1): China demonstrated a remarkably strong performance in this sub-factor. It performed particularly strongly in the area of size of labor force (1), although its performance in the criterion such as monthly compensation for manufacturing workers (25) was relatively lower compared to its performance in other criteria of this sub-factor.

Quality of Workers (41): China indicated medium-level competitiveness in most criteria of this sub-factor including the openness of labor market (31), education (33), literacy rate (33), and attitude and motivation (36).

- Policymakers & Administrators

Policymakers (14): China revealed high-level competitiveness in this sub-factor. Its strong performance is highlighted in the areas of the result of the legislature (11), education level (11), ethics (e.g., bribery and corruption) (15), and international experience (17).

Administrators (30): China displayed medium-level competitiveness in this sub-factor. In this sub-factor, the relatively competitive criteria of China include education level (11) and international experience (18).

- Entrepreneurs

Personal Competence (24): China exhibited a moderate standing in this sub-factor, performing relatively stronger in entrepreneurs' education level (7) and entrepreneurs' core competence (11). However, China's performance in most other criteria remained relatively weaker including the process of decision-making (29), entrepreneurs' international experience (30), and the result of decision-making (46).

Social Context (17): In most criteria, China showed high-level competitiveness such as openness to foreign entrepreneurs (14), support for the social system (15), and availability of entrepreneurs (17). However, the country demonstrated slightly lower competitiveness in areas such as new business (21) and the social status of entrepreneurs (31).

- Professionals

Personal Competence (19): China was classified in the high-performing group for this sub-factor. China showed strong performance in the criteria such as professionals' international experience (18) and decision-making (20), although it only showed moderate performance in many other criteria such as the ability to manage opportunities (29), professionals' core competences (29), and professionals' education level (30).

Social Context (23): China had a medium-level performance in this sub-factor, showing moderate performance in all criteria in this sub-factor including openness to foreign professionals (20), professionals' compensation (20), availability of professionals (22), mobility of professionals (30), and social status of professionals (31).

Constructing a term-priority matrix

The 15 sub-factors listed in Table 6 are organized into a 4 × 3 matrix (Figure 4) to provide an overview for policy recommendations. The sub-factors in the short term (Term 1) in the order of correlation are Administrators, Industrial Infrastructure, Policymakers, and Rivalry. The sub-factors under the midterm (Term 2) are Living Infrastructure, Structure of Business Context, and Processed Resources. The sub-factors in the long term (Term 3) are Social Context of Entrepreneurs, Personal Competence of Entrepreneurs and Professionals, and Quantity of Workers. The sub-factors in the very long term (Term 4) are Demand Quality and Quality of Workers. In this respect, like the explanation in the previous section on the US, it would be more effective for the Chinese government to pay strategic attention to the areas in the upper-left-hand corner of Figure 4.

Table 6.   The key areas of strengths and weaknesses for the US and China.

Criteria of NCR 2022	Rank of the US	Rank of China
Livestock	18	52
Consumer sophistication: design	7	49
Consumer sophistication: new technology	7	43
Vehicles	2	40
Scientific research institutions	1	38
Firm's decision process	11	41
Global standards	9	39
Health, safety, and environmental concerns	8	44
Portfolio openness (Financial outflows as % of GDP)	10	49
The result of decision-making (e.g., the ability to seize opportunities)	1	46
Coal production	8	5
Goods and services: export	2	1
Personal security	45	17
Size of labor force	3	1

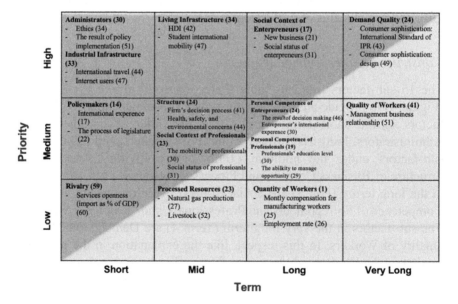

Figure 4.   Term-priority matrix: The case of China

The US and China: Enhanced Competitiveness through Cooperation

Comparing the competitiveness of the two countries, it can be noted that the US outperformed China in more than 80% of the 93 criteria. This was very evident with regards to entrepreneurs (e.g., decision-making), firm strategy (e.g., health, safety, and environmental concerns, global standards), consumer sophistication (e.g., design, new technology), and science and technology (e.g., scientific research institutions), in which the US recorded more than 30 places higher. Conversely, China showed stronger performance in 20% of the total criteria, particularly those with regards to energy resources (e.g., coal production), demand size (e.g., exports of goods and services), personal security, and the size of labor force (see Table 6).

To investigate this further, we classify the competitiveness of a country for each criterion as "high" when its ranking is between 1 and 20, "moderate" when its ranking lies between 21 and 40, and "low" when its ranking is between 41 and 62. This is more apparent when we compare the rankings between the US and China. Among the total of 98 criteria, 70 criteria for the US are classified in the "high" group, and 18 criteria for the US are in the "moderate" group. By contrast, for China, only 25 criteria are classified in the "high" group, while more than 50% are classified in "moderate."

Despite the competitive relationship, the competitiveness structure between the two countries suggests many areas for further potential cooperation, in which one can leverage the strengths to complement the other's weaknesses. However, the growing conflict between the two countries seemingly makes it more difficult to exploit the benefits of economic cooperation. For example, in August 2022, the US passed the Inflation Reduction Act, which provides subsidies for electric vehicles that were produced in the US. This aims to reshore the supply chains back to the US from China (*The Economist*, 2022). Regardless of such efforts, China has been rapidly catching up with the dominant position of the US in certain areas of technological development. For example, China now has a larger e-commerce and mobile payments industries than the US, and China publishes as much research on artificial intelligence (AI) as the US does (*The Economist*, 2018). Yet, Chinese technology firms Baidu, Alibaba, and Tencent (BATs) have mainly focused on the domestic market, and still lack international competitiveness and global brands that can compete against American technology firms such as Facebook, Amazon, Apple, Netflix, and Google's parent, Alphabet.

Such a rivalry over technological development between the two countries is well reflected in our rankings for the related criteria from the sub-factor of Industrial Infrastructure. In the 2022 NCR rankings, the US was ranked in sixth and first place for the criteria of total expenditure on R&D and international patents granted, respectively, while China was placed 12th and third, respectively, in the rankings for the two criteria. The exceptional performance of the US in these two criteria indicates the dominant position of the US in leading technological development in the world. At the same time, China is rapidly catching up with the position of the US, although it is still behind the US in many other criteria as of now. This implies that China needs to undergo some structural adjustments and changes that would only likely be achieved in the long term. In doing so, strategically collaborating with the US or other countries that hold strengths in areas where China has weaknesses would facilitate it to achieve such goals quickly and efficiently.

References

Center for Strategic & International Studies (CSIS). 2019. Are the United States and China in an ideological competition? https://www.csis.org/blogs/freeman-chair-blog/are-united-states-and-china-ideological-competition. Accessed July 5, 2023.

Cho, D. S. and Moon. H. C. 2013. *From Adam Smith to Michael Porter: Evolution of Competitiveness Theory* (extended edition). Singapore: World Scientific Publishing.

Mitter, R. and Johnson, E. 2021. What the West gets wrong about China. *Harvard Business Review*, May–June. https://hbr.org/2021/05/what-the-west-gets-wrong-about-china. Accessed July 5, 2023.

The Economist. 2018. America's tech giants vie with China's in third countries. https://www.economist.com/leaders/2018/07/05/americas-tech-giants-vie-with-chinas-in-third-countries. Accessed July 5, 2023.

The Economist. 2022. China's tech industry is catching up with Silicon Valley. https://www.economist.com/graphic-detail/2018/02/16/chinas-tech-industry-is-catching-up-with-silicon-valley. Accessed July 5, 2023.

Chapter 5

Snapshot of Top 30 Economies[*]

1. Singapore[1]

Singapore demonstrated exceptional performance in the overall national competitiveness ranking, particularly excelling in the areas of Business Context (1), Policymakers and Administrators (1), and Professionals (2). Its economy achieved a remarkable GDP growth of 3.6%. The retail sector remained strong as the country recovered from the COVID-19 pandemic, while the accommodation sector grew by 7.4% and the construction sector experienced a 6.7% growth rate compared to the previous year, contributing to the overall GDP growth. One of the driving factors behind Singapore's strong performance in the hospitality sector was the influx of international travelers throughout the year. The labor market in Singapore also exhibited strength, and the youth unemployment rate dropped by an impressive 7.3% compared to the previous year, largely attributed to the retail sector regaining its strength.

---

[*] The rankings of the top 30 economies are based on the base data without weights across the eight factors of the IPS model.

[1] This information is abstracted and organized from United Overseas Bank (UOB) (2022), Ministry of Trade and Industry Singapore (2022, 2023), HRM Asia (2023), and ISG (2023).

2. Denmark[2]

Denmark showcased strengths in the areas of Policymakers and Administrations (2) and Entrepreneurs (3) as the economy experienced GDP growth of 3.8% in 2022. At the same time, its labor market remained strong throughout the year, experiencing improvement in employment rates. This strengthened business performance resulted in increased personal and income tax revenue, leading to a government surplus of 3.3%. Notably, the pharmaceutical and maritime transport sectors demonstrated robust performance, leading to significant export growth, and thus contributing to overall net export expansion. Investment in construction has also grown due to the strong housing market. Moreover, Denmark is characterized by its leading renewable industries, which have attracted much investment, thus signifying the country's commitment to establishing the necessary infrastructure for producing renewable energy.

3. Canada[3]

Canada's economy demonstrated resilience in 2022 as it recorded GDP growth of 3.4%. This was driven by several positive factors, which are attributed to Factor Conditions (2) and Entrepreneurs (4). Notably, the wholesale sector, consisting of industries such as food and beverage and machinery and equipment, expanded by an impressive 11% compared to the previous year. On the demand side, a notable aspect was the significant increase in household spending, which played a crucial role in boosting economic activity. Additionally, employee compensation witnessed a considerable increase, with wages rising by 3.8% compared to the previous year. An important milestone was the successful reopening of the economy, enabling a rapid restoration of employment levels to pre-pandemic figures. Moreover, the business outlook in Canada remained positive throughout 2022, indicating a robust recovery in the business sector.

---

[2]This information is abstracted and organized from European Commission (2023b) and Reuters (2022b).
[3]This information is abstracted and organized from Forbes (2023), Proof Point (2023), Statistics Canada (2023), and The Real Economy Blog (2022).

4. Netherlands[4]

The Dutch economy performed strongly in 2022 as it experienced a robust expansion of 4.5%. This can be attributed to the areas of Professionals (1), Entrepreneurs (2), and Business Context (3). Despite the rapid rise in inflation, household consumption displayed remarkable resilience, driven by an increase in income and working hours. Conversely, the Netherlands experienced negative growth in exports, mainly due to a slowdown in GDP growth among its main trading partners, such as Germany and the United Kingdom. Moreover, its heavy reliance on European countries for gas imports makes the Netherlands vulnerable to fluctuations in the gas price.

5. United States[5]

The United States (US) demonstrated exceptional performance across various areas, including Demand Conditions (1) and Entrepreneurs (1), which has contributed to it recording a GDP growth of 2.1% in 2022. Reflecting the strong performance of the economy throughout the year, the US experienced a historic job market expansion, marking the second-highest job growth record in the past 40 years. The overall business outlook in the US remained robust with regard to both outward and inward foreign direct investment (FDI). Foreign investment by US multi-national corporations increased by 3.6% compared to the previous year. Conversely, foreign multinational corporations showed increased interest in the US as well, with the growth of inward FDI rising by 1.7%.

6. Switzerland[6]

Switzerland's relative strengths can be seen in various areas, including Policymakers and Administrators (3), Related Infrastructure (4),

---

[4]This information is abstracted and organized from Coface (2023), CBS (2023), European Commission (2023f), and Statistics Netherlands (2023).
[5]This information is abstracted and organized from Economic Policy Institute (2023), Bureau of Economic Analysis (2023), and Washington Post (2023).
[6]This information is abstracted and organized from SWI (2022), IMF (2023b), Allianz (2023), International Monetary Fund (2023), and Reuters (2023).

and Entrepreneurs (7). In 2022, its economy experienced GDP growth of 2.1% and was able to boast robust fundamentals that underpin its economic stability, particularly in areas such as regulatory quality, rule of law, and control of corruption. However, following Russia's invasion of Ukraine, the stock market remained volatile and the bond markets stagnated due to economic slowdown and rising interest rates. Swiss banks also witnessed a decrease in the volume of transactions. In addition to these challenges, the situation of the country's second-largest bank, Credit Suisse, deteriorated significantly throughout 2022 as it recorded its worst annual losses since the financial crisis of 2008.

7. Sweden[7]

Sweden excelled in several key areas, including Related Infrastructure (5), Policymakers and Administrators (5), Entrepreneurs (5), and Business Context (7). Although it experienced a GDP growth of 2.6%, there was a slowdown in economic growth. Particularly, the country's performance in factors such as workers (19) was lower due to its relatively high unemployment rate, which increased to 7.4%. This was due to adverse economic conditions affecting the construction and real estate sectors. The surge in energy prices had a detrimental impact on domestic demand, causing stagnation and a decline in real wages. Moreover, this negatively affected the housing market with higher mortgage rates and lower purchasing power. As a result, private consumption faced pressure, leading to a contraction of the overall economy.

8. UAE[8]

The United Arab Emirates (UAE) holds strengths in areas such as Professionals (3) and Factor Conditions (5) as its economy achieved a remarkable growth rate of 7.4% in 2022, which was double the rate recorded in the previous year. This is attributed to higher energy prices and the active implementation of various strategies to cultivate a diverse economy, including trade agreements, investments in energy transition,

---

[7]This information is abstracted and organized from European Commission (2023g) and Statista (2023).
[8]This information is abstracted and organized from Reuters (2023).

and the promotion of foreign trade. Moreover, in 2022, the UAE's foreign trade exhibited significant growth, with a 17% increase compared to the previous year. These developments highlight the UAE's proactive efforts and successful initiatives aimed at driving economic expansion and enhancing international trade relations.

9. Australia[9]

Australia revealed a robust performance in areas such as Factor Conditions (1) and Policymakers and Administrators (8) as its economy remained positive in 2022 with signs of recovery, overall recording GDP growth of 3.6%. Throughout the year, higher exports and lower imports contributed to a favorable net export situation. However, Australia's heavy reliance on low-complexity categories such as mining and agriculture for primary exports created risk, especially considering the potential decline in demand for coal, gas, and iron ore due to the COVID-19 pandemic. In addition, high inflation and low wage growth were significant concerns. These inflationary pressures and increasing interest rates affected the spending power of individuals and businesses, potentially leading to a decline in economic activity. The combination of these factors, including lower savings rates and declining property prices, has dampened the likelihood of a significant increase in household spending for the near term.

10. Finland[10]

The Finnish economy recorded a moderate growth rate of 2.1% in 2022. This performance is attributed to Related Industries (1), Demand Conditions (5), and Policymakers and Administrators (6). However, the net export performance was weak, mainly due to subdued export growth, particularly in the services sector, which was influenced by weakening economic conditions in major export markets. In addition, Finland experienced an exceptionally high inflation rate of 7.2%. This had a negative effect on consumer confidence and posed difficulties for consumer purchasing power and cost competitiveness. The rise in inflation was driven

---

[9]This information is abstracted and organized from ING (2023a), The Diplomat (2022), and ABC News (2022).

[10]This information is abstracted and organized from European Commission (2023c).

by increases in energy and food prices, adding further pressure to the economy. Furthermore, after maintaining a policy of neutrality since the end of World War II, Finland recently became a member of NATO. This geopolitical shift has created increased risks, particularly concerning escalating tensions on the Finnish border near Russia. The evolving situation adds an additional layer of uncertainty to Finland's geopolitical landscape.

11. New Zealand[11]

New Zealand demonstrated strength in several key areas, particularly in Factor Conditions (4) and Policymakers and Administrators (11), as it experienced robust economic growth in 2022 with a GDP growth rate of 2.2%. This positive performance was largely attributed to the trade sector, which witnessed a significant expansion of 21% compared to the previous year. The surge in crude oil exports was particularly noteworthy, doubling in value as oil prices rose due to the Russia–Ukraine war. Similarly, the value of aluminum exports increased, boosted by a 15% rise in aluminum prices. Additionally, the relaxation of COVID-19 restrictions played a crucial role in the recovery of services exports, which saw an impressive rise of 28%. By the end of December 2022, there was a remarkable surge in travel demands and transportation volume compared to the previous year.

12. Belgium[12]

Belgium continues to recover from the impact of the COVID-19 pandemic as it achieved an economic growth rate of 3.1% in 2022 with strengths in key areas including Business Context (6), Related Industries (9), and Professionals (10). This recovery was largely attributable to effective policy support measures implemented by the government. Notably, both private (household) and public consumption witnessed substantial growth, increasing by 4.3% and 1.4%, respectively. Additionally, the

---

[11] This information is abstracted and organized from New Zealand Foreign Affairs & Trade (2022).

[12] This information is abstracted and organized from ING (2023b), National Bank of Belgium (2023), Belga (2023).

volume of exports also experienced a notable upswing, rising by 4.6% during the same year. Moreover, the labor market demonstrated robust performance with the creation of 100,000 jobs in 2022. This significant increase in employment further bolstered the overall economic stability and growth of Belgium, contributing to a favorable business environment.

13. Hong Kong SAR[13]

Throughout 2022, Hong Kong SAR exhibited strengths in several areas, including Business Context (2), Entrepreneurs (12), Related Industries (13), and Demand Conditions (13). Its economy though faced significant challenges due to a new COVID-19 outbreak, resulting in negative GDP growth of –3.5%. In addition, the monetary policy of the United States imposed a negative impact on the economy, adding to the existing difficulties faced by Hong Kong. As a result, the return of tourists and short-term business travelers remained limited, offering little stimulation to the economy. Hong Kong maintained strict quarantine measures throughout the year 2022. Government revenue recorded its lowest quarterly level in over five years, primarily due to declines in tax revenues, duties, and land sales although government expenditure remained high as the administration implemented measures to address the impact of the pandemic.

14. Austria[14]

Gaining strength, Austria boasts advantages in Related Industries (3), Business Context (11), and Policymakers and Administrators (11). Throughout 2022, the Austrian economy successfully navigated challenges posed by high interest rates and labor costs, with an impressive GDP growth rate of 5.0%. Notably, this positive economic momentum was accompanied by a decrease in the unemployment rate, which signified improved conditions in the labor market. In addition to a robust economic performance, the improvement in the business environment is evident from the growth in income-based tax revenue. As a result, the

---

[13] This information is abstracted and organized from Fitch Ratings (2022).
[14] This information is abstracted and organized from OECD (2023a), Bank Austria (2023), Statistics Austria (2023), and European Commission (2023a).

budget deficit stabilized, and total debt decreased, which indicated positive progress in fiscal management. The tourism sector has also contributed to the country's economic growth. In 2022, overnight stays in Austria increased by an impressive 72% compared to the previous year, reflecting a robust revival in tourism.

15. United Kingdom[15]

For the United Kingdom, Demand Conditions (7), Entrepreneurs (10), and Professionals (11) played pivotal roles as the economy made a notable recovery from the impact of COVID-19, recording GDP growth of 4.1% in 2022. This recovery was largely driven by private consumption, which demonstrated evidence of sustained consumer confidence and spending. British banks increased their loan loss provisions, reflecting the positive outlook on consumer behavior. Additionally, the labor market demonstrated resilience, with the unemployment rate falling below pre-pandemic levels. Alongside this, business confidence remained above pre-pandemic levels, which contributed to a significant surge in business investment. Indeed, business investment increased by 10% in 2022 compared to the previous year, signaling a favorable environment for companies to expand and actively contribute to the overall economic growth of the country.

16. Germany[16]

The strengths of Germany were particularly evident in Demand Conditions (4), Business Context (12), and the actions of Policymakers and Administrators (13). As a result, Germany recorded modest economic growth of 1.8% in 2022, which was primarily driven by the improvement in household consumption, even amidst inflationary pressure. In response to the hike in energy prices, Germany implemented effective measures by imposing price caps on gas and electricity. This proactive approach helped mitigate the impact of rising energy costs and effectively decelerated the inflationary pressure on the economy. Resilient consumer spending also played a pivotal role in bolstering the economy. Additionally, the

---

[15]This information is abstracted and organized from CNBC (2023) and OECD (2022d).
[16]This information is abstracted and organized from European Commission (2023e), Statistisches Bundesamt (2022), and DW (2023).

industrial sector demonstrated remarkable strength by efficiently managing increased production costs and strategically investing in equipment.
The labor market remained robust throughout the year and the country
achieved and sustained a historically low unemployment rate.

17. Taiwan, China[17]

Taiwan, China (hereafter Taiwan) demonstrated strengths in the areas
such as Related Industries (6), Workers (11), and Professionals (12) as the
economy recorded GDP growth of 2.5%. Being an export-oriented economy, Taiwan faced challenges throughout the year due to factors such as
tightening of monetary policies, the Russia–Ukraine war, and weakened
consumer demand. Unlike many other economies, Taiwan managed to
maintain a moderate inflation rate of 3.0%. However, Taiwan's economy,
heavily reliant on trade with China, saw disruptions affecting industries
like semiconductors, electronics, and information technology (IT), influenced by heightened geopolitical tensions between the two sides. Risks
for businesses in Taiwan surged, including economic instability, trade
disruptions, reduced investment opportunities, and a decline in the tourism and hospitality sectors.

18. China[18]

China still performed exceptionally well in certain areas, particularly
Workers (1) and Demand Conditions (2). GDP growth reached 3.0% in
2022, which is the second-lowest growth rate over the past 50 years. Much
of the year was characterized by China's ongoing zero-COVID policy,
which is characterized by frequent quarantines, regional lockdowns, and
significant government spending on testing equipment. Although the government decided to relax this approach in December 2022, it led to a sud-
den and sharp increase in COVID-19 cases, which created uncertainty and
challenges for economic recovery from the pandemic. Furthermore, China

---

[17]This information is abstracted and organized from Reuters (2022a), Beroe (2023), ING
(2023c), *The Economist* (2023), and National Statistics (2023).
[18]The information is abstracted and organized from BBC (2023a), NYT (2023), CNN
(2023a), RBC (2023), Rhodium Group (2023), OECD (2023b), and The World Bank
(2023).

experienced a slowdown in FDI inflow in comparison to the previous year. This slowdown can be attributed to sporadic COVID-19 outbreaks and the stringent control measures implemented throughout the year, impacting business confidence in the Chinese market.

19. Korea, Republic of[19]

Korea, Republic of (hereafter Korea) showcased robust performance in the areas of Related Industries (12) and Demand Conditions (14) as it achieved a commendable GDP growth of 2.6% in 2022. Throughout the year, it witnessed an increase in foreign investment, driven by the strong performance of computer chips and automobile industries. The value of foreign investments made by Korean companies improved compared to the previous year, with notable growth observed in the manufacturing sector, which saw a 28.9% increase. Additionally, FDI increased by 3.2% compared to the previous year. The property market experienced a 0.6% growth, signaling positive developments in the real estate sector. For 2023, the anticipated reopening of China is expected to mitigate supply disruptions, which will facilitate the recovery of demand for computer chips and electric components. This positive development presents a significant opportunity for Korea's high-tech industries to regain momentum and further enhance their position in the global market.

20. Kuwait[20]

Kuwait showcased robust performance in key areas, particularly in Factor Conditions (3) and Workers (8). The country achieved an impressive economic growth rate in 2022, recording an 8.2% increase in GDP. The increase in oil prices significantly boosted government revenue compared to the previous year and contributed to the maintenance of macroeconomic stability. This surge in revenue also played a crucial role in reducing the government budget deficit, marking the first time such a significant improvement has been seen in the past three years. However, Kuwait's

---

[19]The information is abstracted and organized from YNA (2023), Ministry of Trade (2023), Bloomberg (2022), and Yonhap News Agency (2023).
[20]The information is abstracted and organized from Oxford Business Group (2023), Arab News (2022), Union of Arab Chambers (2023), and Fitch Solutions (2022).

heavy reliance on oil revenue poses a significant risk due to market volatility. The improved economic conditions and the shrinkage of the budget deficit have created a conducive environment for investment. Consequently, Kuwait experienced an expansion in investment activities, with outward FDI increasing by an impressive 55.6% in 2022.

21. France[21]

France's relative strengths lie in areas such as Demand Conditions (12) and Related Industries (16) as it recorded a GDP growth rate of 2.6%. Inflation surged to 5.9% in 2022 but remained the lowest in the EU due to government interventions. The labor market in France was dynamic, and the unemployment rate in the fourth quarter was the lowest since 2008. Notably, France's fiscal conditions improved significantly, as the government deficit decreased from 6.5% of GDP in 2021 to 4.7% in 2022. This reduction was facilitated by a decrease in pandemic-related measures, enhanced tax revenues due to high inflation, and reduced expenditure under the "France Relance" initiative. As a result, France maintained stable macroeconomic conditions when compared with the previous year. External factors, like global geopolitics, and internal challenges, such as social unrest and supply chain disruptions, are anticipated to shape the country's economic trajectory in the next few years.

22. Czech Republic[22]

The country holds strengths in the areas of Related Industries (11) and Entrepreneurs (17), which are driven by increased investment and inventories. Its economy has experienced a GDP growth of 2.5%, signaling a recovery from the impact of the COVID-19 pandemic. This positive trend was reflected across various sectors of the economy, including retail sales, fuel sales, and non-food sales, and is an indicator of a strong rebound in consumer confidence and spending. The unemployment rate, which had started declining after the easing of pandemic restrictions in 2021,

---

[21]The information is abstracted and organized from European Commission (2023d), INSEE (2023), CNBC (2023), CNN (2023b), and Statista (2023).

[22]*Ibid.*

continued to decrease, reflecting improved labor market conditions and economic stability. Furthermore, the country's trade sector performed well, with transaction volumes in the first quarter reaching 210% of the same period in 2021. Additionally, the investment volume for the first quarter exceeded the average of the past 12 quarters by 45%, showcasing a robust investment climate.

23. Saudi Arabia[23]

Saudi Arabia demonstrated strengths in several key areas, including Factor Conditions (8), Policymakers and Administrators (23), and Demand Conditions (23). Notably, in 2022, the country experienced a robust GDP growth rate of 8.7%. Boosted by rising oil and gas prices and a growing non-oil sector, the nation has been witnessing record trade surpluses and is set to be among the fastest-growing economies in the G20. However, despite the economic growth Saudi Arabia achieved in 2022, the political situation remained negative, which is reflected in the ongoing domestic challenges surrounding political rights and freedom of speech. Moreover, Saudi Arabia's heavy dependence on oil revenue continues to pose a challenge to the country's economic diversification efforts. While progress has been made in recent years to reduce the reliance on oil and promote other sectors, further steps are necessary to achieve a more balanced and sustainable economy.

24. Italy[24]

Italy holds strengths in areas such as Business Context (19) and Demand Conditions (20), while it recorded a positive economic performance in 2022, achieving 3.7% of real GDP growth. The recovery in domestic demand was the primary driver for this growth, while there was a notable improvement in gross fixed capital formation. This indicates a substantial increase in investment in fixed assets, reflecting heightened business confidence and a proactive approach to expanding and modernizing infrastructure. Moreover, a significant contributing factor to the positive

---

[23]The information is abstracted and organized from Freedom House (2023) and New Zealand Foreign Affairs & Trade (2022).

[24]The information is abstracted and organized from Istat (2022) and Nova News (2023).

economic activity in 2022 was the remarkable export growth in the country. The sales of non-durable consumer goods and intermediate goods played a crucial role, contributing to impressive export growth. The labor market in Italy also exhibited resilience and positive trends as the employment rate went through a notable increase, reflecting the creation of new jobs and opportunities for workers. Additionally, the unemployment rate showed a significant decrease, suggesting improved job market conditions.

25. Israel[25]

Israel still managed to demonstrate its economic prowess in areas of Entrepreneurs (19) and Related Industries (20) as its economy achieved an economic growth rate of 6.5% in 2022. Israel though faces challenges due to rising prices as well as the high cost of living. This inflationary environment is expected to have a negative effect on private consumption growth and exports, as the demand from trading partners remains moderate. Additionally, the increase in interest rates is anticipated to slow down investment growth, as businesses face higher borrowing costs. This can potentially hinder investment projects and limit economic expansion. Moreover, the ongoing Israeli–Palestinian conflict added to the geopolitical risks faced by the country. The conflict escalated in March 2022, leading to a decrease of investment in start-ups, which poses a threat to the technological advancement of the country. Start-ups have been a driving force behind Israel's innovation and economic growth, and a decline in investment could impact the country's further technological development.

26. Japan[26]

Japan has demonstrated notable strengths in three critical areas — Demand Conditions (9), Policymakers and Administrators (18), and Related Industries (19). Its economy grew by 1.1% in 2022 over the previous year, marking its second consecutive year of growth as the country bounced back from the ramifications of the COVID-19 pandemic.

---

[25]The information is abstracted and organized from The Medialine (2023), OECD (2023c), United Nations (2023), BBC (2023b), and Ctech (2023).
[26]The information is abstracted and organized from Deloitte (2023), Humble Bunny (2022), Nikkei Asia (2023), The Japan Times (2023), and Xinhua News (2023).

However, the growth rate was lower than that in 2021. Currently, Japan is investing heavily in renewable energy and climate technology, and sectors like pharmaceuticals, medical equipment, and healthcare services, especially those serving the aging population, are witnessing growth. While Japan showcased strengths such as a high savings rate, diversified industrial sector, and resilient domestic demand, it also faced significant challenges. These ranged from an aging population and tensions with neighboring countries to economic stagnation and vulnerabilities associated with high global oil prices and reliance on China for manufacturing investments. The rise in fuel costs, prompted by the Russia–Ukraine war, and the depreciation of the Japanese currency contributed to higher import costs. These factors, in turn, impacted upon Japan's trade performance, with exports experiencing slower growth.

27. Poland[27]

Poland has showcased notable strengths in two crucial areas, Workers (10) and Factor Conditions (22), as it witnessed a robust economic growth of 4.9% in 2022, primarily propelled by a significant increase in private consumption and inventories. The country's stable macroeconomic framework and comparatively lower public debt levels compared to its peers contributed to its favorable economic performance. Both industrial output and retail sales experienced strong expansion during the first half of 2022, indicating a vibrant domestic market. Private consumption was further bolstered by spending from Ukrainian refugees and a rebound from the effects of the pandemic. Notably, Poland has maintained a low unemployment rate of around 3.0% in recent years, showcasing the resilience of its labor market in the face of challenging circumstances.

28. Chile[28]

Chile has demonstrated relative strengths in two key areas, Factor Conditions (12) and Entrepreneurs (20). In 2022, it witnessed a remarkable expansion of its economy, recording a GDP growth of 2.4%, driven

---

[27]The information is abstracted and organized from Deloitte (2024), IMF (2023a), and Property Forum (2023).

[28]The information is abstracted and organized from Credit Agricole Group (2023a).

by a robust recovery from the COVID-19 pandemic and strong private consumption. Notably, the country's relatively high unemployment rate dropped to 7.9%, primarily due to the recovery of sectors such as construction, commerce, and transport that rebounded strongly after the pandemic. The government's efforts to stimulate private consumption and restore business activities have played a crucial role in revitalizing the economy. The construction sector's rebound has led to increased infrastructure projects, while the recovery of the commerce and transport sectors has provided employment opportunities and restored business confidence. These developments have had a positive impact on reducing the unemployment rate and fostering economic growth.

29. Vietnam[29]

Vietnam has had a commendable performance in two crucial areas, Workers (9) and Professionals (14), while it experienced a remarkable economic rebound, achieving a growth rate of 8.0%. This strong economic performance in 2022 can be attributed to the recovery of domestic private consumption and the robust performance of the export-oriented manufacturing sector. Additionally, Vietnam witnessed a significant increase in the disbursement of FDI, with a growth rate of 13.5% compared to the previous year, the highest in the past five years. This influx of foreign capital has played a crucial role in stimulating investment and supporting the country's economic expansion. Vietnam's trade turnover reached a new record high in 2022, resulting in a trade surplus three times higher than that of 2021. This underscores the country's strong export performance and its ability to capitalize on global market opportunities. Furthermore, the tourism sector in Vietnam experienced a robust recovery after the country reopened its borders in March 2022. The influx of foreign visitors increased significantly after this date, with the number being 23 times higher than in 2021. This revival of tourism has provided a boost to the sector and contributed to the overall economic growth of Vietnam.

---

[29]The information is abstracted and organized from World Bank (2023) and VietnamPlus (2022).

30. India[30]

India possesses significant strengths in two areas, Workers (3) and Professionals (21). Although India achieved an impressive GDP growth of 7.0% in 2022, it faces significant challenges, particularly in the form of high inflation. This resulted in a 30-year-low household savings rate, as the cost of living increased. The surge in commodity prices, coupled with weak consumer demands, had a dampening effect on industrial output growth. Consequently, the manufacturing sector in India experienced a slowdown in growth during 2022. Additionally, India experienced a period of political turmoil in 2022, with a series of protests taking place on various issues, ranging from the hijab row to the Nupur Sharma and Agniveer protests. These disturbances reflected the diverse range of societal and political tensions within the country.

References

ABC News. 2022. Australia's economy recovered in 2022, will it crash in 2023. https://www.abc.net.au/news/2022-12-21/australia-economy-recovered-in-2022-will-it-crash-in-2023/101705402.

Access Now. 2023. Five years in a row: India is 2022's biggest internet shutdowns offender. https://www.accessnow.org/press-release/keepiton-internet-shutdowns-2022-india/.

Allianz. 2022. Solid economic fundamentals help cushion the growth headwinds. https://www.allianz-trade.com/en_global/economic-research/country-reports/Switzerland.html.

Arab News. 2022. Kuwait narrows its fiscal deficit for first time in 3 years. https://www.arabnews.com/node/2203561/business-economy.

Bank Austria. 2023. Austrian economy. https://www.bankaustria.at/en/markets-research-austrian-economy.jsp.

BBC. 2023a. Covid: China 2022 economic growth hit by coronavirus restrictions. https://www.bbc.com/news/business-64286126.

BBC. 2023b. Why is Israel-Palestinian violence surging? https://www.bbc.com/news/world-middle-east-64757995.

Belga. 2023. 3.1% economic growth in Belgium in 2022. https://www.belganewsagency.eu/31-economic-growth-in-belgium-in-2022.

---

[30]The information is abstracted and organized from Trading Economics (2023), The Wire (2023), India Today (2022), The Times of India (2023), India CSR (2023), and Access Now (2023).

Beroe. 2023. China-Taiwan conflict: Business impact and advisory. https://www.beroeinc.com/blog/china-taiwan-conflict-business-impact-advisory/.

Bureau of Economic Analysis. 2023. U.S. economy at a glance. https://www.bea.gov/news/glance.

CNBC. 2023. UK economy in 'a lot better shape' than bleak figures suggest, fund manager says. https://www.cnbc.com/2023/02/23/uk-economy-in-a-lot-better-shape-than-bleak-figures-suggest-fund-manager-says.html.

CNN. 2023a. China sets lowest GDP growth target in decades as Beijing tightens its belt. https://edition.cnn.com/2023/03/06/economy/china-two-sessions-lowest-gdp-target-analysis-intl-hnk/index.html.

CNN. 2023b. May Day protest erupts in Paris as France seethes about a hike in the retirement age. https://edition.cnn.com/2023/05/01/europe/france-pension-protests-explainer-intl/index.html.

Coface. 2023. Netherlands. https://www.coface.com/Economic-Studies-and-Country-Risks/Netherlands.

Credit Agricole Group. 2023a. Chille. https://international.groupecreditagricole.com/en/international-support/chile/economic-overview.

Ctech. 2023. Investments in Israeli startups plummeted 42% in 2022, cybersecurity hit hardest. https://www.calcalistech.com/ctechnews/article/b16n1jc9o.

Deloitte. 2023. Japan economic outlook, July 2023. https://www2.deloitte.com/us/en/insights/economy/asia-pacific/japan-economic-outlook.html.

Deloitte. 2024. Analysis of the impact of refugees from Ukraine on the economy of Poland. https://data.unhcr.org/en/documents/details/106993.

DW. 2023. Germany's economy grew by 1.9% in 2022, latest data shows. https://www.dw.com/en/germanys-economy-grew-by-19-in-2022-latest-data-shows/a-6437626.

Economic Policy Institute. 2023. Historic job growth in 2022 reflects strong but uneven economic recovery. https://www.epi.org/blog/historic-job-growth-in-2022-reflects-strong-but-uneven-economic-recovery-state-and-local-lawmakers-should-prioritize-rebuilding-the-public-sector-in-2023.

European Commission. 2023a. Economic forecast for Austria. https://economy-finance.ec.europa.eu/economic-surveillance-eu-economies/austria/economic-forecast-austria_en.

European Commission. 2023b. Economic forecast for Denmark. https://economy-finance.ec.europa.eu/economic-surveillance-eu-economies/denmark/economic-forecast-denmark_en.

European Commission. 2023c. Economic forecast for Finland. https://economy-finance.ec.europa.eu/economic-surveillance-eu-economies/finland/economic-forecast-finland_en.

European Commission. 2023d. Economic forecast for France. https://economy-finance.ec.europa.eu/economic-surveillance-eu-economies/france/economic-forecast-france_en.

European Commission. 2023e. Economic forecast for Germany. https://economy-finance.ec.europa.eu/economic-surveillance-eu-economies/germany/economic-forecast-germany_en.

European Commission. 2023f. Economic forecast for Netherlands. https://economy-finance.ec.europa.eu/economic-surveillance-eu-economies/netherlands/economic-forecast-netherlands_en.

European Commission. 2023g. Economic forecast for Sweden. https://economy-finance.ec.europa.eu/economic-surveillance-eu-economies/sweden/economic-forecast-sweden_en.

Forbes. 2023. Leading experts weigh in on growing Canada's economy in 2023–24. https://www.forbes.com/sites/ankitmishra/2023/05/17/leading-experts-weigh-in-on-growing-canadas-economy-in-202324/?sh=e46e7371b0ac.

Fitch Ratings. 2022. Quarantine tweaks unlikely to end Hong Kong's economic troubles. https://www.fitchratings.com/research/sovereigns/quarantine-tweaks-unlikely-to-end-hong-kongs-economic-troubles-09-08-2022.

Freedom House. 2023. Freedom in the world 2023. https://freedomhouse.org/country/saudi-arabia/freedom-world/2023.

HRM Asia. 2023. Singapore's youth unemployment hits 24-year low in 2022. https://hrmasia.com/singapores-youth-unemployment-hits-24-year-low-in-2022.

Humble Bunny. 2022. Starting a business in Japan — A guide for 2022. https://www.humblebunny.com/starting-business-in-japan-guide-for-2022/.

India CSR. 2023. India: Manufacturing growth falls short of GDP projections. https://indiacsr.in/india-manufacturing-growth-falls-short-of-gdp-projections/#:~:text=sustain%20economic%20growth.-,Manufacturing%20Growth%20Slows%20in%202022%2D23,NSO)%20by%202.5%20percent-age%20points.

India Today. 2022. From hijab row to Nupur Sharma to Agniveer protests, five controversies that rocked India in 2022. https://www.indiatoday.in/news-analysis/story/from-hijab-row-to-nupur-sharma-to-agniveer-protests-five-controversies-that-rocked-india-in-2022-2314383-2022-12-28.

ING. 2023a. Australia: GDP growth to remain below 2% this year. https://think.ing.com/articles/australia-the-economy-is-slowing/#a3.

ING. 2023b. Belgium: Short-term resilience, medium-term challenges. https://think.ing.com/articles/belgium-short-term-resilience-medium-term-challenges/#a1.

ING. 2023c. Taiwan's economic outlook: A challenging year as global semiconductor sales slump. https://think.ing.com/articles/economic-outlook-for-taiwan-challenging-year-semiconductor-sales-slump/#:~:text=Taiwan's%20real%20GDP%20growth%20was,the%20fourth%20quarter%20of%202022.

INSEE. 2023. In 2022, the public deficit reached 4.7% of GDP, the public debt 111.6% of GDP. https://www.insee.fr/en/statistiques/7233185.

International Monetary Fund. 2023a. Poland: Staff Concluding Statement of the 2023 Article IV Mission. https://www.imf.org/en/News/Articles/2023/03/24/poland-staff-concluding-statement-of-the-2023-article-iv-mission.

International Monetary Fund. 2023b. Switzerland: Staff Concluding Statement of the 2023 Article IV Mission. https://www.swissinfo.ch/eng/business/looking-ahead--switzerland-s-economic-outlook-for-2023/48151238.

ISG. 2023. Sustainable growth beckons for Singapore's hospitality sector. https://www.isgltd.com/sg/en/what-we-think/sustainable-growth-beckons-for-singapores-hospitality-sector. Accessed July 31, 2023.

National Bank of Belgium. 2023. Economic projections for Belgium. https://www.nbb.be/en/publications-and-research/economic-and-financial-publications/economic-projections-belgium.

New York Times (NYT). 2023. China's economy stumbled last year with covid lockdowns hobbling growth. https://www.nytimes.com/2023/01/16/business/china-gdp-fourth-quarter-2022.html.

New Zealand Foreign Affairs & Trade. 2022. Saudi Arabia: The fastest growing economy fighting for its future — November 2022. https://www.mfat.govt.nz/en/trade/mfat-market-reports/saudi-arabia-the-fastest-growing-economy-fighting-for-its-future-november-2022/.

Nikkei Asia. 2023. Japan's GDP slows to 1.1% in 2022 on weaker export growth. https://asia.nikkei.com/Economy/Japan-s-GDP-slows-to-1.1-in-2022-on-weaker-export-growth.

Nova News. 2023. In 2022, Italian exports grow by 19,9 percent, imports soar to +36,5 percent. https://www.agenzianova.com/en/news/in-2022-Italian-exports-grow-by-199-percent-imports-fly-by-365-percent.

OECD. 2023a. Austria economic snapshot. https://www.oecd.org/economy/austria-economic-snapshot/.

OECD. 2023b. China economic snapshot. https://www.oecd.org/economy/china-economic-snapshot/.

OECD. 2023c. Israel economic snapshot. https://www.oecd.org/economy/israel-economic-snapshot/.

OECD. 2023d. United Kingdom economic snapshot. https://www.oecd.org/economy/united-kingdom-economic-snapshot/.

Property Forum. 2023. Poland's retail market closes stable year in 2022. https://www.property-forum.eu/news/polands-retail-market-closes-stable-year-in-2022/14600.

Reuters. 2022a. China-Taiwan: Why tensions are rising and what could happen in 2023. https://www.reuters.com/world/asia-pacific/yearender-eye-storm-taiwan-centre-sino-us-tensions-2022-12-06/.

Reuters. 2022b. Orsted plans large-scale green hydrogen project in Denmark. https://www.reuters.com/business/sustainable-business/orsted-plans-large-scale-green-hydrogen-project-denmark-2022-12-06/.

Reuters. 2023. Swiss government expects economy to grow by weaker than average 1.1% in 2023. https://www.reuters.com/markets/europe/swiss-government-expects-economy-grow-by-weaker-than-average-11-2023-2023-03-16/.

RBC. 2023. Proof point: Canada's economy can't afford a slump in business investment. https://thoughtleadership.rbc.com/proof-point-canadas-economy-cant-afford-a-slump-in-business-investment/.

Rhodium Group. 2023. Chinese FDI in Europe: 2022 update. https://rhg.com/research/chinese-fdi-in-europe-2022-update/.

Statista. 2023. Inflation rate in France from 2004 to 2022. https://www.statista.com/statistics/470313/inflation-rate-in-france/#:~:text=In%20France%2C%20the%20inflation%20rate,and%20sustained%20increase%20in%20prices.

Statistics Austria. 2023. Overnight stays strongly increased in 2022. https://www.statistik.at/fileadmin/announcement/2023/01/20230127Tourismus2022EN.pdf.

Statistics Canada. 2023. Wholesale sales decline in December. https://www150.statcan.gc.ca/n1/daily-quotidien/230215/dq230215b-eng.html.

Statistics Netherlands. 2023. Dutch economy grew by 4.5 percent in 2022. https://www.cbs.nl/en-gb/news/2023/08/dutch-economy-grew-by-4-5-percent-in-2022.

The Diplomat. 2022. Australia's lack of economic complexity is a problem. https://thediplomat.com/2022/03/australias-lack-of-economic-complexity-is-a-problem/.

The Economist. 2023. It is time to divert Taiwan's trade and investment from China. https://www.economist.com/special-report/2023/03/06/it-is-time-to-divert-taiwans-trade-and-investment-from-china.

The Japan Times. 2023. Panasonic resists decoupling trend to boost China investment. https://www.japantimes.co.jp/news/2023/01/06/business/corporate-business/panasonic-china-invest/.

The Medialine. 2023. As Israeli Gov't focuses on judicial reforms, consumers struggle with rising prices. https://themedialine.org/by-region/as-israeli-govt-focuses-on-judicial-reforms-consumers-struggle-with-rising-prices/.

The Real Economy Blog. 2022. Canada's economy cools but outlook remains positive. https://realeconomy.rsmus.com/canadas-economy-cools-but-outlook-remains-positive/.

The Times of India. 2023. One year of Russia-Ukraine war: How the conflict impacted Indian economy. https://timesofindia.indiatimes.com/business/india-business/one-year-of-russia-ukraine-war-how-the-conflict-impacted-indian-economy/articleshow/98214568.cms?from=mdr.

The World Bank. 2023. China economic update — December 2022. https://www.worldbank.org/en/country/china/publication/china-economic-update-december-2022.

The World Bank. GDP growth (annual %). https://data.worldbank.org/indicator/NY.GDP.MKTP.KD.ZG.

The Wire. 2023. Five issues that are hurting the Indian economy. https://thewire.in/economy/indian-economy-inflation-adani-press-freedom-politics.

Trading Economics. 2023. India GDP annual growth rate. https://trading economics.com/india/gdp-growth-annual. Accessed July 31, 2023.

Union of Arab Chamber. 2023. 55.63% Increase in Kuwaiti investment abroad during 2022. https://uac-org.org/en/News/details/5110/55-63.

United Nations. 2023. With 2022 deadliest year in Israel-Palestine conflict, reversing violent trends must be international priority, Middle East coordinator tells security council. https://press.un.org/en/2023/sc15179.doc.htm.

United Overseas Bank (UOB). 2022. Quarterly global outlook 2Q 2022. https://www.uobgroup.com/web-resources/uobgroup/pdf/research/SG_2q22.pdf.

Vietnamplus. 2022. Vietnam — Silver lining in the world economy in 2022. https://en.vietnamplus.vn/vietnam-silver-lining-in-the-world-economy-in-2022/246396.vnp.

Washington Post. 2023. U.S. economy grew 2.1 percent in 2022, but recession fears linger. https://www.washingtonpost.com/business/2023/01/26/gdp-2022-q4-economy/.

Xinhua News. 2023. 3 factors weigh on Japan's delayed economic recovery. https://english.news.cn/20230216/5064b5e30b20480d9885c956da5bada6/c.html.

Yonhap News Agency. 2023. S. Korea's overseas investment hits fresh high in 2022. https://en.yna.co.kr/view/AEN20230324002700320. https://www.cnbc.com/2023/01/26/south-koreas-economy-growth-expected-from-china.html.

Part II

Special Topic: Introduction

The second part of this book delves into a comprehensive and thought-provoking discussion on this edition's special topic: Emerging Technologies and the Fourth Industrial Revolution. This is addressed by Chapter 6, titled "ABCD Technologies in the Fourth Industrial Revolution," which conceptualizes the key technologies collectively known as ABCD technologies: Artificial Intelligence, Big Data Analytics, Cloud Computing, and Digital Technology. The fourth revolution (Industry 4.0 or I4.0), began in the early twenty-first century with the integration of cyber and physical systems, evolving from purely technological to also encompass managerial and strategic perspectives. I4.0 originated in manufacturing but now includes various sectors. Despite the universal acknowledgment of I4.0's technologies, no universally accepted definition exists. Technologies like the Internet of Things (IoT), big data, cloud computing, and AI are often cited as drivers, but grouping them under the label of "digital technologies" can be misleading given their distinction from traditional digital processes.

Chapter 6 introduces the ABCD technologies as foundational for the Fourth Industrial Revolution, emphasizing their synergistic interactions and varying significance across different emerging technologies.

By doing so, it aims to highlight their crucial role in various industries and their significant impacts on the competitiveness to develop applied technologies such as ChatGPT, IoT, and Blockchains. Furthermore, this chapter explores how these foundational technologies will continue to play a pivotal role in shaping the future of technology and business. It is essential to recognize that these advancements are built upon the solid foundation laid by ABCD technologies. By understanding their significance and interplay with applied technologies, a deeper insight can be gained into the dynamics of the Fourth Industrial Revolution, thereby preparing sufficiently for the next challenges and future opportunities.

Chapter 6

ABCD Technologies in the Fourth Industrial Revolution

Dong-sung Cho, Hwy-chang Moon, Wenyan Yin, Minji Hong, and Dilong Huang

Abstract

This chapter proposes four key foundational technologies in the era of the Fourth Industrial Revolution, collectively termed ABCD technologies: artificial intelligence, big data analytics, cloud computing, and digital technology. While the four technologies emerged independently across different time frames, they have become increasingly interwoven over time, driving the advent of new technologies. This chapter delves into the dynamics of their interplay and articulates their critical role in catalyzing a variety of emerging technologies. This study also highlights how their relevance differs across the emerging technologies, as illustrated by three examples: ChatGPT, the Internet of Things (IoT), and blockchains. Moreover, the study provides implications for both firms and policymakers on how to effectively leverage the four foundational technologies and respond to the fast-changing technology environment in the era of the Fourth Industrial Revolution and beyond.

Keywords: Fourth Industrial Revolution, digitization, big data, artificial intelligence, cloud computing, ChatGPT, IoT, blockchains

Introduction

The history of modern capitalism has so far experienced four industrial revolutions. The first industrial revolution took place between the late 18th and early 19th centuries, characterized by the invention of the steam engine. This technological breakthrough expedited the transition from farming to new manufacturing processes. The second industrial revolution took place between the late 19th and early 20th centuries, characterized by mass production powered by electric energy, which enabled the efficient production of goods on a large scale. The third industrial revolution emerged in the latter half of the 20th century, driven by information and communication technologies (ICTs) such as computers and the internet. This technological shift fostered new forms of automation and communication, and fundamentally changed the way people live and work. All of these industrial revolutions have been propelled by significant technological shifts, and their cumulative influence has contributed to economic development (Taalbi, 2019). Yet, the Fourth Industrial Revolution, which began in the early 21st century, is fueled by the synergistic interaction of multiple technologies that were developed previously.

The Fourth Industrial Revolution is widely recognized by academics and practitioners under the term Industry 4.0, or I4.0. The terminology can be traced back to 2011, when it was first introduced at the Hannover Fair in Germany. Industry 4.0 addresses the integration of cyber and physical systems in an attempt to make all manufacturing processes integrated and share information in real-time (Agostini and Nosella, 2021; Gupta, 2023). Although I4.0 began in the manufacturing sector, it has since expanded to encompass various sectors and firms, including small- and medium-sized enterprises (SMEs) and startups. Moreover, I4.0 has evolved from a purely technological to a managerial and strategic perspective for a better understanding of value creation through interactions with technological elements (Agostini and Nosella, 2021; Bortoluzzi *et al.*, 2022). While technologies play a pivotal role as the backbone of the fourth industrial revolution, previous studies did not distinguish the foundational technologies that particularly enable the emergence of new technologies.

In contrast, existing studies on the technologies driving the fourth industrial revolution are quite fragmented, and there is no universally accepted or adopted definition. For instance, studies by Agostini and Filippini (2019), Tortorella and Fettermann (2017), and Deloitte (2015) proposed that Industry 4.0 has been influenced by several technologies, including the Internet of Things (IoT), big data and analytics, cloud computing, cybersecurity, and additive manufacturing. Other studies, such as Coreynen *et al.* (2017), Frank *et al.* (2019), and Paiola *et al.* (2022), proposed that I4.0 technologies differ depending on the areas of adoption. For example, for servitization, I4.0 technologies can encompass IoT, big data analytics, software simulation, and cloud computing. Klaus Schwab, who was Chairman of the World Economic Forum and first coined the concept of "fourth industrial revolution," emphasized that the fusion of more sophisticated technologies and their interconnection across the physical, digital, and biological domains has made it fundamentally different from the previous three revolutions (Schwab, 2016). However, he did not distinguish the foundational technologies from others.

On the other hand, previous studies often categorize the cluster of emerging technologies under the general term "digital technologies" (Parida *et al.*, 2019; Warner and Wager, 2019). However, "digital technology" originally refers to the technological process of converting analog content into a digital format. Newly emerging technologies, such as IoT, artificial intelligence (AI), and big data analytics, should function based on digital content or data. Therefore, they are distinct from digital technology, and labeling all these enabling or emerging technologies in the Fourth Industrial Revolution as simply "digital technologies" will not be appropriate. In this regard, it is necessary to distinguish precisely the key foundational technologies, along with all other applied technologies that function based on these foundational ones, to understand the patterns of technological development. To this end, this chapter introduces the four fundamental technologies, collectively referred to as the ABCD technologies (AI, big data analytics, cloud computing, and digital technology). It further demonstrates that the four foundational technologies play a crucial role in fostering the emergence of new technologies in the era of the Fourth Industrial Revolution by taking the examples of IoT, blockchains, and ChatGPT. Moreover, this chapter further addresses the fact that while the four foundational technologies collectively contribute to the development of new emerging technologies, their respective importance or significance may vary across different emerging technologies.

The rest of the chapter is organized as follows. First, we provide a comprehensive review and description of the historical evolution of the four fundamental technologies. We then delve into the mechanisms of interactions among these technologies, forming a system that fosters a wide range of emerging technologies and applications. To illustrate the significance of these four technologies, we present three specific examples: ChatGPT, IoT, and blockchains. Finally, this chapter concludes by emphasizing the contribution of this study and the implications of the four foundational technologies for managers and policymakers in the era of the Fourth Industrial Revolution and beyond.

Literature Review on the Four Foundational Technologies

While the four technologies are labeled as ABCD in alphabetical sequence, this section presents them in the order of digital technology, big data, AI, and cloud computing to elucidate their interactions more effectively. This sequence illustrates how each preceding technology serves as the foundation for the development and functioning of the subsequent one.

Digital technology

Although the term "digital technology" encompasses a variety of emerging technologies in the literature, its original meaning pertains specifically to the technical process of converting analog information into a digital format of 1s and 0s (Brennen and Kreiss, 2016). The increasing use of digital technologies has enabled connecting and converging people and things, or the real and virtual worlds (Kagermann, 2015; Coreynen *et al.*, 2017). This has been achieved over the past decades through several waves of technological development.

Since the introduction of digital computers in the 1930s and 1940s, the technologies relevant to the process of digital transformation have undergone continuous development, thanks to various enabling tools such as hardware, software, and infrastructure (Kagermann, 2015). The widespread adoption of computing technology between the 1970s and the mid-1980s facilitated the accumulation of immense amounts of data (Bumblauskas *et al.*, 2017). The proliferation of the internet in the mid-1990s and the subsequent use of the World Wide Web in the early 2000s revolutionized data accessibility, enabling real-time data sharing among individuals, organizations, and nations. As a result, the production of vast quantities of data soared. The advent of smartphones in the late 2000s further accelerated the pace of digitization at an exponential speed, empowering a huge number of mobile users worldwide, particularly in developing countries, to generate and exchange data across various sectors of the global economy.

In addition, the digitization process has been bolstered by technologies, including radio frequency identification (RFID) and wireless communications such as wireless local area network (WLAN). Systems embedded with RFID technology and equipped with sensors possess the capability of recording, storing, and processing a wide variety of data from their surroundings (Kagermann, 2015). RFID technology further helps track and monitor the products through the scanning of physical things and the transmission of information via wireless networks (Peris-Lopez *et al.*, 2011). Furthermore, wireless communications and WLAN have triggered the expansion of the internet (Kagermann, 2015). These technologies have then facilitated the emergence of IoT technologies, which accelerated the process of digitization and the integration between the physical and virtual realms (Ben-Daya *et al.*, 2019). By connecting diverse physical devices to the internet, IoT devices equipped with computing and communication capabilities enable the use of real-time data and information (Guo *et al.*, 2013).

Nowadays, countless everyday objects are equipped with advanced sensors, wireless networks, and computing capabilities (Sestino *et al.*, 2020). Digital technology has a significant impact on the way firms conduct business in terms of what they serve and how they serve the market (Ritter and Pedersen, 2020). Digital technology has also contributed to businesses by improving cost efficiency and effectiveness with regard to customer satisfaction, thereby helping firms enhance their performance in a dynamic environment. The adoption and implementation of digitization across supply chain management empower firms to effectively trace and enhance the visibility of product flows. This, in turn, improves the ability of firms to respond to environmental uncertainties with flexibility and resilience (Gupta *et al.*, 2021). However, reaping the benefits of digitization and creating value for firms requires the complementary technologies of analyzing large and complex data, commonly known as big data analytics. Big data analytics enhances the decision-making process and outcome of firms by extracting valuable insights from vast and intricate datasets. The following section explores the historical evolution and significance of big data analytics.

Big data analytics

Thanks to the advancement in digital technology, we are witnessing an unprecedented level of data generation in history (Smolan and Erwitt, 2012). From the beginning of recorded history to 2003, approximately 5 billion gigabytes of data were generated, and this number skyrocketed to 2 zettabytes in 2010 and further surged to 64.2 zettabytes in 2020

(Koh *et al.*, 2023; Statista, n.d.). However, it becomes more difficult for firms to handle such large-scale, fast-moving, and complex datasets using traditional tools and techniques (Elgendy and Elragal, 2014). As a result, the field of big data analytics has emerged, offering a range of tools and techniques to analyze and interpret data in real-time, enabling organizations to derive meaningful insights and make informed decisions.

The term "big data" was first mentioned in the mid-1990s (Diebold, 2012). However, it was in the 2010s that the hype and widespread adoption of big data truly took off, largely due to promotional initiatives by IBM and other leading technology firms (Gandomi and Haider, 2015). Several characteristics of big data have been identified, and among them, the framework proposed by Laney (2001), known as the "Three Vs," has emerged as a common way to describe big data, along with other notable features (Chen *et al.*, 2012). The Three Vs stand for volume, variety, and velocity. *Volume* refers to the magnitude or size of data flows. *Variety* refers to the structural heterogeneity of a dataset, encompassing not only structured data but also unstructured data, such as text, images, audio, and video. It also refers to a wide range of data sources, such as photos, tweets, posts, and information from IoT devices (*Economist*, 2010). *Velocity* refers to the rate at which data are generated and the speed at which they are processed and analyzed (Gandomi and Haider, 2015). Building upon the concept of the Three Vs, subsequent studies have proposed additional characteristics. These include veracity, which pertains to the reliability of the data (Hilbert, 2016); variability, emphasizing the context in which data are generated (Gandomi and Haider, 2015); and visualization, a critical aspect of presenting data effectively (Sivarajah *et al.*, 2017).

The value of big data relies on the ability to convert meaningful and relevant data into useful information, or knowledge, which then helps firms make better decisions and take action in a timely fashion (Gandomi and Haider, 2015; Bumblauskas *et al.*, 2017; Janssen *et al.*, 2017; Davenport *et al.*, 2012). Big data analytics is thus necessary to deal with the challenges of data for firms to transform their way of making decisions and create values. With regard to big data analytics, there are various classifications of analytical techniques for structured and unstructured data. Gandomi and Haider (2015) highlighted five techniques for text, audio, video, social media, and predictive analytics, tailored according to the typology of big data. On the other hand, Lee (2017) introduced various data analytics for processing structured and unstructured data based on the evolution of big data since the mid-1990s. Lee identified three development stages of big data: stage 1 (1994–2004) focused on web content and web mining techniques; stage 2 (2005–2014) saw the emergence of the social media phenomenon, necessitating analytics such as sentiment analysis, lexical-based methods, and machine learning; the third stage (2015–present) is driven by the rise of IoT applications and the importance of streaming analytics involving real-time event analysis to discover data patterns.

While big data analytics addresses technologies with regard to interactions with big datasets and the extraction of insights from the data, the emergence and evolution of AI implies that a portion, or even a substantial part, of decision-making processes, could be executed by machines.

Artificial intelligence

Despite various definitions of AI, it is commonly defined as "a system's ability to interpret external data correctly, to learn from such data, and to use those learnings to achieve specific goals and tasks through flexible adaptation" (Kaplan and Haenlein, 2019: 17). The history of AI dates back to the 1950s, when the term "artificial intelligence" was first officially introduced in 1956 by Marvin Minsky and John McCarthy[1] at the Dartmouth Conference, which is considered the birthplace of AI. Although the concept and various AI techniques were developed earlier than big data analytics, there have been ups and downs over the past decades.

The 1950s and 1960s marked the first wave of widespread enthusiasm for AI. In the early days of AI research, the focus was on developing expert systems, which were rule-based systems designed to mimic the decision-making processes of human experts in a particular field. Although there was some technological advancement during the initial stages, progress in the AI field was slow due to limited capabilities and underwhelming performance. Skepticism about its potential, coupled with the inability of early AI systems to fulfill their projected promises, led to a reduction in government financial support.[2] The lack of funding has also

---

[1]They were two of the pioneers of AI technology in the 1950s. John McCarthy is widely regarded as the father of AI, and along with Marvin Minsky, he co-founded the MIT AI Lab in 1959, which became a hub for AI research and development.

[2]According to the ALPAL report, during the Cold War, automatic machine translation was of great interest and had received large funding from the US government since 1956.

contributed to a dramatic decrease in AI research in both industry and academia. This led to the first AI winter in the 1970s. During this time, the poor performance was partly due to technological barriers, mainly the limitations of computing power, memory, and processing speed to handle the work required by AI systems (Dasgupta, 2014; Farrow, 2019).

Since the 1990s, there has been a renewed interest in AI research, with the focus shifting toward developing intelligent agents that could interact with their environment and make decisions based on their observations. The rebound growth of AI technology was driven by advances in computing power, the availability of large amounts of data, and the development of new machine learning techniques. The development of faster and more powerful processors and the availability of cloud computing resources made it possible to train and run more complex machine learning algorithms.

Another important factor was the availability of large amounts of data. The growth of the internet in the 1990s led to an explosion of available data, which could be used to train machine learning algorithms. This data included everything from scientific research to user-generated content and provided a rich source of information for AI systems. This is because the limited data quantity could constrain AI capabilities or performance, thus reflecting real-world scenarios, and more data will help produce better models (Delipetrev, 2020). The development of new machine learning algorithms and techniques, such as neural networks and deep learning, opened up new possibilities for AI applications. These algorithms were better able to process and analyze data and could be used for a wider range of tasks.

Since the 1990s, there have been three milestones with regard to AI research that received public attention. They are IBM's chess-playing computer *Deep Blue* (1997), IBM's computer *Watson* (2011) with the explicit goal of joining the quiz show *Jeopardy!*, and Alphabet's

---

However, due to slow progress, the report stated that machine translation did not provide adequate improvements in quality, speed, and cost, and overall, the machine translation was of poor quality. On the other hand, the British Scientific Research Council published a report that provided a similar pessimistic evaluation and highlighted that the conventional engineering approach with radio waves performed better than AI methods. Furthermore, the report pointed out that the application of AI technologies was still very limited, suited to labs and small domains but not to large-scale real-world problem solutions (Delipetrev, 2020).

AlphaGo (2015), which succeeded in beating the world champion in the board game Go (Fjelland, 2020). The impressive performance of Alphabet's AlphaGo program can be attributed to deep learning, a specific type of artificial neural network. This advanced form of AI technology has been widely adopted for commercial purposes, such as the image recognition algorithms used by Facebook, speech recognition algorithms used by smart speakers, and self-driving cars (Haenlein and Kaplan, 2019).

ChatGPT, an AI chatbot, was released by OpenAI in November 2022 and has taken the web by storm. It represents a general-purpose technology, which can boost productivity across a wide range of industries and occupations (*Economist*, 2023).[3] The substantial improvement in the capabilities of ChatGPT should be attributed to large language models (LLMs), a type of generative AI. These models are capable of producing poetry, coding, generating images, sound, and video — tasks that typically necessitate a highly skilled workforce or professionals.

Unlike big data analytics, which often requires a significant amount of human expertise to design and implement analytical models and interpret the results, AI, on the other hand, is designed to make decisions based on data with little or no human intervention. Hence, the fast development of AI technology brings a big consideration regarding the risks of losing control of our civilization. Compared to other technologies, AI is also subject to government regulations.

Cloud computing

John McCarthy first mentioned the concept of cloud computing in 1961 by stating, "… The computer cloud become the basis of a new and important industry." (Qian *et al.*, 2009: 627), but cloud computing services were first introduced into the market in 2006 by Amazon, Google, and other service producers (Yang and Tate, 2012). Although there has been no standard definition, the concept defined by the National Institute of Standards and Technology (NIST) is used most widely (Yoo and Kim, 2019). It describes cloud computing as "a model for enabling ubiquitous,

---

[3]Please refer to Chapter 1, which looks at the systematic analysis of ChatGPT's overall economic impact by investigating its influences on the eight determinant factors of national competitiveness.

convenient, on-demand network access to a shared pool of configurable computing resources (e.g., networks, servers, storage, applications, and services) that can be rapidly provisioned and released with minimal management effort or service provider interaction." (Satyanarayana, 2012: 76).

Cloud computing has firmly positioned itself as a cornerstone in the next generation of the IT industry and business (Hashem *et al.*, 2015; Majid Al-Ruithe *et al.*, 2018). The increasing use of wireless networks and mobile devices has driven unprecedented demand for cloud computing because of the limited processing capability, storage capacity, and battery lifetime of traditional devices. The management and analysis of big data necessitate substantial on-demand computational power and distributed storage. Cloud computing is well suited to meet these requirements, providing scalable, on-demand, integrated computing resources, along with the requisite storage and computing capacity (Muniswamaiah *et al.*, 2019). As such, data can be processed and stored outside of mobile devices onto mobile cloud applications, such as Gmail, iCloud, and Dropbox, which improves not only mobile cloud performance but also user experience (Hashem *et al.*, 2015). Therefore, the recent scientific and technological literature on cloud computing has pivoted toward exploring various storage technologies within the cloud designed to provide data analytics and AI services, as well as multi-level cloud computing systems (Yoo and Kim, 2019).

NIST suggested five essential characteristics of cloud computing: on-demand self-service, broad network access, resource pooling, rapid elasticity, and measured service. Cloud computing has been shifting from computing as a product to computing as a service to consumers over the internet (Khajeh-Hosseini *et al.*, 2010). There are three fundamental service models with regard to cloud computing: Infrastructure as a Service (IaaS), Platform as a Service (PaaS), and Software as a Service (SaaS). In particular, the visualization technology of cloud computing can help present analytical results visually through various graphs, facilitating decision-making. Consequently, big data can leverage distributed storage technology based on cloud computing, as opposed to relying on local storage connected to a computer or electronic device (Hashem *et al.*, 2015). Thanks to the significant advantages of cloud computing, there has been an emerging trend of adoption in both the public and private sectors.

Interactions Among the Four Technologies

The development of the four major technologies, collectively referred to as ABCD technologies, took place at distinct periods in history. As highlighted in the literature review section on the historical evolution of the four technologies (Table 1), digital technology emerged as the earliest, dating back to the 1930s. AI followed suit in the 1950s. The concept of big data gained attention in the mid-1990s, and cloud computing began its development in the mid-2000s. However, it was during the 2010s, coinciding with the advent of Industry 4.0, that all four technologies experienced significant popularity and widespread adoption.

This trend is also evident in the growing number of academic papers dedicated to research in the four technology domains. A bibliometric analysis was conducted using published data on emerging technologies based on these four foundational technologies. The analysis employed the Web of Science database, and the scope was limited to articles included in the database, with no restrictions on publication year. The search was

Table 1.   Historical evolution of the four technologies.

Four Technologies	Description	Evolution
Digital technology	• Transitioning from analog to digital contents • Enabling factors: PCs, internet, web browsers, RFID, smartphones, IoT	Start: 1930s and 1940s Popularity: 1990s
Big data analytics	• 3Vs: high volume, velocity, and variety • Enabling factors: big data analytics, such as web mining, social media analytics, and machine learning	Start: mid-1990s Popularity: 2010s
Artificial intelligence	• Machines mimicking human intelligence • Enabling factors: computing power, big data, machine learning techniques, government regulations	Start: 1950s Fall: 1970s and 1980s Reemergence: 1990s and 2000s Popularity: 2010s
Cloud computing	• Wireless networks and mobile devices • Enabling factors: big data analytics and AI services	Start: mid-2000s Popularity: 2010s

performed four times, each time focusing on one of the four technologies: "digital technology," "big data or big data analytics," "artificial intelligence," and "cloud computing," using relevant keywords. For instance, for articles related to digital technology, the keyword used was "digital technology" in the title or abstract.

Figure 1 illustrates a consistent increase in the number of papers discussing these four technologies in the context of emerging technologies. Among the four technologies, AI publications have the highest count, totaling 65,335, with the earliest cited publication dating back to 1960. In comparison, digital technology publications amount to 14,115 (with the earliest cited publication in 1968), big data publications total 43,528 (with the earliest cited publication in 1993), and cloud computing publications amount to 25,461 (with the earliest cited publication in 2007). It is worth noting that these articles span multiple subject areas, ranging from science to social sciences and interdisciplinary studies.

As shown in Figure 1, until the 2000s, the annual number of publications related to the four technologies was relatively small, with little variation from year to year. However, beginning in the 2010s, the volume of publications on each of the four technologies started to grow exponentially, albeit with slight differences in the timing of inflection points. This upward trend continues, demonstrating an unceasing interest in these fields. Notably, while the growth rate of relevant articles published from 2020 to 2022 dipped slightly due to the impact of the COVID-19 pandemic, the overall trajectory remained sharply upward.

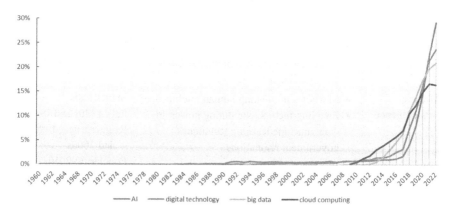

Figure 1.   Distribution of cited publications on the ABCD technologies over the years (1960–2022)

Although the foundational technologies have evolved independently, they are becoming more and more interconnected over time. This convergence of the four technologies creates new opportunities and fosters the emergence of novel applications in various fields. The subsequent sections delve into the utilization of this convergence in areas such as ChatGPT, IoT, and blockchains. The rapid growth and widespread adoption of all four technologies in recent years can be attributed to their interplay and mutually reinforcing relationships. The combination of these technologies not only leads to significant productivity gains at the firm level through process and business model innovation but also enhances the flexibility of economic interactions among a broader range of economic actors, facilitated by the emergence of digital platforms. This cluster of technologies has triggered a profound restructuring and transformation across industries, such as the automotive industry (Pardi *et al.*, 2020), blurring and redefining sectoral boundaries (Lee and Gereffi, 2021) and enabling data-driven business models and platform strategies (Butollo *et al.*, 2022). Digital platform firms have emerged as influential players, particularly in transactional sectors such as logistics, retail, and the distribution of intangible goods such as media and software. Their activities have progressively expanded into other sectors (Butollo *et al.*, 2022). The interconnection of the four foundational technologies is illustrated in Figure 1, and their synergistic relationship significantly impacts the business and social demand for ABCD technologies, as well as their performance capabilities.

Digital technology acts as the foundation for the other three enabling technologies, as it allows the conversion of analog information into digital formats that can be stored, processed, and transmitted by computing systems. Digitization has given rise to an exponential growth in the volume and variety of data generated by various sources, such as business transactions, social media, sensors, and machines. This increasing availability of digital data has paved the way for the development and application of big data analytics, AI algorithms, and cloud computing infrastructure. By transforming analog information into digital formats, digitization enables organizations to access, analyze, and leverage data more effectively, driving improvements in efficiency, decision-making, and innovation.

Big data features a vast and complex collection of data generated by various sources, such as social media, sensors, machines, and human interactions. Digital technology has significantly contributed to the growth of big data as more information becomes available in digital formats. This thus encourages a growing demand for the technologies and

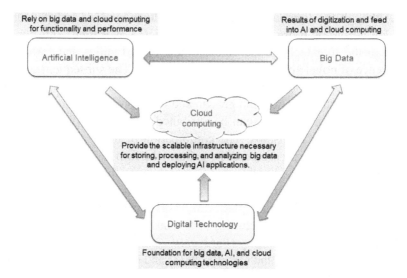

Figure 2.   Interactions among the four base technologies

techniques used to process, manage, and analyze these large datasets. AI encompasses a range of technologies and algorithms that enable machines to simulate human intelligence and perform tasks that typically require human cognitive capabilities. Machine learning, in particular, often relies on big data to learn patterns automatically, make predictions, and improve their performance over time. Lastly, cloud computing provides the necessary infrastructure for storing, processing, and analyzing big data and deploying AI applications. It allows organizations to access and utilize massive computing resources without investing in costly hardware, enabling faster and more efficient development of AI systems. Therefore, big data analytics is the immediate outcome of digitization, and AI and cloud computing technologies rely on big data to perform complex tasks and deliver scalable services (see Figure 2).

Emerging Technologies and Their Relevance to the ABCD Technologies

ChatGPT and the ABCD technologies

ChatGPT, a breakthrough language model released by OpenAI in November 2022, is well known as an AI chatbot. After only three months, in May 2023, ChatGPT appeared on the cover of TIME magazine, reflecting its popularity and sensational impacts on society. Nevertheless, its operations and improved performance should also depend on the sophisticated integration and improvement of the four foundational technologies: digital technology, big data analytics, AI, and cloud computing. These four technologies have jointly played a pivotal role in transforming OpenAI's GPT models, from the debut of GPT-1 in 2018 to the latest version, GPT-4.

Without digitization, none of the advanced AI applications that we see today would exist. For ChatGPT, foundational digital data include a vast compilation of text data scraped from the internet (e.g., web pages, articles, books, and social media platforms) and real-time conversations in several languages (Hassani and Silva, 2023). Such digital data are the lifeblood of the model, providing the language patterns, structures, and contexts that the model learns to understand and generate human-like text. During the COVID-19 pandemic in particular, several driving forces, such as remote working, increased the daily time spent with digital media. Moreover, consumer preferences toward online shopping have contributed to the rapid creation and growth in volume of data worldwide (McKinsey, 2020), which grew substantially from 41 zettabytes in 2019 to 64.2 zettabytes in 2020.

The size and complexity of the data used to train ChatGPT require big data analytics, which primarily involves the techniques and technologies used to handle the vast amounts of data required for training. GPT-3 utilized 175 billion parameters, making it one of the largest language models available as of today. Yet, its initial model of GPT-1 is based on only 117 million parameters, compared to 1.5 billion parameters for GPT-2. For GPT-4, the most recent model, Open AI did not disclose the exact number of parameters used for training. ChatGPT uses natural language processing (NLP) as a type of big data analytics to understand and respond to human queries.

Next, we consider the role of AI, which is at the heart of ChatGPT. For ChatGPT, the most relevant branch of AI is machine learning, particularly a sub-branch known as deep learning. More specifically, ChatGPT employs a type of deep learning model known as an LLM. The success of ChatGPT is due to the transformer architecture, which was introduced in 2017. This architecture has been incredibly successful in NLP tasks and has revolutionized the field of NLP. The primary innovation in the Transformer model is the introduction of the "attention mechanism," which allows the model to make connections between different parts of the prompt when producing an output (*Economist*, 2023). This mechanism makes Transformers especially effective and fine-tuned for a wide range of language-related tasks, which often require consideration of their context.

Finally, cloud computing has been pivotal in the development and deployment of ChatGPT. Cloud computing provides the necessary infrastructure to store large amounts of data used for training and the high computational power required to process these data (*New York Times*, 2023). Without cloud computing, training advanced models like ChatGPT would be out of reach for most organizations due to the cost and complexity of setting up and maintaining the necessary infrastructure (*Economist*, 2023). Moreover, once the model is trained, cloud computing enables it to be deployed at scale, serving millions of users simultaneously, regardless of their location.

ChatGPT's functionality and performance are reliant on these four base technologies. The digitization of text data provides the raw material that the model learns from. Big data analytics involves processing and understanding large amounts of data, which is critical for training LLMs, and cloud computing provides the infrastructure for training and deploying the model. AI, and specifically Transformer-based LLM, is the mechanism by which the model learns from data and generates contextual answers in response to specific questions. Without any one of these technologies, a language model like ChatGPT would not be possible. The advancements in these areas have not only made ChatGPT possible but also continue to push the boundaries of what language models can achieve.

IoT and the ABCD technologies

Since the International Telecommunications Union (ITU) first published an impactful report on IoT in 2005, this concept has been in frequent use (Sorri *et al.*, 2022). Since then, IoT has attracted growing interest from both academics and practitioners, given its significant impact on individuals, businesses, and even the overall economy. Yet, there is no universally accepted definition of IoT in academia. Despite the inconsistency in the definition, most previous studies agree that the IoT features of "things" — virtual and physical — have some sort of interconnection or interaction among these things. Although most studies consider IoT as an emerging technology or digital technology in general, Sorri *et al.* (2022) suggested that IoT should be an entity, an ecosystem, or a business enabler by addressing the business component as part of IoT. They suggested three core components — data, information, and services — which help transform existing technologies into businesses. The following breaks down and analyzes IoT within the lens of ABCD technologies.

IoT fundamentally relies on the digitization of physical phenomena. Sensors play a crucial role in IoT because these sensors attached to IoT devices convert real-world observations into digital signals (Sinha, 2023). For example, a temperature sensor on a smart thermostat converts the analog temperature into digital data that can be processed and analyzed. All the functions and performance of IoT are enabled by collecting data from processes with sensors and actuators. The data are then used for analysis, process control, and development (Sorri *et al.*, 2022). On average, each new IoT device that comes online is equipped with four sensors. Given the estimated 14 billion active IoT connections, this suggests that more than 50 billion sensors have been deployed and are currently connected (Sinha, 2023).

IoT devices can effortlessly generate and share a huge volume of data. Yet, collecting a huge amount of data alone is insufficient. To generate benefits from IoT, it requires new ways for firms to create networks and ecosystems to capture value and turn them into advantages against rivals (Tiwana, 2014). The process is not automatically achieved but requires firms to adopt big data analytics to process, analyze, and derive insights from this data. Analyzing the data derived from IoT provides firms with huge opportunities to develop new markets and consumer insights, thereby improving the firm's performance and creating new competitive advantages (Erevelles *et al.*, 2016).

AI is also crucial to determining the degree of smartness or sophistication of the actions that IoT devices can perform. An IoT-enabled device can sense its environment, gather data, transmit and store it, and then act based on the processed information. The sophistication of an IoT service is ultimately determined by the degree of processing it can perform and the subsequent actions it can undertake (Debauche *et al.*, 2020). A non-smart IoT system will have limited capabilities, whereas a smarter IoT system equipped with AI will have the capability of automation and adaptation. For instance, AI could analyze data from a network of environmental sensors to predict weather patterns or identify anomalies in machine operations in an industrial IoT setting.

Cloud computing provides the infrastructure to store and process the large amounts of data generated by IoT devices. It enables scalable storage solutions and offers powerful computing capabilities to process and analyze the data in real-time. Furthermore, cloud platforms often provide services to manage IoT devices, making it easier to operate IoT networks.

Each technology serves a different purpose within the IoT framework, and thus, the "most related" can vary based on the specifics of the use case. For instance, a simple sensor network may depend more heavily on digitization and cloud computing, while an AI-driven predictive maintenance system for industrial machinery may lean more on AI and big data analytics. It is the combination of these technologies that influences the operations and performance of IoT. Take Amazon's Echo, for example. It is an intelligent home assistant, or IoT hub, which takes voice commands from users to control itself and other connected devices and sensors, such as smart lights, smart kettles, and smart doors (Li *et al.*, 2019). The voice commands are interpreted and performed by Amazon's Alexa, a virtual assistant AI technology, through which Echo controls other IoT devices (Jackson and Camp, 2018).

Blockchain and the ABCD technologies

Blockchain is defined as "a decentralized peer-to-peer (P2P) network of personal computers called nodes, which maintains, stores, and records historical and transaction data" (Haleem *et al.*, 2021: 131). As no records involved can be changed retroactively without changing any blocks afterward, this technology provides a good deal of accountability and is very useful for exchanging critical data and keeping it secure and confidential (Haleem *et al.*, 2021). There are different types of blockchain technologies, such as public, private, hybrid, and consortium (Haleem *et al.*, 2021). Bitcoin and other cryptocurrencies are good examples of adopting the public blockchain. In this case, blockchain is a distributed and decentralized ledger system and also has connections to the four technologies: digitization, AI, big data analytics, and cloud computing.

Blockchain relies on digitization because all transactions recorded on the blockchain must be in digital format. Digitization provides the prerequisite for blockchain, enabling the conversion of assets, contracts, and other types of information into digital form so they can be used in blockchain transactions. The nature of blockchain, with its numerous and complex transactions, generates a large amount of data that can be analyzed. Big data analytics can provide insights into blockchain transactions, detect anomalies indicating potential fraud, and predict trends in blockchain networks, such as the fluctuation of cryptocurrency values. AI can be used in various ways within the context of blockchain. For example, machine learning algorithms can be employed to detect fraudulent patterns in blockchain transactions. AI can also enhance the efficiency of blockchain mining processes, and it could be used to automate decision-making in decentralized autonomous organizations (DAOs). Blockchain and cloud computing are often intertwined. Blockchain as a Service (BaaS) is a cloud-based service that enables users to develop, host, and use their own blockchain apps, smart contracts, and functions on the cloud-based infrastructure developed by a vendor. This enables organizations to experiment with blockchain solutions without the need for extensive in-house expertise or infrastructure.

While each of these technologies intersects with blockchain in different ways, digitization can be considered the most fundamentally linked to the basic operations of this technology. Blockchain technology inherently relies on digitization. All the transactions and data stored on the blockchain are digital. Moreover, the concept of digital trust is fundamental to blockchain operations. For instance, digitization enables assets and contracts to be tokenized and transacted on the blockchain. Thus, the fundamental operation of blockchain is highly reliant on digitization.

Blockchain does generate a vast amount of data that can be analyzed, but its operation is not primarily about analyzing or extracting insights from data. Instead, blockchain focuses on recording and securing data. While AI can provide enhancements to blockchain technology, such as improving efficiency or enabling automation in blockchain operations, its core function does not inherently rely on AI. Blockchain can function independently of cloud computing and can run on any type of computing infrastructure. However, cloud computing does offer advantages such as scalability and ease of deployment for blockchain systems, especially in the form of BaaS offerings.

Although the three emerging technologies rely on the four foundational technologies, their significance and contribution to each of the emerging technologies vary, as depicted in Table 2. We used the ChatGPT application to assess the relevance and importance of the four foundational technologies for the three emerging technologies, using a scoring scale of up to five, where a higher score indicates

Table 2.   The significance of the four technologies: comparison among ChatGPT, IoT, and blockchain.

	Digital Technology	Artificial Intelligence	Big Data Analytics	Cloud Computing
ChatGPT	4	5	5	5
IoT	5	4	5	4
Blockchains	5	2	2	3

greater relevance. As shown in Table 2, ChatGPT exhibits a high dependence on all four technologies, scoring five in three areas. In contrast, IoT demonstrates a complete score in digital technology and big data analytics and a score of four in the areas of AI and cloud computing. Blockchains, however, display a different distribution pattern across the four foundational technologies. The table also implies the core competencies or focus areas of different emerging technologies, suggesting where firms should allocate resources to strengthen their competitive advantages against rivals.

Conclusion and Implications

The Fourth Industrial Revolution, beginning with Industry 4.0 in the early 2010s, marks a significant shift in the technological landscape, not merely due to the emergence of new, disruptive technologies but also the way these technologies interact and integrate. This chapter proposes that the four foundational technologies, namely ABCD technologies (AI, big data, cloud computing, and digitization), are crucial drivers behind this revolution. These technologies, while powerful individually, have even more profound implications when used in synergy, driving far-reaching changes across businesses, industries, and even society as a whole.

The historical evolution of these foundational technologies and their subsequent interaction and integration have significantly transformed the business landscape. Their mutual reinforcement and confluence have expedited the process of innovation, opening up new avenues for value creation. Moreover, their integration provides the necessary technological infrastructure that enables the emergence and function of more advanced, applied technologies such as GPT family products, IoT, and blockchain.

Regarding AI, examples such as ChatGPT underscore the powerful convergence of these foundational technologies. Built on the four base technologies, ChatGPT is a testament to the potential of ABCD technologies in revolutionizing communication and information dissemination. Similarly, emerging technologies such as IoT and blockchains exhibit a similar reliance on ABCD technologies, despite the variant degree of dependence on the four base technologies.

As ABCD technologies serve as the bedrock for technological advancement in the era of the Fourth Industrial Revolution, it is vital for firms, especially technology firms such as Microsoft, Apple, Alphabet, Facebook, Amazon, and Tesla, to understand and strategically leverage these foundational technologies, which influence their core competences and portfolio development. Being proficient in ABCD technologies and knowing how to integrate them effectively can be a critical differentiator in the competitive landscape. A firm's ability to navigate and innovate within these technologies could determine its resilience against disruptive changes and its capacity to lead in the new technology era. The understanding of the foundational technologies also provides implications for policymakers. As ABCD technologies reshape economic landscapes, they inevitably bring about societal changes, requiring new regulatory frameworks and educational approaches. Policymakers need to understand these technologies and their implications to facilitate an enabling environment that fosters innovation while mitigating potential risks.

References

Agostini, L. and Nosella, A. 2021. Industry 4.0 and business models: A bibliometric literature review. *Business Process Management Journal*, 27(5): 1633–1655.

Agostini, L. and Filippini, R. 2019. Organizational and managerial challenges in the path toward Industry 4.0. *European Journal of Innovation Management*, 22(3): 406–421.

Ben-Daya, M., Hassini, E., and Bahroun, Z. 2019. Internet of things and supply chain management: A literature review. *International Journal of Production Research*, 57: 4719–4742.

Brennen, J. S. and Kreiss, D. 2016. Digitalization. In K. B. Jensen and R. Craig (Eds.), *The International Encyclopedia of Communication Theory and Philosophy* (pp. 1–11). Hoboken, NJ: John Wiley & Sons.

Bortoluzzi, G., Chiarvesio, M., Romanello, R., Tabacco, R., and Veglio, V. 2022. Servitisation and performance in the business-to-business context: The moderating role of Industry 4.0 technologies. *Journal of Manufacturing Technology Management*, 33(9): 108–128.

Bumblauskas, D., Nold, H., Bumblauskas, P., and Igou, A. 2017. Big data analytics: Transforming data to action. *Business Process Management Journal*, 23(3): 703–720.

Butollo, F., Gereffi, G., Yang, C., and Krzywdzinski, M. 2022. Digital transformation and value chains: Introduction. Global Networks, 22(4): 585–594.

Chen, H., Chiang, R. H., and Storey, V. C. 2012. Business intelligence and analytics: From big data to big impact. *MIS quarterly*, 36: 1165–1188.

Coreynen, W., Matthyssens, P., and Van Bockhaven, W. 2017, Boosting servitization through digitization: Pathways and dynamic resource configurations for manufacturers. *Industrial Marketing Management*, 60: 42–53.

Davenport, T. H., Barth, P., and Bean, R. 2012. How 'big data' is different. *MIT Sloan Management Review*, 54(1): 22–24.

Debauche, O., Mahmoudi, S., Mahmoudi, S. A., Manneback, P., and Lebeau, F. 2020. A new edge architecture for AI-IoT services deployment. *Procedia Computer Science*, 175, 10–19.

Delipetrev, B., Tsinaraki, C., and Kostic, U. 2020. Historical evolution of artificial intelligence. Luxembourg: Publications Office of the European Union, Luxembourg.

Deloitte. 2015. Industry 4.0: Challenges and solutions for the digital transformation and use of exponential technologies. www2.deloitte.com/content/dam/Deloitte/ch/Documents/manufacturing/ch-en-manufacturing-industry-4-0-24102014.pdf. Accessed June 10, 2023.

Diebold, F. X. 2012. On the origin(s) and development of the term 'Big Data'. *PIER Working Paper No. 12-037*. https://ssrn.com/abstract=2152421. Accessed June 10, 2023.

Economist. 2015. Data, data everywhere. https://www.economist.com/special-report/2010/02/27/data-data-everywhere. Accessed June 1, 2023.

Economist. 2023. Large, creative AI models will transform lives and labour markets. https://www.economist.com/interactive/science-and-technology/2023/04/22/large-creative-ai-models-will-transform-how-we-live-and-work. Accessed July 27, 2023.

Elgendy, N. and Elragal, A. 2014. Big data analytics: A literature review paper. *Advances in Data Mining. Applications and Theoretical Aspects: 14th Industrial Conference*, St. Petersburg, Russia, July 16–20, 2014.

Erevelles, S., Fukawa, N., and Swayne, L. 2016. Big Data consumer analytics and the transformation of marketing. *Journal of Business Research*, 69(2): 897–904.

Fjelland, R. 2020. Why general artificial intelligence will not be realized. *Humanities and Social Sciences Communications*, 7(1): 1–9.

Farrow, E. 2019. To augment human capacity — Artificial intelligence evolution through causal layered analysis. *Futures*, 108: 61–71.

Frank, A. G., Mendes, G. H., Ayala, N. F., and Ghezzi, A. 2019. Servitization and Industry 4.0 convergence in the digital transformation of product firms: A business model innovation perspective. *Technological Forecasting and Social Change*, 141: 341–351.

Gandomi, A. and Haider, M. 2015. Beyond the hype: Big data concepts, methods, and analytics. *International Journal of Information Management*, 35(2): 137–144.

Guo, B., Zhang, D., Wang, Z., Yu, Z., and Zhou, X. 2013. Opportunistic IoT: Exploring the harmonious interaction between human and the internet of things. *Journal of Network and Computer Applications*, 36(6): 1531–1539.

Gupta, R. 2023. Industry 4.0 adaption in Indian banking sector — A review and agenda for future research. *Vision*, 27(1): 24–32.

Gupta, H., Kumar, S., Kusi-Sarpong, S., Jabbour, C. J. C., and Agyemang, M. 2021. Enablers to supply chain performance on the basis of digitization technologies. *Industrial Management & Data Systems*, 121(9): 1915–1938.

Haenlein, M. and Kaplan, A. 2019. A brief history of artificial intelligence: On the past, present, and future of artificial intelligence. *California Management Review*, 61(4): 5–14.

Haleem, A., Javaid, M., Singh, R. P., Suman, R., and Rab, S. (2021). Blockchain technology applications in healthcare: An overview. *International Journal of Intelligent Networks*, 2, 130–139.

Hashem, I. A. T., Yaqoob, I., Anuar, N, B., Mokhtar, S., Gani, A., and Khan, S. U. 2015. The rise of big data on cloud computing: Review and open research issues. *Information Systems*, 47: 98–115.

Hassani, H. and Silva, E. S. 2023. The role of ChatGPT in data science: How ai-assisted conversational interfaces are revolutionizing the field. *Big Data and Cognitive Computing*, 7(2): 62.

Hilbert, M. 2016. Big data for development: A review of promises and challenges. *Development Policy Review*, 34(1): 135–174.

Jackson, R. B. and Camp, T. 2018. Amazon echo security: Machine learning to classify encrypted traffic. In *2018 27th International Conference on Computer Communication and Networks (ICCCN)* (pp. 1–10). IEEE.

Janssen, M., vander Voort, H., and Wahyedi, A. 2017. Factors influencing big data decision-making quality. *Journal of Business Research*, 70: 338–345.

Kagermann, H. 2015. Change through digitization — Value creation in the age of Industry 4.0. Management of permanent change. In H. Albach, H. Meffert,

A. Pinkwart, and R. Reichwald (Eds.), *Management of Permanent Change* (pp. 23–45). New York, NY: Springer.

Kaplan, A. M. and Haenlein, M. 2019. Siri, Siri, in my hand: Who's the fairest in the land? On the interpretations, illustrations, and implications of artificial intelligence. *Business Horizons*, 62(1): 15–25.

Khajeh-Hosseini, A., Sommerville, I., and Sriram, I. 2010. Research challenges for enterprise cloud computing. https://arxiv.org/abs/1001.3257.

Koh, S., Lee, H. H., Perdana, A. 2023. Accountancy programme: The spaced retrieval method. In Rana, T., Svanberg, J., Öhman, P., and Lowe, A. (Eds.), *Handbook of Big Data and Analytics in Accounting and Auditing* (pp. 415–437). Singapore: Springer Singapore.

Laney, D. (2001). 3-D data management: Controlling data volume, velocity and variety. *META Group Research Note*, February, pp. 1–4.

Lee, I. 2017. Big data: Dimensions, evolution, impacts, and challenges. *Business Horizons*, 60(3): 293–303.

Li, S., Choo, K.-K. R., Sun, Q., Buchanan, W. J., and Cao, J. 2019. IoT forensics: Amazon echo as a use case. *IEEE Internet of Things Journal*, 6(4): 6487–6497.

New York Times. 2023. The chatbots are here, and the internet industry is in a tizzy. https://www.nytimes.com/2023/03/08/technology/chatbots-disrupt-internet-industry.html. Accessed July 27, 2023.

McKinsey. 2020. How COVID-19 has pushed companies over the technology tipping point—and transformed business forever. https://www.mckinsey.com/capabilities/strategy-and-corporate-finance/our-insights/how-covid-19-has-pushed-companies-over-the-technology-tipping-point-and-transformed-business-forever. Accessed July 27, 2023.

Muniswamaiah, M., Agerwala, T., and Tappert, C. 2019. Big data in cloud computing review and opportunities. arXiv preprint arXiv:1912.10821.

Paiola, M., Agostini, L., Grandinetti, R., and Nosella, A. 2022. The process of business model innovation driven by IoT: Exploring the case of incumbent SMEs. *Industrial Marketing Management*, 103: 30–46.

Pardi, T., Krzywdzinski, M., and Lüthje, B. 2020. Digital manufacturing revolutions as political projects and hypes: Evidences from the auto sector. ILO Working Paper.

Parida, V., Sjödin, D., and Reim, W. 2019. Leveraging digitalization for advanced service business models: Reflections from a systematic literature review and special issue contributions. *Sustainability*, 11(2): 391.

Peris-Lopez, P., Orfila, A., Mitrokotsa, A., and Van der Lubbe, J. C. 2011. A comprehensive RFID solution to enhance inpatient medication safety. *International Journal of Medical Informatics*, 80(1): 13–24.

Qian, L., Luo, Z., Du, Y., and Guo, L. 2009. Cloud computing: An overview. In *Cloud Computing: First International Conference*, Beijing, China,

December 1–4, 2009. Proceedings 1 (pp. 626–631). Springer, Berlin Heidelberg.

Ritter, T. and Pedersen, C. L. 2020. Digitization capability and the digitalization of business models in business-to-business firms: Past, present, and future. *Industrial Marketing Management*, 86, 180–190.

Satyanarayana, S. 2012. Cloud computing: SAAS. *Computer Sciences and Telecommunications*, 4(36): 76–79.

Schwab, K. 2016. *The Fourth Industrial Revolution*. Geneva, Switzerland: World Economic Forum.

Sestino, A., Prete, M. I., Piper, L., and. Guido, G. 2020. Internet of Things and Big Data as enablers for business digitalization strategies. *Technovation*, 98: 102173.

Sinha, S. 5 IoT sensor technologies to watch. https://iot-analytics.com/5-iot-sensor-technologies/. Accessed July 27, 2023.

Sivarajah, U., Kamal, M. M., Irani, Z., and Weerakkody, V. 2017. Critical analysis of Big Data challenges and analytical methods. *Journal of Business Research*, 70: 263–286.

Smolan, R. and Erwitt, J. 2012. *The Human Face of Big Data*. Sausalito, CA: Against All Odds Productions.

Sorri, K., Mustafee, N., and Seppänen, M. 2022. Revisiting IoT definitions: A framework towards comprehensive use. *Technological Forecasting and Social Change*, 179, 121623.

Statista. n.d. https://www.statista.com. Accessed June 10, 2023.

Taalbi, J. 2019. Origins and pathways of innovation in the third industrial revolution. *Industrial and Corporate Change*, 28(5): 1125–1148.

Tiwana, A. (2014). Separating signal from noise: Evaluating emerging technologies. *MIS Quarterly Executive*, 13(1): 45–61.

Tortorella, G. L. and Fettermann, D. 2017. Implementation of Industry 4.0 and lean production in Brazilian manufacturing companies. *International Journal of Production Research*, 56(8): 2975–2987.

Yoo, S. K. and Kim, B. Y. 2019. The effective factors of cloud computing adoption success in organization. *The Journal of Asian Finance, Economics and Business*, 6(1): 217–229.

Warner, K. S. and Wäger, M. 2019. Building dynamic capabilities for digital transformation: An ongoing process of strategic renewal. *Long Range Planning*, 52(3): 326–349.

Part III

Cases: Introduction

The final section of the book delves deep into emerging technologies amid the fourth industrial revolution, highlighting various perspectives on how they have affected firms, workers, and regions. This part of the book is organized into seven chapters, as follows.

The first three chapters in this section offer detailed analyses on the effects of emerging technologies at the regional or national level. Specifically, Chapter 7, titled "AI and Destructive Creation: Toward a New AI Urban Regime?", examines the opportunities and risks associated with the new urban AI regime, which involves integrating AI into the development of smart cities. However, this process of "destructive creation" may introduce negative externalities, risking public space centrality and human interactions. This chapter addressed that it is essential to discuss and define "smart and just sustainability" to guide AI's integration into urban areas. Chapter 8, titled "Corporate Strategy and Government Policy for Technological Development in Poland's Peripheral Region," discusses the strategies and policies for adopting technological innovations in the peripheral regions with the specific example of Poland. This chapter analyzes the influence of government policies on corporate strategies concerning technological adoption. It suggests that government policies should prioritize the development of infrastructure as a crucial foundation during the early stages of technological advancement. Chapter 9, titled "Indigenous Knowledge Management in the Fourth Industrial Revolution: A Reflection on the Emerging Technologies and Development Strategies in Tanzania," addresses the need to use emerging technologies in preserving and managing indigenous knowledge with a specific focus on Tanzania. This chapter proposes strategies for integrating emerging technologies into the management of indigenous knowledge.

The following two chapters discuss the significance of emerging technologies in relation to human capital. Chapter 10, titled "Developing Human Capital for Competitiveness: A Study of Singapore's Artificial Intelligence Apprenticeship Program (AIAP) from a Systems Thinking Viewpoint," discusses the role of artificial intelligence in the development of human capital, addressing Singapore's AIAP as an example. Chapter 11, titled "Factors Influencing the Future of Work 4.0: Technological Competitiveness, Education, and Policy Coordination," delves into the correlation between technological competitiveness and education, while also assessing the impact of the fourth industrial revolution on the future job creation in Latin America. This chapter thus emphasizes the importance of adequately preparing the future labor force to meet the challenges of disruptive and emerging technologies.

The final two chapters explore the effects of emerging technologies on firms and their respective response strategies. Chapter 12, titled "Analyzing the Digital Entrepreneurial Ecosystem: Evidence from the Information Technology-Related Small and Medium Enterprises in an Emerging Economy," presents the ways in which small and medium companies (SMEs) can leveraging digital technology to secure their competitiveness. Conversely, Chapter 13, titled "The Role of MNEs in Industry 4.0 Transformation in ASEAN," assesses the significance of the role played by multinational corporations in leading the Industry 4.0 Transformation, specifically in ASEAN countries. It emphasizes the implementation of relevant policies aimed at incentivizing the adoption of emerging technologies to enhance business efficiency.

Chapter 7

AI and Destructive Creation: Toward a New AI Urban Regime?

Gerardo del Cerro Santamaría

Abstract

Despite the diffuse, diverse, and controversial meaning of the "smart city" concept, its proponents assume that a smart city is capable of better addressing the challenges of urban resilience and sustainability. The evolution of "smart cities" toward a widespread use of artificial intelligence (AI) techniques, processes, and devices indicates that a new urban AI regime will expand in the coming years, and therefore it is necessary to analyze both the benefits and the risks of this strategy. This disruptive urban AI regime (which I describe as "destructive creation") generates a critical mass of negative externalities in the development process of smart cities, derived initially from the contemporary hegemonic nature of technological innovation in urban socioeconomic processes. Such a disruptive thrust represents a risk for the centrality of public spaces and the civic friction between humans that should occur, according to Jane Jacobs, in the core of the urban as self-organized complexity. The intelligent disruption (destructive creation) produced by AI systems is no longer avoidable, although we can debate about what kind of sustainability we want for ourselves and for future generations. There should be analyses and discussions around the notion of "smart and just sustainability" as a normative horizon setting the framework to decide what technological innovations and what AI applications we need.

Keywords: Artificial intelligence, destructive creation, AI urban regime, urban technopoles, smart cities, competitiveness, sustainability, cohesion, public value

Introduction

It has long been known that cities and urban areas significantly contribute to economic development, and the classic work by Paul Bairoch on the matter still stands today as a prominent example of this idea (Bairoch, 1988). In recent decades, however, the prominent role of urban regions in growth and development has expanded. The wave of globalization that started roughly in the 1980s, enhanced by neoliberal capitalism, and the simultaneous rapid urbanization of the planet in recent decades has placed urban areas, cities, world-city regions, and megaregions as the axes and foundations to understand the world economy, its evolution, and transformations.

Competitiveness amidst global social change cannot be understood without focusing on the links between urbanism and the global economy. The issue at stake here is not so much to zoom in to the particularities of city life as opposed to other forms of life, but rather to grasp how what we commonly call "the economy" takes place and is shaped in urban areas. By adopting this approach, we are indeed *materializing* the economy and shifting away from the explanatory excesses of abstract global arguments that the economic science too often utilizes. Urbanists who understand the economy through the prism of cities are in fact very well positioned to untangle the complexities of the global economy as they attach to place and context.

The relevance of information and virtuality in the knowledge economy can lead us to underestimate or misunderstand the importance of infrastructure, merchandise and commodity chains, trade and transport, logistics, spatial planning, or the geo-biological and environmental processes in the configuration of the globalized economy. This tangible dimension of economic processes is clearly seen from the perspective of urban planning, since urban planning and global cities constitute the materiality of globalization.

High-tech in the city

As part of this materiality, we are witnessing the movement of advanced manufacturing and high-tech business activities to urban regions years after the creation of producer services complexes in cities (Sassen, 2011; Zukin, 2020). In their worldwide study of high-tech industrial complexes, Castells and Hall (1994) emphasized the significance of technopoles for the growth of urban and regional areas. The modern equivalents of technopoles, such as factories of the future and innovation districts, are brand-new megaprojects that profoundly alter the urban fabric and the socioeconomic structure of entire neighborhoods in distinct, specialized ways (Castells and Hall, 1994; del Cerro Santamaría, 2020a). A simultaneous and significant reorganization of production is occurring in many cities around the world by utilizing new technologies, particularly "smart" innovations and AI, in old technopoles, new factories of the future, and innovation districts, while many countries have resourced to infrastructure development via megaprojects in the form of industrial corridors (e.g., in India) and reterritorialization via megaregions (e.g., in China) (ADB, 2016; Li and Wu, 2020). As Zukin (2020) puts it:

> Since the economic crisis of 2008, city governments have aggressively pursued economic growth by nurturing these ecosystems. Elected officials create public–private-nonprofit partnerships to build an "innovation complex" of discursive, organizational, and geographical spaces; they aim not only to jump-start economic growth but to remake the city for a new modernity.

Corporate policies, especially those relating to the use of high-tech like AI, have a direct impact on urban sustainable development insofar as these new centers of corporate activity are situated in cities, megacities, megaregions, and urbanized areas. The impact is specifically more pronounced on the centrality of advanced infrastructure for sustainability. In this context, the newer spatial reorganization of production is fundamentally urban and presents formidable challenges for sustainability: it enables it and constrains it to an unprecedented scale (Leigh *et al.*, 2014). Despite the diffuse, diverse, and controversial meaning of the "smart city" concept, its proponents assume that a smart city is capable of better addressing the challenges of urban resilience and sustainability.

Smart cities are presumably more liveable, sustainable, and resilient. They are presented to us as better prepared to respond to urban challenges than the more traditional and transactional forms of urban governance. Given that the development of smart cities toward the widespread application of artificial intelligence techniques, processes, and devices suggests that a new urban AI regime will expand in the coming years, it is vital to evaluate both the advantages and risks of this approach.

Despite the incremental nature of smart city implementation, its disruptive character is undeniable. This disruptive urban AI regime (which I describe as "destructive creation") generates a critical mass of negative externalities in the development process of smart cities, derived initially from the contemporary hegemonic nature of technological innovation in urban socioeconomic processes. Such a disruptive thrust represents a risk for the centrality of public spaces and the civic friction between humans that should occur, according to Jane Jacobs, in the core of the urban as self-organized complexity (Jacobs, 1961). Technological gentrification (interrelated with green gentrification) is already an emerging feature in spaces adjacent to innodistricts and other tech neighborhoods. There are other risks and ethical dilemmas brought about by the smart city strategy that have to do with control, privacy, and security. For all these reasons, *smart* megaprojects are indeed landscapes of disruption, albeit exhibiting a particular genesis, development, and impact. The intelligent disruption (destructive creation) produced by artificial intelligence systems is no longer avoidable, although we can debate about what kind of sustainability we want for ourselves and for future generations. Existing and forthcoming analyses and discussions would gain by focusing on the notion of "smart and just sustainability" as a normative horizon setting the framework to decide what technological innovations and what AI applications we need and want to see implemented.

This chapter analyzes the pervasive expansion of the smart city paradigm and its gradual evolution into a nascent AI urban regime. Such an AI regime is characteristically disruptive, and it begins to show some distinct features that impose valuation and devaluation strategies over entire neighborhoods and urban areas, thus reinforcing marked inequalities and a dual pattern of benefits and high risks in already "quartered" cities (Marcuse, 1989). By focusing on high-tech development and utilization, particularly new kinds of automation capabilities and AI, this chapter offers some elements for a critical analysis of the "smart city" paradigm and the promises and discontents of urban sustainable infrastructure centered on those new technologies. The paradox of artificially intelligent urban environments lies in the promise of attaining a certain kind of sustainability at the risk of further jeopardizing urbanity, equality, and liveability. We argue that AI can contribute to improving urban management (and the management of megaprojects), but if we use a relational concept of urbanism that highlights the *embeddedness* of cities with the wider economy and society (del Cerro Santamaría, 2013), it is then questionable that a better urban management can by itself contribute to fostering urban sustainability. Put differently, AI by itself does not necessarily foster urban sustainability, even if some specific AI innovations could. Further, in the case of those innovations that do foster sustainability, one needs to factor in both the benefits and the risks of innovation strategies. The key question, then, is how to craft and build a framework for sustainability that is able to discriminate and tell which innovations can contribute to the desired sustainability outcomes.

Destructive Creation: An Era of Disruptive Innovation

Beginning in the 1980s, a new round of global capital accumulation started to focus on the extraction of value added from the innovations in science and technology (and digital information technologies) that were taking place in the United States, specifically around Silicon Valley and Boston Route 128 (Castells, 2009; Saxenian, 1994). In the following decades, the information revolution expanded to other areas within the United States and around the world, particularly in the Global North (North America, Europe, Asia-Pacific), but also in some areas in the Global South (Chib, 2015). While emerging market economies continue to increase investment in R + D + i, advanced economies have experienced a slowdown since 2000 relative to both prior periods and to other, less advanced economies. In contrast to newer revolutionary technologies like AI, machine learning, and automation, experts generally agree that the impact of ICTs is waning. Significant technological advancements may be difficult to maintain over time, but persistent disparities allow emerging countries to catch up through adoption as well as their own adaptation and invention (UNCTAD, 2021).

The diffusion of knowledge and technology promoted by the functioning of a global economy operating in real time at a planetary scale accelerates and strengthens incentives to adopt new technologies and innovate (IMF, 2018). With globalization, new ideas and technologies can spread quickly around the world. Increased exposure to a highly diverse cultural world results in the blending and hybridization of established ideas, which both drive and produce process- and product-innovation (IMF, 2018). One of the benefits of globalization has been its promotion of productivity-enhancing technology transfer and innovation worldwide. The April 2018 World Economic Outlook by the International Monetary Fund (IMF) highlights freer trade, increased foreign direct investment, and the international use of patents and copyrights as some of the pillars of the increased transnational exchange in trade, goods, services, capital, and information that characterize globalization (IMF, 2018). To be sure, the hyper-globalization of the neoliberal period from roughly 1990 to 2020 is today severely undermined, even if the pace of technological innovation shows no signs of slowing down, and a perennial need for more inclusive growth still reflects global capitalism (Korinek *et al.*, 2021). That we live in the era of the so-called "knowledge-based economy" has also major implications for the ways in which states, cities, and even supranational political units are spatially planned, governed, and developed, which suggests that knowledge-based "economization" can be understood as a geopolitical process that produces territories of wealth, security, power, and belonging (Moisio, 2018).

What is known today as the Fourth Industrial Revolution represents the evolution, transformation, and maturation of the information technology revolution around digitalization, biotechnologies, materials and nanotechnologies, and environmental and energy technologies. Schwab (2018) proposed the following classification of new processes and technologies in the Fourth Industrial Revolution:

1. Extending digital technologies — ubiquitous computing, mesh computing (distributed computing across many devices on a network), the Internet of Things (IoT) and technologies that increase the possibilities for a two-way flow of information between humans and our environment.
2. Reforming the physical world — AI and robotics, advanced materials, nanotechnologies, additive manufacturing and multidimensional printing.
3. Altering the human being — biotechnologies, neurotechnologies, and virtual and augmented realities.

4. Integrating the environment — energy capture, storage and transmission, geo-engineering, space technology.

Urban Technopoles

The coming of an "industrial renaissance" in advanced economies can turn into a major development in the global political economy due to the end of hyper-globalization and the return of geo-politics to the global stage. Coupled with this, risk materializations in global supply chains under pandemic conditions are shifting foreign, commerce, industrial, and economic priorities among Western and East Asian countries, toward a realignment of trade blocks based on political affinities. In this context, urban technopoles can constitute "central knowledge districts" in cities, whereas factories of the future can be part of those districts or be located in industrial districts in surrounding metropolitan areas. The primary drivers for the urbanization of technopoles in central knowledge districts (CKDs) are new reindustrialization plans, support for urban development, and the establishment of synergies between actors and stakeholders. Metropolitan regions are once more considered to be the best locations for the growth of new industries, and technopoles serve as new Marshallian industrial districts that specialize heavily in a few key industrial sectors (Zukin, 2020). Building the urban fabric and luring a knowledge community have taken place simultaneously, and there has been much conflict between the interests of investors and scientists and entrepreneurs. The nature and perception of proximity have changed, and various technopoles place differing emphasis on various forms of territoriality and proximity (organizational, cognitive, geographical, cultural, and social) (Miao *et al.*, 2015).

Due to the necessity for coordination between levels of government to suit the needs of industry, governance has taken on a more significant role in the past 30 years in determining the emergence of technopoles. Additionally, we have observed the rise of so-called "open innovation" and the absorption of the idea in campus architecture, synergy management, connections between production and R&D, and the development of dynamic company ecologies. From inflexible structures to dynamic and unstable ecosystems, more recent urban technopoles arise in the context of extremely dynamic and loosely connected ecosystems. Furthermore, synergy management necessitates a deeper comprehension of how collective leadership processes work in relation to the concepts of innovation ecosystems and innovation districts (Miao *et al.*, 2015).

With the growing significance of STEM subjects at universities as anchors for technopole activity and for continuously nourishing innovation ecosystems, corporate innovation has evolved from merely tech development to building start-ups. According to the characteristics of interactivity (interdependence, hybridization, and reciprocity), the entrepreneurial university is actually designed specifically to develop inside complex network innovation ecosystems. With the advent of new platform technologies that are causing shifts in regime, technopoles are increasingly integrated into lengthier cycles of technological change and have a great deal of potential to act as change agents. Technopoles are responding to the great challenges of the 21st century, such as resource scarcity, global warming, urban inclusion/sustainability, access to energy, and civic security, as they become more integrated into national technical innovation networks. As the idea of "living labs" has been extended to the level of the urban fabric, they are also becoming more integrated inside cities (Benneworth *et al.*, 2015).

Urban technopoles and science cities are closely related to urban developments, and in some instances the two labels designate the same phenomenon that locates science-based economic development within established metropolitan areas. During the mid-2000s, the UK's government declared six English cities to be "science cities." The Northern Way, a strategy to revitalize the North of England, was tied to the first announcement of three cities in Northern England in 2004 (Manchester, Newcastle, and York). Birmingham, Nottingham, and Bristol were added as three more in the Midlands and South West in 2005, but London and the South East with Oxford and Cambridge were left out because the policy was primarily intended to spur growth in underdeveloped regions. Even though the cities had to have a solid scientific foundation, science cities in England were more about rebalancing the nation's economy than they were about recognizing current scientific capabilities.

Smart Cities and Intelligent Environments

A smart city is not a territorially bounded strategy. Its concept (and the practice) exhibits an expansive scope with an encompassing and relentless nature. As such it is not static, with no absolute definition or end point, but rather it is a process or a series of steps. Smart city applications are developed to manage urban flows and allow for real-time responses.

Despite the fuzzy, diverse, and contested meaning of the concept of a smart city, it is assumed by proponents that a smart city is capable of better addressing the challenges of urban resilience and sustainability. Smart cities are presumably more liveable, sustainable, and resilient, which can be a contested proposition (Caragliu *et al.*, 2009; Mitchell, 2007; Marrone and Hammerle, 2018). They are presented as better prepared to respond to challenges than more traditional and transactional forms of urban governance (Chan, 2017; Komninos 2013; Nisenbaum, 2019; Schaffers *et al.*, 2011; Yovanof and Hazapis, 2009).

Production, adoption, and governance are three salient aspects of smart city developments:

- From the production side, expertise in the development of smart technologies, programming, and coding tends to concentrate in specific urban areas (innodistricts termed TAMI, i.e., technology, advertising, media, and information), such as the Flatiron District, DUMBO, Brooklyn Tech Triangle, and Lower Manhattan/Wall St in New York City, or King's Cross, Tech City, Here East, and Canary Wharf in London.
- Regarding implementation and adoption, some urban areas are more technologically advanced and make use of different electronic methods, voice activation devices and methods, and sensors to collect specific data. It is hardly the case that the smart city reaches all urban neighborhoods similarly: a "smart city divide" separates early adoption areas from the rest.
- From the viewpoint of urban governance, smart city technology is intended to allow city officials to interact directly with both community and city infrastructure and to monitor what is happening in the city and how the city is evolving. ICT and IoT are generally used to enhance the quality, performance, and interactivity of urban services. They also reduce costs and resource consumption and increase contact between citizens and the government (Nam and Pardo, 2018; Peris-Ortiz *et al.*, 2016; Zhao and Ge, 2013).

Smart city programs have been developing in line with the concept and practices related to the Internet of Things (IoT). The drop in the production cost of environmental sensors and network devices, as well as the increased use of reliable mobile telecommunications and cloud computing, is enabling the spread of IoT strategies, processes, and devices (McLaren and Agyeman, 2015).

In essence, IoT is a coordinating and maximizing data strategy deployed across various built environment systems and equipment to speak to one another. This increases both the volume and velocity of data movement and creates new opportunities to interconnect physical operations. Thus, the common element in smart city programs is the use of interconnected sensors, data management, and analytical platforms to enhance the quality and operation of built environment systems (Hollands, 2008; Komninos, 2008, 2009). As the Fourth Industrial Revolution develops, expands, and becomes a key component of the socioeconomic productive fabric, cities are increasingly characterized as *complex adaptive innovation ecosystems* (Cooke, 2012; Gu *et al.*, 2021). In such an ecosystem, "intelligent environments" (Augusto *et al.*, 2013) function via computers, sensors, and machine learning algorithms that are being built in roads, bridges, buildings, homes, transport systems, and other urban amenities and facilities.

Toward a New AI Urban Regime

The emerging AI regime epitomizes the maturation of both the information economy (where maximizing data and information is a key generator of economic value) and the expansion of the so-called Fourth Industrial Revolution (where autonomous decision-making by machines promises to enhance efficiency and effectiveness in all kinds of productive processes). The evolution of smart cities toward a widespread utilization of AI techniques, processes, and devices indicates the rise of *a new AI urban regime* that is set to expand in the coming years.

We can define an AI urban regime as *a stage of evolution in urban "growth machines"* (Logan and Molotch, 1992), *characterized by a set of formal and informal arrangements between public bodies and private interest that (1) prioritizes smart city development, particularly algorithm-based technologies, and (2) puts forward the necessary institutional frameworks enabling the realization of the goals and objectives of the AI industry, which would allegedly trickle down for the benefit of all segments of the urban population.*

AI is a collection of programmed algorithms to mimic human decision-making. It refers to a variety of computer systems and applications that can sense their environment, think, learn, and act in response to what they sense and their programmed objectives. AI is relatively worthless without a set of intentional goals to complement it. Thus, the initial task facing the individuals who plan, build, and manage physical systems is to determine the kind of outcomes they want machine-learning algorithms to pursue (Tomer, 2019).

Generally speaking, one can identify four key components in smart cities processes: (1) data sets, (2) communication platforms, (3) timely decision-making, and (4) effective action. As a specific technology, AI adds to smart city processes some key features: machine learning abilities, automation processes, and autonomous decision-making as well as, with so-called *deep learning*, forecasting capabilities that can combine with digital twinning and simulation techniques (Berryhill *et al.*, 2019).

As Guo and Curugullo (2022) remind us, scholars recognize that AI represents one of the critical elements in the development of smart cities. In conjunction with machine learning, AI is well suited to form the analytical foundation of smart city programs. Research in this is still in its infancy, even if AI is expected to become a critical feature of an ever-increasing share of smart city applications.

AI urban spaces

AI is already playing a role in contemporary high-tech clusters and spaces (mainly innodistricts and factories of the future, but increasingly science cities, smart seaports and city-ports, networked producer service areas, and eco-industrial parks). These spaces share with old technopoles a concentration in advanced, innovative manufacturing as well as information-based industries. Some innodistricts combine AI and robotic platforms with both mature start-up ecosystems and established high-tech companies newly relocated to city centers in the past 10–15 years (Vermesan *et al.*, 2020).

Advanced manufacturing research and innovation taking place in "Factories of the Future" located in urban areas and metropolitan regions is making extensive use of autonomous decision-making processes and devices to optimize manufacturing production. An example is "lights out manufacturing" where production sites are fully automated and processes such as computer numeric control (CNC) machining require no human presence on site (Masami, 2003; Brumson, 2017).

Entire urban areas (for example, in London and New York) are becoming AI production spaces where programming and algorithm summits — hackathons — are organized to produce code. Some innodistricts host these gatherings, which are set as *design thinking* events. The goal of a hackathon is to create functioning software or hardware by the end of the event. According to critics, sponsors take advantage of free labor to create "fictional expectations of innovation" (Griffith, 2018).

AI in megaconstruction

At some point in the recent past, the biggest challenge for megaprojects shifted from the ability to overcome engineering hurdles and workloads to administrative, management, and planning processes. In other words, it is seldom the case that builders and engineers cannot build: it is bureaucratic complexities and uncoordinated design efforts that prevent megaprojects from being carried out in the first place, or from succeeding when they are implemented — and consequently, there have been more than just a few failed megaprojects (Hu *et al.*, 2018).

At some point in the near future, one can imagine that megaprojects will be completely designed with Building Information Management (BIM) systems, manufactured by means of CNC systems or 3D printers and installed by robots. Due to cost reduction factors, the world will be built by machines, which for critics and the public probably constitutes an Orwellian scenario.

Implementation of AI technologies in several industry sectors is increasing and is now attracting the attention of the megaconstruction sector, which as we know has been plagued by problem and shortcomings, including massive cost overruns, high incidence of failure, and other difficulties (Dimitriou *et al.*, 2013; Flyvbjerg, 2014). Sarkheyli (2022), for example, discussed the utilization of Artificial Neural Networks and Adaptive Neural Fuzzy Interface Systems for risk control and better management of megaprojects.

The main usage of AI is as an analytic tool to quickly discover trends, patterns, and meaning in data. Megaproject planners are also turning to AI expecting productivity increases. Bechtel, for example, created a Big Data & Analytics Center of Excellence (BDAC) in partnership with data science firm Miner and Kasch so that project teams could simulate modularity and construction sequencing (Garza, 2018).

AI can handle scheduling, follow-ups and reminders, evaluation, risk identification, and mitigation. Reinforced learning, an AI technique based on trial and error, can assess combinations and alternatives based on analysis of similar projects as well as other project planning optimization tasks. Furthermore, robots can be designed to learn from simulations and help in tasks that are set to become common, such as on-site prefabrication (Chui *et al.*, 2018). The megaconstruction sector could benefit from using AI innovations from other industries. Commentators suggest megaproject planners become more engaged and become a part of the industry ecosystem in order to benefit from cross-fertilization and synergies (Blanco *et al.*, 2018). Given the current situation of relatively limited high-tech utilization in the megaconstruction industry, decision-makers would also need to increase investment in R&D to foster digitalization (Skinner, 2020).

Disruptive AI for disruptive megaprojects

In spite of the incremental nature of smart city implementation, its disruptive character is undeniable (Batty, 2016). To be sure, disruptive innovation develops within the overall framework of capitalist creative destruction (Schumpeter, 1994 [1942]); Schneider, 2017). Such a disruptive thrust adds to the process of megaproject development as an essentially disruptive and contentious enterprise (del Cerro Santamaría, 2019).

The disruptive AI urban regime effectively responds to biased strategic interests among entrepreneurial, technology stakeholders and the urban growth machine. A consequence is the lack of exploration of alternative venues for urban development based on other models, values, priorities, and regulatory frameworks (Graham and Marvin, 1996).

This scientifically planned blue ocean strategy, which knocks down all alternatives and turns AI into a necessary and unavoidable component in urban development (potentially leading to monopolization), is a major threat to the chaotic and haphazard character of cities (Sennett, 2012). It is also a risk to the centrality of public spaces and the human–civic friction at the core of urban life as self-organized complexity (Jacobs, 1961).

Conversely, relying on a single, encompassing, and interrelated set of strategies for urban development that are delivered by a single industry — the tech industry — presents serious risks of dependency on capital mobility. Since the "spatial fix" process is decided fully by tech corporations, private interests can determine the success or failure of urban policy and urban development (Hollands, 2008). The failed negotiations by the City of New York in 2019 to try to have Amazon build a new corporate headquarters in the borough of Queens is a case in point (Goodman, 2019).

The mode of production promoted by Facebook, Google, and Amazon claims to be run on "artificial intelligence." However, it is actually held together by tens of millions of anonymous workers "tucked away in ware-houses, data centers, content moderation mills, electronic sweatshops, lithium mines, industrial farms, meat-processing plants, and prisons, where they are left unprotected from disease and hyperexploitation" (Klein, 2020).

As a top-down strategy, the nascent AI regime would likely foster a race for biased valuations in actions, processes, devices, and out-comes tilting urban economies toward a heightened focus on networked land and intellectual property rights. Tech gentrification (interrelated with green gentrification) is already an emerging feature in spaces adja-cent to innodistricts and other tech urban quarters (Catanzaro, 2017). As a consequence, large segments of urban populations (those living in poverty, without access to basic services, or with accessibility problems due to disabilities) can potentially be left behind (Watson, 2013). These are some of the shortcomings in the political economy of the nascent AI urban regime (see also Bird *et al.*, 2020). Other risks, disruptions, and ethical dilemmas triggered by the smart city strategy are as follows:

- Control, privacy, and security in a situation of "surveillance capitalism" derived from the high level of big data collection, analytics, scanning, and identification for predictive policing (Zuboff, 2019).
- Cognitive risks, such as "intellectual automation" and "automation complacency" (Carr, 2014).
- Deep learning operates on a black box model that is not always under-standable for humans (Rudin, 2019).
- AI could potentially be hacked, enabling bad actors to interfere with energy, transportation, early warning, or other crucial systems (Comiter, 2019).
- Since AI systems interact autonomously, they can produce unpredict-able outcomes; uncontrolled AI could potentially represent an existen-tial danger to humans (Brundage, 2018).
- AI-based automation may lead to massive job losses in any industry, including the megaconstruction industry.

Sustainability in the AI Urban Regime

Decision-making around AI will have to effectively integrate different smart city domains by optimizing communication between systems (Zhang, 2015). Legislators, policymakers, and society, rather than algorithms, would need to prioritize the various smart city goals. Regulatory frameworks would need to ensure trust without hindering innovation and development.

High-tech innovation and the smart city strategy, including decision-making algorithms, hardly constitute a normative framework for urban environments. In fact, the focus on high-tech capacities and big data, particularly AI technologies, automation, machine learning, deep learning, and bot autonomous decision-making capabilities, is shifting attention away from key issues in urban governance. It also prevents a careful reconsideration of what could constitute a restructured "growth machine" capable of fostering urbanity, equality, and liveability in cities (Greenfield, 2013).

Framing AI innovation

In order to promote urban sustainability, we need to evaluate the objectives that the AI decision tools try to serve. In fact, the linkage between artificial intelligence and sustainability would require a wider policy framework that would specify priorities and expected outcomes so that we can understand precisely under what conditions AI innovation leads to urban sustainable scenarios and outcomes.

The nascent AI regime would also need to be scrutinized alongside the following fundamental questions: (1) What are the benefits that megaproject bring to cities? (2) Which megaprojects ought to be built and which should be discarded? (3) And how to mitigate the wider socioeconomic impacts of large-scale development projects? (Sturup and Low, 2019).

Arguably, AI and innovation technology would more effectively contribute to quality improvements in the management or sustainability of projects if they are framed within a robust process of conceptual, analytical clarification and grounded theory building regarding goals and priorities that are fed by both experience and experimentation (Köhler *et al.*, 2019). Class reference experimentation and tested results about safety, explainability, transparency, and validity would contribute to improving the record of smart city and AI disruptions in megaproject planning, implementation, and success (Ryan and Gregory, 2019).

Besides concerns about improved megaproject management via high-tech innovation and AI, researchers ought to develop analytical blueprints to account for megaprojects as socioeconomic particles producing negative externalities and hugely negative societal impacts (Grubbauer and Čamprag, 2018; del Cerro Santamaría, 2019). Ultimately, the values and objectives of human development and sustainability would have to determine which tech innovations we need.

Put differently, technological innovation and AI by themselves do not necessarily foster urban sustainability, even if some specific innovations (technological or otherwise) do. In the case of those innovations and AI technologies that do foster sustainability, one needs to factor in both their benefits and risks, and thus seriously consider matters of resilience or "antifragility" (Taleb, 2012). The key question, then, is how to craft and build a framework for sustainability that is able to discriminate and tell which AI innovations can contribute to the sustainability outcomes at hand, rather than initiating work for sustainability from the innovation side.

Cohesion versus Competitiveness

One of the factors contributing to the essentially complex nature of sustainability is that, in conceiving and presenting the goals of preserving sustainable strategies, sustainability appears as interdependent on the dimensions of entrepreneurship, innovation, and competitiveness of economies. Indeed, the goal that is presented to us in the majority view on sustainability is "green capitalism," that is, not a sustainable global society with clearly established limits to growth, but rather the sustainability of the information and knowledge economy, through which reformers and planners add relatively ambitious commitments to the environment (Meadows *et al.*, 2004).

Let us take a Chinese case to illustrate this point. In early 2019, the Chinese government approved three sustainable development zones in Shenzhen, Guilin, and Taiyuan, which form the leading axis in Chinese innovation and are also implementing the 2030 United Nations Sustainable Development Goals (Ness, 2018).

One way toward that goal would be rethinking the competitiveness–cohesion binary at a time of policy experimentation under the perception that we are witnessing the dawn of neoliberal practices. One of the shifts operated during neoliberalism has been that, rather than being a source of competitiveness, social cohesion is seen as predominantly an effect and treated as a by-product, outside of the concern of public policies. This has been portrayed as a widespread evolution in urban and national political economies, in spite of the fact that, in order to handle shifting policy issues and opportunities, various national welfare systems, political cultures, and socioeconomic realities combine and recombine. The competitiveness component of the equation receives more attention in programs with a "competitiveness and cohesiveness" focus, with the cohesion component acting more as a consequence and being justified by its purportedly positive effects on competitiveness.

Urban megaprojects, as emblems of global capitalism, have become a main spatial manifestation of this dynamic. The adoption of neoliberal policies from center to periphery (and research on urban policy mobilities) has been made possible by this dominant discourse, which is imposed on a variety of urban and regional realities as a de-contextualized universal analysis and policy direction. It also minimizes the significance of addressing contextual specificity in order to address local challenges. As a result, beyond the agendas of place competition, knowledge economies, and cluster-based growth strategies, there has been a glaring lack of meaningful alternative agendas.

Further, even if research highlights the significance of internal forces, disputes, and resolutions in urban communities, as well as the variety of responses to global concerns and interpretations of shared policies, we know that the still prevailing neoliberal narrative has conveyed that cities that became more competitive have a greater potential to create tools for social cohesiveness and for addressing social issues. Urban entrepreneurship is more likely to trigger win–win scenarios, not only because these cities have been likely to create better (and more) policy solutions but also because the social dynamics in these cities have been (and are) directly impacted by the economic development they experience.

Still, increased economic competitiveness does not always translate into improved forms of social cohesion unless certain conditions are met. For example, new urban governance models must be developed to address challenges, structural changes must be implemented to promote competitiveness without increasing exclusion, low-skilled labor must be stimulated without being marginalized, and new socialization and social control mechanisms must be organized (Vranken, 2008).

Despite their alleged propensity to balance their two components, competitiveness–cohesion discourses end up representing a significant regression and shrinkage of equity policies and discourses. Cohesion discourses and policies prioritize protecting the most vulnerable from significant marginalization rather than promoting social justice. In Istanbul, one of the cases included in this book, global trade and export activities have significantly increased the number of new jobs, particularly for disadvantaged groups like women from low-income households. However, the majority of these positions were low-wage and unprotected. Residential segregation decreased as a result of reforms to the educational system, increased opportunities for upward mobility, and rising female labor market involvement, even though the economic gap between poorer and higher-income groups in society remains wide. Households leave their neighborhoods as possibilities grow, and the growth of mixed-character neighborhoods was also compelled by the new opportunities offered by the urban land market. The evidence in this instance demonstrates that oversimplifying the relationships between social cohesiveness and competitiveness may be insufficient or even deceptive in comprehending the dynamics of development in various cities.

The discussion on sustainability is now present in all policy objectives and statements. Sustainability seems to give fresh perspectives on how economic growth might be used to further social and environmental goals. It forces decision-makers to consider the broader implications of economic "progress" and some of the connections between economic growth and the larger contexts in which it occurs. According to Krueger and Savage, there has been a growing understanding that the availability of top-notch social infrastructure and natural resources is necessary for the sustainability of economic prosperity (Krueger and Savage, 2007). For example, housing and transportation are essential for ongoing development. These more widely acknowledged connections appeared to be producing promising grounds for additional investigation into what causes economic growth and how larger agendas might be reshaped to promote subsequent development cycles (Jessop, 2002; While, 2004). Despite its almost utopian appeal, however, results have been largely disappointing at the public policy level. It is this realm — that of public policy — that we see as holding the potential for utopian pragmatist policy experimentation in the quest for reconstruction after neoliberalism's wide-spread damage to urban societies. In this respect, it is worth reflecting upon the pathways and accomplishments of welfare statism in Britain after World War II, as described by Gold (2007).

Early in the 1950s, Great Britain undertook efforts to repair the damage from World War II and modernize its infrastructure, which was known as the "reconstruction" era. Funds from large-scale projects like town center renovation had been redirected due to the necessity-driven programs for the construction of houses, schools, and factories. Due to the extensive rehabilitation required following World War II, the expansion of the role of public sector architects acquired importance (Guillén, 2006). Local authorities were given this responsibility, and the private sector was used because the public sector lacked the capacity or knowledge to carry out all of the work necessary to reconstruct Britain. Planning ministries were known for their ability to award large public sector contracts without a formal bidding process. In the 1960s, the government-sponsored shift toward industrialized building coincided with the crucial phase of construction for high-rise apartments, while neither of these developments was required to occur and did not always do so.

In hindsight, industrialized construction does increase efficiency. Modernism became inextricably linked in England and Wales to social housing that became the homes of the underprivileged. Modern architecture and design did not merely supply housing; they also stood for social change since they believed that certain dwelling types might promote certain lifestyles and that better housing could lead to a better society. Due to predictions of significant population growth through the year 2000, two not-all-that-new concepts were adopted by modernist architects in the 1970s for experimentation. The first attempted to contain explosive urban growth by directing new construction into predetermined corridors or linear areas. Although it never enjoyed much popularity as the formula for a whole community, the advantages of this strategy included transport efficiency and the opportunity for close relationships between city inhabitants and the countryside. The second idea was a megastructure, which consisted of enormous, multipurpose metropolitan complexes with movable, smaller pieces that could adapt to changing needs (Gold, 2007).

There are still a significant number of unanswered problems regarding the definitions of sustainability that are used throughout the world and the manner in which the concept of sustainability has been interpreted and used as a policy discourse. A reconfiguration of social cohesion via welfare statism would not suffice as an effective strategy for urban sustainability without a simultaneous refocusing on preventing further damage by neoliberal individualism and breakdowns in community structures. Strong communities serve as a barrier against social exclusion and alienation as well as the foundation for the promotion of social cohesiveness and stability. A social strategy based on the premise that much social conduct is supported and influenced by the informal web of social ties and by the moral voices of the community is advocated by Etzioni (1998), who describes his work as the direct descendent of Tönnies. Accepting the idea that the self is an innately social being who is born with group identities and a strong longing for community is the first step toward communitarianism. Therefore, if people are social beings by nature, then powerful communities will provide desirable goods.

A communitarian approach to social policy prioritizes societal and civic values over individual ones, while acknowledging the interconnectedness and embeddedness of human life. Thus, communitarianism positions itself as both a complement to social democracy under the control of the state and a challenge to traditional liberal-individualist ideas of society. In response to the current social breakdown in cities, one would anticipate an increase in state intervention, as well as the promotion and strengthening of communal social ties (Driver and Martell, 1997). There is a pressing need to get past the focus on cultural and religious identities and discuss more prominently about the practical issues of gendered violence, poverty, and unemployment as well as the need to fight for safe working conditions, quality healthcare, and inclusive public education in urban areas. We must rediscover a language of universality, democratic rights, and secularist politics in order to do this.

Conclusion: Rescuing Public Value

In this chapter, we have presented sustainability as a complex assemblage in the socioeconomic realm revolving around four axes: the need to go beyond green capitalism (or, decoupling sustainability from profitability), sustainable innovation in the new AI urban regime (or, framing innovation around sustainability goals), cohesion versus competitiveness (or, finding ways to design equity policies with a local focus), and public value (or, developing bottom-up market shaping and value-co-creating strategies). These four axes represent fundamental vectors or directions for urban sustainability that dispute some existing strategic public policy and private priorities (Davidson, 2009). The argument could be extended to smart city regions and poli-nucleated cities by taking into consideration the notion of spatial clusters. As a way of concluding remarks, let us briefly address the matter of public value.

We believe it is important to reflect on the notion of "value" and how to develop an understanding of "value" that is decoupled from, and goes beyond, the market and the private sector. In fact, the issue of how value should be distributed arises when we acknowledge that value is created collaboratively by public, commercial, third-sector, and social movement organizations (Mazzucato and Ryan-Collins, 2019; Mazzucato and Kattel, 2019). Regarding high-tech solutionism, one must come up with fresh ideas for data ownership and governance that take into account human intelligence as well as technological independence. Public investments in the underlying technology have directly benefited digital companies, and the data they monetize comes from citizens.

To maintain sustainable capital and resources for ongoing innovation, the benefits of innovation should also be shared since the value is created jointly via the participation of public and private actors. The issue of inclusive growth must also include how to ensure that the production and distribution of value are in constant communication. The narratives and stories about how and where value is created are important for this reason. Value can, at best, be redistributed from the risk-takers to the others if the story is that value creation and risk-taking only happen in the commercial world, with the public sector merely serving to reduce risk in the private sector. Instead, the question of how to ensure that not only risks but also rewards are socialized arises if we have a true communal understanding of value, and the market itself is regarded as a result of the way that public and private spheres connect. Mazzucato and Ryan-Collins (2019) argue:

> There are many publics in 'the public.' In the public value framework, contestation of actual value production and evaluation systems is a critical success factor. Involving civil society organisations in framing public policy goals (missions) is a central part of the co-creation process. Producing public value requires collaboration and co-creation; public value cannot be created from the top down. Missions present an opportunity to put citizen participation at the heart of innovation policy and to directly connect R&D spending and broader policy measures to issues

that matter to people [...] This is a 'market-shaping' and 'market-creating' role rather than a 'market-fixing' role [...].

Following this characterization, it is important to recognize that value creation in high-tech ecosystems is an outcome of a wide variety of stakeholders. Private firms could also contribute to tackling social and environmental issues as long as they commit to preserving public value for all citizens. Further, the question about market-shaping and market-creating mechanisms in the AI urban regime leads us to interrogate the concepts of action, ethics, responsibility, distributed morality, and public. Planning has tended to be haunted by a fraught relationship between plans and the consequences meant to follow. This is why it is necessary to consider the shifts and alterations from intentions, to knowledge, to actions, and to consequences in a planner's work. Planners need to connect knowledge to action "by translating between possibilities (truths) and the material manifestations of those possibilities (realities)." In describing the formation of publics (alliances, assemblages), Beauregard's new materialism is not interested in "facts" or "measures" but rather in "matters of concern." While matters of fact are a combination of models and measures, matters of concern also include actor-networks that help entangle ideas and reality into the world, thus becoming harder to oppose. Planners, then, would play an important role in deciding how value should be distributed (Beauregard, 2015).

Does the public sector have the resources to learn from and try out such things? Innovative thinking, flexibility, and adaptability are abilities that managers of private businesses are taught; they are at the core of MBA programs globally in strategic management, organizational behavior, and decision sciences. The role we give bureaucracy has everything to do with the reality that they frequently lack certain talents. Many public organizations have been concentrating on improving the marginal efficiency of their operations over the last few decades, which has hurt their capacity to develop strategic goals (within the bounds of political and legal constraints) and align organizational resources to achieve these goals. Governments are becoming more aware of the need for more dynamic capabilities, but they do not have a theory to support this transformation. We know relatively little about what makes governments and particular public organizations dynamic and capable of responding to shifting societal demands and requirements, which has been recognized by both policymakers and scholars (Mazzucato and Kattel, 2019).

Co-creative approaches see individuals as active participants in their communities rather than passive recipients of services, prioritize cultural change over immediate problems or successes, and involve the entire community rather than just a subset of it. Citizen-centered and co-creative approaches assist people in forming and promoting their own decisions, creating new stakeholder maps, building capacities for self-government, and developing open-ended civic processes rather than asking them to "plug into" already-existing, pre-determined programs, initiatives, or campaigns. Co-creation has the potential to be used as a tool to include citizens and demand openness and cooperation from the government. Co-creation has been used for some time in the private sector by businesses hoping to benefit from client feedback, but it is also becoming more widely acknowledged as a useful tool for the public sector. It can be one of the tools among many to be used to enhance capabilities as we focus our efforts on the key notion of public value.

References

Ache, P., Anderson, H. T., Maloutas, T., Raco, M., Tasan-kok, T. 2008. *Cities between Competitiveness and Cohesion*. Springer Science+Business Media B.V.

ADB. 2016. Scaling new heights. *Vizag–Chennai Industrial Corridor. India's First Coastal Corridor*. Manila: Asian Development Bank.

Atkinson, R. 2012. *Innovation Economics: The Race for Global Advantage*. New Haven, CT: Yale University Press.

Augusto, J., Callaghan, V., Cook, D., Kameas, A., and Satoh, I. 2012. Intelligent environments. A manifesto. *Human-centric Computing and Information Sciences*, 12.

Bairoch, P. 1988. *Cities and Economic Development: From the Dawn of History to the Present*. Translated by Christopher Braider. Chicago: University of Chicago Press.

Batty, M. 2016. How disruptive is the smart cities movement? *Environment and Planning B Planning and Design*, 43(3): 441–443.

Beauregard, R. A. 2015. *Planning Matter. Acting with Things*. Chicago, IL: University of Chicago Press.

Benneworth, P., Miao, J. T., and Phelps, N. A. 2015. Old and new lessons for in Miao. In J. T. P. Benneworth and N. A. Phelps (Eds.), *Making 21st Century Knowledge Complexes. Technopoles of the World Revisited*, technopoles (pp. 275–295). New York: Routledge.

Berryhill, J., Heang, K., Clogher, R., and McBride, K. 2019. Hello, World: AI and its use in the public sector, OECD working papers on public governance, no. 36. https://dx.doi.org/10.1787/726fd39d-en. Accessed July 17, 2023.

Bird, E., Fox-Skelly, J., Jenner, N., Larbey, R., Weitkamp, E., and Winfield, A. 2020. The ethics of artificial intelligence: Issues and initiatives. Panel for the Future of Science and Technology (STOA), European Parliament. https://www.europarl.europa.eu/RegData/etudes/STUD/2020/634452/EPRS_STU(2020)634452_EN.pdf. Accessed July 17, 2023.

Blanco, J. L., Fuchs, S., Parsons, M., and Ribeirinho, M. J. 2018. Artificial intelligence — Construction technology's next frontier, McKinsey & Co. 2018. https://www.mckinsey.com/business-functions/operations/our-insights/artificial-intelligence-construction-technologys-next-frontier. Accessed July 17, 2023.

Brumson, B. 2017. Robotic industries association. *RoboticsoOnline.* https://roboticsonline.wordpress.com/tag/robotic-industries-association/. Accessed July 17, 2023.

Brundage, M. 2018. The malicious use of artificial intelligence: Forecasting, prevention and mitigation. Future of Humanity Institute paper, February. https://arxiv.org/pdf/1802.07228.pdf. Accessed July 17, 2023.

Caragliu, A., Del Bo, C., and Nijkamp, P. 2009. Smart cities in Europe. *Serie Research Memoranda 0048,* VU University Amsterdam, Faculty of Economics, Business Administration and Econometrics.

Carnes, S. 2016. The case for the innovation district as a sustainable economic development tool in the knowledge economy. Georgia Tech Center for Urban Inovation, February 1. https://gtcui.wordpress.com/2016/02/01/the-case-for-the-innovation-district-as-a-sustainable-economic-development-tool-in-the-knowledge-economy/. Accessed July 17, 2023.

Carr, N. 2014. *The glass cage. Where Automation is Taking Us.* New York: W. W. Norton.

Castells, M. 2009. *The Rise of the Network Society* (second edition). London: Wiley-Blackwell.

Castells, M. and P. Hall 1994. *Technopoles of the World. The Making of 21st Century Industrial Complexes.* London: Routledge.

Catanzaro, M. 2017. *Interview with Isabelle Anguelovski.* Barcelona Metropolis, 102, January.

Chan, K. 2017. What is a 'smart city'? *Expatriate Lifestyle,* January 24. Accessed July 17, 2023.

Charles, D. 2015. From technopoles to science cities: Characteristics of a new phase of science cities. https://www.researchgate.net/publication/323308836_From_technopoles_to_science_cities_characteristics_of_a_new_phase_of_science_cities. Accessed July 17, 2023.

Chib, A. 2015. Research on the impact of the information society in the global South: An introduction to SIRCA. In A. Chib, J. May, and R. Barrantes (Eds.), *Impact of Information Society Research in the Global South*, Singapore: Springer. https://doi.org/10.1007/978-981-287-381-11. Accessed February 22, 2023.

Chui, M., Manyika, J., and Miremadi, M. 2018. What AI can and can't do (yet) for your business. *McKinsey Quarterly*, January.

Comiter, M. 2019. Attacking artificial intelligence: AI's security vulnerability and what policy makers can do about IT. Belfer Center for Science and International Affairs, Harvard Kennedy School. https://www.belfercenter. org/publication/AttackingAI.

Cooke, P. 2012. *Complex Adaptive Innovation Systems.* London: Routledge.

Davidson, M. 2009. Social sustainability: A potential for politics? *Local Environment*, 14(7): 607–619.

De Oliveira, S. P. and Carayannis, E. G. 2017. *The Quadruple Innovation Helix Nexus. A Smart Growth Model, Quantitative Empirical Validation and Operationalization for OECD Countries.* London: Palgrave Macmillan.

del Cerro Santamaría, G. (Ed.) 2013. *Urban Megaprojects. A Worldwide View.* Bingley, UK: Emerald Publishing.

del Cerro Santamaría, G. 2018. Megaprojects, sustainability and competitiveness in the United Arab Emirates. Unpublished fulbright scholar project proposal.

del Cerro Santamaría, G. 2019. Disruptive and contentious enterprises: Megaprojects in Bilbao, Istanbul and Hong Kong. In *XIII CTV 2019 Proceedings: XIII International Conference on Virtual City and Territory: "Challenges and Paradigms of the Contemporary City"*. UPC, Barcelona, October 2–4.

del Cerro Santamaria, G. 2020a. Innovation districts, complex sustainability and urban redevelopment. Evaluating multiple success factors. *IJEBMR*, 4(6): 279–290.

del Cerro Santamaría, G. 2020b. Complexity and transdisciplinarity. The case of iconic urban megaprojects, transdisciplinary. *Journal of Engineering and Science*, 11: 19–33.

Dimitriou, H., Ward, J., and Wright, P. 2013. Mega transport projects — Beyond the iron triangle: Findings from the OMEGA research programme. *Progress in Planning*, 86(November): 1–43.

Driver, S and Martell, L. 1997. New labour's communitarians. *Critical Social Policy*, 17(52): 27–46.

Etzioni, A 1998. Introduction. In A. Etzioni (Ed.), *The Essential Communitarian Reader* (pp. ix–xxiv). Lanham, MD: Rowman & Littlefield.

Flyvbjerg, B. 2014. What you should know about megaprojects and why. An overview. *Project Management Journal*, 45(2): 6–19.

Garza, A. 2018. Sequencing made simpler: Bechtel is turning to artificial intelligence for megaprojects. *PM Network*, 32(11): 14.

Gold, J. 2007. *The Practice of Modernism: Modern Architects and Urban Transformation, 1954–1972.* London: Taylor & Francis.

Goodman, D. 2019. Amazon pulls out of planned New York City headquarters. *The New York Times,* February 14, https://www.nytimes.com/2019/02/14/ nyregion/amazon-hq2-queens.html, Accessed July 17, 2023.

Graham, S. and Marvin, S. 1996. *Telecommunications and the City: Electronic Spaces, Urban Place.* London: Routledge.

Greenfield, A. 2013. *Against the Smart City.* London: Verso.

Griffith, E. 2018. Sociologists examine hackathons and see exploitation, Wired (business Section), March. https://www.wired.com/story/sociologists-examine-hackathons-and-see-exploitation/. Accessed July 17, 2023.

Grubbauer, M. and Čamprag, N. 2018. Urban megaprojects, nation-state politics and regulatory capitalism in Central and Eastern Europe: The Belgrade Waterfront project. *Urban Studies* 56(4).

Grunert, K. G. and Ellegaard, C. 1992. The concept of key success factors. Theory and method, MAPP Working Paper No. 4, October. ISSN 09072101. https://pure.au.dk/portal/files/32299581/wp04.pdf.

Gu, Y., Hu, L., Zhang, H. and Hou, C. 2021. Innovation ecosystem research: Emerging trends and future research. *Sustainability*, 2021, 13(20): 11458,

Guillén, M. 2006. The taylorized beauty of the mechanical. *Scientific Management and The Rise of Modernist Architecture,* Princeton, NJ: Princeton University Press.

Guo, Z. and Curugullo, F. 2022. Artificial intelligence, healthcare and megaprojects in the Chinese smart city: The case of Guangzhou. *Journal of Mega Infrastructure and Sustainable Development.* Special issue on *Artificially Intelligent Megaprojects, Benefits, Risks and Sustainable Development.*

Harris, M. 2017. Competitive precinct projects. The five consistent criticisms of "global" mixed-use megaprojects. *Project Management Journal*, 48(6): 76–92.

Hollands, R. G 2008. Will the real smart city please stand up? *City*, 12(3): 303–320.

Hu, Y., Le, Y. Gao, X., Li, Y., and Liu, M. 2018. Grasping institutional complexity. *Management*, 5(1): 52–63.

IMF World Economic Outlook. 2018. Cyclical upswing, structural change, The IMF, Washington, DC. www.imf.org/en/Publications/WEO/Issues/2018/ 03/20/world-economic-outlook-april-2018.

Jacobs, J. 1961. *The Death and Life of Great American Cities*, New York: Random House.

Jessop, B. 2002. Liberalism, neoliberalism, and urban governance: A state–theoretical perspective. *Antipode*, 34(3), July.

Kahneman, D. and Tversky, A. 2000. *Choices, Values, and Frames.* New York: Cambridge University Press.

Kahneman, D. 2013. *Thinking fast and slow*, New York: Farrar, Straus and Giroux.

Katz, B. and Wagner, J. 2019. The evolution of innovation districts. The new geography of global innovation. Brookings Institution. https://www.giid.org/the-evolution-of-innovation-districts-download/. Accessed July 17, 2023.

Klein, N. 2020. Screen new deal. *The Intercept.* https://theintercept.com/2020/05/08/andrew-cuomo-eric-schmidt-coronavirus-tech-shock-doctrine/.

Köhler, J., Geels, F., Kern, F., and Markard, J. 2019. An agenda for sustainability transitions research: State of the art and future directions. *Environmental Innovation and Societal Transitions*, 31: 1–32.

Komninos, N. 2008. *Intelligent Cities and Globalisation Of Innovation Networks*. London: Routledge.

Komninos, N. 2009. Intelligent cities: Towards interactive and global innovation environments. *International Journal of Innovation and Regional Development*, 1(4): 337.

Komninos, N. 2013. What makes cities intelligent? In Deakin, Mark (Ed.), *Smart Cities: Governing, Modelling and Analysing the Transition* (pp. 77–91). London: Taylor & Francis.

Korinek, A., Schindler, M., and Stiglitz, J. 2021. Technological progress, artificial intelligence and inclusive growth. IMF eLibrary, Issue 166. https://www.elibrary.imf.org/view/journals/001/2021/166/article-A001-en.xml. Accessed July 17, 2023.

Krueger, R. and Savage, L., 2007. City-regions and social reproduction: A 'place' for sustainable development? *International Journal of Urban and Regional Research*, 31(1), March.

Leigh, N., Hoelzel, N., Kraft, B., and Dempwolf, C. 2014. Sustainable urban industrial development. London: Routledge.

Li, Y. and Wu, F. 2020. Territory, the state and geopolitics of mega city-region development in China. In Sami Moisio, Natalie Koch, Andrew E.G. Jonas, Christopher Lizotte and Juho Luukkonen (Eds.), *Handbook on the Changing Geographies of the State* (pp. 343–354). London: Edward Elgar.

Logan, J and Molotch, H. 1992. Urban fortunes. In *The Political Economy of Place.* Berkeley, CA: University of California Press.

Marcuse, P. 1989. 'Dual city': A muddy metaphor for a quartered city. *International Journal of Urban and Regional Research*, 13(4), December.

Marrone, M. and Hammerle, M. 2018. Smart cities: A review and analysis of stakeholders' literature. *Business & Information Systems Engineering*, 60(3): 197–213.

Masami, T. 2003. Realizing unattended hours of continuous operation of machining center with addition of intelligent function. *Subaru Technical Review* (in Japanese), 30: 251–256.

Mazzucato, M. and Kattel, R. 2019. Getting serious about value. UCL Institute for Innovation and Public Purpose, Working Paper No. 7.

Mazzucato, M. and Ryan-Collins, J. 2019. Putting value creation back into public value: From market fixing to market shaping. UCL Institute for Innovation and Public Purpose, Working Paper No. 5.

McLaren, D. and Agyeman, J. 2015. *Sharing cities: A Case for Truly Smart and Sustainable Cities.* Cambridge, MA: MIT Press.

Meadows, D. H., Randers, J. and Meadows, D. L. 2004. *Limits to Growth: The 30-Year Update.* New York: Chelsea Green Publishing.

Miao, J. T., Benneworth, P. and Phelps, N. A. 2015. Technopoles of the world: Changes, dynamics and challenges. In J. T. Miao, P. Benneworth, and N. A. Phelps (Eds.), *Making 21st Century Knowledge Complexes. Technopoles of the World Revisited* (pp. 3–20). New York: Routledge.

Mitchell, W. 2007. Intelligent cities. *e-Journal on the Knowledge Society.* Inaugural lecture of the UOC's 2007–2008 academic year. https://www.uoc.edu/uocpapers/5/dt/eng/mitchell.html. Accessed July 17, 2023.

Moisio, S. 2018. *Geopolitics of the Knowledge-Based Economy.* London: Routledge.

Nam, T. and Pardo, T. A. 2018. Conceptualizing smart city with dimensions of technology, people, and institutions. Center for Technology in Government University at Albany, State university of New York, U.S. *The Proceedings of the 12th Annual International Conference on Digital Government Research.* https://intaaivn.org/images/cc/Urbanism/background%20documents/dgo_2011_smartcity.pdf. Accessed July 17, 2023.

Ness, D. 2018. Sustainable urban infrastructure in China: Towards a factor 10 improvement in resource productivity through integrated infrastructure systems. *The International Journal of Sustainable Development and World Ecology*, 15 (4): 288–301.

Nisenbaum, A. 2019. What's holding smart cities back? *Scientific American Blog Network.* Archived from the original on June 29, 2019. Accessed July 17, 2023.

Paquot, T. 2013. cited in Ecodistricts: A sustainable utopia? Paris innovation review, April. http://parisinnovationreview.com/articles-en/ecodistrict-a-sustainable-utopia.edn. Accessed July 17, 2023.

Peris-Ortiz, M., Bennett, D. R, and Pérez-Bustamante Yábar, D. 2016. *Sustainable Smart Cities: Creating Spaces for Technological, Social and Business Development.* Cham: Springer.

Rudin, C. and Radin, J. 2019. Why are we using black box models in AI when we don't need to? A lesson from an explainable AI competition. *HDSR*, 1.2, Fall. https://hdsr.mitpress.mit.edu/pub/f9kuryi8/release/6. Accessed July 17, 2023.

Ryan, M. and Gregory, A. 2019. Ethics of using smart city AI and big data: The case of four large European Cities. *RBIT Journal*, 2(2).

Sarkheyli, A. and Sarkheyli, E. 2022. Dynamic intelligent risk management in megaprojects case study: Transportation megaprojects in Sweden. *Journal of Mega Infrastructure and Sustainable Development*, Special Issue on *Artificially Intelligent Megaprojects, Benefits, Risks and Sustainable Development*.

Sassen, S. 2011. *Cities in a World Economy*. Thousand Oaks, CA: SAGE.

Saxenian, A. L. 1994. *Regional Advantage: Culture and competition in Silicon Valley and Route 128*. Cambridge, MA: Harvard University Press.

Schaffers, H., Komninos, N., Pallot, M. Trousse, B., and Nilsson, M. 2011. Smart cities and the future internet: Towards cooperation frameworks for open innovation, Lecture notes in computer science. *The Future Internet*, 6656: 431–446.

Schiavone, F., Appio, F. P., Mora, L. and Risitano, M. 2020. The strategic, organizational and entrepreneurial evolution of smart cities. *International Entrepreneurship and Management Journal*, 16: 1155–1165.

Schneider, H. 2017. *Creative Destruction and the Sharing Economy*. London: Edward Elgar Publishing.

Schumpeter, J. A. 1994 [1942]. *Capitalism, Socialism and Democracy*. London: Routledge. Schwab, K. 2018. *Shaping the Future of the 4th Industrial Revolution*. New York: Penguin.

Sennett, R. 2012. No one likes a city that's too smart, *The Guardian*. Archived from the original on March 18, 2017. Accessed July 17, 2023.

Skinner, L. 2020. Artificial Intelligence for megaprojects — Association for project management. https://hub.apm.org.uk/news/295212. Accessed July 17, 2023.

Sturup, S. and Low, N. 2019. Sustainable development and mega infrastructure: An overview of the issues. *Journal of Mega Infrastructure and Sustainable Development*, 1(1): 8–26.

Taleb, N. 2012. *Antifragile. Things That Gain from Disorder*. New York: Random House.

Tomer, A. 2019. Artificial intelligence in America's digital city, Brookings Institution report, https://www.brookings.edu/research/artificial-intelligence-in-americas-digital-city/. Accessed July 17, 2023.

UNCTAD 2021. Catching technological waves. Innovation with equity. UNCTAD 2021 Innovation Report, https://unctad.org/system/files/official-document/tir2020_en.pdf.

Vermesan, O., Bahr, R., Ottella, M., Serrano, M., Karlsen, T., Wahlstrøm, T., Sand, H., Ashwathnarayan, M. and Gamba, M. 2020. Internet of robotics things. Intelligent connectivity and platforms. *Frontiers in Robotics and AI*, 25(7), September.

Watson, V. 2013. African urban fantasies: Dreams or nightmares? *Environment and Urbanization*, 26(1): 215–231.

WEF 2018. Harnessing artificial intelligence for thee Earth. Report. https://www3.weforum.org/docs/Harnessing_Artificial_Intelligence_for_the_Earth_report_2018.pdf. Accessed July 17, 2023.

While, A., Jonas, A. E. G., and Gibbs, D. 2004. The environment and the entrepreneurial city: Searching for the urban 'sustainability fix' in Manchester and Leeds. *International Journal of Urban and Regional Research*, 28(3), September.

Yovanof, G., and Hazapis, G. N. 2009. An architectural Framework and enabling wireless technologies for digital cities & intelligent urban environments. *Wireless Personal Communications*, 49(3): 445–463.

Zhang, J., Hua, X., Huang, J., Shen, X., Chen, J., Zhou, Q., Fu, Z., and Zhao, Y. 2015. The city brain: Practice of large-scale artificial intelligence in the real world. *IET Smart Cities*, 1(1): 28–37.

Zhao, K. and Ge, L. 2013. A survey on the internet of things security. In *2013 Ninth International Conference on Computational Intelligence and Security*, pp. 663–667.

Zuboff, S. 2019. *The Age of Surveillance Capitalism: The Fight for a Human Future at the New Frontier of Power*. New York: Public Affairs.

Zukin, S. 2020. Seeing like a city: How tech became urban. *Theory and Society*, 49(5–6): 941–949.

Chapter 8

Corporate Strategy and Government Policy for Technological Development in Poland's Peripheral Regions

Arkadiusz Mironko and Mariusz Sagan

Abstract

This chapter contributes to the understanding of technology adoption and innovation in peripheral regions, with a specific focus on Poland. It addresses the challenges faced by these regions, including insufficient support from state institutions, limited investment capital, and infrastructural inefficiencies. Despite these barriers, this chapter identifies several development opportunities. Overall, we observed that local companies are demonstrating adaptability to new technologies and leveraging local scientific communities, indicating a promising technological future. This chapter highlights the importance of evidence-based policies that consider regional needs and capabilities. It emphasizes the need for collaboration between local governments, businesses, academic institutions, and community organizations to support innovation, entrepreneurship, and job creation. By providing insights into the strategies and initiatives that can enhance technological development in peripheral regions, this chapter contributes to the literature on technology adoption and innovation in developing economies. The findings offer valuable guidance for policymakers and stakeholders seeking to promote economic growth and prosperity in peripheral areas.

Keywords: Emerging technologies, competitiveness, peripheral regions, government policy, innovation ecosystems, corporate strategies, technology adoption

Introduction

The rapid advancement of emerging technologies has disrupted various industries, from information technologies (IT) to healthcare and artificial intelligence (AI), requiring firms and countries to respond to the changing environment to enhance their competitiveness. Such a trend has been pointed out by Luo and Zahra (2023), especially under fast-paced change and possible vulnerability, uncertainty, complexity, and ambiguity (VUCA) scenarios that we experienced since the 2000s. This chapter aims to explore the ways in which firms and countries like Poland, specifically its peripheral regions of Eastern Poland, are responding to the rise of the latest technologies. It will also examine the impact of government policies on corporate strategies and how they affect the ability of firms to leverage new technologies (Pang *et al.*, 2019).

The case of Poland, specifically its peripheral regions, provides an interesting example of the challenges and opportunities associated with emerging technologies. These regions have historically faced challenges related to infrastructure, talent retention, and access to funding, which can hinder their ability to respond to emerging technologies (Guellec and Wunsch-Vincent, 2009). However, government policies aimed at promoting innovation and economic development have created new opportunities for firms in these regions.

The Polish economy has grown substantially over the past 30 years, mainly due to foreign investment and exports. However, peripheral regions with predominantly rural populations and low development potential are lagging behind. Although regional capitals have the potential to drive development, they still face challenges of low growth rates and depopulation. For the period 2010–2020, all peripheral regions, on average, recorded low and very low rates of development in relation to the national average rate of development. Furthermore, the COVID-19 pandemic caused some of these subregions to record a decline in real GDP. One reason for this poor rate of development is the negligible inflow of foreign investment, with most being directed toward traditional, low-value-added industries. Only a few regions, such as Podlaskie located east of Warsaw, have attracted investment in the manufacturing sector.

To address this issue, policies need to be implemented to facilitate the adaptation of local companies to technological change and innovation, thus making them more competitive and attractive to foreign investors. As we see from the aforementioned cases, investment in high-tech industries such as artificial intelligence, nanotechnology, and biotechnology would help create highly skilled jobs and drive economic growth. Additionally, supporting entrepreneurship in peripheral regions by providing financial and non-financial support, such as mentoring and training, can help create a supportive environment for start-ups. Furthermore, providing incentives for foreign investors to invest in peripheral regions can help create jobs and drive economic growth. Finally, improving infrastructure, including roads, public transport, and telecommunications, is crucial for facilitating economic development in these regions.

The main research purpose of this chapter is to identify the challenges faced by firms and countries, especially those in the peripheral regions of Central Europe, in responding to the rapid advancement of emerging technologies. As industries across various sectors including IT, healthcare, and AI continue to be disrupted by new technologies, firms and countries need to respond quickly to remain competitive (Dwivedi *et al.*, 2021; also. Markolf *et al.*, 2018). This chapter aims to explore how firms and countries in Poland's peripheral regions are responding to these changes and how government policy is impacting their ability to leverage new technologies. It also seeks to examine the impact of fast-paced change and possible VUCA scenarios, such as pandemics or war, on the ability of firms and countries to adapt to emerging technologies. The research purpose, therefore, revolves around the challenge of responding to emerging technologies in order to enhance competitiveness in an environment characterized by rapid change and potential uncertainties.

Literature Review

Previous research has identified distinct phases in the pattern of FDI inflows to peripheral regions, starting from low-cost and medium-tech investments and progressing toward more high-tech focused investments (see, for example, Barry, 2007; Crescenzi and Iammarino, 2017). This progression is supported by earlier studies that have examined the evolution of FDI in peripheral regions.

During the initial phase of FDI inflows to peripheral regions, the focus is primarily on low-cost and medium-tech investments (Acs *et al.*, 2012).

This phase is characterized by foreign investments targeting industries that benefit from the region's cost advantages such as lower labor costs or access to natural resources (Caves, 1971). These investments often involve manufacturing activities that require moderate levels of technological sophistication. Research conducted by Dunning (1994) and Cantwell and Iammarino (2002) have provided insights into this phase of FDI inflows to peripheral regions. As peripheral regions develop and gain experience in attracting and hosting foreign investments, they enter a subsequent stage, characterized by a shift toward more high-tech-focused investments. This phase reflects a maturing of the region's capabilities and infrastructure, as well as an increased emphasis on innovation and knowledge-intensive activities.

Further, evidence from an earlier study of FDI in peripheral regions of Poland by Chidlow *et al.* (2009) supports the progression from low-cost and medium-tech investments to more high-tech-focused investments. They found that over time, as the peripheral regions developed their technological capabilities and improved their attractiveness to investors, there was a noticeable shift toward higher-tech investments (see also Chidlow *et al.*, 2015).

Similarly, a paper by Cantwell and Iammarino (2005) focuses on the role of multinational corporations (MNCs) in the development of European regional systems of innovation. The authors argue that MNCs can contribute to regional economic development through the transfer of knowledge, technology, and skills. However, the extent to which MNCs can promote regional innovation depends on the nature of their activities, the level of interaction with local firms and institutions, and the capacity of local actors to absorb and utilize the knowledge spillovers generated by MNCs.

The authors also discuss the impact of FDI on regional systems of innovation, highlighting the importance of local absorptive capacity and the need for policies that encourage collaboration between MNCs and local actors (Cantwell and Iammarino, 2005). They contend that peripheral regions can benefit from FDI if they are able to create an environment that is conducive to innovation and knowledge creation. This requires investment in education, research and development, and infrastructure, as well as the development of institutional frameworks that support innovation and entrepreneurship.

More specifically, the paper by Santangelo (2004) explores the relationship between foreign direct investment (FDI) and local capabilities in peripheral regions, using the case study of the Etna Valley in Italy, which is a peripheral region that has experienced significant FDI inflows, but also faces challenges related to its peripheral location and limited local capabilities.

Although, FDI has played a role in upgrading the local industrial structure and increasing the competitiveness of local firms in the Etna Valley, the impact of FDI on local capabilities has been mixed, as it has often led to a reliance on foreign technology and limited technology transfer to local firms. The paper argues that to maximize the benefits of FDI for peripheral regions, it is important to focus on building local capabilities and promoting technology transfer between foreign and local firms. The Etna Valley case study provides examples of successful collaborations between foreign and local firms, as well as the role of local institutions in supporting the development of local capabilities.

Overall, the paper emphasizes the importance of balancing the benefits of FDI with the need to build local capabilities and promote technology transfer in peripheral regions.

Further research by Pavlínek (2004) highlights the main points regarding the development of peripheral regions and FDI in Central Europe by examining whether FDI has been an important factor in the economic development of Central Europe, especially in the post-socialist period after the 1990s. It has contributed to economic growth, employment, and technology transfer. However, FDI has not always benefited peripheral regions equally (see also Mironko, 2014). While some regions have attracted a significant amount of FDI and have experienced economic growth, others have been left behind and continue to struggle with low levels of FDI and economic underdevelopment.

Pavlínek believes that the success of FDI in peripheral regions is dependent on a variety of factors such as the availability of skilled labor, the presence of a supportive institutional environment, and regional connectivity. He also highlights the importance of regional policies in attracting and maximizing the benefits of FDI. Effective policies should aim to improve the investment climate, support the development of local capabilities and entrepreneurship, and enhance the connectivity of peripheral regions with national and international markets. The research finds that FDI can have positive impacts on peripheral regions, but it is not a panacea for regional development. Thus, it is necessary to implement effective policies that address the specific needs and challenges of peripheral regions to ensure that they can fully benefit from FDI.

Generally, FDI is considered to have a positive impact on regional innovation and economic growth of host regions (Li *et al.*, 2018). According to Li *et al.* (2018) and Mironko (2018), the positive effect of FDI on regional innovation efficiency is contingent upon the level of human capital and the level of openness in a region. In this respect, they find that FDI has a stronger positive effect on regional innovation efficiency in areas with higher levels of human capital and greater openness. The effect of FDI on regional innovation efficiency is stronger for high-tech industries (Li *et al.*, 2018). The authors find that FDI has a stronger positive effect on regional innovation efficiency in high-tech industries compared to other industries.

Research by Bhawe and Zahra (2019) explores the concept of heterogeneity in local entrepreneurial ecosystems and the role it plays in promoting entrepreneurship. The authors argue that a diverse set of actors, resources, and networks is essential for creating a vibrant and successful entrepreneurial ecosystem. Similarly, Motoyama and Knowlton (2017) also suggest that policymakers and ecosystem builders should focus on inducing heterogeneity in local ecosystems by creating policies and programs that promote diversity and inclusiveness. They also emphasize the importance of leveraging social networks to create connections between diverse actors and resources. Their study presents findings from a case study of the entrepreneurial ecosystem in St. Louis, Missouri, which was intentionally designed to induce heterogeneity. They found that the deliberate promotion of diversity and inclusiveness led to a more robust and resilient ecosystem, with increased levels of entrepreneurship and innovation.

Motoyama and Knowlton (2017) further discuss the potential challenges of inducing heterogeneity, such as resistance from established actors and difficulties in coordinating diverse resources. However, they argue that these challenges can be overcome through collaborative efforts and a shared vision for promoting entrepreneurship. Following this pattern, Kociuba *et al.* (2023) propose a Smart City Ecosystem Model (SCEM) that can be implemented by using tailored strategic thinking, adapting to global trends, and engaging stakeholders. Their study provides novel insights into smart governance, leadership, and strategic choices in creating a sustainable and people-centered smart city. The findings indicate that effective smart city ecosystems can be created by exploiting development opportunities and smart specializations to design and implement smart city strategies. Ultimately, this study offers a comprehensive policy framework for managing smart and sustainable cities at both strategic and operational levels.

Ning and Wang (2018) examine the relationship between foreign direct investment and environmental knowledge spillovers in developing countries (also, Mironko, 2014). They investigate whether FDI can bring environmentally friendly knowledge to these countries and whether the local industrial structure plays a role in facilitating or hindering this process. They find that FDI can indeed bring environmental knowledge spillovers to developing countries, but the effects are contingent on the local industrial structure. Specifically, the research finds that FDI is more likely to bring environmental knowledge spillovers to countries that have a diversified industrial structure. In contrast, FDI is less likely to bring environmental knowledge spillovers to countries, or locations within them, that have a specialized industrial structure (Ning *et al.*, 2016, among others).

Similarly to Bhawe and Zahra (2019), Ning and Wang (2018) argue that the result of their study can be explained by the fact that a diversified industrial structure allows for more cross-sectoral learning, which can facilitate the transfer of environmental knowledge from foreign firms to local firms. In contrast, a specialized industrial structure limits cross-sectoral learning and may result in a more insular business environment (Mironko, 2020). Overall, the findings suggest that FDI can bring important environmental knowledge spillovers to developing countries, but policymakers must consider the local industrial structure when designing policies to attract foreign investment. Specifically, policies that promote a diversified industrial structure may be more effective in fostering environmental knowledge spillovers from foreign firms.

Kottaridi (2005) highlights the core–periphery pattern of FDI-led growth and production structure in the EU, emphasizing regional disparities and the need for targeted policies to promote balanced development. In line with this, the export-focused industries in Lublin indicate its integration into the global economy and early stages of economic integration. Also, Mudambi and Santangelo (2016) argue that MNE subsidiaries can facilitate the transition of peripheral areas into emerging clusters by leveraging their resources and capabilities. They emphasize the importance of policy interventions to attract and retain MNE subsidiaries in peripheral regions while promoting linkages and knowledge spillovers with local firms.

Overall, the research on the subject suggests that FDI and MNE subsidiaries can play a positive role in promoting the economic development of peripheral regions incrementally by contributing to the emergence of new clusters and industries, and by enhancing the innovation and upgrading capabilities of local firms. Nevertheless, the relationship between more advanced clusters and peripheral regions is not prescriptive and often requires different approaches, which this chapter aims to demonstrate.

Research Methods

FDI plays a crucial role in economic growth and development, but its impact varies across regions, particularly in peripheral areas (Iammarino *et al.*, 2019). Pavlínek *et al.* (2009) conducted a mixed-method study on industrial upgrading in Central European automotive manufacturing, combining quantitative analysis and qualitative case studies to explore the regional implications of FDI-driven upgrading. Their research highlights the transition from low-value-added to higher-value-added activities through FDI inflows. Similarly, Ascani *et al.* (2016) employed a mixed-methods approach to analyze FDI in Italian regions, revealing positive economic impacts as well as challenges related to labor skills and capital availability in peripheral areas. These studies emphasize the significance of FDI in peripheral regions while acknowledging the unique challenges they face. The utilization of diverse research methods provides a comprehensive understanding of the impact of FDI and the factors influencing its success in peripheral regions.

Additionally, the paper by Nielsen *et al.* (2017) addresses the methodological challenges encountered in studying FDI location choice. It discusses issues related to data availability, measurement, and reliability in FDI research. The authors highlight the complexity of the FDI decision-making process and the need for robust methodologies to capture the multidimensional aspects of location choice. Recognizing the challenges, here we present some statistical data analysis along with the specific cases to demonstrate the most current scenario in the region of Lublin.

For this chapter, a survey was conducted of companies representing the technology sector in Lublin, southeast Poland. A dozen companies from different industries, as well as with contrasting scales of operations and business life cycles, were selected for analysis. The survey was conducted using an unstructured Intercultural Development Inventory (IDI) questionnaire from October 2022 to February 2023 with high-level executives and owners. The survey lasted approximately one hour and was recorded and subsequently transcribed. The presented case studies provide a cross-sectional picture of the technology environment in Lublin, although not aspiring to full representativeness, due to the adopted research method (qualitative research).

Corporate Strategy and Government Policy in Peripheral Regions of Developing Economies of Central Europe

Further in this chapter, we focus on the corporate strategies for leveraging emerging technologies in the peripheral regions of Poland. The examination of the approaches to technology adoption and innovation among firms in the region will be accompanied by an analysis of the challenges and opportunities in leveraging emerging technologies for competitive advantage in the region (Almeida *et al.*, 2020).

The role of government policy in promoting technology adoption and innovation in peripheral regions of Poland will be discussed here further. The next section includes an examination of the regulatory framework and policy measures for promoting technology adoption and innovation in the regions and cities, as well as government-led initiatives to support the development of innovation ecosystems (Appio *et al.*, 2019). This chapter further introduces case studies of firms in the region that have successfully adapted their strategies to take advantage of emerging technologies. The analysis of these cases will also consider the factors that contributed to their success and the challenges they face.

Peripheral Regions in Poland: Development Context

Poland is now internationally recognized as an example of a country that has most successfully carried out a socioeconomic transformation from a centrally planned economy to a market one, pursuing a path of continuous GDP growth for almost 30 years. Poland's economy has been boosted by numerous foreign investments, and the country has built a strong export position mainly as a sub-supplier and cooperator in the automotive industry, an exporter of processed food and furniture, and a major seller of IT and outsourcing services in foreign markets. As a result, with a GDP per capita of nearly $16,000, Poland ranks among wealthy countries, albeit at the bottom of the group (World Bank, 2022).

The success of the Polish economy has not been evenly distributed spatially, which is characteristic of most global economies. Poland's problem, however, is that the scale of the country's economic peripheralization is very large, as it covers almost 1/3 of its area, de facto excluded from development processes. The reasons for this state of affairs are very complex and have a historical, structural, and contemporary character, related to the shortcomings and mistakes of Poland's industrial, infrastructural, and regional policies over the past 30 years. The less developed peripheral regions in Eastern and Northeastern Poland include Lubelskie, Podlaskie, Podkarpackie, Świętokrzyskie, and Warmińsko-Mazurskie voivodeships. At the same time, these are one of the lowest levels of GDP per capita in PPP among the European Union's regions. It should be noted that before 1991, these regions bordered the countries of the former USSR, which today include Belarus, Lithuania, Russia, and Ukraine.

As already noted, the peripheral character of the above-mentioned regions influenced their development opportunities for practically the entire post-World War II period. Their location, first near the border of the Soviet Union, and after 1990 in the vicinity of Ukraine and Belarus, which were slow to transform economically, was not conducive to the development of these areas on the basis of the trade exchange infrastructure. This was compounded by structural problems (the traditionally agricultural character of these areas, with low-productivity farms) and limited communication (Jóźwik, 2013: 26–28). Between 1990 and 2010, highways were built in all areas other than Eastern Poland, and the situation only began to improve in the second decade of the 21st century. An international paradox is the fact that the largest city and economic center of Eastern Poland, Lublin, only gained full access to the Polish highway network in 2021, more than 30 years after the start of the country's social and economic transformation.

As already noted, the development problems of Poland's peripheral regions have not been entirely solved in the 21st century. These provinces still suffer from low FDI inflows, and the relatively high state aid from the EU does not materialize in the form of higher innovation and productivity in this part of Poland. In addition to the lack of effective support from Polish government institutions, which *de facto* leaves this part of the country to fend for itself (Jóźwik and Sagan, 2013: 18–19), the low level of social capital on the ground caused passivity and perpetuation of a culture of waiting for help for many years. Only in the last 10 years, in some of the urban centers of peripheral Eastern Poland, has there been a shift from a mindset of waiting for the "invisible market forces" or decision-makers from Warsaw to remedy this unfavorable situation (Jóźwik and Sagan, 2013: 60) to moving ahead with the implementation of individual endogenous development strategies and the construction of local innovative business ecosystems (Kociuba *et al.*, 2023). However, this does not solve the problems with the demographic drain of Eastern Poland, which has been intensifying since 2010.

Poland's peripheral regions are characterized by a predominance of the rural population, while among cities, only the regional capitals (Bialystok, Kielce, Lublin, Olsztyn, and Rzeszow) have significant potential. They are hypothetically centers of development for the surrounding peripheral areas, although some of these cities still face low development and depopulation problems. At the same time, these centers cannot break the rapid GDP growth rate barrier and catch up with other metropolitan cities in the western and central parts of Poland. Table 1 provides data on the change in GDP among the cities of the capitals in the peripheral regions of Eastern Poland, along with their functional/metropolitan areas. In the period 2010–2020, all of them, on average, recorded low or very low rates of development in relation to the average rate of development of Poland as a whole. As many as three cities, despite a positive GDP growth rate, saw a decline in relation to the average national GDP, in the case of Kielce by as much as 5%. A slight improvement in indicators was noted in the richest subregion of Eastern Poland — Lublin, and to a lesser extent in Rzeszów. Still, none of these cities and agglomerations exceeded 100% of the Polish average wealth. The COVID-19 pandemic also caused some of Poland's peripheral subregions to record a decline in real GDP in 2020. This was the case, among others, for the Rzeszów subregion, with an undiversified economy dependent on low-innovation aerospace cooperative manufacturing, which was witnessing real GDP decline.

One of the reasons for the poor rate of development in Poland's peripheral regions is the negligible inflow of foreign investment (except for reinvestment). The annual level of FDI in individual regions ranged from a few million USD to a maximum of $250 million in the period under review, while in many cases the average annual rate of inflow did not exceed $30–50 million (see Table 2).

However, it should be noted that some regions are increasingly successful in attracting foreign investment in the manufacturing sector, such

Table 1. GDP per capita changes in Poland's peripheral subregions.

	GDP Per Capita, Poland = 100 [%]											Change 2020/2019	Change 2020/2010
	2010	2011	2012	2013	2014	2015	2016	2017	2018	2019	2020		
Olsztyn subregion	81.0	81.2	80.7	82.2	81.7	80.5	80.5	78.2	76.9	77.0	79.3	3.0%	−2.1%
Kielce subregion	83.0	82.2	81.4	80.1	79.7	79.0	78.3	78.3	79.3	77.3	78.4	1.4%	−5.5%
Lublin subregion	**89.1**	**88.1**	**92.1**	**94.4**	**94.7**	**91.6**	**92.2**	**92.0**	**91.1**	**91.4**	**89.9**	**−1.6%**	**0.9%**
Rzeszów subregion	83.4	84.7	86.6	87.9	87.4	89.2	87.8	86.7	87.8	88.4	84.1	−4.9%	0.8%
Białystok subregion	85.5	84.5	84.8	84.7	84.2	82.7	82.4	82.0	82.1	82.6	82.9	0.4%	−3.0%

Source: Główny Urząd Statystyczny (2023).

Table 2.   FDI changes in Poland's peripheral regions (excluding reinvestments).

Sources of Funding for Investment in Enterprises (Funds Directly from Abroad) [in mln PLN]

	2010	2015	2016	2017	2018	2019	2020	Change 2020/2019	Change 2020/2010
Warmińsko-Mazurskie	73.8	146.1	8.0	22.8	973.9	235.6	162.7	−30.9%	120.4%
Świętokrzyskie	246.6	140.2	2.4	8.0	59.7	71.8	117.1	62.9%	−52.5%
Lubelskie	215.2	154.7	59.8	75.0	120.4	201.3	222.3	10.4%	3.3%
Podkarpackie	112.2	223.3	66.6	81.1	398.7	557.9	289.5	−48.1%	157.3%
Podlaskie	81.5	103.1	3.1	160.0	175.4	378.6	326.7	−13.7%	300.8%

Source: Główny Urząd Statystyczny, 2023. The following USD/PLN exchange rate was assumed for the calculation — 4.0.

as the Podlaskie region (with capital city Białystok), where the value of new FDI (excluding reinvestment) increased by 300% in 2020–2010. However, it should be remembered that the vast majority of FDI in this part of Poland is directed to traditional industries (low value added), i.e., furniture, metal processing, and food processing, and partly only to more technological sectors, such as automotive and aerospace.

Government Policies Shaping the Innovation Ecosystems in Peripheral Regions of Poland

The role of public institutions in supporting the innovation of regions, including peripheral regions, is widely discussed in the literature. In practical terms, since 2010, Polish government institutions have been conducting an increasingly sophisticated ecosystem support program in the country, especially in large Polish cities. However, these processes are still in their infancy, and impediments to the effectiveness of public policies include the low culture of innovation in Poland, the lack of widely implemented innovations in enterprises, low business–university cooperation, and low rates of internationalization of Polish small and medium-sized businesses. These problems are even more pronounced in the analyzed Polish peripheral regions. These regions are usually classified not only as underdeveloped but also as not very innovative. For example, in the innovation ranking of 16 Polish regions, the most innovative region of Eastern Poland, Lubelskie, was ranked 8th in 2020, while all other peripheral regions were ranked in the bottom half of the list (Indeks Millenium, 2020).

The regional system of supporting entrepreneurship in Poland's peripheral regions is based primarily on using regions as local government units to transmit financial resources from the national and EU levels to entrepreneurs located in a given region. This is done in a grant model (transfer of EU funds to local entrepreneurs, mainly from the SME sector) and through repayable financing (regions provide financing to independent repayable financial institutions or directly create or manage such institutions) (Angowski and Sagan, 2023). The structure of business financing in the regions of Poland is most often derived from the guidelines and strategies of the European Union, contextualized by the development situation of the region and the smart specializations implemented there. In 2007–2020, during EU budget perspectives, the priority was to support basic investments of enterprises, regardless of the sector, and to strengthen the competence of employees. In the sub-perspective of 2014–2020, funding was mainly provided for innovative projects, research and development, and investments to improve the energy efficiency of enterprises (Kawałko and Sagan, 2015).

Regional support for the enterprise sector in Polish regions includes promotional and informational activities. Polish regions, especially those from the areas in the east, have implemented several activities to support, for example, the internationalization processes of their entrepreneurs. This is done by financing participation in various activities including foreign missions, international trade fairs, and study visits, among others. This seems to have been an important factor in the transfer of knowledge and new technological solutions from around the world to Poland. Another element of supporting regional entrepreneurship was preparing and providing companies with business infrastructure. Local governments and their dedicated companies (institutions) have carried out a number of activities in building infrastructure for fairs and exhibitions, congresses, meetings, incubators, and technology parks, to facilitate innovations.

The importance of local government support for the development of regional entrepreneurship, innovation, and competitiveness of urban economic ecosystems is highlighted in the literature as conclusive. The concept of coordinating local entrepreneurial ecosystems in a model of cooperation of key stakeholders is slowly ceasing to be just an academic theory, and becoming a developmental paradigm in many cities. Furthermore, authorities in Polish cities are pursuing policies to support local businesses, mainly through available tax tools. Very few Polish cities implement sophisticated support tools, coordinating the cooperation of key stakeholders, such as businesses and universities (Brooks *et al.*, 2019), in order to implement joint projects between urban actors, share resources, and build a climate for creating and implementing innovations. In peripheral Eastern Poland, such as Lublin, they are building a contextual smart city ecosystem including innovation (Kociuba *et al.*, 2023). The toolkit of entrepreneurial support in Eastern Poland cities and other local communities is mainly traditional in nature. It includes the following tools: (a) financial (real estate tax exemptions for companies investing in SEZs or for the creation of new jobs), (b) investment (preparation of investment areas, mainly for large companies, construction of business infrastructure such as technology parks and innovation laboratories as well as subsidizing micro-businesses with funds from labor offices),

(c) competence (training for entrepreneurs), (d) relational (participation in the co-creation of clusters), and (e) educational (entrepreneurship support programs for young people).

Despite the wide instrumentation of support for the innovativeness of Polish enterprises and regions, their effectiveness has been repeatedly criticized, and this is particularly true for peripheral regions. For example, from the cross-sectional research conducted by Sagan (2023), a highly differentiated picture of the evaluation of public institutions operating in Eastern Poland emerges, which can be very aptly put by the following opinion of one entrepreneur operating in a peripheral region: "the more local the better, and the more central the worse — government institutions are almost exclusively interested in politics." The IDI survey conducted for this study includes 20 large multinational companies operating in Eastern Poland. From the respondents' indications, it is clear that they evaluate Poland's central/government institutions, foreign institutions, local governments, and clusters differently (see Figure 1). Respondents

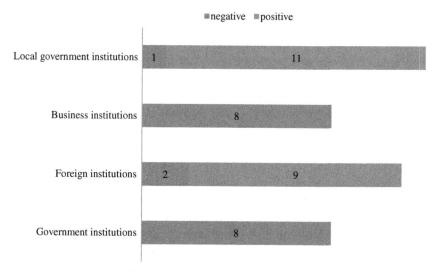

Figure 1.   Business opinions on various Polish institutions (IDI study, 2022)

Notes: *The numbers in the chart represent the responses of the surveyed companies — positive or negative opinions.
**Government institutions — represent the Polish government in Warsaw, Local government institutions — represent the Polish government in the regions, Foreign institutions — government institutions from other countries, Business institutions — institutions that support entrepreneurs in Poland.
Source: Adopted from Sagan (2023).

often indicate that Poland is at a developmental stage in this aspect, modeling itself on good foreign practices, but still deviating in the quality of institutions from those of the United States and Western Europe.

The evaluation of the functioning of institutions at the central level was negative and devastating (8 negative indications, 0 positive indications), and the majority of companies felt that these institutions do not care about supporting regional development. Particularly disturbing seem to be the statements regarding Poland's economic diplomacy, which, according to the companies surveyed, simply does not exist. As for organizations operating at a lower level, a clear distinction should be made between them, as a bipolar picture of industry organizations and local government emerges from the statements among respondents, e.g., clusters were evaluated very negatively (8 indications of negative evaluation), while local government institutions were perceived positively (11 indications of positive evaluation) and usually rated very highly (as initiators of ecosystem cooperation with universities, supporting foreign investment, knowledge transfer, and innovation) (Sagan, 2023). It is symptomatic that in the institutional system of Poland, especially in its peripheral regions, a significant lack of trust in the actions of the state is noticeable, while trust in local institutions and city governments is high. Business understands that the failure to support the underdevelopment of peripheral regions for many years may be structural and permanent, so local actions aimed at endogenously building their own competitiveness and innovation at the bottom, i.e., local business and smart city ecosystems, should be supported (Kociuba *et al.*, 2023).

Corporate Strategy in Peripheral Regions of Developing Economies of Central Europe — The Case of Lublin

The peripheral region of Eastern Poland, despite its economic stagnation and low innovation rates, boasts a handful of technologically progressive economic ecosystems. Such an example is the city of Lublin, a major business, academic, cultural, and infrastructure center of Eastern Poland. The city built an interesting contextual model of smart socioeconomic development between 2011 and 2022, creating conditions for attracting technology companies, foreign students, and talent, despite its peripheral location in an underdeveloped part of Poland (Kociuba *et al.*, 2023).

Key factors in the city's success include long-term strategic thinking, creating infrastructural conditions for development, building partnerships among key stakeholders in the city and a culture of cooperation and trust, and attracting nearly 100 companies in the technology sector, including numerous foreign companies. These activities have resulted in the fact that after a decade of change, not only have successfully adapted global technologies appeared in Lublin and local companies but their own innovations are being created, which is a kind of a rarity in peripheral Polish regions.

The strategies of companies in Lublin and the surrounding region are characterized in many cases by the implementation and contextual adaptation of the latest global technologies and attempts to create their own unique technological solutions. Due to the fact that Lublin's economy is very diversified, these solutions are created in various industries and sectors, both in services and industrial processing. The technological responses of some of the local companies are very fast, which is due to their technological competence, internationalization, ongoing contacts with world technology or through ownership structures or transfer of know-how to Poland. Some of them benefit from the local innovative environment and the knowledge produced by Lublin's universities, especially the Lublin University of Technology, which is the leading technical university in Poland in terms of patents and inventions.

The case studies of technology companies from Lublin and the surrounding region (that have successfully adapted their strategies to take advantage of emerging technologies) are presented below and cover various sectors, including IT, artificial intelligence, automotive, and medical robotics, among others. IDI interviews were conducted with the owners of these companies or their managers, during the months from October 2022 to February 2023.

The summaries of each case are as follows.

Accrea, a robotics company based in Lublin, Poland, is owned by Bartłomiej Stańczyk and specializes in creating robots for medical and care settings. The company was founded while Bartłomiej was pursuing his PhD in Germany where he collaborated with colleagues from Lublin. The team consists of around 30 people, including mechanics, electronics engineers, electricians, automation engineers, and programmers who work with the company permanently. They also collaborate with designers and psychologists as needed. Accrea's first successful project was a robotic arm for individuals who are paralyzed and rely on a wheelchair for mobility. They have two additional projects in the works: a system designed to assist minimally invasive surgeons who use laparoscopic instruments for procedures and a biopsy needle guidance system for cancer diagnosis. The company's current sales achievements include their automatic wheelchair arm, which is selling well. Bartłomiej believes that robots do not eliminate jobs but rather create them, as they require skilled workers to program, install, integrate, and maintain them. He suggests that Lublin needs more innovative solutions and creative employees interested in new technologies, as well as more maker spaces.

BioMinds Healthcare Ltd. is a company founded in 2019 that develops a rehabilitation system for patients with neurological conditions such as strokes, brain injuries, Alzheimer's, Parkinson's, and various other types of dementia. They use virtual reality and artificial intelligence solutions to provide a tool that supports therapists in their daily work and brings better results for patients. The prototype system currently reflects the gold standard of neurological rehabilitation in motor, cognitive, and psychological areas.

The founder(s) of BioMinds Healthcare Ltd. identified the need for medical products that use virtual reality to treat neurological patients more effectively. The company's mission is to provide an opportunity to increase the ability of medical facilities to provide services to patients with limited access to qualified staff and at the same time an ever-growing demand for professionally conducted neurological rehabilitation. They plan to start the Food and Drug Administration (FDA) certification and introduce their therapeutic system to the United States within two years.

Cortivision is a Lublin-based company that manufactures a wireless and fully mobile near-infrared spectroscope based on Functional near-infrared spectroscopy (fNIRS) technology, which is used to study brain activity, mainly for scientific purposes. The company's co-founders are Sławomir Sobótka and Wojciech Broniatowski. The company's product differs from electroencephalogram (EEG) technology in terms of the type of signal it registers. fNIRS technology measures the level of oxygen in the blood flowing through selected areas of the brain, while EEG technology registers changes in the electric field generated by groups of neurons in the brain. Cortivision's solution is available in Poland and abroad, and its main customers are scientists, scientific institutes, or university laboratories that study brain activity. Its product can be useful in areas other than science, such as neuromarketing or biofeedback. The device works on near-infrared and detects the reflected light to determine what percentage of oxygenated blood is in a particular area of the cortex, allowing it to test whether someone is relaxed, concentrated, or distracted, and ultimately to teach a person to control attentiveness.

CosmoEye is a Lublin-based start-up that offers an artificial intelligence (AI) system to improve and optimize business processes, quality control, and work safety. It is a unique system that allows real-time monitoring of activities in manufacturing and logistics companies. The company was founded in February 2022 and has finished working on the minimum viable product (MVP) concept. They are currently in the production and testing phase and plan to sign the first three contracts within a month.

The AI industry has gained significant attention in recent years due to its potential to revolutionize various fields. CosmoEye operates in the business optimization and work safety segment of the AI industry.

HD Air Studio operates in the unmanned aviation industry, which is generating a new market full of innovative drone solutions. Although there are many companies on the market that offer stabilizers for different types of sensors, there are few companies on the market that specialize in mainly "tailor-made products" for a specific project.

HD Air Studio has identified a significant opportunity to develop their technology by working with universities or research units that conduct very specialized research. They have also identified the opportunity to optimize the management of wind farms and provide comprehensive drone services, revolutionizing the performance of such inspections. Furthermore, they offer large gyro heads and stabilizers that carry the heaviest cameras used on TV and film sets.

HD Air Studio is managed by Jakub Jakubczyk, the managing director, and Urszula Jakubczyk, the marketing director. The company has a micro-enterprise structure, but it gathers all the competences necessary to create complex technical solutions — from design to production and brand promotion. The core team is made up of people responsible for research and development as well as the supervision and production of stabilizers. They also have a long-standing cooperation with a partner from Latvia who supports them on the software side.

Plastic Omnium Group is a global company operating in the automotive industry, with 137 production facilities located in 25 countries. The company's core business includes several business lines, such as Clean Energy Systems, Intelligent Exterior Systems, HBPO, New Energies, and Lighting Division. Clean Energy Systems is responsible for the production of fuel systems and exhaust emissions, including the

Selective Catalytic Reduction (SCR) system, which reduces diesel-powered cars' exhaust gas emissions. Plastic Omnium supplies its products to major automotive companies worldwide, including Dacia, BMW, Bentley, Porsche, VW, PSA Group — Stallantis, Renault, Chrysler, Ford, and GM. The company is a market leader with more than 20% market share in the Clean Energy Systems branch. Plastic Omnium's development strategy is based on three pillars, including innovation, and the Lublin plant is involved in the R&D activities for the product design department and the production of special production means. The company cooperates with Lublin universities and is open to closer collaboration with science, offering opportunities for students to gain practical knowledge. Plastic Omnium's employment focuses on hiring mechatronics, mechanics, electronics, and electrical engineering professionals, among others, with language skills being a crucial requirement.

Pyramid Games is a Lublin-based game development company that began its operations in 2010 and currently employs around 60 people. They have transformed into a public limited company and made their debut on the NewConnect market in 2020. Apart from game production, the company focuses on creating a friendly and creative place to work and developing their employees' skills.

The computer games industry or gamedev (video game development) is a dynamic and growing sector of the creative industries. Polish game developers generated a revenue of almost one billion euros in 2020. The industry is not only about satisfying entertainment needs but also involves the increased popularity of game mechanics in other high-tech service and production industries.

Pyramid Games Academy program trains students and people who want to change careers, and academy graduates are ready to enter the workforce after a few months of intensive training. Experienced people who began their careers with Pyramid Games are now training others themselves. The company operates in multiple ways, with several in-house projects and commissioned projects, and provides comprehensive services from programming, graphics, animation, testing, partly marketing and everything up to the release of the game.

Jacek Wyszynski is the CEO of Pyramid Games and Julia Żurakowska is the company's Operations Director. The company cooperates with various universities in Lublin, where they run mentoring programs and help with curriculum development and support events. Pyramid Games hires mainly IT graduates, and 60–70% of their employees are people who have previously worked for them, for example, as interns or trainees. Pyramid Games' standard training program lasts about three months, and they hire graduates from the program or interns.

Quantum Blockchains is a start-up company located in Lublin that specializes in providing security solutions for blockchain systems using quantum technology. The company was founded by three experts in the field of quantum computers and quantum mechanics who shared a passion for blockchain technology. The team has since expanded to include a cyber-security financier and a business affairs manager, bringing the total to 15 employees.

The company operates in the technology industry, specifically in the field of blockchain technology and quantum computers. Quantum Blockchains aims to provide complete safety and security to blockchain networks by creating a security system that is based on quantum technology. The company focuses on developing solutions that can be implemented in blockchain systems and ensure complete safety.

Professor Piotr Kulicki, the scientific director of Quantum Blockchains, was a founding member of the company. He is a specialist in quantum computers and quantum mechanics and holds a position at the Department of the Foundations of Computer Science at the Catholic University of Lublin. The company's founding members are all experts in the field of quantum computers and quantum mechanics.

Virtuar is a dedicated platform for training radiologists using virtual reality and was created by Professor Agnieszka Trojanowska from the Department of Radiology at the Medical University of Lublin. The company was established in 2006, and since then, it has trained over a thousand radiologists every year.

The healthcare sector is facing mounting challenges, including the growing need to educate new generations of medical professionals. Advances in information technology are addressing these challenges and providing increasingly accessible and effective educational tools. Virtuar provides an interactive and immersive learning experience for radiology residents at different levels and specialists who want to deepen or refresh their knowledge. It is an innovative and engaging solution that enhances the learning experience by providing virtual reality modules regarding pathologies of the brain, chest, prostate, and sinuses.

Professor Agnieszka Trojanowska is a radiologist who founded the company Entomografia in 2006 to train radiologists using a workshop method. She was inspired to start Virtuar after recognizing the need for interactive and immersive learning experiences, particularly for the younger generation of radiologists who are accustomed to short-form stimuli. Trojanowska's partner, who is a radiologist and computer scientist, helped create the architecture for the Virtuar programme. The company has worked with teams of IT specialists from different countries, including programmers, medical graphic designers, and IT specialists as needed.

The Implication of the Findings

What is a very positive trend is the use of algorithms and artificial intelligence in the surveyed companies in the peripheral regions of Eastern Poland. In the previously cited survey, out of 20 large companies in Eastern Poland, as many as 13 declared the use of such solutions inside their organizations (Sagan, 2023). Artificial intelligence and algorithms are mainly used in the areas of customer contact and service, organizational management, process improvement, production process management, development of proprietary products and services, and logistics including warehouse space management or the use of autonomous vehicles. Only 6 of the surveyed companies indicated that they are not using AI solutions but intend to implement them in their structures soon. In contrast to the increasing use of AI by companies in Poland's peripheral regions, they very rarely use another technological tool that is a key success factor for many global companies — technology platforms. Functioning in the platform model in the referenced survey was declared by only one company, while in the partial (or unnamed) technology platform model by another five companies (Sagan, 2023).

Table 3 summarizes the competitive advantages of the examined technology companies from Lublin. These are potential advantages related to the unique technology owned and the business model implemented. The main challenges, in turn, include the issues of commercialization of technology and finding customers and potential investors.

To overcome challenges and engage international investors and partners, companies need to develop strategies that ensure their value propositions meet their target audience's needs, understand and manage risks, and engage stakeholders effectively. In the case of Accrea, the company could consider attending international conferences and trade shows to display their products, establish collaborations with international medical equipment distributors, and partner with medical facilities abroad. BioMinds

Table 3.   Summary of key competitive advantages of the surveyed companies (case studies).

Technology	Business Models
1. Ownership of disruptive technologies (medical robotics, AI, blockchains)	1. Advanced collaboration with local stakeholders
2. Integration of technological solutions from different areas of high-tech	2. Attempt to build business solutions/products based on the platform model
3. High competence in prototyping solutions	3. Advanced international cooperation and technology flow
4. Integration of technology and education	4. Looking for profitable market niches

Healthcare Ltd. could consider conducting clinical trials and gathering data that prove the effectiveness of its products, and reaching out to international neurological associations to market its services. CosmoEye could consider partnering with international logistics companies to test and validate its product and participating in international events or business competitions to attract potential investors. HD Air Studio could establish partnerships with universities and research units that conduct specialized research and participate in international conferences to showcase its products. Finally, Plastic Omnium Group could continue its collaborations with Lublin universities and expand its scope of activities in R&D and special production means. Additionally, the company could explore new market opportunities and establish joint ventures with local partners in other regions.

Conclusion

The implications for policymakers, entrepreneurs, and managers regarding FDI attraction, clustering of firms, innovation, and emerging technologies in the economic development of peripheral regions differ from earlier research in a few important aspects. Despite the many challenges and barriers to technological development in Poland's peripheral regions (such as insufficient support from state and government institutions and lack of investment capital, weakness of business environment institutions, mismatch with the degree of development of local enterprises support programs promoted and financed by the EU, and years of infrastructural backwardness), there now seems to be many development opportunities for the area, also in the context of technological development of local companies.

First, there is a shift in global value chains toward their regionalization and the relocation/opening of new ventures in Europe (Radło and Sagan, 2021). Although thus far without discernible growth in inquiries from prospective investors directed towards urban centers and other local government entities within this periphery this shift in global value chains may create new prospects for Eastern Poland.

Second, positive scenarios for the end of the armed conflict in Ukraine provide an opportunity for the reconstruction of that neighboring country. This can be exploited by the Polish border regions described in this chapter, as a place for intensive economic cooperation, consulting, and locating foreign investment, both from Ukraine and other countries. Although the Ukrainian capital fled eastern and southern Ukraine in 2022 after Russia started its war, relatively few chose Eastern Poland as a safe haven, investing mainly in western Poland, the Czech Republic, or Germany. The end of the war though could radically reverse such a trend.

Third, local companies are quickly adapting to new technologies, being agile, buying technology and developing it. They are also taking advantage of the local scientific community and technology base, working closely with the city government and the business ecosystem. This bodes very well for the technological future of the region.

Overall, this chapter contributes to the literature by providing insights into the ways in which firms and countries can respond to emerging technologies in developing economies, with a focus on the peripheral regions of Poland, and the impact of government policy on corporate strategies for technology adoption and innovation. Policies must be evidence-based and should consider regional needs and capabilities as well as be more involved in providing infrastructure and direction in the early stages of development. Additionally, local governments should work in partnership with businesses, academic institutions, and community organizations to develop strategies and initiatives that support innovation, entrepreneurship, job creation, and reduce brain drain in peripheral regions.

References

Acs, Z. J., Brooksbank, D. J., O'Gorman, C., Pickernell, D., and Terjesen, S. 2012. The knowledge spillover theory of entrepreneurship: An application to foreign direct investment. *International Journal of Entrepreneurship and Small Business*, 15(2): 237–261.

Almeida, F., Santos, J. D., and Monteiro, J. A. 2020. The challenges and opportunities in the digitalization of companies in a post-COVID-19 World. *IEEE Engineering Management Review*, 48(3): 97–103.

Angowski, M. and Sagan, M. 2024. The Entrepreneurial Ecosystems in Poland: A Panacea for Growth? In E. Bukalska, T. Kijek, B. S. Sergi (Eds.), *Modeling Economic Growth in Contemporary Poland*. London: Emerald Publishing.

Appio, F. P., Lima, M., and Paroutis, S. 2019. Understanding smart cities: Innovation ecosystems, technological advancements, and societal challenges. *Technological Forecasting and Social Change*, 142: 1–14.

Ascani, A., Crescenzi, R., and Iammarino, S. 2016. What drives European multinationals to the European Union neighbouring countries? A mixed-methods analysis of Italian investment strategies. *Environment and Planning C: Government and Policy*, 34(4): 656–675.

Barry, F. 2007. Foreign direct investment and institutional co-evolution in Ireland. *Scandinavian Economic History Review*, 55(3): 262–288.

Bhawe, N., and Zahra, S. A. 2019. Inducing heterogeneity in local entrepreneurial ecosystems: The role of MNEs. *Small Business Economics*, 52: 437–454.

Brooks, Ch., Vorley, T., and Gherhes, C. 2019. 'Entrepreneurial ecosystems in Poland: Panacea, paper tiger or Pandora's box?', *Journal of Entrepreneurship and Public Policy*, 8(3): 319–338.

Cantwell, J. and Iammarino, S. 2005. *Multinational Corporations and European Regional Systems of Innovation*. London: Taylor & Francis.

Caves, R. E. 1971. International corporations: The industrial economics of foreign investment. *Economica*, 38(149): 1–27.

Chidlow, A., Salciuviene, L., and Young, S. 2009. Regional determinants of inward FDI distribution in Poland. *International Business Review*, 18(2): 119–133.

Chidlow, A., Holmström-Lind, C., Holm, U., and Tallman, S. 2015. Do I stay or do I go? Sub-national drivers for post-entry subsidiary development. *International Business Review*, 24(2): 266–275.

Crescenzi, R. and Iammarino, S. 2017. Global investments and regional development trajectories: The missing links. *Regional Studies*, 51(1): 97–115.

Dunning, J. H. 1994. Reevaluating the benefits of foreign direct investment. *Alliance Capitalism and Global Business*. Oxfordshire: Routledge.

Dwivedi, Y.K., Hughes, L., Ismagilova, E., Aarts, G., Coombs, C., Crick, T., Duan, Y., Dwivedi, R., Edwards, J., Eirug, A. and Galanos, V., 2021. Artificial intelligence (AI): Multidisciplinary perspectives on emerging challenges, opportunities, and agenda for research, practice and policy. *International Journal of Information Management*, 57: 101994.

Guellec, D. and S. Wunsch-Vincent. 2009. Policy responses to the economic crisis: Investing in innovation for long-term growth, *OECD Digital Economy Papers*, No. 159. Paris: OECD Publishing.

Iammarino, S., Rodriguez-Pose, A., and Storper, M. 2019. Regional inequality in Europe: Evidence, theory and policy implications. *Journal of Economic Geography*, 19(2): 273–298.

Indeks Millenium. 2020. Potencjał innowacyjności regionów, The innovation potential of regions Warszawa. Millenium_201027_Raport_index2020.pdf (bankmillennium.pl). Accessed March 15, 2023.

Jóźwik, B. 2013. Economic growth and competitiveness. In B. Jóźwik and M. Sagan (Eds.), *Eastern Poland. Development Challenges* (pp. 25–46). Lublin: Instytut Europy Środkowo-Wschodniej.

Jóźwik, B. and Sagan, M. 2013. Introduction. In B. Jóźwik and M. Sagan (Eds.), *Eastern Poland. Development Challenges* (pp. 17–23). Lublin: Instytut Europy Środkowo-Wschodniej.

Kawałko, B. and Sagan, M. 2015. Lubelskie Voivodeship Development Strategy for the Years 2014-2020: Context of metropolitan Lublin. In Z. Pastuszak, M. Sagan, and K. Żuk (Eds.), *Peripheral Metropolitan Areas in the European Union*. Bangkok-Celje-Lublin: ToKnowPress.

Kociuba, D., Sagan, M., and Kociuba, W. 2023. Toward the smart city ecosystem model. *Energies*, 16(2795): 1–26.

Li, Z., Li, J., and He, B. 2018. Does foreign direct investment enhance or inhibit regional innovation efficiency? Evidence from China. *Chinese Management Studies*, 12(1): 35–55.

Luo, Y. and Zahra, S. A. 2023. Industry 4.0 in international business research. *Journal of International Business Studies*, 54: 403–417.

Markolf, S. A., Chester, M. V., Eisenberg, D. A., Iwaniec, D. M., Davidson, C. I., Zimmerman, R., Miller, T. R., Ruddell, B. L. and Chang, H. 2018. Interdependent infrastructure as linked social, ecological, and technological systems (SETSs) to address lock-in and enhance resilience. *Earth's Future*, 6(12): 1638–1659.

Mironko, A. 2014. Determinants of FDI flows within emerging economies. *Studies in Economic Transition*. https://www.palgrave.com/gp/book/9781137372154. London: Palgrave Macmillan.

Mironko, A. 2018. The impact of human capital and skill availability on attraction of foreign direct investment (FDI) into regions within developing economies. *International Journal of Management (IJM)*, 9(3): 139–163.

Mironko, A. 2020. To make or to serve — Regional industrial specialization patterns of foreign subsidiaries in service and manufacturing sectors across regions in a transition economy. *International Journal of Business and Applied Social Science*, 6(3): 1–26.

Motoyama, Y. and Knowlton, K. 2017. Examining the connections within the startup ecosystem: A case study of St. Louis. *Entrepreneurship Research Journal*, 7(1), 20160011.

Mudambi, R. and Santangelo, G. D. 2016. From shallow resource pools to emerging clusters: The role of multinational enterprise subsidiaries in peripheral areas. *Regional Studies*, 50(12): 1965–1979.

Nielsen, B. B., Asmussen, C. G., and Weatherall, C. D. 2017. The location choice of foreign direct investments: Empirical evidence and methodological challenges. *Journal of World Business*, 52(1): 62–82.

Ning, L., Wang, F., and Li, J. 2016. Urban innovation, regional externalities of foreign direct investment and industrial agglomeration: Evidence from Chinese cities. *Research Policy*, 45(4): 830–843.

Ning, L. and Wang, F. 2018. Does FDI bring environmental knowledge spillovers to developing countries? The role of the local industrial structure. *Environmental and Resource Economics*, 71(2): 381–405.

Pang, C., Wang, Q., Li, Y., and Duan, G. 2019. Integrative capability, business model innovation and performance: Contingent effect of business strategy. *European Journal of Innovation Management*, 22(3): 541–561.

Pavlínek, P., Domański, B., and Guzik, R. 2009. Industrial upgrading through foreign direct investment in Central European automotive manufacturing. *European Urban and Regional Studies*, 16(1): 43–63.

Radło, M.-J. and Sagan, M. 2021. Opportunities and challenges for moving up the value chains before and after the pandemic. The case of Central and Eastern European countries. In A. Chłon-Domińczak, R. Sobiecki, M. Strojny, and B. Majewski (Eds.), *Report of SGH Warsaw School of Economics and the Economic Forum 2021* (pp. 341–374). Warsaw: SGH Publishing House.

Sagan, M. 2023. *Institutional Advantage: The Case of Poland* (pp. 1–57). Warsaw: SGH Publishing House (in print).

Santangelo, G. D. 2004. FDI and local capabilities in peripheral regions: The Etna Valley case. *Transnational Corporations*, 13: 73–108.

Chapter 9

Indigenous Knowledge Management in the Fourth Industrial Revolution: A Reflection on the Emerging Technologies and Development Strategies in Tanzania

John Jackson Iwata

Abstract

Developing countries are witnessing an increased use of indigenous knowledge (IK) products by people of all backgrounds who use them for various purposes including maintenance of human health. In recognizing the importance of indigenous knowledge, several initiatives have been taken by governments. This chapter explores the impact of the Fourth Industrial Revolution (4IR) and its emerging technologies on the management of indigenous knowledge in Tanzania. It also discusses the background information on Tanzania and its indigenous knowledge. This chapter argues that Tanzania has made considerable progress in recognizing the value of indigenous knowledge for competitiveness advantages, but more needs to be done to address the identified challenges in managing such knowledge in the context of the Fourth Industrial Revolution. This chapter offers recommendations on how to harness the potential of the 4IR to the management of indigenous knowledge. The conclusion explains that emerging technologies have not been sufficiently and effectively used in managing indigenous knowledge as has been done in education, banking, and other industrial sectors. Some strategies are discussed to address these challenges in managing indigenous knowledge including capacity building through education to all indigenous knowledge stakeholders.

Keywords: Development strategies, emerging technologies, Fourth Industrial Revolution, indigenous knowledge (IK), indigenous knowledge management, Tanzania

Introduction

In the era of the Fourth Industrial Revolution, technology is increasingly shaping the ways in which people live, work, and communicate. This revolution is characterized by the convergence of technologies that are blurring the lines between digital, physical, and biological systems. Such advances are sometimes referred to as emerging technologies, which entails an innovative achievement in various fields that are still in the early stages of development or adoption but with the potential to revolutionize the way tasks are performed. The most prominent ones include Artificial Intelligence (AI), Internet of Things (IoT), and Blockchain. All these have the potential to revolutionize the way people interact with each other and the environment. Hence, they offer promising opportunities, particularly in managing and preserving indigenous knowledge. However, the impact of these technologies on indigenous communities and knowledge must be considered, as they risk eroding the knowledge and practices that have been passed down through the generations. More importantly, impacts of these technologies on traditional knowledge systems, particularly on indigenous knowledge (IK), have been a subject of debate in this chapter. The use of such technologies can facilitate the development of new solutions to pressing societal challenges including the management of IK. Conversely, the 4IR can pose a threat to the survival of IK as it promotes homogenization and standardization of knowledge systems (Dube and Mutanga, 2020).

According to the Tanzania Commission for Science and Technology (COSTECH), IK is "a vital resource for sustainable development" (COSTECH, 2018). In this context, IK is defined as the knowledge, innovations, and practices developed by local communities over time and generations often through trial and error while interacting with their environment (Kikwilu, 2019). This knowledge is based on a deep understanding of the nature and environment, and is often passed down through generations (COSTECH, 2018). In Tanzania, IK has played a critical role in the development of agriculture, medicine, and other key areas in the community (Nhemachena *et al.*, 2019). In the country, IK systems are diverse and include practices related to agriculture, natural resource management, health, and spirituality (Nnko and Nyange, 2020). A study by Nhemachena *et al.* (2019) notes that there is a need for greater recognition and protection of IK in Tanzania, because the rapid pace of technological change in 4IR may undermine and threaten practices and sustainability of such knowledge.

An example in this regard is the use of AI and Big Data analytics in agriculture, which can help farmers make informed decisions on crop selection, irrigation, and pest control (Komba, 2020). However, the adoption of new technologies without considering the local context can have negative implications for IK management. For instance, the introduction of new seeds and irrigation methods can lead to the loss of traditional crop varieties and knowledge of water harvesting and conservation (Kikwilu, 2019). Furthermore, the introduction of new agricultural practices and technologies may lead to the displacement of traditional farming methods and the loss of IK related to crop diversity and soil management (COSTECH, 2018). Moreover, 4IR can exacerbate the existing digital divide between rural and urban areas, gender, and age groups, hindering the access and transmission of IK. The digital divide can further marginalize indigenous communities and weaken their traditional knowledge systems (Nnko and Nyange, 2020). It is therefore crucial that the potential impacts of new technologies on indigenous communities are carefully considered, and that efforts are made to integrate IK into the development and deployment of new technologies.

In this chapter, the concept of IK management in the context of 4IR has been explored, with a focus on Tanzania. The ways in which emerging technologies and development strategies can be harnessed to support the preservation and dissemination of IK has also been examined. Therefore, this chapter reflects on the emerging technologies and development strategies for managing IK in Tanzania within the context of 4IR. It focuses on how emerging technologies can be integrated in IK management. Furthermore, it will explore how IK can be harnessed to inform the development of new technologies and how new technologies can support the preservation and dissemination of IK. This chapter is organized as follows: First, it provides an overview of IK and its importance in Tanzania. Next, it will discuss the 4IR and its key technologies as well as their impact on IK management. Then, the chapter presents development strategies that integrate IK with emerging technologies. Finally, the conclusion will highlight the implications of 4IR on IK management in Tanzania and suggest future directions for research.

Initiatives for promoting indigenous knowledge management in Tanzania

It is important for the readers to note that, Tanzania is a country in East Africa with a population of over 60 million people. It is home to over 120 ethnic groups, each with its unique culture and IK systems (Nnko and Nyange, 2020). The country has a rich history of IK that has been passed down from generation to generation through oral traditions, rituals, and practices. Tanzania's IK covers a wide range of areas, including agriculture, natural resource management, health, and spirituality. For example, the Maasai pastoralists have a deep understanding of the behavior and movements of their cattle and have developed effective herding strategies that have sustained their livelihoods for centuries (Kikwilu, 2019). The Chagga people have developed innovative terracing methods that enable them to farm on steep slopes without soil erosion (Machumu, 2016).

However, the transmission and preservation of IK in Tanzania have faced various challenges. The colonial legacy and the subsequent adoption of Western education systems have led to the marginalization of IK systems. As a result, indigenous languages and cultures have been suppressed in favor of Western languages and practices, leading to the erosion of IK systems (Nnko and Nyange, 2020). Additionally, rapid urbanization and modernization have contributed to the loss of traditional knowledge systems as the younger generation adopts Western lifestyles and practices. Despite these challenges, there have been efforts and initiatives for promoting the management of the IK systems both at the international and local levels.

At the international level, the United Nations Educational, Scientific, and Cultural Organization (UNESCO) has established a program on IK Systems to promote the recognition and valorization of IK as a tool for sustainable development (UNESCO, n.d.). Similarly, the World Intellectual Property Organization (WIPO) has established a Traditional

Knowledge Division to support the protection and promotion of traditional knowledge and its integration into modern technologies and practices (WIPO, n.d.).

At the local level, Tanzania has established several initiatives to promote IK management and its integration into development strategies. The government of Tanzania has recognized the importance of IK in sustainable development and has incorporated it into various policies and programs. The Tanzania Commission for Science and Technology (COSTECH) has established a program on IK Systems and Practices (IKSP) to promote the documentation, preservation, and dissemination of IK in Tanzania (Makate, 2019). Similarly, the University of Dar es Salaam has established a Centre for Indigenous Knowledge and Organizational Development (CIKOD) to promote the integration of IK into development policies and programs (CIKOD, n.d.).

Additionally, non-governmental organizations and community-based organizations' initiatives have also been established and play a crucial role in promoting IK management through documentation, research, and advocacy (Machumu, 2016). For example, the Kagera Basin Organization (KBO), a community-based organization in North-Western Tanzania, has established a program on IK Systems and Practices (IKSP) to promote the integration of IK into agricultural practices (KBO, n.d.). Similarly, the *HakiElimu* organization has established a program on IK and Learning (IKL) to promote the integration of IK into education policies and practices in Tanzania (*HakiElimu,* n.d.). All, these international and local initiatives reflect a growing recognition on the importance of IK in promoting sustainable development and preserving cultural heritage in Tanzania.

Aim, justification, and rationale for the chapter

The aim of this chapter is to explore the challenges and opportunities posed by the 4IR to the management of IK in Tanzania. Specifically, it aims to:

1. Provide an overview of the 4IR and its impact on IK management.
2. Discuss the background information on Tanzania and its indigenous knowledge.
3. Identify the challenges and opportunities facing the management of IK in Tanzania in the context of the 4IR.

4. Highlight the emerging technologies and development strategies that can be used to promote the preservation and utilization of IK in Tanzania.
5. Offer recommendations for policymakers, researchers, and practitioners on how to harness the potential of the 4IR to enhance the management of IK in Tanzania.

In Tanzania, the management of IK faces various challenges, including the marginalization of IK systems, loss of traditional knowledge systems, and the impact of modernization and urbanization (Nnko and Nyange, 2020). However, there are also opportunities to leverage emerging technologies, such as natural language processing and machine learning in analyzing and organizing large volumes of indigenous knowledge. Also, the virtual and augmented reality (VR/AR) technologies can enable creating virtual environments or overlaying digital information on the real world. VR/AR can be utilized to preserve and showcase indigenous cultural practices, rituals, and historical sites. Conversely, the blockchain technology can be utilized to protect and authenticate indigenous intellectual property rights to ensure fair and transparent sharing of such knowledge. More importantly, mobile applications, which are part of the emerging technologies, can serve as platforms for indigenous communities to promote the preservation, accessibility, and utilization of IK (Kikwilu, 2019).

In the developing countries including the East African countries (Tanzania, Uganda, Kenya, Rwanda, and Burundi) and South African countries including Botswana, Zimbabwe, and others, there is increased use of IK products by people of all ages and socioeconomic statuses. The increased use of such knowledge has been observed in various sectors such as agriculture, medicine, and education. In East Africa, particularly in Tanzania, IK has been integrated into various agricultural practices, such as agroforestry, soil and water conservation, and pest control. In this country, IK has also been used to develop and promote traditional medicines and healing practices, particularly in rural areas where modern healthcare services are limited (Iwata and Hoskins 2017). In the education sector, IK has been used to develop curriculum materials that reflect local cultures and traditions. Similarly, in Uganda IK has been utilized in agriculture, particularly in the production of staple crops such as cassava and millet (Nabalegwa *et al.*, 2020). IK has also been used to develop traditional medicines and healing practices, particularly in the treatment of common ailments such as malaria, diarrhea, and respiratory infections.

While in Kenya, IK has been utilized in the management and conservation of natural resources, particularly in wildlife conservation and ecotourism (Mugambi *et al.*, 2017). IK has further been used to promote sustainable agriculture practices, particularly in the production of traditional crops such as sorghum, maize, and millet. In Rwanda, IK has been utilized in the production of traditional crops such as beans, cassava, and sweet potatoes, as well as in the management and conservation of natural resources (Kamanzi *et al.*, 2018). IK has also been used to develop traditional medicines and healing practices, particularly in the treatment of common ailments such as malaria and diarrhea (Bimenyimana *et al.*, 2019). And in Burundi, IK has been utilized in the management and conservation of natural resources, particularly in the development of community-based conservation programs (Ndayizeye *et al.*, 2019). In addition, IK has been used in agriculture, particularly in the production of traditional crops such as cassava, beans, and sorghum.

In South Africa, the country adopted a policy framework on the promotion and protection of IK systems through the Ulwazi Program. Through this program, the documentation of various forms of South African indigenous cultures and histories, like a local celebration of the rite of passage specifically in Durban, have been preserved via online media. This has also been the case in Botswana where IK has been used in the management and conservation of natural resources, particularly in the development of community-based natural resource management programs. IK has further been utilized in the development of traditional medicines and healing practices, particularly in the treatment of chronic illnesses such as diabetes, hypertension, and HIV/AIDS. In Zimbabwe, IK has been utilized in agriculture, particularly in the development of drought-resistant crops such as sorghum and millet (Mhlanga *et al.*, 2018). And it has been used in the management and conservation of natural resources, particularly in the development of community-based wildlife conservation programs.

Historical and Cultural Context of Indigenous Knowledge in Tanzania

As earlier stated, IK refers to the knowledge, innovations, and practices that have been developed by local communities over time, and that are based on their experience and understanding of the natural environment

(UNESCO, 2002). In Tanzania, IK is a vital part of the country's cultural heritage, and it plays a critical role in various sectors, including agriculture, health, and education. In the country, IK has been passed down from generation to generation, mainly through oral traditions, storytelling, and community practices (Nnko, 2017). For example, the Maasai, one of Tanzania's indigenous communities, have a vast knowledge of herbal medicine, which they use to treat various ailments. Additionally, the Sukuma and Nyamwezi are indigenous communities with extensive knowledge of traditional hunting and agriculture including soil and water conservation practices.

Therefore, IK in Tanzania is deeply rooted in the country's cultural traditions, social relations, and spiritual practices, and it reflects the deep connection that indigenous communities have with their environment. Hence, IK is essential for the sustainable development of many regions of the world, including Tanzania, as it provides local communities with tools to manage their resources, mitigate environmental risks, and adapt to changing conditions (FAO, 2019). In Tanzania, IK has played a critical role in various sectors, including agriculture, health, and education. It has further promoted sustainable development, especially in rural areas, where communities rely on traditional practices for their livelihoods (Nnko, 2017). However, the rapid technological changes brought about by the 4IR and emerging technologies pose a challenge to the preservation and transmission of IK in Tanzania. The emergence of new technologies, such as AI and big data, has the potential to transform various sectors of the economy in Tanzania, including agriculture, health, and education (Sawe, 2021).

In this respect, it is essential to recognize the value of IK in Tanzania and develop strategies to integrate it with emerging technologies for sustainable development. This can be achieved through partnerships between local communities, government, and private sector organizations to promote the preservation and transmission of IK while also leveraging emerging technologies for development. In the agriculture sector, IK has contributed to the development of sustainable farming practices that conserve soil and water resources (Nnko, 2017). IK has also helped in the identification and cultivation of local crops that are adapted to the local climate and soil conditions. In the health sector, IK has contributed to the development of herbal medicine that is used to treat various ailments (Nnko, 2017). Traditional healers in Tanzania continue to play a vital role in providing healthcare services to rural communities.

The importance of IK in Tanzania cannot be overstated. It helps local communities to preserve the identity of indigenous people, their cultural heritage, and resilience to environmental challenges. IK is also utilized as a tool to fight poverty by supporting indigenous people to overcome their social and economic problems as well as to promote human growth. Crucially, IK has the historical significance of establishing the reliability of data for future references and comparative studies about knowledge. As previously indicated, it is significant to note that there are numerous IK systems, and the value of each one needs to be recognized because they all influence social identity and human lives. In other communities, IK is locally used as the basis for decision-making, ensuring food security, animal and human health, education, the management of natural resources, and other crucial activities. Thus, IK as a unique knowledge covers a wide range of aspects including education, health (human and animal), natural resource management, agriculture, food preparation, communication and conflict resolution, institutional management, and governance (Dixit and Goyal, 2011; Msuya, 2007). However, the rapid changes brought about by the 4IR and emerging technologies pose a threat to the preservation and transmission of IK in Tanzania. More importantly, these technologies may overshadow or displace IK and its practices, leading to the loss of valuable cultural heritage.

Types of indigenous knowledge in Tanzania

There are many types of IK in Tanzania. Although some IK may not seem worth using today, others are very useful and are in high demand. Authors including Iwata and Hoskins (2017), Lwoga (2009), and Msuya (2007) have noted diverse categories of IK encompassing various fields such as traditional medicine, agriculture, wildlife management, food security, weather forecasting, communication and conflict resolution, religious beliefs, politics and human resources, education, witchcraft, divination, and sorcery and magic, among others. This section provides an overview of the types of IK in Tanzania.

Traditional medicine

Traditional medicine is an essential part of the healthcare system in Tanzania, especially in rural areas. In such a practice, traditional healers use a combination of herbs, minerals, and animal products to treat various ailments. The use of traditional medicine is often associated with cultural and spiritual beliefs and practices, and it reflects the deep connection that indigenous communities have with their environment (Nnko, 2017). Traditional medicine is also an affordable and accessible option for many Tanzanians who cannot afford modern medical services. The Hadzabe people, who live in the Lake Eyasi area in Northern Tanzania, are known for their extensive knowledge of traditional medicinal plants. They use plants such as the stem bark of Acacia mellifera and the roots of Entada abyssinica to treat various ailments, including diarrhea, malaria, and skin infections (Hunn *et al.*, 2010).

Tanzania is endowed with a rich diversity of flora and fauna, which has led to the development of a wealth of IK practices. The use of traditional plants for medicinal purposes is one of the most prominent examples of IK practices in Tanzania. Traditional medicine in Tanzania has a long history, and its importance is evident in the fact that it is estimated that up to 60–80% of the Tanzanian population rely on traditional medicine for their primary healthcare needs (Moshi *et al.*, 2010). Traditional medicine in Tanzania involves the use of plant extracts, animal parts, and minerals for treating various ailments. The knowledge on the use of these resources has been passed down from generation to generation, and it is considered an important cultural heritage in Tanzania (Bodeker *et al.*, 2007).

Agriculture

Agriculture is the backbone of the Tanzanian economy, and IK has played a significant role in its development. IK has contributed to the development of sustainable agricultural practices that conserve soil and water resources, promote crop diversity, and reduce the reliance on chemical inputs (Nnko, 2017). Traditional agricultural practices include crop rotation, intercropping, and the use of organic fertilizers. IK has also facilitated the identification and cultivation of local crops that are adapted to the local climate and soil conditions. Indigenous agricultural knowledge includes the application of local knowledge for plant and animal disease management, livestock management, and crop cultivation. In this context, controlling animal diseases such as livestock fungal diseases entails using local herbs whereas controlling plant diseases such as treating the effects and implementing organic farming which involves crop husbandry. Various pharmaceutical businesses are currently exploring a variety of conventional medications made from plant and animal remains. Crop cultivation involved the improvement of soil fertility using manure to produce various products, thinning, and plant spacing and weeding. Livestock keeping involves animal husbandry and ethnic-veterinary medicine.

Another good example of IK practices in Tanzania in the field of agriculture is that of the Wagogo people, who live in the Dodoma region of Tanzania. The Wagogo have developed a unique farming system that involves intercropping and crop rotation to maximize crop yields and maintain soil fertility. The system is based on IK that has been passed down through generations and has proven to be effective in sustaining agricultural productivity in the region (Brown *et al.*, 2018; Nan *et al.*, 2021).

Food and technology

In today's modern world, food and technology have become increasingly intertwined. This process has revolutionized various aspects of the food industry, including production, processing, preservation, distribution, and consumption. Technology has brought about significant advancements that have both positive and negative impacts on food systems, nutrition, and society as a whole. The increase in agricultural production is a good example of where technology has made a significant impact through advancements such as the use of precision farming techniques, genetically modified organisms (GMOs), and hydroponics. These have increased crop productions, reduced water usage, and minimized the need for chemical inputs. As far as IK is concerned in agriculture and food security, the related technology involves fermentation and other practices to ensure food security. It starts with seed treatment and storage methods, then tools and equipment used for planting and harvesting, and finishes with cooking pots and implements.

In Tanzania, food security and technology are based on indigenous agricultural practices and local knowledge. They revolve around small-scale farming, subsistence agriculture, and communal sharing of resources. As stated earlier, farmers in the country rely and focus on traditional seeds, crop rotation, and natural fertilizers. This involves practices such as intercropping and agroforestry, to maximize production and minimize risks. In recent years, Tanzania has embraced various technologies to enhance food security including improved seeds through hybridization and genetically modified varieties to increase crop productivity and resilience against pests and diseases; the adoption of modern irrigation systems, such as drip irrigation and sprinklers, has enhanced agricultural production by mitigating the effects of erratic rainfall patterns.

Wildlife management

Tanzania is home to some of the most iconic wildlife species in the world, including elephants, lions, and giraffes. IK has played a significant role in the conservation and management of wildlife in Tanzania. Indigenous communities have developed various techniques for managing wildlife resources sustainably, including the use of fire to maintain grasslands and the creation of sacred areas where hunting is prohibited (Nnko, 2017). In Tanzania, IK practices related to wildlife management are common to the Hadzabe, Nyamwezi, and Maasai people, who are also known as pastoralists and hunters in Tanzania. These societies have developed a unique system of wildlife management that involves co-existing with wild animals, such as lions and elephants. For example, the Maasai use their IK to maintain a balance between human activities and wildlife conservation, which has been crucial in the conservation of wildlife in Tanzania (Goldman *et al.*, 2010).

Handicrafts and traditional arts

Indigenous communities in Tanzania have a rich cultural heritage that is reflected in handicrafts such as baskets, mats, and pottery using traditional techniques and materials. They are also seen in traditional arts such as music, dance, and storytelling, which are an important part of the cultural identity of indigenous communities (Mhando, 2004).

Incorporating IK with emerging technologies can enhance the sustainability and productivity of these sectors. For example, the use of drones and other technologies can improve wildlife management and conservation efforts, while the use of precision agriculture can enhance crop productivity while reducing environmental impacts.

Information, communication, and conflict resolution

In some traditional societies, animal sounds, earthquakes, trees, and plants carry messages to inform society on various issues including weather and volcanic eruptions. For example, in pastoral societies such as the Maasai of Tanzania, their migration patterns for effective land use and conservation are determined by the type of trees or plants that grew or did not grow well in a particular year. Hence, they are important for traditional weather forecasting. In addition, the dissemination of information is done locally to inform people through storytelling. Thus, weather forecasting through traditional means assists in determining various challenges that face farming and livestock keeping.

Politics and human resources

This entails the ways in which indigenous people organize and choose leaders in their localities such as local organizations such as kinship groups, councils of elders, or groups that share and exchange labor. In Tanzania, IK influences various aspects of social organization and livelihoods. Indigenous communities possess rich knowledge about local ecosystems, natural resources, and sustainable practices for agriculture, hunting, and gathering. This knowledge is often integrated into their daily lives and economic activities, contributing to their resilience and adaptation to the local environment.

Tanzania recognizes the importance of IK in both politics and human resources. Efforts have been made to incorporate indigenous perspectives into national policies and legislation, promoting the inclusion and protection of indigenous rights. However, challenges such as land rights, cultural preservation, and equitable representation persist, and there is ongoing work to ensure the full recognition and integration of IK in these areas.

The Fourth Industrial Revolution and Emerging Technologies

The 4IR and emerging technologies are interconnected although they have distinct characteristics. Chui *et al.* (2016) are of the view that emerging technologies provide potential opportunities for creating new foundations for business and societal value; in this context, as stated earlier, the term "emerging technologies" is used to refer to the novel and innovative advancements that are currently in the early stages of development or adoption and have the significant potentials on industries and society as a whole. Conversely, Schwab (2016) contends that the 4IR is a fusion of technologies that is blurring the lines between the physical, digital, and biological spheres; as stated in the introduction of this chapter, 4IR is characterized by the integration of advanced technologies such as AI, robotics, IoT, blockchain, 3D printing, big data, and cloud computing, among others, to drive innovation and productivity in various sectors. The 4IR thus represents a broader socioeconomic paradigm shift driven by the integration of the mentioned technologies into various aspects of society. With the emergence of these technologies, a profound impact has been felt on how we live, work, and interact with each other. In Tanzania, like in other countries, 4IR is transforming the economy and the way people do business in various sectors such as agriculture, healthcare, and finance, which improves efficiency and productivity (UNDP, 2021).

In the emerging technologies, AI is a key technology in the 4IR related to the development of intelligent machines that can perform tasks that usually require human intelligence, such as visual perception, speech recognition, decision-making, and language translation. For instance, AI is being used in Tanzania to develop predictive models for crop yield and disease outbreaks in agriculture (Kavishe *et al.*, 2021). The IoT is another key technology in the 4IR that involves the interconnection of physical devices, vehicles, buildings, and other objects embedded with sensors, software, and network connectivity. In Tanzania, IoT is being used in various sectors, such as energy, transportation, and healthcare. For instance, IoT is being used in Tanzania to develop smart grids for efficient energy management (Kavishe *et al.*, 2021). Blockchain is a distributed ledger technology that enables secure and transparent transactions without the need for intermediaries. It has the potential to transform various sectors, such as finance, healthcare, and supply chain management. In Tanzania, blockchain is being used to develop digital identity systems and secure land registries (World Bank, 2021). Other key technologies in the 4IR include robotics, 3D printing, and virtual reality, among others. These technologies have the potential to transform various sectors in Tanzania and enhance the country's economic development.

One of the main challenges of 4IR is the potential to marginalize IK and undermine local knowledge systems (LKS) (Mutula and van Brakel,

2019). The introduction of new technologies may disrupt traditional ways of life, causing the erosion of IK systems, which are closely linked to the cultural identity and practices of local communities. In Tanzania, IK has played a vital role in various sectors, such as agriculture, medicine, and wildlife management among other sensitive areas (Tengia-Kessy and Mushi, 2018). Therefore, it is essential to ensure that 4IR is leveraged in a way that supports and strengthens IK systems rather than eroding them.

Several emerging technologies have the potential to enhance IK management in Tanzania. For example, some AI chatbots facilitate engagement with indigenous communities, answer their questions, and provide information about their culture, language, and traditional practices. Virtual Reality/Artificial Reality (VR/AR) technologies can recreate traditional ceremonies or rituals, allowing people to experience them firsthand and understand their significance. Alongside this, IoT sensors can be deployed in traditional lands to monitor changes in temperature, air quality, or water levels, providing valuable information for indigenous communities regarding the health of their environment. Blockchains can be used to create a registry of indigenous cultural expressions, artworks, or indigenous knowledge, providing a transparent and immutable record of ownership and usage rights; the mobile applications can also be used to enable indigenous language speakers to connect with each other, share stories, and access resources for language revitalization. Hence, the emerging technologies can facilitate the documentation and sharing of IK, making it accessible to a wider audience (Mutula and van Brakel, 2019). Additionally, the use of AI and big data analytics can help to preserve and analyze IK, providing insights that can be used to inform policies and decision-making (UNDP, 2021). However, it is crucial to ensure that the adoption of these technologies is done in a way that respects the cultural context and values of the local communities.

Impacts of technologies in indigenous knowledge management

4IR technologies such as AI, IoT, and Blockchain are transforming the way information is generated, managed, and disseminated. These technologies are providing new opportunities for the preservation and management of IK in Tanzania. For instance, the use of AI can assist in the identification, classification, and storage of IK data. IoT can be used to monitor and manage natural resources, such as water, forests, and wildlife, which are central to the IK practices of many Tanzanian communities. Blockchain technology can be used to create secure and transparent systems for the management of IK, such as the ownership and rights to traditional knowledge. However, the adoption of these technologies must be done with caution and with the participation of the communities holding the IK. It is essential to ensure that the ownership, control, and benefits of these technologies remain within these communities and avoid the exploitation of the IK holders or their resources.

The integration of 4IR technologies should not overlook the unique characteristics of IK. The knowledge is often embedded in cultural practices, rituals, and social norms, which can be challenging to translate into data or algorithms. This highlights that it is essential to consider the context and relevance of IK practices when integrating these technologies. Tanzania is currently implementing various initiatives to integrate 4IR technologies into different sectors, including education, agriculture, health, and natural resource management. For example, the government has launched an initiative to digitize the country's archives and museum collections, which contain valuable information on the country's history and culture. The initiative aims to preserve and make such information accessible to future generations.

It is evident that the use of ICT tools to manage and disseminate IK in Tanzania is gaining momentum. The emerging technologies in 4IR have the potential to significantly impact IK management and innovation by providing new tools and platforms for the documentation, preservation, and dissemination of IK. For instance, the Indigenous and Traditional Knowledge Management System (ITKMS) is a web-based platform that allows communities to document, store, and share their IK. The platform was developed through a partnership between the government of Tanzania, UNESCO, and the World Intellectual Property Organization (WIPO). The platform enables communities to retain ownership and assert control over their IK as well as provide a secure and transparent system for the management of this knowledge. Hence, emerging technologies such as mobile applications and the IoT provide a means for remote communities to access and share traditional knowledge (Mkandawire *et al.*, 2019). Additionally, geographic information systems (GISs) can be used to map and analyze IK related to natural resources, such as medicinal plants, and support their sustainable use (DeVore *et al.*, 2019).

In Tanzania, the government has established several development initiatives to support the integration of emerging technologies into IK management and innovation. For example, the Tanzania Commission for Science and Technology (COSTECH) has established a program on Science, Technology, and Innovation (STI) to promote the use of emerging technologies in various sectors, including agriculture, health, and education (COSTECH, n.d.-a). Similarly, the Tanzania Industrial Research and Development Organization (TIRDO) has established a program on Innovation and Technology Development (ITD) to support the evolution and commercialization of innovative technologies in Tanzania (TIRDO, n.d.). These initiatives can help to facilitate the integration of emerging technologies into IK management and innovation in Tanzania and support the sustainable development of local communities.

In this context, therefore, one of the key impacts of emerging technologies in IK management is the ability to document and store traditional knowledge using digital tools. This can help to preserve traditional knowledge for future generations and make it accessible to a wider audience. For example, in Tanzania, the COSTECH-led Tanzania Open Data Initiative (TODI) has facilitated the development of a digital repository of IK on agriculture, biodiversity, and traditional medicine (COSTECH, n.d.-b). This digital repository provides a platform for sharing and disseminating traditional knowledge to farmers, researchers, and policymakers.

Another impact of emerging technologies in IK management is the potential to support the sustainable use of natural resources. Geographic Information Systems (GIS) can be used to map and analyze traditional knowledge related to natural resources, such as medicinal plants, and support their sustainable use (DeVore *et al.*, 2019). In Tanzania, the Ministry of Agriculture has partnered with the International Centre for Tropical Agriculture (CIAT) to develop a GIS-based system for mapping and managing soil fertility using IK (CIAT, 2018). This system has helped to improve the productivity and sustainability of smallholder farming systems in Tanzania. Moreover, emerging technologies can also support the commercialization of traditional knowledge by facilitating its integration into modern industries. For example, in Tanzania, COSTECH has established an STI program to support the development and commercialization of innovative technologies, including those based on traditional knowledge (COSTECH, n.d.-a).

The use of emerging technologies and 4IR poses additional challenges to IK management. For instance, there are concerns about the commercialization and misappropriation of IK, where private companies use traditional knowledge for their own profit without sharing the benefits with the indigenous communities that own the knowledge (Chen *et al.*, 2020). Thus, the government has established the National Council for Technical Education (NACTE) to regulate and oversee technical education and training in the country, including the promotion of IK-based skills and knowledge (NACTE, 2021).

Development Strategies for Indigenous Knowledge Management in Tanzania

Tanzania has recognized the value of IK and has put in place policies and strategies to manage and promote it. The Tanzania National Science and Technology Policy emphasizes the importance of traditional knowledge in development, and the National Strategy for Growth and Poverty Reduction (NSGRP) recognizes the need to integrate IK into modern technologies and development plans (URT, 2005). One key strategy for promoting and managing IK in Tanzania is through documentation and preservation. The Tanzania Traditional Knowledge Documentation, Inventory, and Management Project (TRAKDIMP), which was initiated in 2001, is an example of such an effort. The project aimed to collect, document, and preserve traditional knowledge and practices in various sectors, including agriculture, health, and natural resource management (URT, 2005).

Another strategy is the incorporation of IK into formal education systems. The Tanzanian Ministry of Education and Vocational Training has recognized the importance of IK and has included it in the primary and secondary school curricula (URT, 2005). Additionally, there is a need for collaboration between traditional knowledge holders and modern technology experts to promote innovation and development. The integration of modern technologies, such as ICTs, with IK can lead to the development of new products and services that are locally relevant and environmentally sustainable. However, there are challenges on the effective management and promotion of IK in Tanzania. One of the challenges is lack of legal protection of indigenous knowledge owners and their intellectual property. This has led to exploitation and misappropriation of traditional knowledge by external actors (Chambers *et al.*, 1989). Another challenge is the lack of recognition and support for traditional knowledge holders and practitioners. Many traditional knowledge holders are marginalized, and their knowledge is not valued in modern society (Mbilinyi, 2010). To address these challenges, there is a need for policy and legal frameworks that protect traditional knowledge holders and their intellectual property, as well as efforts to raise awareness and promote the value of traditional knowledge in modern society.

Use of digital platforms to preserving and promoting indigenous knowledge

The emergence of new technologies has presented an opportunity to complement IK management in Tanzania. Traditional methods of managing and transmitting knowledge are facing various challenges, such as the loss of traditional knowledge holders and the impact of climate change. Therefore, emerging technologies such as digital platforms can be used to preserve and promote IK. For instance, the use of mobile phones and the internet can be used to disseminate information on IK to a wider audience, including young people who are disconnected from their cultural heritage. Additionally, digital platforms can be used to create databases of IK to ensure that the knowledge is not lost, but rather available for future generations.

Tanzania has already made efforts toward the preservation and promotion of IK through the establishment of the Traditional Knowledge Digital Library (TKDL). It provides digital access to traditional knowledge related to health, agriculture, and biodiversity conservation. Through this platform, traditional knowledge holders can document their information in a digital format that can be accessed by others. This approach ensures that traditional knowledge is preserved and protected from misappropriation. More importantly, the use of blockchain technology can be applied to protect the intellectual property rights of traditional knowledge holders. It can help to create a permanent and unalterable record of traditional knowledge, making it easier to identify and prevent unauthorized use and appropriation of the knowledge.

With all these initiatives there is still a limited use of emerging technologies in IK (IK) management, despite the potential benefits that could be achieved. The reasons for this include inadequate infrastructure, lack of funding, limited awareness, and the challenge of balancing the benefits of technology with the preservation of cultural traditions and practices. In Tanzania, for instance, limited access to infrastructure such as electricity and the internet hinders the use of emerging technologies in IK management. This limits the opportunities for indigenous communities to share and access information, as well as to participate in the digital economy (Kasente *et al.*, 2019).

Another reason for the limited use of emerging technologies in IK management is the lack of funding for research and development in this area. This hinders the development of appropriate technologies and tools that could facilitate the management of IK using modern methods (Chen *et al.*, 2020). Moreover, there is limited awareness among indigenous communities on the potential benefits of emerging technologies for the preservation and management of their traditional knowledge. This limits their ability to leverage the available technologies to document and share their knowledge with other communities and with the broader public (Kasente *et al.*, 2019). Finally, the challenge of balancing the benefits of technology with the preservation of cultural traditions and practices poses a significant challenge to the use of emerging technologies in IK management. Indigenous communities may view the use of modern technologies as a threat to their cultural identity and values, and as a result, they may be hesitant to adopt these technologies in their traditional practices (Chen *et al.*, 2020).

Challenges constraining indigenous knowledge management in Tanzania

IK is an essential component of the cultural heritage of Tanzania. However, despite its importance, IK is facing numerous challenges that are threatening its survival. One of the major ones is the lack of recognition by the formal education systems and policymakers, who tend to prioritize Western approaches over IK (Mwansasu, 2002). This has led to a decline in the transmission of IK from generation to generation, as younger generations are not taught to value their traditional knowledge. Additionally, there is a risk of cultural erosion as younger generations adopt Western lifestyles, leading to the loss of traditional practices and knowledge (Nkya *et al.*, 2021).

The integration of emerging technologies into IK management has brought about a new set of challenges. For instance, the use of digital platforms to preserve and promote IK may not be accessible to everyone, especially those in rural areas who lack access to technology and the Internet. The lack of financial resources and technical expertise among IK holders is also a significant challenge that hinders the effective use of emerging technologies in IK management (Kapinga *et al.*, 2020). To overcome these challenges, several development strategies have been proposed. One strategy is the establishment of community-based organizations to promote and protect IK. These organizations aim to involve community members in IK documentation, management, and dissemination, thereby ensuring its sustainability (Mwansasu, 2002). Another strategy is the integration of IK into the formal education system. This involves the recognition and validation of IK as a legitimate form of knowledge, which can be achieved through the inclusion of IK in the school curriculum (Nkya *et al.*, 2021).

Strategies to integrate indigenous knowledge with emerging technologies

The integration of IK with emerging technologies can lead to the preservation, promotion, and sustainable development of indigenous communities. One strategy is the use of social media platforms to promote and share IK. Facebook, Twitter, and Instagram can all be used to share traditional practices and beliefs with a global audience. They can be further used to connect IK holders with each other and with researchers and policymakers who are interested in working with them.

Another strategy is the use of mobile technologies to enhance the documentation and dissemination of IK. Mobile phones and tablets can be used to capture audio, video, and images of traditional practices and beliefs. These technologies can then be used to share information and connect IK holders with each other and with researchers and policymakers. In Tanzania, the use of mobile technologies has been successful in the documentation and dissemination of IK. For example, the Tanzania Traditional and Alternative Medicine Act of 2009 recognizes traditional medicine as an important part of the country's healthcare system. To support the integration of traditional medicine with modern healthcare, the government established an app for smart devices that provides information on traditional medicine to healthcare providers and the public. This app also enables users to report adverse reactions to traditional medicines and to communicate with traditional healers.

The use of GIS technology can help to map IK systems and resources. This can provide valuable information for policymakers, researchers, and indigenous communities themselves to make informed decisions about the sustainable management of natural resources.

Education plays a critical role in ensuring that emerging technologies in the fourth industrial revolution are used effectively for IK management. Capacity building through education can be achieved through a variety of approaches, including training workshops, seminars, and online courses. These programs should focus on increasing awareness of the importance of IK, promoting the use of emerging technologies, and building the necessary skills and knowledge to manage IK effectively. By doing so, stakeholders can be empowered to preserve and protect IK, while also ensuring that it remains relevant and accessible in today's rapidly changing world.

In Tanzania, initiatives such as the Tanzania Traditional Knowledge Digital Library (TTKDL) have been established to promote the management and preservation of IK using modern technologies (Ngulube, 2014). This initiative has provided a platform for indigenous communities to share and document their knowledge, while also enabling researchers and policymakers to access and utilize this knowledge. Additionally, the University of Dodoma has established a Bachelor of IK Science (BIKS) program aimed at developing the necessary capacity and skills for managing IK (University of Dodoma, 2021).

Community participation in indigenous knowledge management

Indigenous knowledge management involves a collective effort that requires the participation of the community where the knowledge resides. According to UNDP (2008), communities play a crucial role in safeguarding, promoting, and transmitting IK from one generation to another. Therefore, community participation is essential for the successful management of IK.

In Tanzania, community participation is considered vital in the preservation and promotion of IK. This is because IK in Tanzania is rooted in cultural traditions that have been passed down from one generation to another. Community participation is crucial in the preservation and transmission of this knowledge, as it ensures that the knowledge is not lost or eroded over time. Communities can contribute to the management of IK by providing information on the various aspects of their cultural heritage, including traditional medicine, agriculture, and wildlife management (Njau, 2016).

Community participation can help in identifying and addressing the challenges facing IK management in Tanzania. The participation of local communities can provide valuable insights into the unique needs and priorities of the communities, which can help in the development of appropriate policies and strategies for IK management. For instance, community-based organizations such as the Tanzania Indigenous Peoples Organization (TAIPO) have been actively involved in advocating for the recognition and protection of IK in Tanzania (Mbwambo, 2018).

Implications of the Fourth Industrial Revolution on indigenous knowledge management

4IR has brought about significant changes in the way knowledge is produced, distributed, and utilized. The emergence of new technologies such as AI, IoT, and blockchain has presented new opportunities and challenges for the management of IK in Tanzania. It is important to recognize that the integration of IK and emerging technologies should be done with caution to avoid disrupting the culture and traditions of indigenous communities. As the adoption of technology continues to grow in Tanzania, there is a risk of the younger generation losing interest in traditional knowledge, which could lead to its loss.

One of the implications of 4IR on IK management in Tanzania is the potential loss of cultural heritage and traditional knowledge as the younger generation becomes increasingly assimilated into a digital culture. As access to modern technologies increases, young people may lose interest in traditional practices and beliefs, leading to the erosion of cultural heritage. This highlights the need for innovative strategies to preserve and promote IK in the digital age. Another implication of 4IR on IK management in Tanzania is the potential for increased visibility and recognition of IK. With digital platforms and social media, IK holders can share their knowledge and practices with a wider audience, potentially leading to increased recognition and appreciation of their contributions to society. However, this also poses challenges related to intellectual property rights and the protection of traditional knowledge from exploitation by external actors.

There is a need for government policies to prioritize the recognition, preservation, and promotion of IK in Tanzania. These policies should be designed in collaboration with indigenous communities to ensure their participation and ownership of the IK management processes. Additionally, there is a need to establish partnerships between the government, private sector, and indigenous communities to develop innovative solutions that blend traditional knowledge with emerging technologies. It is important to recognize that the use of technology can facilitate the preservation and promotion of IK. For example, the use of social media platforms such as Facebook, WhatsApp, and Instagram can provide a platform for indigenous communities to share their knowledge with a wider audience. Furthermore, the use of blockchain technology can enable the creation of a transparent and secure database of IK, which can be accessed by researchers and policymakers. Still, the adoption of emerging technologies in managing IK should be done in a way that respects the cultural diversity of indigenous communities. It is important to ensure that the IK is not commodified, and that the intellectual property rights of indigenous communities are protected.

It is important to note that the implications of 4IR on IK management in Tanzania are complex and multifaceted. While there are risks associated with the increasing influence of technology on traditional knowledge systems, there are also opportunities to leverage emerging technologies to preserve and promote IK. It is therefore important to develop context-specific strategies that enable IK holders to navigate these changes and adapt to the new realities of the digital age. It is also worth noting that in Tanzania, the government has recognized the importance of IK management and has taken steps to promote and preserve traditional knowledge systems. For example, the Tanzania Traditional Medicine Policy of 2009 was developed to provide a framework for the regulation and promotion of traditional medicine in the country, while the Zanzibar Cultural Policy of 2009 aims to promote and protect the cultural heritage of that region. These policies provide a foundation for the development of context-specific strategies to integrate IK with emerging technologies and promote the sustainable development of Tanzania.

The integration of emerging technologies brought by the fourth industrial revolution has the potential to greatly leverage IK and make it more accessible to the newer generations. The following are some suggestions and discussions on how this can be achieved:

(i) Documentation and preservation of IK through digital technology. Emerging technologies like AI, machine learning, and virtual reality can be suitable ways for digitally documenting and preserving IK.

This could involve creating or having in place digital libraries, databases, and virtual museums where IK in its various forms, such as traditional practices, languages, storytelling, and ecological wisdom, can be stored and shared.

(ii) Since many indigenous languages are at risk of extinction, integrating emerging technologies can help preserve and revitalize these languages. Natural language processing and machine learning algorithms can be used to develop language learning applications, translation tools, and voice recognition systems that support indigenous languages. This would not only help preserve linguistic diversity but also facilitate the transmission of IK.

(iii) With the emerging technologies, people have to start planning the creation of collaborative platforms that connect indigenous communities, researchers, and policymakers. Such platforms can enable the sharing of IK, ideas, and best practices across geographically dispersed communities. By doing that and with the availability of these platforms, future generations can actively participate in the management of IK, contribute their own experiences, and learn from elders and experts.

(iv) Emerging technologies and the widespread use of smart devices provide an opportunity to develop apps that cater to the needs and interests of newer generations while incorporating IK. These apps can provide interactive learning experiences, storytelling, indigenous art and music, and sustainable practices based on traditional IK. By making IK easily accessible through smart devices, younger generations can engage with and appreciate their cultural heritage.

(v) Gamification techniques can be employed for the purpose of making learning about IK more engaging and enjoyable. Some serious games, interactive simulations, and virtual reality experiences can immerse users in indigenous cultures and traditions, allowing them to explore more about IK and learn in a hands-on, interactive manner. By gamifying IK, it can become more appealing to future generations while encouraging their active participation in the processes of managing such knowledge.

Therefore, integrating emerging technologies in 4IR can bridge the gap between IK and newer generations. By making it more accessible, engaging, and relevant, it can ensure that IK continues to thrive and meet the evolving needs of society. This, in turn, will spark increasing interest among younger generations to actively participate in the preservation and management of this valuable knowledge in Tanzania.

Conclusion

This chapter highlights IK management in the context of the Fourth Industrial Revolution. It is focused on discussing the impact of emerging technologies in managing IK. In the discussion it was noted that technologies in the 4IR could complement IK management and there is then a need for a holistic approach to integrate IK with technologies in the 4IR. Additionally, the integration of technologies in managing IK requires addressing the current challenges facing IK management in Tanzania, such as lack of recognition and cultural erosion. This can be made successful through the implementation of development strategies that are context-specific and consider the unique needs and values of the communities involved. In Tanzania, community based approaches to IK management have been implemented in various sectors, such as agriculture and natural resource management (Mwageni, 2011; Mwalyosi and Yanda, 2017). These approaches emphasize the importance of community participation in knowledge generation, sharing, and dissemination.

In this respect, 4IR has presented both opportunities and challenges for the management of IK in Tanzania where the emerging technologies in the 4IR have significant potentials for managing IK, including documentation, storage, dissemination, and commercialization of such knowledge. By integrating emerging technologies, such as IoT, blockchain, and data analytics, indigenous communities can leverage their knowledge to contribute to sustainable development. For example, IoT sensors can monitor ecological systems, blockchain can enable fair trade practices, and data analytics can provide valuable insights for ecosystem conservation. Hence, national strategies, such as the National Research and Innovation Policy, have also played a crucial role in leveraging emerging technologies for IK management, thereby enhancing competitiveness in the 4IR era. It is in this context that the government of Tanzania has recognized the importance of IK and has put in place various initiatives to promote the use of modern technologies in IK management. Such initiatives include the establishment of the Tanzania COSTECH and the National IK Systems Office (NIKSO). However, there are still challenges that need to be addressed to fully realize the potential of emerging technologies in IK management. These include the need for continued investment in research and development, infrastructure, and capacity building. Furthermore, the use of emerging technologies for IK management raises ethical and legal issues, such as the protection of traditional knowledge and the rights of indigenous peoples.

Future directions for research

As the use of emerging technologies in IK management is still in its infancy, it is important to conduct further research to fully understand their potential and limitations in the Tanzanian context. One area that warrants further investigation is the use of platforms brought by the 4IR in promoting and preserving IK. Research can also be conducted on how the use of emerging technologies in 4IR can be tailored to different communities and contexts, considering local beliefs, practices, and values. Another important area for research is the role of education and training in promoting the use of emerging technologies in the 4IR for IK management. Additionally, research can be conducted on how such technologies can be used to support the recognition and protection of IK.

References

Bimenyimana, E., Bizuru, E., Dusabeyezu, J., and Nshimiyimana, E. 2019. Ethnobotanical study of medicinal plants used in the treatment of malaria in Bugesera District, Rwanda. *Journal of Medicinal Plants Studies*, 7(4): 98–103.

Bodeker, G., Ong, C. K., and Grundy, C. 2007. *Traditional Medicine: A Global Perspective*. Geneva: World Health Organisation.

Brown, S. E., Miller, D. C., Ordonez, P. J. and Baylis, K. 2018. Evidence for the impacts of agroforestry on agricultural productivity, ecosystem services, and human well-being in high-income countries: A systematic map protocol. *Environmental Evidence*, 7: 24.

Chambers, R., Pacey, A., and Thrupp, L. A. 1989. *Farmer First: Farmer Innovation and Agricultural Research*. London: Routledge.

Chen, L., Zhang, J., Wang, Y., and Wang, L. 2020. The protection of indigenous knowledge under the influence of the Fourth Industrial Revolution. *Journal of Intellectual Property Rights*, 25(3): 182–189.

Chui, M., Manyika, J., and Miremadi, M. 2016. Where machines could replace humans and where they can't (yet). *McKinsey Quarterly*. Retrieved from https://www.mckinsey.com/business-functions/mckinsey-digital/our-insights/where-machines-could-replace-humans-and-where-they-cant-yet. Accessed November 17, 2022.

CIAT. 2018. Mapping soil fertility with indigenous knowledge in Tanzania. Retrieved from https://www.ciatnews.cgiar.org/2018/08/17/mapping-soil-fertility-with-indigenous-knowledge-in-tanzania/. Accessed October 3, 2022.

CIKOD. n.d. Centre for Indigenous Knowledge and Organisational Development. Retrieved from http://www.cikod.org/. Accessed February 20, 2023.

COSTECH. 2018. Indigenous knowledge systems. Retrieved from https://www.costech.or.tz/indigenous-knowledge-systems/. Accessed December 19, 2022.

COSTECH. n.d-a. Science, Technology and Innovation (STI). Retrieved from http://www.costech.or.tz/science-technology-and-innovation-sti/. Accessed November 10, 2022.

COSTECH. n.d.-b. Tanzania Open Data Initiative (TODI). Retrieved from http://www.costech.or.tz/tanzania-open-data-initiative-todi/. Accessed January 11, 2023.

DeVore, J., Blackmore, C., and Murphy, S. 2019. GIS as a tool for integrating traditional ecological knowledge and western science in natural resource management. *Environmental Management*, 63(3): 358–367.

Dixit, U. and Goyal, V. C. 2011. Traditional knowledge from and for elderly. *Indian Journal of Traditional Knowledge*, 10(3): 429–438.

Dube, K., and Mutanga, O. 2020. Indigenous knowledge and the fourth industrial revolution: Implications for Africa's development agenda. In *Indigenous Knowledge and the Sustainable Development Goals* (pp. 205–222). London: Springer.

Food and Agriculture Organization (FAO). 2019. Indigenous knowledge and its contribution to sustainable development. Retrieved from http://www.fao.org/3/ca6687en/CA6687EN.pdf. Accessed November 21, 2022.

Goldman, M. J., Roque de Pinho, J., Perry, R., and Maginnis, S. 2010. Integrating customary management into national policy and legal frameworks in Tanzania: Implications for community-based wildlife management in developing countries. *Environmental Science and Policy*, 13(2): 164–172.

HakiElimu. n.d. Indigenous knowledge and learning (IKL). Retrieved from http://www.hakielimu.org/index.php?option=com_content&view=article&id=75&Itemid=150. Accessed January 27, 2023.

Hunn, E. S., Etkin, N. L., and Turner, N. J. 2010. Introduction: Indigenous peoples' innovations in sustainable harvesting and management of biodiversity for traditional medicine. *Journal of Ethnobiology and Ethnomedicine*, 6(1): 1–12.

Iwata, J. J. and Hoskins, R. G. M. 2017. Managing indigenous knowledge in Tanzania: A business perspective. In P. Jain and N. Mnjama (Eds.), *Managing*

Knowledge Resources and Records in Modern Organizations. Hershey: IGI Global Publishers.

Kagera Basin Organisation (KBO). n.d. Indigenous knowledge systems and practices (IKSP). Retrieved from http://www.kagera.org/iksp.html. Accessed February 20, 2023.

Kapinga, G. M., Buberwa, J., and Sangeda, A. Z. 2020. Challenges and opportunities of indigenous knowledge in Tanzania: The role of digital platforms in indigenous knowledge management. *International Journal of Advanced Research in Computer Science and Software Engineering*, 10(11): 97–103.

Kasente, D., Muwanguzi, A., and Masaba, G. 2019. Emerging technologies and the preservation of indigenous knowledge in Africa. *Journal of Education and Practice*, 10(9): 129–135.

Kavishe, F. P., Kamala, J. M., Kimaro, H. C., and Mvuma, B. M. 2021. Agriculture 4.0: A review of artificial intelligence applications in agriculture. In *2021 IEEE International Conference on Emerging Technologies and the Internet of Things (ETIOT)* (pp. 1–7).

Kikwilu, E. N. 2019. Indigenous knowledge, cultural practices and climate change adaptation: A case of the Maasai pastoralists in Northern Tanzania. *International Journal of Climate Change Strategies and Management*, 11(4): 501–518.

Komba, C. M. 2020. Technological advancements in agriculture in Tanzania: An analysis of opportunities and challenges. *Journal of Agricultural Extension and Rural Development*, 12(3): 61–73.

Lwoga, E. 2009. Application of knowledge management approaches and information and communication technologies to manage indigenous knowledge in the agricultural sector in selected districts of Tanzania. Doctoral thesis. Pietermaritzburg: University of KwaZulu-Natal.

Machumu, H. 2016. Promoting and preserving indigenous knowledge systems in Tanzania: The role of non-governmental organisations. In *Indigenous Knowledge and the Environment in Africa and North America* (pp. 67–78). New York: Palgrave Macmillan.

Makate, C. 2019. Local institutions and indigenous knowledge in adoption and scaling of climate-smart agricultural innovations among sub-Saharan smallholder farmers. *International Journal of Climate Change Strategies and Management*, 12(2): 270–287.

Mbilinyi, B. P. 2010. Indigenous knowledge management: Challenges and opportunities for indigenous knowledge holders in Tanzania. *The Electronic Journal of Knowledge Management*, 8(1): 71–80.

Mbwambo, L. 2018. Indigenous knowledge systems and management practices in Tanzania. In *Indigenous Knowledge Systems and Practices in Africa* (pp. 149–161). New York: Palgrave Macmillan.

Mhando, D. 2004. The role of traditional arts in building local economies in Tanzania. *Journal of Social Development in Africa*, 19(2): 113–133.

Mkandawire, A., Otiato, R., and Wahome, R. 2019. Mobile phones, social media, and indigenous knowledge dissemination in Africa. *International Journal of Information Management*, 44: 98–107.

Moshi, M. J., Otieno, D. F., Weisheit, A., and Mbabazi, P. K. 2010. Ethnomedicine of the Kagera Region, northwestern Tanzania. Part 2: The medicinal plants used in Katoro Ward, Bukoba District. *Journal of Ethnobiology and Ethnomedicine*, 6(1): 1–16.

Msuya, J. 2007. Challenges and opportunities in the protection and preservation of indigenous knowledge in Africa. In R. Capurro, J. J. Britz, T. J. D. Bothma, and B. C. Bester (Eds.), *Africa Reader on Information Ethics* (pp. 343–349). Pretoria: Department of Information Science, University of Pretoria.

Mugambi, E. N. and Karugu, W. N. 2017. Effect of entrepreneurial marketing on performance of real estate enterprises: A case of Optiven Limited in Nairobi, Kenya. *International Academic Journal of Innovation, Leadership and Entrepreneurship*, 2(1): 46–70.

Mutula, S. M., and van Brakel, P. 2019. Indigenous knowledge and the Fourth Industrial Revolution: Opportunities and challenges for information management in Africa. *Journal of Librarianship and Information Science*, 51(1): 162–173.

Mwageni, E. A. 2011. Participatory knowledge management: An approach to empowering communities in Tanzania. *Journal of Knowledge Management Practice*, 12(2): 1–11.

Mwalyosi, R. B., and Yanda, P. Z. 2017. Community participation in indigenous knowledge systems: A strategy for conservation and management of natural resources in Tanzania. *Journal of Environmental Science and Management*, 20(2): 39–49.

Mwansasu, B. 2002. Indigenous knowledge and its implications for education: A case study of Tanzania. *International Journal of Lifelong Education*, 21(6): 561–572.

Nabalegwa, M.W., Asaba, J., Othieno, E. & Nabatta, C. 2020. Adoption of water conservation technologies among small scale farmers in Lwengo district-Uganda. *African Journal of Inter/Multidisciplinary Studies*, 1(1): 84–96.

NACTE. 2021. About NACTE. Retrieved from https://www.nacte.go.tz/about-nacte. Accessed March 4, 2023.

Nan, M., Lun, Y., Qingwen, M., Keyu, B., and Wenhua, L. 2021.The significance of traditional culture for agricultural biodiversity: Experiences from GIAHS. *Journal of Resources and Ecology*, 12(4): 453–461.

Ndayizeye, R., Sibomana, E., Nyaziyose, I., Conard, C. J., and Cartledge, P. 2019. Neonatal antibiotic use at a district and teaching hospital in Rwanda: A retrospective descriptive study. *Rwanda Medical Journal*, 76(2): 1–6.

Ngulube, P. 2014. The role of modern technology in the preservation and promotion of indigenous knowledge: The case of the Tanzania Traditional

Knowledge Digital Library. *International Journal of Information Management*, 34(1): 28–35.

Nhemachena, A., Makumbe, M., and Ndlovu-Gatsheni, S. 2019. Indigenous knowledge systems and decolonization in Africa: The case of Zimbabwe and Tanzania. In S. Ndlovu-Gatsheni, E. Mawere, and K. Tawodzera (Eds.), *Decolonising the Academy in Africa* (pp. 195–215). Bamenda, Cameroon: Langaa RPCIG.

Njau, P. N. 2016. Preserving indigenous knowledge: A challenge for Tanzania. *International Journal of Humanities and Social Science Research*, 6(1): 30–35.

Nkya, A. M., Komba, S. S., and Mbise, E. R. 2021. Current challenges facing indigenous knowledge in Tanzania and their implications on socio-economic development. *International Journal of Indigenous Knowledge Systems*, 1(1): 1–12.

Nnko, J. 2017. Indigenous knowledge and practices in Tanzania: The case of the Kuria people. *Journal of Indigenous and Traditional Community Health*, 24(3): 1–8.

Nnko, M. A., and Nyange, D. W. 2020. Indigenous knowledge systems: A review of concepts, definitions, and theoretical framework. *Journal of Education and Practice*, 11(12): 124–129.

Sawe, B. E. 2021. The Fourth Industrial Revolution and its potential for Africa: A review. *Journal of Innovation and Entrepreneurship*, 10(1): 1–14.

Schwab, K. 2016. The Fourth Industrial Revolution. World Economic Forum. Retrieved from https://www.weforum.org/about/the-fourth-industrial-revolution-by-klaus-schwab. Accessed February 20, 2023.

Tengia-Kessy, A., and Mushi, H. R. 2018. Indigenous knowledge systems and sustainable development in Tanzania. *Journal of Indigenous Social Development*, 7(1): 58–73.

TIRDO. Innovation and Technology Development (ITD). Retrieved from https://www.tirdo.or.tz/innovation-and-technology-development/. Accessed December 23, 2022.

UNDP. 2008. Indigenous knowledge management: A framework for UNDP. United Nations Development Programme.

UNDP. 2021. Tanzania Accelerator Lab. Retrieved from: https://acceleratorlabs.undp.org/tanzania/. Accessed November 21, 2022.

UNESCO. n.d. Local and indigenous knowledge systems (IKS). Retrieved from https://en.unesco.org/links. Accessed January 15, 2023.

UNESCO. 2002. Local and indigenous knowledge systems. Retrieved from https://en.unesco.org/themes/local-and-indigenous-knowledge-systems. Accessed February 18, 2023.

University of Dodoma. 2021. Bachelor of indigenous knowledge science (BIKS). Retrieved from https://www.udom.ac.tz/programmes/bachelor-of-indigenous-knowledge-science-biks/. Accessed February 27, 2023.

URT. 2005. Tanzania national strategy for growth and reduction of poverty: National report 2005. United Republic of Tanzania.

WIPO. n.d. Traditional knowledge division. Retrieved from https://www.wipo.int/tk/en/. Accessed December 16, 2022.

World Bank 2021. Tanzania: Towards a digital economy. Retrieved from https://www.worldbank.org/en/country/tanzania/publication/tanzania-towards-a-digital-economy. Accessed November 13, 2022.

Chapter 10

Developing Human Capital for Competitiveness: A Study of Singapore's Artificial Intelligence Apprenticeship Program (AIAP) from a Systems Thinking Viewpoint

Ashish Kumar, Kirankumar S. Momaya, Laurence Liew, and Sean Shao Wei Lam

Abstract

The human capital required to develop and sustain competitive advantage in Artificial Intelligence (AI) is in short supply globally. In this context, Singapore's Artificial Intelligence Apprenticeship Program (AIAP) is a leading example of a public–private partnership that has fostered the growth of an indigenous talent pool in Singapore. We aim to elicit the systemic structure of AIAP in the form of a Causal Loop Diagram (CLD), and to derive actionable insights to support policymakers, managers, and researchers who are interested in the development of AI talents. Our CLD reflects the diversity of factors and their interactions that need to come together to make AIAP work. The design of AIAP reflects a pragmatic partnership between stakeholders who are interested in national competitiveness, making their own industries and firms more competitive, furthering the use of AI, and developing careers in a field with promising future prospects. To our knowledge, this is the first study of AIAP from a systems thinking viewpoint. The shared understanding of stakeholders reflected in the CLD provides insight for policymakers who seek to develop national competitiveness through investment in human capital for AI.

Keywords: Artificial intelligence, human capital building, systems thinking, causal loop diagrams, country competitiveness rankings, cooperation strategies, public–private partnership (PPP), Singapore

Introduction

The Fourth Industrial Revolution (4IR) has been described as a fusion of technologies that is blurring the lines between the physical, digital, and biological spheres (Schwab, 2015). It is seen as a disruption that presents possibilities for sustainable productivity gains, while it also raises concerns of rising inequity (Fox and Signé, 2022). Furthermore, 4IR will be powered by reinforcing breakthroughs in many fields such as artificial intelligence (AI), robotics, the Internet of Things (IoT), nanotechnology, biotechnology, material science, energy storage, additive manufacturing, and quantum computing. AI through digitalization stimulates digital innovation (Nambisan *et al.*, 2020) and the applications of AI in furthering 4IR are diverse, ranging from computer vision for industrial automation to disease identification and diagnosis (Chakraborty *et al.*, 2022). While there are differing views (optimists, pessimists, pragmatists, and doubters) on the likely scenarios resulting from the adoption of AI (Makridakis, 2017), there is greater consensus that it will indeed profoundly impact nations and firms; hence, there is a need for effective governance and regulation (Haenlein and Kaplan, 2019; Korinek and Stiglitz, 2021) and AI is a driver of national competitive advantage (Lee, 2018; Waltzman *et al.*, 2020).

Recurring uncertainties including financial crises, climate change, the US–China trade war, and the COVID-19 pandemic point to the need for better strategy and international systems, where growing contributions from Asian economies can be integrated (Cho and Moon, 2022). As new dimensions of international competition over the past decades emerge, they demand innovation in assessing and enhancing competitiveness (across levels from country and industry to firm) and strategy (Moon, 2016; Teece, 2020; Yin *et al.*, 2022). From a national as well as an industry perspective, driving forces of competitiveness are changing in the face of discontinuities, such as the COVID-19 global pandemic that has disrupted not only supply chains but also the trust among and within countries (Cho and Moon, 2022).

Recognizing the limitations of Porter's Diamond Model (Porter, 1990) in explaining competitiveness, several extensions have been developed, such as the model developed by the Institute of Policy Studies (IPS) (Cho *et al.*, 2009). The competitiveness Assets–Processes–Performance (APP) framework (Ajitabh and Momaya, 2004) has been proposed for contexts of competitiveness ranging from software engineering (Bhardwaj *et al.*, 2011) to emerging industries such as nanotech (Momaya, 2011). Human capital is central in these models and the sources of national competitiveness can be derived from both physical factors[1] and human factors.[2] In line with the importance accorded to human capital in these frameworks (Ajitabh and Momaya, 2004; Cho *et al.*, 2009), a recent review finds that 4IR, with AI as one of its drivers, brings major changes to the labor market through the reduction in jobs allocated to human labor, the allocation of labor to alternate higher added value areas, and increasing demand for a labor force endowed with the skills required by new technologies (Sima *et al.*, 2020).

Human factors play a more critical role in enhancing the competitiveness of countries than physical factors (Cho and Moon, 2022), particularly in countries with limited natural resources and physical factors (Porter, 2011). However, the human capital required to develop and sustain competitive advantage in AI is in short supply worldwide (Su *et al.*, 2021). In this context, Singapore's Artificial Intelligence Apprenticeship Program (AIAP) is a leading example of a public–private partnership that has fostered the growth of an indigenous talent pool in Singapore. Though Singapore is already globally competitive in terms of human talent (Appendix A.2, Table A.2), AIAP was born out of a specific need to develop human capital in AI (AI Singapore [AISG], 2023a).

Cooperative strategies have relevance across levels (from country to industries and firms) for innovation. The role of cooperative strategies for innovation has been explored in the context of emerging industries (Momaya, 2009) and global value chains (Yin *et al.*, 2022). Similarly,

---

[1] Physical factors consist of demand conditions, related industries, factor conditions, and business context.

[2] Human factors consist of workers, politicians and bureaucrats, entrepreneurs, and professionals.

cooperation among key stakeholders for competitiveness in an emerging industry such as AI can play an enabling role but has been researched less. The strategic aspects of the management of technology and innovation (MoT) discipline are emerging as a hot topic (Srivastava and Jain, 2023) and demand cooperative strategies for effective implementation.

The linkages of 4IR and AI to competitiveness, rising inequality in an era threatened by the disruptions mentioned above, and the centrality of human capital as an enabler of advancement in AI suggest that the problem that AIAP attempts to solve is a complex phenomenon. Thus, policymakers, managers, and researchers would benefit from an in-depth understanding of the complex inter-relationships within the technology and education ecosystem that underpins it. Systems thinking recognizes that certain systems such as efforts to improve human capital have structures that result in "policy resistance," meaning that actions taken to solve problems end up exacerbating them because of unintended consequences (Forrester, 1987; Sterman, 2000).

Understanding the relationship between the structure of a complex system and its behavior can result in a better understanding of the system and offer actionable insights needed to produce more desirable behavior patterns (Meadows, 2008). Causal Loop Diagrams (CLDs) are useful systems thinking tools to study the interactions and understand the emergent behavior of complex systems. CLDs have been used to map the CASE (Connected, Autonomous, Shared, and Electric) technological disruptions in the automotive retail industry in South Korea (Kim *et al.*, 2021) and to explain the industrial cluster effect through manpower, money, technology, and market flows on competitiveness in general (Lin *et al.*, 2006). In other applications, they have been applied to study the competitiveness of particular industries (Nguyen *et al.*, 2017), the effect of a soft factor such as reputation on competitiveness (Brønn and Brønn, 2015), and Amazon's business model diversifications (Haefliger *et al.*, 2020).

The unfolding of 4IR, powered by numerous technological innovations (e.g., computational efficiency), AI, Internet of Things, and 3D printing (Kim and Hwang, 2022), is a complex phenomenon with implications for the competitiveness of nations, industries, and firms. In this case study, we utilize CLD as a systems thinking tool to understand the complex system that underpins human capital development with a specific focus on AI through Singapore's AIAP. To the best of our knowledge, this is the first study that applies systems thinking, encapsulated in a CLD, to study the dynamics of human capital development in AI for Singapore.

AIAP is the first unique collaborative program that brings together multiple stakeholders — governments, academicians, firms, research institutions, and potential AI engineers — to take collective action that enhances the future-readiness of the AI ecosystem in Singapore through the development of an AI-ready workforce. In this case study, our objectives are two-fold: (1) to elicit the systemic structure of AIAP and (2) to encapsulate this systemic structure in the form of a CLD to derive actionable insights to support policymakers, managers, and researchers who are interested in the development of AI talents. We aim to present an initial analysis of the systemic structure through CLDs to identify the enablers of AI talent development with the AIAP as a specific case.

Systems model for AI talent development

CLDs are tools that enable systems thinking practitioners to elicit a shared understanding of relationships and assumptions and serve as visual representations of mental models that can "facilitate understanding, dynamic reasoning, and formal modeling" (through quantifiable simulation models) (Crielaard *et al.*, 2022; Ford, 2019: 370). In this context, mental models are "relationships and assumptions about a system held in a person's mind" (Ford, 2019: 375). They typically form the first step toward the formalization of organizational dynamics to facilitate quantifiable simulations to derive robust strategies through rigorous scenario planning and analysis (Groesser and Schaffernicht, 2012). A brief introduction to CLD modeling is provided in Appendix A.1.

AIAP is a 9-month long program offered by AI Singapore (AISG) in collaboration with the Singapore Infocomm Media Development Authority (IMDA) to develop a pipeline of indigenously trained AI engineers (AISG, 2023a). Applicants having a base level of skills at the point of selection are first evaluated. These skills can then be acquired through self-learning in accordance with a "field guide" (AISG, 2023b). In the course of the AIAP, apprentices are then first put through a two-month intensive training and deployed on real-world projects based on industrial problems for which Commercial Off The Shelf (COTS) solutions do not exist. In 2023, AIAP admitted its 13th, 14th, and 15th group of apprentices.

The development of the CLD representing the systemic structure of AIAP has been led by one of this chapter's authors. Three interviews were conducted with stakeholders of AIAP (the developer of AIAP, an alumnus of AIAP, and a current apprentice of AIAP). For reference, Appendix A.3 provides the complete text of these interviews. Based on these interviews, and also drawing from open source information available in the public domain on AIAP (AISG, 2023a; AISG 2023b), an initial CLD was created. The finalized CLD, adopted after a review by this chapter's four authors together with the public domain knowledge base, comprises 21 variables organized in a network composed of four reinforcing loops and one balancing loop. We explain the CLD through four phases of development (Figures 1–4). Figures 1 and 2 (baseline dynamics) describe

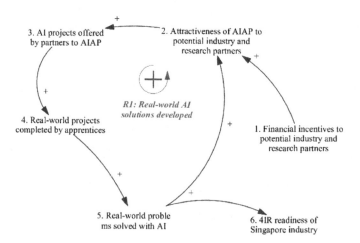

Figure 1.   Real-world AI solutions developed (baseline dynamics)

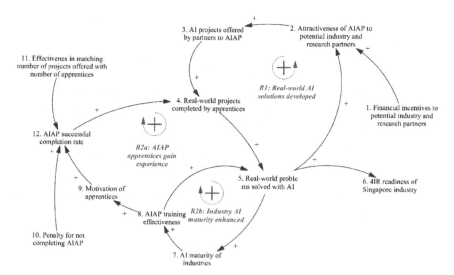

Figure 2.   Industry AI maturity is enhanced with human factors (baseline dynamics with human factors)

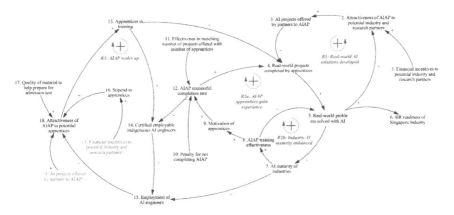

Figure 3.   AIAP scales up (scaling up)

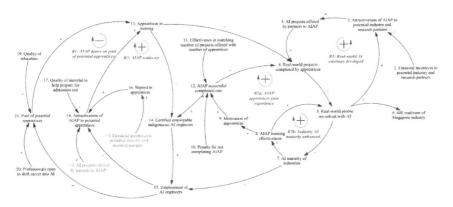

Figure 4.   Sustaining the AI industry through structured development of an AI-ready workforce (sustainability)

the processes underpinning the importance of human factors corresponding with the development of the AI industry within Singapore. Figure 3 (scaling up) further describes the expansion of the AI industry in conjunction with the scaling up of the AIAP. Figure 4 (sustainability) provides a more complete outlook of the pool of potential apprentices that can continue to sustain the next generation of AI talents in driving the AI industry within Singapore. Analyses 1–4 provide the explanation for the dynamic structures underpinning the evolution and success of the AIAP and Table 1 summarizes the more relevant feedback loops and the impact of the AIAP program.

Table 1.   Summary of feedback loops in the CLD.

Loop	Description	Variables
R1	Real-world AI solutions developed	$2 \rightarrow 3 \rightarrow 4 \rightarrow 5 \rightarrow 2$
R2a	AIAP apprentices gain experience	$5 \rightarrow 7 \rightarrow 8 \rightarrow 9 \rightarrow 12 \rightarrow 4 \rightarrow 5$
R2b	Industry AI maturity enhanced	$5 \rightarrow 7 \rightarrow 8 \rightarrow 5$
R3	AIAP scales up	$15 \rightarrow 18 \rightarrow 13 \rightarrow 14 \rightarrow 15$
B1	AIAP draws on pool of potential apprentices	$13 \rightarrow 14 \rightarrow 15 \rightarrow 21 \rightarrow 13$

Analysis 1

Figure 1 shows the key relationships that can facilitate the real-world successful implementation of AI solutions being developed in Singapore. In addition to human capital, AI Singapore provides funding of up to SG$330,000 per project offered by an industry or research partner under AIAP (the partner is required to match the funding from AI Singapore). Variable 1 labeled "Financial incentives to potential AIAP industry and research partners" in Figure 1 refers to this joint funding. Joint investments into the development of AI solutions increase the need for them to be impactful for the partners (Bauer 2018; Thurbon and Weiss 2021). As Variable 1 increases, this makes Variable 2, labeled "Attractiveness of AIAP to potential... partners", as well as Variable 3, labeled "AI projects offered by the partners to AIAP", higher. As Variable 4 labeled "Real-world projects completed by AIAP apprentices" grows, Variable 5, labeled "Real-world problems solved with AI", also increases. The latter boosts the attractiveness of AIAP to potential partners, while enhancing Variable 6, labeled "4IR readiness of Singapore industry". The circular sequence of Variables 2, 3, 4, 5, and back to 2 form the Loop R1, which is reinforcing, i.e., increasing one of the variables along this loop will produce positive feedback.

The CLD describing the baseline dynamics is aligned with existing findings. For example, Guan and Yam (2015) find that market-driven financial incentives were more effective in stimulating the innovation performance of firms than centrally planned direct funding in China during the country's period of economic transition in the 1990s. Furthermore, in the United States of America, Bell *et al.* (2019) show that some financial incentives have limited potential to increase innovation, while "increasing exposure to innovation (e.g., through mentorship programs)" potentially has a much higher impact. Supporting the hypotheses that the successful solution of real-world problems enhances 4IR readiness, Davenport and Ronanki (2018) demonstrate that "moon shot" projects in AI are less likely to be successful than "low hanging fruit" projects focused on business needs; according to Lee and Lee (2022), "rapid and flexible commercialization capability" is the most pivotal factor among those that strengthen the success of Korean venture companies in 4IR. Joint investment in projects is an instance of cooperation, a solution to the problem that "during the innovation process firms might be limited by their knowledge sets or internal resources" (Freire and Gonçalves, 2022: 3370).

Analysis 2

In Figure 2, Reinforcing Loops R2a and R2b are added to describe the impact in consideration of AI talents. As Variable 5 increases, the Variable 7, labeled "AI maturity of industries," is enhanced, leading to greater Variable 8, labeled "AIAP training effectiveness". This, then, has a positive effect on the Variable 9, called "Motivation of apprentice," bolstering Variable 12, labeled "AIAP successful completion rate". Variable 10 labeled "Penalty for not completing AIAP" refers to the financial penalty that must be paid by an AIAP apprentice who does not complete the apprenticeship successfully. Along with Variable 11, which is labeled "Effectiveness in matching the number of projects with the number of apprentices," it has a positive effect on Variable 12.

Variable 11 refers to the ability of AISG to ensure that there is an optimal balance between the number of real-world projects offered and the number of apprentices available at that point of time. A sub-optimal ratio of projects to apprentices would adversely affect the quality of the solution, or the quality of learning. As Variable 12 increases, so does Variable 4, labeled "Real-world projects completed by AIAP apprentices," which then feeds back into Variable 5. Thus, the circularity of Variables 5, 7, 8, 9, 12, 4, and back to 5 forms the Reinforcing Loop R2a labeled "AIAP apprentices gain experience." Similarly, the circularity of Variables 5, 7, 8, and back to 5 forms a smaller Reinforcing Loop R2b labeled "Industry AI maturity enhanced," which represents the enhancement of the AI maturity of Singapore's industry. It is worth noting that frameworks and approaches for measuring AI maturity are available (Chen *et al.*, 2022; Fountaine *et al.*, 2019; Lichtenthaler, 2020).

Analysis 3

Figures 1 and 2 reveal the underlying basis of the AIAP: its apprentices gaining experience while industry AI maturity is enhanced. In Figure 3, we further add Variables 13 through 18 and their associated relationships to discuss the scaling up of the AIAP. The Reinforcing Loop R3 labeled "AIAP scales up" (along with its adjacent variables), is introduced. As Variable 15 labeled "Employment of AI engineers" expands, Variable 18, labeled "Attractiveness of AIAP to potential apprentices," likewise increases; this in turn enhances Variable 13, called "Apprentices in training". This then has a positive effect on Variable 14, labeled "Certified employable indigenous AI engineers,", which is then directly associated with Variable 15. Thus, Variables 15, 18, 13, 14, and back to 15 form the Reinforcing Loop R3 labeled "AIAP scales up."

Here, a key distinguishing feature of the AIAP is Variable 16, titled "Stipend to apprentices," that is competitive with market salaries during the program, which helps to stimulate interest in AIAP among potential apprentices. The prospect of working on Variable 3 labeled "AI projects offered by partners to AIAP" with positive impact on business value, as opposed to synthetic data sets, also attracts potential apprentices; the pragmatic approach followed by AISG of helping candidates follow a structured capability development path (see Variable 17) is also a factor in increasing the attractiveness of AIAP. By looking at the larger perspective of enhancing industry competitiveness, stakeholders in Singapore have taken the path of providing AIAP apprentices a means of sustaining themselves even as they shift into a field that holds the promise of higher future earnings through the dynamics of scaling up AIAP.

Analysis 4

The addition of Variables 19 through 21 in Figure 4 creates the first balancing feedback loop to the CLD that can impact the sustainability of the AIAP.

Figure 4 shows that Variable 21, labeled "Pool of potential apprentices," which in itself is positively influenced by Variable 15 ("Employment of AI engineers"), Variable 20 ("Professionals open to shifting career into AI"), and Variable 19 ("Quality of education"), will have an impact on the sustainability of the AIAP. While Variable 15 is linked to the activities under AIAP itself, Variable 19 reflects the accumulated stock of Singapore's past successes in providing high quality education and Variable 20 reflects the Singaporean government's active promotion of AI as an enabler of future competitiveness and a field with good career prospects. Variable 21 and Variable 18 together have positive effects on Variable 13. Thus, Variables 13, 14, 15, 21, and back to 13 form the Balancing Loop B1, so named as it has a single negative link.

The more the apprentices drawn from the pool, the smaller the pool becomes (other variables being constant). The combination of Reinforcing Loop R3 and the Balancing Loop B1 is an example of a systemic structure that is likely to produce S-shaped growth (Meadows, 2008) across the sustaining phase of the program. This also indicates that growth cannot persist indefinitely without the corresponding growth of AI technologies and markets. Regardless, the recent advent of natural language processing through Large Language Models (LLM) provides some evidence that AI technology and markets have a large room for continuous development and sustainable growth in driving the economic growth of nations, depending on whether the balance of AI's application tilts toward augmentation or elimination of human effort (Brynjolfsson, 2023).

Implications

The systemic structure that sustains AIAP throughout the development of a sustainable AI industry has implications at the policy and managerial level, which we will discuss in this section. We will also discuss the limitations of the current study with suggestions for further research.

Policy implications

Our proposed CLD has four interlocking reinforcing loops, reflecting the diversity of factors that need to come together to make a program such as AIAP work. The successful implementation and sustenance of AIAP must be seen in a larger context. In Singapore, human resource strategies have been continuously revised and adjusted in conjunction with other national strategic economic policies, with the policy infrastructure for human capital development resting on two pillars. These are a tripartite approach including employers, unions, and governments and a multidepartment approach involving all relevant government agencies (Osman-Gani, 2004). For example, in 1998, a report titled *Manpower 21: Vision of a Talent Capital* was produced through a partnership among the government ministries, unions, and more than 100 participants from the private sector (Ministry of Manpower Singapore, 1999). The report was driven by the idea of Singapore as a "talent capital" where actions are taken to develop skills and practices relevant to the new economy. Such a pragmatic practice is provided by the Skills Development Levy (SDL), collected by the Central Provident Fund Board on behalf of the SkillsFuture Agency (Central Provident Fund Board, 2023). The SDL is a compulsory levy paid by employers for all employees, including foreigners, and channeled to a Skills Development Fund. Furthermore, as reflected in the CLD presented in the previous section, the pool of professionals who are potential apprentices is a key ingredient to AIAP; the transition of the education system from one that was "survival-driven" (Goh and Gopinathan, 2008) to a high- performing education system (HPES) (Deng and Gopinathan, 2016; Tan and Ng, 2021) has an important role in this regard.

Policymakers seeking to develop programs equivalent to AIAP need to keep this larger context of interlocking and reinforcing mechanisms in mind, and develop a supporting ecosystem that channels financial, human, and information capital efficiently. Focusing on a single dimension, such as training, without linking it to industry AI maturity and the consequent wider benefits from solving of real-world problems as in the case of AIAP, will be counterproductive.

Policymakers in low- and middle-income countries should be particularly concerned about the potential of AI and related technologies that can result in significant divergence of national productivity (Alonso *et al.*, 2020). They could consider the local equivalents of AIAP, tailored to their contexts (e.g., city/federal/state level) where appropriate. Funding for translation of learning materials could be an important enabler in some contexts. In emerging countries, where capital is scarce, policymakers can benefit from selecting key geographic or industry clusters that have greater potential for deployment of human capital for AI solutions leading to 4IR readiness.

While the full contours of the impact of the current evolution of AI, such as the advent of successful LLMs, are not fully known yet (Birhane *et al.*, 2023), policymakers will be able to account for their disruptive capabilities through structured industry development programs. Mitchell and Krakauer (2023: 1) note that "(the) inner workings of these networks are largely opaque; even the researchers building them have limited intuitions about systems of such scale." Researchers from OpenAI (Eloundou *et al.*, 2023) assert that what the AI community calls a GPT, that is, a Generative Pre-trained Transformer (a type of LLM), is in fact, also what economic historians have traditionally called a GPT, i.e., a General Purpose Technology (technology, such as steam engines, that drove industrial revolutions). Alongside this, Marcus (2022) points out the possibility of "dark risks" from LLMs. Policymakers considering the development of programs like AIAP must be able to provide rapid responses to such disruptive innovations that could include developing the skill sets among apprentices and the framing of real-world problems. In the larger context of AI governance during this challenging cusp of evolution, there is a need for "plural institutional logics" and "public–private interaction" (Radu, 2021).

Managerial implications

Managers who seek to apply the principles of AIAP can benefit from understanding the main drivers of its sustenance. As a starting point, the CLD representing the systemic structure of AIAP has three exogenous variables that could be considered macro-level factors: financial incentives and joint investment to potential AIAP industry and research partners (which is Variable 1 of the CLD), long-term growth and short-term financial incentives to AIAP apprentices (Variable 12), quality of education (Variable 19), and professionals open to shift career into AI (Variable 20). Further, there are two exogenous variables, Variable 10 ("Penalty for not completing AIAP") and Variable 11 ("Effectiveness in matching number of projects with number of apprentices"), that are more tactical in nature.

The idea proposed by Dana Meadows (2008) on the points of leverage or "places to intervene in a system" is relevant here. The highest leverage is attained through aligning goals and changing and transcending paradigms. The overall incentives of AIAP are directed toward a new paradigm, that of developing a cohort of locally trained AI engineers by solving real-world problems in the local industry. Industry and research partners are supported, but they must have so-called "skin in the game." Similarly, apprentices are encouraged to work toward their own employability in a fast-changing environment. Apart from facing penalties for not completing their apprenticeships, the successful completion of a funded industry project would mean they will be highly desirable for the company that supported the AIAP project.

For managers in low AI maturity industries, there is a need to create business cases for investment in human capital development and to convince stakeholders of the financial returns from solving real-world problems. A core principle of AIAP is that all managers can benefit from emulating its systems thinking approach, with pragmatic partnership between stakeholders who are interested in national competitiveness, making their own industries and firms more competitive. This will in turn further the beneficent use of AI, and develop a competitive industry in a field that is rapidly evolving with promising future prospects. The alignment of goals of these stakeholders is a true achievement in synergy, where the whole is greater than the sum of its parts.

Limitations and Future Research

This study has limitations that point to opportunities for future research. The CLD presented here is an initial elucidation of the systemic structure of AIAP. We expect that the CLD will be a living document that may evolve through wider consultations with stakeholders. Our present CLD is based on the views of stakeholders and public material on AIAP. Empirical studies to test the hypothesized relationships would add to the understanding of the domains of human capital development in AI and 4IR readiness. There may be certain contexts in which specific loops need to be studied in more detail. For example, the Reinforcing Loop R1 could be the subject of study for those seeking to gain deeper insight into the choice of projects that maximize return on investment.

Our work is limited to qualitative analysis. Quantitative system dynamics modeling and simulation of the economic impact of human capital enhancement, which builds on the CLD presented here, presents further opportunities for researchers. A prospective quantitative study would operationalize the variables shown conceptually in the CLD and hence provide insight into the driving power of factors that influence the ultimate outcome, namely, the 4IR readiness of Singapore industry (Variable 6). Integrating such modeling with approaches that measure overall 4IR readiness (Lin *et al.*, 2019, 2020; Singapore Economic Development Board, 2020) would further help planners to quantify the benefits of developing human capital in AI.

Singapore's cooperative strategies to develop human capital and leverage it to differentiate and sustain competitiveness need adaptation for different contexts. From a larger perspective, research opportunities are perhaps in how to adapt such strategies for complex contexts in other countries. Singapore has existing stocks of human capital and digital competitiveness to play the platform roles, e.g., in global value chains (Yin *et al.*, 2022). How a city or state in a much more complex macro environment, perhaps without the benefit of these stocks, can execute a win–win cooperative strategy is also a potential topic for research.

A city-state such as Singapore may be able to transform human capital and enhance AI readiness much faster. At the same time, leaders in business, policy, and society in the more populous countries such as China, India, or Indonesia will need to think deeply about the responsible adaptation of their AI readiness initiatives to enhance the quality of the significantly larger human capital pool, while minimizing the negative spill-over effects of new technologies in the economy and society at scale. Mapping the context to tested frameworks such as the APP and IPS frameworks is another fertile topic for research.

Finally, we hope that our work stimulates the study on the role of programs such as AIAP in mitigating the effects of deglobalization, which may limit the effects of deglobalization on the manpower pool of small countries.

Conclusion

In the era of multiple discontinuities, skills and capabilities of human capital play a key role in strengthening competitiveness. A systems thinking view of Singapore's AIAP can provide useful insights for policy and management decision-making. Systematic development and evolution of such AI-centric manpower development programs and policies is a factor that gives Singapore higher strength and agility in shaping future competitiveness.

Acknowledgments

We would like to acknowledge Abigail Toh, Head of Marketing Communications, and Kevin Chng, Asst. Head of AIAP, at AISG, who helped us with inputs for this study. We would also like to acknowledge Karthik Prathaban (AIAP alumnus) and Yong Xianbin (current AIAP apprentice) for their inputs to the study as key stakeholders for the AIAP.

References

AI Singapore (AISG). 2023a. AI apprenticeship program. https://aisingapore.org/innovation/aiap/. Accessed April 23, 2023.

AI Singapore (AISG). 2023b. AIAP field guide. https://epoch.aisingapore.org/aiap-field-guide/. Accessed April 20, 2023.

Ajitabh, A. and Momaya, K. 2004. Competitiveness of firms: Review of theory, frameworks and models. *Singapore Management Review*, 26: 45–61.

Alonso, C., Berg, A., Kothari, S., Papageorgiou, C., and Rehman, S. 2020. Will the AI revolution cause a great divergence? IMF Working Paper No. 20/184. Available at SSRN: https://ssrn.com/abstract=3721209. Accessed April 10, 2023.

Bauer, M. 2018. Online platforms, economic integration and Europe's rent-seeking society: Why online platforms deliver on what EU governments fail to achieve (No. 9/2018). ECIPE Policy Brief. https://www.econstor.eu/handle/10419/202508. Accessed May 22, 2023.

Bell, A., Chetty, R., Jaravel, X., Petkova, N., and Van Reenen, J. 2019. Do tax cuts produce more Einsteins? The impacts of financial incentives versus exposure to innovation on the supply of inventors. *Journal of the European Economic Association*, 17(3): 651–677.

Bhardwaj, B. and Momaya, K. 2011. Drivers and enablers of corporate entrepreneurship: Case of a software giant from India. *Journal of Management Development*, 30: 187–205.

Birhane, A., Kasirzadeh, A., Leslie, D., and Wachter, S. 2023. Science in the age of large language models. *Nature Reviews Physics*, 5: 277–280.

Brønn, C. and Brønn, P. S. 2015. A systems approach to understanding how reputation contributes to competitive advantage, *Corporate Reputation Review*, 18: 69–86.

Brynjolfsson, E. 2023. The turing trap: The promise & peril of human-like artificial intelligence. In *Augmented Education in the Global Age* (pp. 103–116). Oxfordshire: Routledge.

Central Provident Fund Board. 2023. Skills development levy. https://www.cpf.gov.sg/employer/employer-obligations/skills-development-levy. Accessed April 15, 2023.

Chakraborty, U., Banerjee, A., Saha, J. K., Sarkar, N., and Chakraborty, C. 2022. *Artificial Intelligence and the Fourth Industrial Revolution*. Florida: CRC Press.

Chen, W., Liu, C., Xing, F., Peng, G., and Yang, X. 2022. Establishment of a maturity model to assess the development of industrial AI in smart manufacturing. *Journal of Enterprise Information Management*, 35: 701–728.

Cho, D. S. and Moon, H. C. 2022. Highlights of IPS national competitiveness research 2021. *The Competitiveness of Nations 1: Navigating the US–China Trade War and the COVID-19 Global Pandemic.* Singapore: World Scientific.

Cho, D. S., Moon, H. C. and Kim, M. Y. 2009 Does one size fit all? A dual double diamond approach to country-specific advantages. *Asian Business & Management*, 8: 83–102.

Crielaard, L., Uleman, J. F., Châtel, B. D., Epskamp, S., Sloot, P., and Quax, R. 2022. Refining the causal loop diagram: A tutorial for maximizing the contribution of domain expertise in computational system dynamics modeling. *Psychological Methods*, 12 (May): 1–33.

Davenport, T. H. and Ronanki, R. 2018. Artificial intelligence for the real world. *Harvard Business Review*, 96(1): 108–116.

Deng, Z. and Gopinathan, S. 2016. PISA and high-performing education systems: Explaining Singapores education success. *Comparative Education*, 52: 449–472.

Dettmer, H. W. 2018. *The Logical Thinking Process — An Executive Summary.* College Station, TX, USA: Virtualbookworm.com Publishing.

Eloundou, T., Manning, S., Mishkin, P., and Rock, D. 2023. Gpts are gpts: An early look at the labor market impact potential of large language models. arXiv preprint arXiv:2303.10130.

Ford, D. N. 2019. A system dynamics glossary, *System Dynamics Review*, 35: 369–379.

Forrester, J. W. 1987 Lessons from system dynamics modeling, *System Dynamics Review*, 3: 136–149.

Fountaine, T., McCarthy, B., and Saleh, T. 2019 Building the AI-powered organization, *Harvard Business Review*, 97: 62–73.

Fox, L. and Signé, L. 2022. From subsistence to disruptive innovation: Africa, the fourth industrial revolution, and the future of jobs. Brookings Institution Report. https://www.africaportal.org/publications/subsistence-disruptive-innovation-africa-fourth-industrial-revolution-and-future-jobs/. Accessed April 24, 2023.

Freire, J. A. F. and Gonçalves, E. 2022. Cooperation in innovative efforts: A systematic literature review. *Journal of the Knowledge Economy*, 13(4): 3364–3400.

Goh, C. B. and Gopinathan, S. 2008. Education in Singapore: Development since 1965. In B. Fredriksen & J. P. Tan (Eds.), *An African Exploration of the East Asian Education* (pp. 80–108). Washington, DC: The World Bank.

Groesser, S. N. and Schaffernicht, M. 2012. Mental models of dynamic systems: Taking stock and looking ahead. *System Dynamics Review*, 28(1): 46–68.

Guan, J. and Yam, R. C. 2015. Effects of government financial incentives on firms' innovation performance in China: Evidences from Beijing in the 1990s. *Research Policy*, 44(1): 273–282.

Haefliger, S., Hueller, F., and Reza, D. 2020. Customer complementarity in the digital space: Exploring Amazons business model diversification. *Academy of Management Proceedings*. New York: Academy of Management.

Haenlein, M. and Kaplan, A. 2019. A brief history of artificial intelligence: On the past, present, and future of artificial intelligence. *California Management Review*, 61: 5–14.

Kim, H. S. and Hwang, W. S. 2022. Absorption trajectories of 4IR technologies: Evidence from Korea. *Technology Analysis & Strategic Management*, 36(1): 105–121.

Kim, S., Connerton, T. P., and Park, C. 2021. Exploring the impact of technological disruptions in the automotive retail: A futures studies and systems thinking approach based on causal layered analysis and causal loop diagram. *Technological Forecasting and Social Change*, 172: 121024.

Korinek, A. and Stiglitz, J. E. 2021. Artificial intelligence, globalization, and strategies for economic development. National Bureau of Economic Research (NBER) Working Paper 28453. Available at https://www.nber.org/papers/w28453. Accessed April 10, 2023.

Lee, K. F. 2018. *AI Superpowers: China, Silicon Valley, and the New World Order*. Boston: Houghton Mifflin.

Lee, D. and Lee, S. 2022. A study of the competitiveness and development strategy of Korean venture companies in the fourth industrial revolution using SWOT/AHP. *Sustainability*, 14(9): 5154.

Lichtenthaler, U. 2020. Five maturity levels of managing AI: From isolated ignorance to integrated intelligence. *Journal of Innovation Management*, 8: 39–50.

Lin, C.-H., Tung, C.-M., and Huang, C.-T. 2006. Elucidating the industrial cluster effect from a system dynamics perspective. *Technovation*, 26: 473–482.

Lin, T.-C., Wang, K. J., and Sheng, M. L. 2020. To assess smart manufacturing readiness by maturity model: A case study on Taiwan enterprises. *International Journal of Computer Integrated Manufacturing*, 33: 102–115.

Lin, W., Low, M. Y., Chong, Y., and Teo, C. 2019. Application of SIRI for industry 4.0 maturity assessment and analysis. In *2019 IEEE International Conference on Industrial Engineering and Engineering Management (IEEM)*. IEEE.

Makridakis, S. 2017. The forthcoming artificial intelligence (AI) revolution: Its impact on society and firms. *Futures*, 90: 46–60.

Marcus, G. 2022. The dark risk of large language models. *Wired* December 2022. https://www.wired.co.uk/article/artificial-intelligence-language. Accessed May 10, 2023.

Ministry of Manpower, Singapore. 1999. *Manpower 21—Vision of a Talent Capital.*

Mitchell, M. and Krakauer, D. C. 2023. The debate over understanding in AI's large language models. *Proceedings of the National Academy of Sciences,* 120(13): e2215907120.

Meadows, D. H. 2008. *Thinking in Systems: A Primer.* White River Junction, Vermont (USA): Chelsea Green Publishing.

Momaya, K. 2009. Exploring cooperative strategies for innovation: Case of bio-pharmaceutical firms from India and Japan. *The Journal of Science Policy and Research Management,* 23: 327–338.

Momaya, K. 2011. Cooperation for competitiveness of emerging countries: Learning from a case of nanotechnology. *Competitiveness Review: An International Business Journal,* 21: 152–170.

Moon, H. C. 2016. *The Strategy for Korea's Economic Success.* Oxford: Oxford University Press.

Nambisan, S., Lyytinen, K., and Yoo, Y. 2020. Digital innovation: Towards a transdisciplinary perspective. *Handbook of Digital Innovation* (pp. 2–12). Cheltenham, UK: Edward Elgar Publishing.

Nguyen, T. V., Nguyen, N. C., and Bosch, O. J. 2017. Enhancing the competitive advantages of Vietnamese coffee through the exploration of causal loop modelling in the supply chain. *International Journal of Logistics Systems and Management,* 26: 17–33.

Osman-Gani, A. M. 2004. Human capital development in Singapore: An analysis of national policy perspectives. *Advances in Developing Human Resources,* 6: 276–287.

Porter, M.E. 1990. The competitive advantage of nations. *Harvard Business Review,* 90: 73–93.

Porter, M. E. 2011. *Competitive Advantage of Nations: Creating and Sustaining Superior Performance.* New York: Simon and Schuster.

Radu, R. 2021. Steering the governance of artificial intelligence: National strategies in perspective. *Policy and Society,* 40(2): 178–193.

Schwab, K. 2015. The fourth industrial revolution: What it means and how to respond? *Foreign Affairs.* December 2012.

Sima, V., Gheorghe, I. G., Subić, J., and Nancu, D. 2020. Influences of the industry 4.0 revolution on the human capital development and consumer behavior: A systematic review. *Sustainability,* 12: 4035.

Singapore Economic Development Board. 2020. The smart industry readiness index. https://www.edb.gov.sg/en/about-edb/media-releases-publications/advanced-manufacturing-release.html. Accessed April 24, 2023.

Srivastava, M. and Jain, K. 2023. Tracing Evolution of Management of Technology Discipline. *IEEE Transactions on Engineering Management.*

Sterman, J. 2000 *Business Dynamics: Systems Thinking and Modeling for a Complex World.* Boston: Irwin/McGraw-Hill.

Su, Z., Togay, G., and Côté, A.-M. 2021. Artificial intelligence: A destructive and yet creative force in the skilled labour market. *Human Resource Development International*, 24: 341–352.

Tan, C. and Ng, C. S. 2021. Cultivating creativity in a high-performing education system: The example of Singapore. *Journal of Curriculum and Pedagogy*, 18: 253–272.

Teece, D. J. 2020. Fundamental issues in strategy: Time to reassess. *Strategic Management Review*, 1: 103–144.

Thurbon, E. and Weiss, L. 2021. Economic statecraft at the frontier: Korea's drive for intelligent robotics. *Review of International Political Economy*, 28(1): 103–127.

Waltzman, R., Ablon, L., Curriden, C., Hartnett, G. S., Holliday, M. A., Ma, L., Nichiporuk, B., Scobell, A., and Tarraf, D. C. 2020. *Maintaining the Competitive Advantage in Artificial Intelligence And Machine Learning.* Santa Monica: RAND Corporation.

Yin, W., Seo, J., and Kwon, A. 2022. Building resilient global value chains in the pandemic era: A conceptual framework and case studies of Singapore and Vietnam. In D. S. Cho and H. C. Moon (Eds.), *The Competitiveness of Nations 1: Navigating the US–China Trade War and the COVID-19 Global Pandemic* (pp. 131–162). Singapore: World Scientific.

Appendix

A.1 Introduction to causal loop diagramming

CLDs follow certain conventions and practices as outlined by Sterman (2000). The variables in a CLD and the causal links between these variables are depicted as nodes and arrows, respectively. In Table A.1, an arrow with a positive polarity between two variables signifies that the driving variable has a causal link to the driven variable and that the relationship is a direct one. In contrast, an arrow with a negative polarity implies an inverse causal relationship.

A feedback loop is formed when there is a series of links such that a variable, through a set of connected causal links, "feeds back" to itself. Feedback loops may be either reinforcing or balancing. In a reinforcing loop, an increase in a variable sequentially affects other variables along the loop such that the combined effect is to further increase the originally increased variable. In a balancing loop, an increase in a variable has a series of effects that ultimately result in a decrease in the originally

Table A.1.   An explanation of CLD notation.

Visual Representation in a CLD	Interpretation	Example
X1 ⌒ + Y	Other things being equal, an increase (decrease) in X1 will make Y increase (decrease) to a level higher (lower) than Y would otherwise have been.	Demand for property ⌒ + Property price
X2 ⌒ − Y	Other things being equal, an increase (decrease) in X2 will make Y decrease (increase) to a level higher (higher) than Y would otherwise have been.	Supply of property ⌒ − Price of property

Source: Adapted from Sterman (2000).

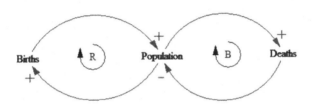

Figure A.1.   An illustration of feedback loops

increased variable. Figure A.1 illustrates a case with two simple feed-back loops. As there are more births (all else being equal), the population increases; as the population increases with all else being equal, there are more births. Thus, the two variables "Births" and "Population" have joined by links forming a reinforcing loop. Reinforcing feedback loops produce spiraling growth. Conversely, balancing loops, such as the one formed by the links connecting the variables "Deaths" and "Population," exhibit goal-seeking behavior. As seen in Figure A.1, feedback loops are labeled either "R" for reinforcing loops or "B" for balancing loops.

Reviewers of CLDs are encouraged to follow the approach of "legitimate reservations" (Dettmer, 2018), which is designed to provide checks for the soundness of logic diagrams.

A.2 A glimpse of relative positions of countries on the competitiveness factor "professionals"

Table A.2.   Relative position of select countries on the factor "Personal competence of professionals" in year 2021.

Countries by Size	Average Score of Sub-Criteria
Small	
Austria	69.14
Singapore	83.51
Switzerland	79.15
Medium	
France	44.32
Germany	67.80
Korea	66.20
United Kingdom	49.27
Large	
Canada	75.65
China	72.87
India	69.88
Japan	44.08
United States	73.99
Average of the sample	66.32

Notes: For personal competence of professionals, the five criteria are as follows: (1) education level, (2) the process of decision-making, (3) core competence, (4) the ability to manage opportunities, and (5) international experience.
Source: Adapted from National Competitiveness research 2021 (Cho and Moon, 2022).

A.3 Interviews with AIAP stakeholders

A.3.1 Interview with Laurence Liew, Director, AI Innovation, AI Singapore

Interview conducted by Ashish Kumar over video conference on April 17, 2023

1. *When was the first batch of AIAP apprentices admitted to the program, and how much time was spent in preparing for the commencement of the program?*
   AI Singapore (AISG) was launched in May 2017. The original "KPI" was to solve 100E problems, i.e., real-world problems posed by Singaporean firms. AI engineers were needed to work on these problems and there was a shortage of such engineers. AIAP was conceived to solve this practical issue around August 2017 and the first batch of AIAP apprentices was admitted in February 2018. A committed team was ready to mentor the apprentices. It was clear that the focus was not to "train" the apprentices but help them to learn on their own, with mentoring, and get to work.

2. *What are the main aims of AIAP today?*
   The main aim is to bring in Singaporeans who are at a certain level of technical competency. We can then "deep skill" them and get them working on 100E projects. We "over-train" people, meaning that we train more than the number strictly needed by AISG, so that we can benefit the industry when apprentices we are not able to hire join the industry. Within the team, we have grown from about 4 to about 40 AI engineers.

3. *Have these aims evolved since inception?*
   The aims remain unchanged.

4. *What measures/metrics do you use to assess how successful AIAP is?*
   The focus is on 100E projects and Singaporeans trained. 250 Singaporeans have been trained so far.

5. *What would you say are the main enablers that helped AIAP to scale up?*
   We started with the fundamentals: identifying people with the right attitude. Technical skills are also required. But we look for a certain attitude. Further, once the apprentices are with us, we look for those who are committed to grooming the next generation. We cannot match the salaries of the big tech companies. We can offer those who are passionate about making a difference the opportunity to do so. When these passionate engineers stay back with us, it is for a contract period of two years, over which they will train five to six batches. We encourage them to think of this as a kind of second national service.[3]

---

[3] https://www.mindef.gov.sg/web/portal/mindef/national-service/discover-ns. Accessed July 16, 2023.

6. *What were the main barriers in scaling up?*

We have to constantly match the number of real-world industry projects and the number of apprentices. This is a delicate balance. Further, the rapid rate of change makes it challenging to keep up with technology — obvious examples are in NLP and LLM.

7. *Are there factors specific to Singapore that contribute to the pool of potential AI apprentices here?*

Some factors are now widely available and hardly unique to Singapore. These include MOOCs and material on YouTube, and so on. What could be rare outside of Singapore is the co-funding approach. To those who are willing to learn, the government channels funding. Apprentices are paid a stipend of SG$3500 to SG$5500 (US$2600 to 4100) per month, depending on their credentials.

8. *What makes AIAP attractive to apprentices?*

It is mainly real-world projects that help them move beyond artificial data sets like New York taxis and so on. The stipend also makes the apprenticeship sustainable for them.

9. *What helps AIAP apprentices to complete the program? Are there significant dropouts?*

Once they are in, apprentices are in a culture of openness and collaboration. There are people from different domains, and there are shared goals. If technical weaknesses are found, help is provided. There are financial penalties for dropping out — the stipend paid has to be returned and a course fee is payable. There have not been drop outs.

10. *What makes AIAP attractive to industry and research partners?*

The 100E projects result, at least, in minimum viable products that are well documented for the sponsor's engineers to take over, even in those cases where the apprentices do not join the sponsor. Partners do return with additional projects, but there are restrictions on giving too many project opportunities to a single sponsor.

11. *Among the real-world projects that apprentices did, which were the few that were most impactful in your view?*

The projects are driven by sponsor ROI, and not so much by larger impact. One example of national impact that comes to mind is AISG's Speech Lab,[4] which helps convert audio to text and is unique in that it accommodates Singlish.[5]

---

[4]https://aisingapore.org/aiproducts/speech-lab/. Accessed July 16, 2023.
[5]https://eresources.nlb.gov.sg/infopedia/articles/SIP_1745_2010-12-29.html. Accessed July 16, 2023.

12. *Is it acceptable for real-world projects to "fail," in the sense of not meeting their original aims? Are there some examples that you could talk about?*

We use agile approaches to minimize failures. There can be external events like funding for a project being canceled because the sponsor company has problems. In about 100 projects, there was only one where the sponsor was not technically satisfied; the AI Singapore mentors stepped in to help resolve the issue.

13. *What changes do you see in AIAP in future? Will AIAP ever stop?*

Both the 100E projects and AIAP will be around for the visible future, three to five years. They may be tweaked slightly to cater to different segments, but they will continue.

A.3.2 Interview with Karthik Prathaban, former AIAP apprentice and current AISG engineer

Interview over email dated April 24, 2023

1. *What made AIAP attractive to you when you made up your mind to become an apprentice?*

The opportunity to get mentored in the field was the biggest reason I signed up to join the AIAP. I partook in AI-based projects for my undergraduate dissertation but had to learn about machine learning and deep learning methods on my own. Identifying and selecting useful learning resources in a massive repository on the internet is extremely difficult and tedious, and there was very little expertise in my working environment at the time to guide me through the best practices, whether it was in data exploration or software engineering or modeling. The structured nature of the program that encompassed 2 months of deep skilling and 7 months of pursuing a real-world AI-based business challenge was enticing for me.

2. *What helped you complete the program after you were selected?*

Much of the credit goes to the mentors and my fellow batch-mates for that. Some level of initiative was required on my part to look up online or test resources, to write code and experiment to address challenges presented by the deep skilling assignments and industry project. However, it was the knowledge-exchange between my fellow apprentices, the teamwork in the project phase, and the guidance from my project mentor and manager that ultimately ensured that my learning and project deliverables were accomplished.

3. *What do you think makes AIAP attractive to industry and research partners?*

I think the AIAP ensures that there is a very structured environment around the apprentices throughout their learning and project phases. The exposure to the various methodologies and best practices in the deep skilling phase is extensive. During the project phase, the apprentices are given the support of the project manager, the engineering mentor, and an extremely competent ML-Ops (Machine Learning Operations) team. Many of the risks associated with the project are handled as early as possible by a team of engineers in the pre-sales team. Thus, it's fair to say that the projects we handle are in very capable hands. The apprentices also come from a variety of backgrounds and present a plethora of perspectives and experiences that, coupled with their knowledge in AI, allows them to present useful and unique insights toward building robust engineering solutions.

4. *Looking back, what would you say has changed in your work life since you joined and completed AIAP?*

For starters, I don't work alone now. The collaborative nature of my work environment means that I interact with a lot more people than I used to. Everyone in the engineering team at AI Singapore is interested in certain aspects of AI and is very open to sharing their findings with the rest of the team, be it interesting articles on developments, or their experiences trying different methodologies. The opportunities for me to learn have thus increased greatly. Knowing that I am interested in AI in the medical field, for example, my recent project mentor shared an article on the application of foundation models in medicine and tagged me in it. The engineers have also always been available wherever concerns have emerged throughout the projects I have been partaking in here. It also gives me pleasure to say that I rarely have my lunches alone nowadays.

5. *What do you look forward to in your career in AI over the next few years?*

It's possible to use AI in a wide variety of fields and work with several different data modalities, be it imaging, text, numerical data, and so on. Since commencing my stint as an apprentice, I have been exposed to projects in computer vision and natural language processing already. These projects have presented their unique challenges and learning opportunities. I look forward to the diversity in the projects and challenges that await me as an AI engineer. I also look forward to communicating with apprentices, industrial partners, and the public about the field. It's important that my technical knowledge and pursuits are shared in a manner that can be understood by people from different backgrounds, and I look forward to more opportunities to do that.

A.3.3 Interview with Yong Xianbin, current AIAP apprentice

Interview over email dated April 24, 2023

1. *What made AIAP attractive to you when you made up your mind to become an apprentice?*

   One of the appeals of AIAP was the chance to be able to learn some of the best practices in developing and deploying AI models. This was important as coming from a different career path, it was beneficial to be exposed to various aspects of working with AI models that I might not have known or need to read up more on. Additionally, as part of AIAP involves working on actual AI problems in the industry, this allowed me to gain experience in solving challenges that may arise when dealing with real-world problems. Thus, I found it valuable as it would allow me to move beyond the toy data sets and be better prepared to enter the field of AI.

   Another appeal was the opportunity to learn alongside like-minded peers from varying backgrounds. As each apprentice brings different experiences, I felt it was a good chance to learn from their perspectives. The possibility of networking with other apprentices and mentors was also another plus factor.

2. *What is helping you stay on track and complete the program now that you are an apprentice?*

   What is helping me stay on track would be the collaborative environment among like-minded peers. This has made the learning process more enjoyable as we are able to share our findings among each other. The collaborative aspect also helps whenever any problems are encountered as it is easy to brainstorm solutions with my fellow apprentices and mentors. This has made the learning journey easier and more enjoyable.

3. *What do you think makes AIAP attractive to industry and research partners?*

   AIAP is attractive to industry and research partners as it is a chance for these partners to work with a team of AI engineers that are excited to explore AI solutions for their use cases. The result would be a minimum viable model that can be used to solve some of the challenges that the partners are facing. Given the use of the agile methodology during the program, the partners would also be able to provide inputs, and hence, would have a role in shaping the outcome of the project.

The team has also been exposed to AI best practices and would provide a solution that will be able to work well in the long run. Furthermore, these partners would be able to pick up and adopt some of these practices for future projects.

4. *Looking back, what would you say has changed in your life since you joined AIAP?*

I have gained a new appreciation for what goes into the various AI tools and have a better grasp of some of the technologies and intuitions behind them. As such, hearing about the latest developments in AI feels less daunting. On the contrary, it has sparked my own interest in applying AI to come up with novel solutions that can be applied in my own life.

5. *What do you look forward to in your career in AI over the next few years?*

I look forward to having a role in creating AI solutions that will solve problems and are beneficial to society. There will be many new developments in the next few years, and it would be exciting to be able to be involved in shaping some of these new developments. I also look forward to being able to leverage the skills that I have gained in my past roles to complement those that I have gained through AIAP.

Chapter 11

Factors Influencing the Future of Work 4.0: Technological Competitiveness, Education, and Policy Coordination

Maria M. Feliciano-Cestero

Abstract

Throughout history, advanced technologies have played a vital role in each industrial revolution. The Fourth Industrial Revolution, in particular, strives to make manufacturing smarter, more self-sufficient, and capable of adapting to changes and making informed decisions based on data it collects from its surroundings through technological advancements. This study explores the correlation between technological competitiveness, education, and policy coordination in the Fourth Industrial Revolution and its impact on the future of jobs by focusing on Latin America as a case study. It aims to evaluate national technological competitiveness and disruptions in various Latin American countries, assess the opportunities and challenges of integrating disruptive and emerging technologies into businesses, and identify the knowledge competencies and policies necessary to enhance competitive advantages and prepare the workforce for the demands of this new era.

Keywords: Industry 4.0, Work 4.0, disruptive technologies, emerging technologies, technological competitiveness, technological education, policy coordination

Introduction

Technology is probably the most critical change factor in the modern world, as disruptive and emerging technologies can present innovative solutions to significant global challenges. Technologies allow and facilitate the emergence of new markets (Christensen, 1997); they can also bring uncertainties about an unimaginable and whimsical future. According to Acosta Henríquez (2018), technologies can cause five major disruptions: (1) reduction in manufacturing time, (2) new manufacturing strategies, (3) new revenue streams, (4) new capabilities, and (5) disruptive competition. However, advanced technologies have been seen in every industrial revolution, from steam engines and railways (in the first industrial revolution); to electric motors, mass production, the combustion engine, the airplane, the automobile, the telephone, and the radio (in the second); automation and computing (in the third); and the current cyber-physical systems that collect and process information, make intelligent decisions, and execute tasks in versatile environments (in the fourth) (Joyanes Aguilar, 2017).

Disruptions occur in any business environment (Gutiérrez Arenas and Quintero Arango, 2019) and cause a phase of competition between innovative companies using disruptive or emerging technologies, replacing less innovative companies with those that constantly introduce innovations (Dedehayir *et al.*, 2017). Therefore, companies must be concerned with entering and staying in the market of their choice, finding and maintaining financial success, and focusing on their long-term capabilities, using technological advances to develop or market their products and services quickly, timely, and responsively (Paap and Katz, 2004). Disruptive innovations cause paradigm shifts and establish new trajectories of technological improvement (Christensen, 1997; Dedehayir *et al.*, 2017). Moreover, they involve a launch, adoption, and use plan that consolidates the new technology and replaces the prior one (Vidal Ledo *et al.*, 2019); causes business model changes and establishes new trajectories of technological improvement (Dedehayir *et al.*, 2017); disrupts and displaces leading companies, products, alliances, and markets (Christensen, 1997); and prevents and mitigates disruptions in the supply chain (World Bank, 2020).

At the same time, many companies may not find technologies useful and reject them because they do not know how to identify a strong market within their business model (Cruz Sánchez, 2017). Through technological advancement, the Fourth Industrial Revolution (Industry 4.0) induces manufacturing industries to be intelligent, autonomous, and able to change their configuration and make judgments depending on the information they gather from their environment (Mejía Huidobro *et al.*, 2020). Furthermore, manufacturing and information technologies create innovative business management systems (smart manufacturing) by optimizing production processes, achieving greater flexibility and efficiency, and generating value propositions for customers, which all thus can respond promptly to market needs (Ynzunza *et al.*, 2017). Smart manufacturing contemplates that every aspect of manufacturing is digitally represented, from design to manufacturing processes (Alcácer and Cruz-Machado, 2019). Cyber-physical systems and technological manufacturing allow the digitalization of production, automation, integration of capabilities, and development of the smart factory leveling value chain organization and management (Ynzunza *et al.*, 2017).

Industry 4.0 redefines all life processes while disrupting economies and societies (Schwab, 2018). One of the features of Industry 4.0 is the connectivity reached between machines, suppliers, orders, customers, and workers, due to electronic devices, the Internet of Things (IoT), and artificial intelligence, among others. In this regard, many companies have already adopted and implemented product innovation as a strategy to achieve better business performance (Gutiérrez Arenas and Quintero Arango, 2019). Consequently, firms can produce their products by making decentralized decisions and using autonomous systems (Lopes de Sousa Jabbour *et al.*, 2018). As a result, Industry 4.0 creates new business, government, and individual opportunities (Schwab, 2018) and interconnects advanced technologies and production with management and business governance, enabling communication and cooperation between sectors from different countries (Feliciano-Cestero *et al.*, 2023), allowing faster progress in the international commerce competition.

Some academics indistinctively use disruptive and emerging technologies as the same term, but both refer to something slightly different. Nevertheless, what makes disruptive technology different from emerging technologies? First, emerging technologies (ET) are pioneering fast-growing developments that dramatically impact socioeconomic structures (Li *et al.*, 2018; Rotolo *et al.*, 2016) and may well influence an economy for over a decade after their appearance (e.g., Rotolo *et al.*, 2016; Stahl, 2011). ET has five characteristics: (1) radical novelty, (2) relatively fast growth, (3) coherence, (4) prominent impact, and (5) uncertainty and ambiguity (Rotolo *et al.*, 2016; Li *et al.*, 2018). The leading ET adopted and used by companies is artificial intelligence, computer vision, 5G telecommunications, edge computing technologies, e-commerce, robotic process automation, virtual and augmented reality, and the metaverse. Those technologies continuously develop, making them stronger and better used by many industries.

Next, disruptive technologies (DT) characterize Industry 4.0, encouraging significant changes to goods and services processes instantaneously (Vidal Ledo *et al.*, 2019). Companies have integrated new DT within the digital transformation that distinguishes Industry 4.0 (Joyanes Aguilar, 2017). Some well-known and used DTs are IoT, including 3D and 4D printing, cloud computing, big data and data analytics, machine learning, chatbots, nanotechnology, and cybersecurity. Many of these DTs are rooted in information and communication technologies (ICT) services (Díaz Lazo *et al.*, 2011). To work effectively, they must include three conditions: (1) affordable price, (2) sufficient initial quality, and (3) continuous improvement potential (Ibarra, 2019). DTs can drastically affect or alter a business, such as eliminating products and services from the market or forcing companies to make structural changes so as not to fail (Ynzunza *et al.*, 2017). Consistent with Danneels (2004), they change the foundations of the competition by changing the performance metrics during the competition. So then, the DTs can be directly related to the foundations of competition and structural changes in companies, countries, or globally. At the same time, ETs are somehow associated with governance, policymaking, and the digital economy. Although there are different definitions and categorizations of technologies, this research has considered both.

Artificial intelligence, machine learning, and IoT are just a few examples of cutting-edge technologies that Industry 4.0 incorporates into manufacturing. As a result, the workforce of Industry 4.0 requires a different set of skills than those needed in traditional manufacturing. Due to constant technological changes, increasing globalization not only attracts new challenges but, above all, also new opportunities. Moreover, global digitalization increases competitive advantages in different sectors, increasing opportunities to trade outside a region's geographical and cultural boundaries. Still, technological innovation and advanced technologies have transformed industrial activities in almost all chain links in recent centuries. In a knowledge-based economy, this ongoing evolution is prevalent (Trullén, 2006). Therefore, the workforce's readiness for

Industry 4.0 depends on several key elements: education, competitiveness, and policy coordination.

The structure of the chapter is as follows. The first section, *Technological competitiveness*, will explore the relationship or connection between competitiveness and technology acquisition. The second section, *Technological disruption in developing countries,* will present different case studies evaluating technological disruptions of Latin American countries and their experience with technology acquisition and adoption. *Future of Work 4.0: employment shifts through knowledge factor,* the third section, will examine the importance of intertwining the relationship between technologies and employment status through the lenses of education and training. The fourth section, *Policies and their role in technology-based competitiveness,* will cover the policy coordination on micro and macro levels. Finally, the last thoughts will then be presented in the *Conclusions* section.

Technological Competitiveness

Industry 4.0 is identified by high-tech and advanced information technology strategies; automation of systems, production, and supply chains; the digitalization of processes; product customization; services provision; the creation of value-added businesses; and the competitive advantage offered to companies helping them grow (see Figure 1 for a sample of references). According to Porter (1990), technological change is one of the main drivers of competition since innovation allows firms to create competitive advantages. Therefore, Industry 4.0 is distinguished by the noticeable use of technological innovations and allowing faster progress in international trade.

The key factors that determine technological competitiveness are the participation of the incursion of new markets, the improvement of the performance and sustainability of organizations (Alvarez-Aros and Bernal-Torres, 2021), the interconnection with production, systematic education, the training of human capital, management techniques that align with the global economy, and organizations that encourage innovation, flexibility, and creativity (Lavarello, 2017). Therefore, business leadership is essential in adopting and using these technologies while managing data and improving value chains (Jacobs and Webber-Youngman, 2017). Furthermore, under the complexity of global supply

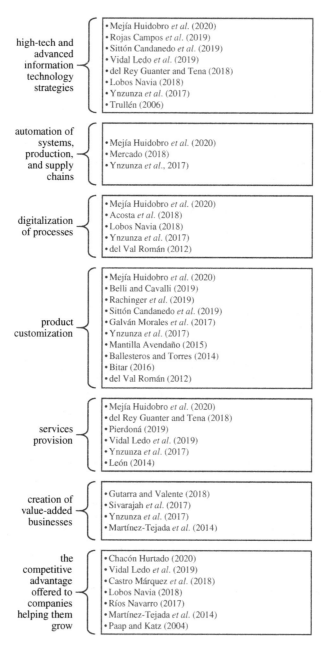

high-tech and advanced information technology strategies
- Mejía Huidobro *et al.* (2020)
- Rojas Campos *et al.* (2019)
- Sittón Candanedo *et al.* (2019)
- Vidal Ledo *et al.* (2019)
- del Rey Guanter and Tena (2018)
- Lobos Navia (2018)
- Ynzunza *et al.* (2017)
- Trullén (2006)

automation of systems, production, and supply chains
- Mejía Huidobro *et al.* (2020)
- Mercado (2018)
- Ynzunza *et al.*, 2017)

digitalization of processes
- Mejía Huidobro *et al.* (2020)
- Acosta *et al.* (2018)
- Lobos Navia (2018)
- Ynzunza *et al.* (2017)
- del Val Román (2012)

product customization
- Mejía Huidobro *et al.* (2020)
- Belli and Cavalli (2019)
- Rachinger *et al.* (2019)
- Sittón Candanedo *et al.* (2019)
- Galván Morales *et al.* (2017)
- Ynzunza *et al.* (2017)
- Mantilla Avendaño (2015)
- Ballesteros and Torres (2014)
- Bitar (2016)
- del Val Román (2012)

services provision
- Mejía Huidobro *et al.* (2020)
- del Rey Guanter and Tena (2018)
- Pierdoná (2019)
- Vidal Ledo *et al.* (2019)
- Ynzunza *et al.* (2017)
- León (2014)

creation of value-added businesses
- Gutarra and Valente (2018)
- Sivarajah *et al.* (2017)
- Ynzunza *et al.* (2017)
- Martínez-Tejada *et al.* (2014)

the competitive advantage offered to companies helping them grow
- Chacón Hurtado (2020)
- Vidal Ledo *et al.* (2019)
- Castro Márquez *et al.* (2018)
- Lobos Navia (2018)
- Ríos Navarro (2017)
- Martínez-Tejada *et al.* (2014)
- Paap and Katz (2004)

Figure 1.   Some bibliographic references of technological characteristics of Industry 4.0.

chains, technological spaces seek to establish markets for disruptive innovations that will lead to new business opportunities.

Developing the business environment in Industry 4.0 uses new technologies to interconnect companies, customers, and suppliers. This trend has redefined business models providing the environment and organization with a fully integrated global perspective (Ynzunza *et al.*, 2017). As the market becomes increasingly dynamic, innovative, and susceptible to various disruptions, companies must begin to innovate and use the technology that best suits their business to stay in the competition. In this way, they will see the return on their investment in disruptive technologies (Gutiérrez Arenas and Quintero Arango, 2019). For Acosta *et al.* (2018), investment is crucial to ensuring technology is used throughout all society, technicalizing the workforce and populace, and advancing to digital economy practices. Unfortunately, most organizations fail to unlock their business value due to mishandling or misunderstanding of data, a dearth of business readiness and appropriate technology, and a lack of communication between a company's employees (Finnegan and Kona, 2020). ICT (e.g., Cloud computing or Internet actions, such as IoT and IoS [Internet of Services]) allows real-time information transfer, maximizing supply chain responsiveness and flexibility while evading and mitigating disruptions (Blackhurst *et al.*, 2005). Therefore, these technologies do not always threaten traditional businesses but represent the opportunity to create commercial alliances and provide value to an international business ecosystem (e.g., Hult *et al.*, 2020).

Technological competitiveness is associated with economic expansion, improved well-being, and job creation (Sánchez de la Vega *et al.*, 2019). Knowing the former, why does a general perception exist in most countries that advanced technology acquisition and technological transformation of businesses and industries will cut jobs and therefore increase unemployment rates? How do academics, entrepreneurs, businesses, and governments not take the same direction and work together?

Technological disruption in developing countries

Many researchers in academia agree that achieving economic development requires increasing productivity, capital intensity, physical and human capital, creating innovations, accumulating knowledge and skills, improving the quality of goods and services, and promoting technological change (e.g., Ahmad and Schreyer, 2016; Benzell *et al.*, 2015; Burke and

Ng, 2006; Nahavandi, 2019; Song and Kim, 2022). Others, such as Rosales (1994), suggest that globalization and technological change shape the international economic order with the help of global financial markets, foreign direct investment, and the export of services. In addition, some scholars concentrate their research on the availability of digital servitization in rural communities or less developed countries and how these regions must utilize strategic planning to reach a technological standard compared to other cities in the same area or another country (e.g., Grimes, 2003; Leong *et al.*, 2016). Finally, other academics have researched leadership roles within business models and management as an essential source in times of technological advances and their implementation (e.g., AlNuaimi *et al.*, 2022). Ultimately, research on disruptive or emerging technology has been conducted, exploring how technologies can help companies and manufacturers to make them smart and improve supply chain processes to avoid disruptions (e.g., Haddud and Khare, 2020). Nonetheless, how can a specific technology be an asset for a particular industry, and how are more resources and research and development of this construct and its aspects needed to achieve direction, reasonable use, and correct management of these technologies?

Innovations and technologies have been widely studied in the literature about developed countries and have been used to improve the performance of companies in emerging market countries (Alfao *et al.*, 2019), including China and India (Cruz Sánchez, 2017), South Africa (International Monetary Fund [IMF], 2020), and Mexico, Colombia, Brazil, Peru, and Argentina (e.g., Ascúa, 2021; Castro Márquez, 2018; Gutarra and Valente, 2018; Huerta Riveros and Navas López, 2006; Martínez-Tejada *et al.*, 2014; Rojas, 2010). However, little research has been done on countries in Africa, Asia, and Latin America. Furthermore, there is a diminishing amount of literature stipulating which competitive advantages disruptive or emerging technologies could offer competitiveness to firms, industries, and supply chains or which specific technology fits each chain link.

Castro Márquez *et al.* (2018) suggest that countries must invest in resources for the technologies implementation to achieve business evolution allowing visibility, venturing into international markets, and, therefore, adaptation to the global economy. According to these authors, the digital economy presents numerous and limitless opportunities for wealth generation and social growth. Thus, Latin America (LATAM) should be part of the challenge of the digital economy to achieve social and global economic inclusion. Acosta *et al.* (2018) suggest increasing the country's digital infrastructure through investment and policy formulation to foster economic development and strengthen the growth of an emerging digital economy. Yet, in LATAM, many people still cannot prove their identity, which is an extreme challenge to the digital economy. Furthermore, a lack of digital distinctiveness is another issue that prevents residents from contributing to the economy.

Internet accessibility in LATAM countries represents another challenge at the public and company level, marked by inequality in gender and social classes. Ascúa (2021) highlights many barriers preventing LATAM firms from reaching their digitalization and technology adoption goals. Some of those barriers are the dearth of knowledge or digital infrastructure, organizational habits and culture, resistance to change, funding challenges, economic instability, deficiencies in the education and training system, and too many unqualified staff. Nevertheless, some LATAM countries have much potential in Internet use, purchases, sales, and media; societies still have a long way to go, especially with the country's indigenous population of LATAM and the inclusion of people with functional diversity as blindness and deafness, among others (Ríos Navarro, 2017). Costa Rica, for example, has developed physical spaces for web accessibility and ICT (Ríos Navarro, 2017). Conversely, Peru needs to design, implement, and carry out a systematic regulatory framework that reflects modern technological trends and considers the country's geographic diversity, biological diversity, and cultural richness to support emerging technology-based businesses (Gutarra and Valente, 2018). Those authors also recommend encouraging long-term strategic studies to back up and strengthen the state-supported productive sectors.

Integrating digital technologies and the digitalization of production is an inevitable requirement across many regions (Belli and Cavalli, 2019). The digital transformation process is fundamental for not losing market competitiveness and continues to be at the technological innovation vanguard (Feliciano-Cestero *et al.*, 2023). Developed countries lead the Industry 4.0 issues. However, even though some developing countries are integrating disruptive technologies in their manufacturing sectors, public policies must be created or reassessed to support digital transformation among firms and industries. For instance, some developing countries are unaware of the advantages digital transformation could bring them.

Conversely, while ICT provides universal accessibility (Ríos Navarro, 2017), many firms are unwilling to face this challenge because they may have different areas of investment priorities or are resistant to change, or do not have the financial resources to implement it (Mejía Huidobro *et al.*, 2020). Additionally, for Castro Márquez *et al.* (2018), in underdeveloped countries, the investment of resources for social and food welfare is super-imposed on investment in technological resources, serving society in the present but eliminating the probability of future economic development of the country. The rest of the section will discuss some LATAM countries' practices in countries established as emerging countries in the MSCI Emerging Market.[1]

In recent years, LATAM countries have made plans to encourage the digitalization of their businesses in order to maintain their competitiveness in the global market (Mejía Huidobro *et al.*, 2020). Mexico is also giving great importance to education and training in Industry 4.0 issues and has created innovation and technology centers, worked on redesigning curricula, and supported programs to promote innovation and train the current workforce (Mejía Huidobro *et al.*, 2020). As part of business globalization, Colombia has developed a holistic method to implement information technologies for governments to be more sustainable and regionally competitive (Castro Márquez *et al.*, 2018). Among the proposed policies is to stimulate private investment in science, technology, and innovation through tax deductions, to achieve the country's digital security (Castro Márquez *et al.*, 2018). According to Mejía Huidobro *et al.* (2020), Mexico has to develop four pillars: (1) training and development of human capital, (2) promotion of innovation, (3) creation of alliances and clusters that result in successful work, and (4) adoption of technologies that mainly support SMEs to increase their level of technological competitiveness. Similarly, the Colombian government has developed economic and social policies to strengthen technologies in the country. Besides having a political, economic, social, and cultural structure focused on globalization, the creation of a technological culture through education and training is required (Castro Márquez *et al.*, 2018). All developing countries, including LATAMs, can replicate these philosophies.

---

[1] Established by the MSCI's emerging market index, in 2023, the emerging market countries are Brazil, Chile, China, Colombia, Czech Republic, Egypt, Greece, Hungary, India, Indonesia, Korea, Malaysia, Mexico, Peru, Philippines, Poland, Qatar, Saudi Arabia, South Africa, Taiwan, Thailand, Turkey, and UAE. For more information, visit https://www.msci.com/our-solutions/indexes/emerging-markets.

To not lose technology competitiveness in the markets, countries like Mexico have implemented strategies to promote the digitalization of their industries (Mejía Huidobro *et al.*, 2020). For a region, digitalizing production processes and assimilating digital technologies are inevitable (Belli and Cavalli, 2019). Therefore, governments must encourage societies to embrace information technologies, achieve competitiveness and sustainability, and continue to evolve at the level of developed countries and globalization, giving significant financial support to micro, small, and medium-sized enterprises (MSMEs). For instance, automotive clusters related to innovation ecosystems were created in Mexico as a regional development strategy immersed in a business culture based on the principles and requirements of Industry 4.0 and remained updated concerning the digital economy (Álvarez Medina and Negrete Martínez, 2019). Still, MSMEs are left behind in the competency since there is no simultaneous advance in the digitalization of all Mexican companies. Even so, Mexico ranked third among LATAM countries in the Global Innovation Index in 2018 (Chile and Costa Rica ranked first and second, respectively) and 56th out of all other 126 countries (Mejía Huidobro *et al.*, 2020).[2]

Over the past 20 years, nanotechnology has raised a trillion US dollars in revenues worldwide. One of the commercial advantages of nanotechnology is the development of value chains between small and large businesses, research institutions or centers, equipment suppliers, intermediaries, the financial and insurance sectors, end users in the public and private sectors, regulatory entities, and other stakeholders (Martínez-Tejada *et al.*, 2014). Brazil, Mexico, and Argentina are the three LATAM countries leading the way in learning and producing nanotechnologies. Therefore, any indication of nanotechnology research in developing or emerging economies should be the basis for projects, programs, and activities promoting national development since nanotechnology maximizes and improves, for example, agricultural crops and inputs, water supplies, and purification systems, the generation of added value to non-renewable resources, energy conversion, and development systems, development of sustainable means of transportation, research, and

[2]"The Global Innovation Index (GII) was launched in 2007 […] with the aim of identifying and determining metrics and methods that could capture a picture of innovation in society that is as complete as possible" (World Intellectual Property Organization [WIPO], 2022: 225).

medical treatments, and the strengthening of the production chain, among others (Martínez-Tejada *et al.*, 2014).

The involvement of institutions should encourage policy development, promote process transformation, and strengthen the institutional efficiency of the State in serving citizens and companies (Castro Márquez *et al.*, 2018). According to Canossa Montes De Oca (2019), companies must temper themselves and formulate business plans, including e-commerce, to increase their chances of success because business methodologies evolve. Firms must adapt to the changing market, and some examples of both successful or unsuccessfully technology adoption are in Ecuador, Peru, and Costa Rica.[3] The first example is when Ecuador's government began planning and constructing the Yachay Knowledge City and the LATAM Silicon Valley in 2013 (Martínez-Tejada *et al.*, 2014). This city was planned in four sectors: (1) the knowledge development sector, (2) the high-tech industrial sector, (3) the tourism sector, and (4) the biotechnology and agriculture sector (Yachay Project, 2013). This city's goal was to train the future local and regional workforce. Unfortunately, 10 years later, some facets of this project have been stocked into government bureaucracy and failed policymaking. The second is the advanced mobile payment initiatives in LATAM, with Peru leading the way (León, 2014), allowing unbanked individuals to interact and exchange money with banked individuals. In this way, this technological tool, known as fintech, has emerged as a market that provides goods and services to the populace via ICTs like websites, social networks, and mobile applications (Gutiérrez Arenas and Quintero Arango, 2019).[4] For its part, Costa Rica changed consumption over the past years because there is a more significant online presence and better offers, representing a tendency to change from physical commercial establishments to online purchases (Canossa Montes De Oca, 2019). Therefore, firms should consider new business strategies and value propositions because

---

[3]Although Costa Rica's nominal gross domestic product (GDP) increased by $20 billion US dollars in the last 10 years, it has a lower GDP than necessary to be categorized as an emerging country. See https://www.worldometers.info/gdp/costa-rica-gdp/.

[4]Fintech is the abbreviation of the combination of the terms finance and technology, referring to the use of new technologies to automate and improve financial services delivery. For more information, visit https://www.investopedia.com/terms/f/fintech.asp#:~:text=Fintech%20refers%20to%20the%20integration,creating%20new%20markets%20for%20them.

this consumer behavior generates global market opportunities; therefore, e-commerce should be part of new business plans worldwide.

Future of Work 4.0: Employment shift through knowledge factor

In an evolving digital world, technologies are advancing progressively, changing the way of doing business, managing knowledge, and undertaking and developing the presence of companies and institutions (Acosta *et al.*, 2018). Industry 4.0 increases the number of new jobs linked to the digital environment, decreasing those jobs without a high degree of automation. In this case, Work 4.0 is the work of the future that constantly develops new technologies. It also refers to how jobs are transforming with the digitalization of ICT, the incorporation of automation in manufacturing, the increasing number of possible remote careers, the growing connectivity with digital infrastructure, the collaboration of humans and robots, and the need to obtain new skills more often, among others.

Being born in the digital age does not necessarily mean a person is tech-savvy, which would suggest that education is the foundation for the Industry 4.0 workforce. Everything depends on the system's resources, opportunities, and curiosity about learning and evolving. Additionally, education must be ongoing to keep up with the rapidly changing technological landscape. Therefore, continuous learning and upskilling programs will be necessary for workers to remain competitive. To succeed in the future job market, individuals must acquire digital and soft skills and develop social and creative intelligence (Zemtsov, 2020). According to Autor (2015), investment in human capital should be the key strategy to produce skills that complement technological change as it transforms occupations. Developing a technological culture through education and training is essential for sustainability and competitiveness in the global market (Castro Márquez *et al.*, 2018). Education must adapt to new digital challenges and provide training for future jobs or Work 4.0.

Ibarra (2019) stipulates that every organization's main support pillars are processes, technology, and human resources. Some authors agree that the main reasons for developing countries to continue lagging is the lack of culture and educational training in new technologies. Therefore, education must be updated to address the new digital challenges and strengthen the skills and training for future jobs when forthcoming human capital confronts global change and the challenges of

integrating disruptive or emerging technologies into business and industrial processes (Asato *et al.*, 2018).

Developing countries need a long-term strategic plan to advance in
the global race. Innovation does not just happen; it needs mechanisms to
stimulate it and a supportive company culture (Gutiérrez Arenas and
Quintero Arango, 2019). LATAM countries' significant problems and
challenges are the lack of technological equipment, poor digital infrastructure, and unemployment. The main challenge is ensuring that all
companies embrace technology in their organizational processes to
decrease the technological gap between developing and developed countries and reduce digital illiteracy (Acosta *et al.*, 2018). Many companies
in LATAM countries are unaware of the benefits of Industry 4.0 and how
to use such advanced technologies, as people without the training to face
new technologies cannot use them efficiently. Therefore, the digital management of human talent with the workforce's training is needed to create
a digital culture in business that will satisfy the knowledge gap. In this
case, several LATAM countries have already begun to focus on education
and acquiring knowledge of these technologies by conducting various
centers of innovation, entrepreneurship, training, and business incubators.
However, education is not everything. In addition to knowledge, to
achieve technological success, create added value, and offer competitive
advantages to a company, it is imperative to have strategic planning, commercial alliances, and real-time communication. These advances will be
essential to improve production, optimize the supply chain, support local
and regional development, enter international markets, and stay in the run.

ICT, the most commonly used technology in society, allows access,
production, processing, data treatment, storage, transmission, and communication of information presented in different codes due to the interaction between computing and telecommunications (Jiménez Bermejo,
2013). Furthermore, ICT produces social changes, including changes in
the working field (Díaz Lazo *et al.*, 2011). Recent studies indicate that
rather than increasing unemployment, there will be a labor transformation
through different industries. Even as overall employment has grown,
advanced economies have undergone profound sectoral changes in
employment. Some academics contend that inadequate skill sets prevent
people from adopting new technologies (Acemoğlu and Autor, 2011;
Acemoğlu, 1998) and succeeding in the future. Although many jobs
would cease, new jobs with specific skills and abilities would be created.
As such, people must learn to use digital technologies, develop soft skills,

and increase their social and creative intelligence (Casey, 2018; Zemtsov, 2020). Autor (2015) argues that investing in human capital should be the primary strategy for developing skills that complement technology expansion as it affects occupations (Acemoğlu and Restrepo, 2018, 2020; Frey and Osborn, 2013).

The scholarly discourse extensively explores theoretical investigations within the economic domain pertaining to the ramifications of technological advancements on the dynamics of workforce engagement, encompassing both employment and unemployment phenomena. Since the past century, many researchers have established that technology will increase unemployment; some believe technology will create new career opportunities, and others understand that technology will transform previously known jobs. The opportunities that digital technologies provide for people (Brynjolfsson and McAfee, 2012), the rise in wages, and the availability of employment are just a few of the advantages of technological progress. Unemployment is lower in businesses that adopt innovations, so these benefits are particularly significant (Acemoğlu, 1997; Author, 2015; Acemoğlu and Restrepo, 2020). Furthermore, technological advancement and automation are inextricably linked to the global economy, and this connection does not inevitably lead to the extinction of human labor.

Conversely, information technology transforms and disrupts every area of the economy, including entire industries and job categories, and new technologies can replace jobs held by workers with a range of skill sets and result in joblessness (Acemoğlu and Autor, 2011; Zemtsov, 2020; Hémous and Olsen, 2015). Moreover, computerization significantly impacts every area of the labor market, bringing about significant changes and elevating some human skills above others in value (Brynjolfsson and McAfee, 2012; Ford, 2013; Frey and Osborn, 2013). For example, robotics is advancing quickly and becoming less expensive, safer, and more flexible (Graetz and Michaels, 2018), increasing the demand for service occupations. Unfortunately, it also tends to cause skills-biased technological shocks and raise labor shortages (Casey, 2018; Ford, 2013; Frey and Osborn, 2013; Mortensen and Pissarides, 1999; Van Roy, Vértesy, and Vivarelli, 2018). Those labor shortages should encourage creativity, innovation, and entrepreneurship.

Every aspect of life is undergoing essential and impending digital transition. Academics must also undergo digital transformation because education cannot be left behind and must continually protect the future employment of those engaged. As with other professions, educational

262 *The Competitiveness of Nations 3*

technologies are becoming increasingly specialized and sophisticated, and each learner groups' demands will determine their use. Technology adoption in education entails, for instance, accepting and using digital tools outside their comfort zone, the same way businesses, especially small and medium enterprises, need to consider technology implementation in their business models. It goes further than any teaching–learning or job-training process and requires digital hands-on skills in all subjects taught at any level. Although future professionals are being prepared at the university level, digital transformation and literacy at this level are even more necessary regardless of the study area. Recognizing this trend, universities have had to redesign their curricula to incorporate the use and management of these technologies in their academic offerings. However, this prerequisite is failing since technology teaching (and adoption) focuses on Science, Technology, Engineering, and Mathematics (STEM) careers (Acosta Henríquez, 2018), and other professional workers are deficient in this competitive advantage.

Nevertheless, why focus only on STEM careers? All academic programs must be reviewed promoting technologies, specialized software, and additional information and communication technologies. Digital transformation must start in schools, training students in the routine and appropriate use of technologies that will be used in the future. Furthermore, since the labor market will continue transforming, a larger workforce with specific skills will be needed to promote labor competence in each industry. Thus, it will encourage the adequate training of future workers in these and other areas of knowledge.

Policies and their role in technology-based competitiveness

Industrial policy (IP) coordination should include delineating objectives, mobilizing economic actors, and assigning public and private institutional roles. Goal setting is fundamental in an industrial strategy that seeks innovation, technological transformations, and structural changes in companies and industries (Suzigan and Furtado, 2006). In addition, global digitalization increases competitive advantages in different sectors, increasing opportunities to trade in foreign markets outside a region's geographical and cultural boundaries. The objectives of effective policy development include growing incomplete markets, achieving increasing returns, and strategic complementarities regulating markets to stimulate systemic technological competitiveness. Yet, why do academics, entrepreneurs, businesses, and governments not take on the same direction and work together?

In the past, economists thought that only state planning and public investment could produce economic development. In contrast, others felt that developing countries could only escape poverty and market failures through "forceful government interventions" (Rodrik, 2004: 2). Then, following the government's inability to steer the economy, economists suggested that they should refrain from including themselves in the decision-making process. IP involves the collective efforts of governments to enhance global competitiveness in high-tech and strategic industries (Zhang, 2020). Government inefficiencies in resource distribution give rise to IP, intended to be a model for direct involvement and alterations to the economy's rules (Costa Campi, 1996).

Moreover, policy coordination that seeks to address complex problems shows a deficit in the linkage between industrial policy and macroeconomic policy (Peres-Núñez, 1993), while underestimating investment programming and overestimating the microeconomic management capacity of governments (Rosales, 1994). IP has been linked to direct government intervention in the productive system, which can help assess a country's economic and scientific significance and contribute to technologies rapidly achieving economies of scale (Suzigan and Furtado, 2006). At this point, goal setting could fail if actors do not accept the uncertainty and take the risk; uncertainty exists over the viability of new or pertinent technologies in goods and services markets and the culture and institutions affecting the adoption of new technologies (Zhang, 2020).

IP understands the nature of technological change and anticipates its economic effects from the cooperative efforts of the public and private sectors (Suzigan and Furtado, 2006). According to Suzigan and Furtado (2006), development involves the accumulation of physical and human capital and learning and mastery of technological skills, peculiarly like the IPS model of competitiveness.[5] According to Peres-Núñez (1993), many traditional ideas about the relationship between entry barriers, concentration, diversification and differentiation of products, and market power must be revised in open and globalizing economies. Regional IP discussion, grounded in Industry 4.0 (Schwab, 2018), centered on measures to boost technological competitiveness in open economies because

---

[5]For details about the model, please see the reference: Porter, M. E. 1990. *The Competitive Advantage of Nations*. The Free Press.

they emphasize developing and disseminating those technologies to improve the positioning of national companies in the international market (Rosales, 1994).

The market explains a country's development and economic progress since it has been used in all industrializations (Amsden, 1992). The objectives of effective development policies include developing incomplete markets, achieving increasing returns and strategic complementarities that stimulate systemic competitiveness, and regulating markets for technological competitiveness. Still, the validity of IP has been questioned because errors overestimate the costs of market failures and underestimate the costs for the government (Peres-Núñez, 1993). This dilemma is due to several factors, including the digitalization of markets, making the government's controlling role increasingly tricky in terms of planning due to the reduction of options open to governments as a result of the progressive internationalization of trade and production; the lack of clear criteria making it difficult to establish market objectives and to evaluate and monitor market policies; and the limited effectiveness of some policies, increasing the likelihood of policy conflict (Peres-Núñez, 1993).

Historically, inequality has been a significant obstacle to LATAM's economic growth (Ocampo, 2005). Unfortunately, economic development in developing countries will never happen on the same path as in developed countries. In LATAM countries, the lack of technological equipment, poor infrastructure, and unemployment pose significant challenges. However, many niches requiring existing technological advances offer venture opportunities in international markets (Arechavala Vargas, 2013). Furthermore, developed countries have an advantage in acquiring and implementing technological resources because of economic fluidity and significant revenues (Castro Márquez *et al.*, 2018), which, conversely, can lead to a further disparity between countries and regions. Still, gaining entry and staying in the global market is challenging and requires considerable economic, social, political, and cultural resources to be invested. Despite frequent policy changes with new administrations, regional industrial policy has demonstrated remarkable consistency over the years (Peres-Núñez, 1993). For instance, legislation has been passed multiple times to replace imports with exports, enhance the production of consumer goods (Peres-Núñez, 1993), and achieve macroeconomic stabilization (Lavarello, 2017). Many countries have also implemented government policies to enable companies, especially MSMEs, to adopt Industry 4.0 technologies and gain a competitive technological advantage (Ynzunza *et al.*, 2017). Still, MSMEs in LATAM may lag in their digital adoption because their peers are not progressing at the same pace.

IP targets new technology and knowledge sectors (Trullén, 2006). Therefore, to reach economic development, IP and global value chains (GVC) must evolve simultaneously, considering other criteria such as governance and power structures, economic rents, barriers to entry, dimensions of modernization, upgrades, and the local and international institutional framework (Pietrobelli and Staritz, 2017). Furthermore, IP should promote the ability of domestic producers to link directly with GVC (Dalle *et al.*, 2013). Therefore, it is crucial to consider and respect technological changes, innovation, knowledge accumulation, competition, market strength, and added value. Finally, the success of IP as an innovation-centered development strategy demonstrates the considerable complexity of the development process (Amsden, 1992) depending on the disarticulation of the instruments, rules, and regulations to which it is bound (Suzigan and Furtado, 2006).

Conclusion

Technology acquisition and adoption is a topic that has been studied since the first industrial revolution. However, a significant percentage of the population still believes that advanced technology acquisition and technological transformation of businesses and industries will lead to a loss of jobs, thus increasing unemployment rates. But why is it still occurring? A possible answer to this question could be that the market "fear" of the unknown (technology) has been perpetuated over the centuries. Hence, this technological feeling in the global population is mainly produced by misleading information and outdated education.

This study highlights the relationship between disrupting and emerging technologies in terms of technological competitiveness, the difficulties and opportunities presented by technological disruptions in developing and emerging countries, the inevitability of preparing the workforce for the future of work or Work 4.0, and the part played by policies in promoting technology-based competitiveness. The goal was to offer a starting point for future studies on the connections between technology, competitiveness, employment, and policies, revealing some potential possibilities and difficulties of new technological advances forging competitive advantages and stimulating market competition.

Technological competitiveness is driven by various factors, such as venturing into unexploited markets, enhancing organizational performance and sustainability, integrating production processes, offering systematic education and training to the workforce, adopting management practices aligned with the global economy, and fostering innovation, flexibility, and creativity within organizations. Furthermore, allocating substantial resources to research and development in this field can lead to effective utilization, optimal management, and a deeper understanding of how specific technologies can benefit particular industries.

Disruptive technologies improve productivity and lead to expansion (World Bank, 2020) and generate essential changes in the manufacturing industry, consumer behavior, and business (Acosta *et al.*, 2018; Ynzunza *et al.*, 2017). In the context of Industry 4.0, technological competitiveness is defined by adopting advanced high-tech strategies, sophisticated information technology initiatives, system and production automation, digitalization of processes, and establishing value-added businesses. Information technologies culture is a central axis for transformation and technological disruption for sustainability and competitiveness demanding market globalization (Castro Márquez *et al.*, 2018).

Conversely, regulations and policies must play a key role in technology-based competitiveness to encourage innovation, technological advancements, and structural changes in businesses and industries. Industrial policy coordination entails establishing objectives, enlisting economic players' aid, and dividing the work among public and private entities. Policymakers and educators must pay close attention to the complex interaction between education, competitiveness, and policy coordination in the workforce of Industry 4.0. Therefore, governments must collaborate with the corporate sector and academic institutions to develop policies that support these elements and the Industry 4.0 workforce, and ensure their implementation.

Although the rate of technological acquisition has increased significantly in recent years, and jobs in manufacturing services have decreased (Gallipoli and Makridis, 2018), it is necessary to evaluate how much of this percentage of the labor decline has been induced by technological acquisition. Even if robots and automation, for example, cause a reduction in the productive workforce, acquiring these will require hiring workers with skills and formal studies to handle these technologies.

Integrating businesses, clients, and suppliers plays a crucial role in shaping the business environment within Industry 4.0.

This interconnectedness redefines business models and provides a global perspective. Effective business leadership is indispensable for adopting new technologies, effective data management, and enhancing value chains. Furthermore, companies need to foster innovation and integrate technologies that align with their business models to maintain competitiveness and ensure a worthwhile return on investment in disruptive technology.

Academics, entrepreneurs, businesses, and governments must take the same direction and work together. Still, the absence of up-to-date statistical data presents a problem in measuring the current situation in digital terms. For example, the Centre for the New Economy and the Society of the World Economic Forum gave leaders a platform to comprehend and forecast new economic and social trends and to adjust policies and practices to every situation (Schwab, 2018). The platform, which strongly emphasizes the significance of human capital, innovation, resilience, and agility to improve the Global Competitiveness Index 4.0 through adopting new tools and executing a successful Industry 4.0 strategy, is intended to benefit as many economies as possible.[6] However, more global resources and research data are needed. In addition, empirical analyses are required to assess the relationship between advanced disruptive technology acquisition and the employment situation in different industries.

The labor force will require a solid technological background, continued education, upskilling opportunities, and an emphasis on innovation, efficiency, and quality. Workers must also be able to adapt quickly to changing circumstances and be open to new challenges. Nevertheless, Industry 4.0 offers many chances to boost output, develop industries, and provide new job scenarios. Additionally, technological education cannot be centered only on STEM careers; the imminence of continuous digital transformation is in every aspect of life and career. Therefore, the relationship between technology and employment is most significant when these components are intertwined, emphasizing the knowledge factor. As the most crucial step to Industry 5.0, LATAM must finally establish a digital business culture to close the knowledge gap and continue scaling internationally.

---

[6]The Global Competitiveness Index 4.0 is a relatively new measure introduced by the World Economic Forum to contribute to the global thinking and the policy-making embedded in the trends of Industry 4.0 while redefining the concept of competitiveness of nations (Schwab, 2018).

References

Acemoğlu, D. 1997. Technology, unemployment, and efficiency. *European Economic Review*, 41(3–5): 525–533.

Acemoğlu, D. 1998. Why do new technologies complement skills? Directed technical change and wage inequality. *The Quarterly Journal of Economics*, 113(4): 1055–1089.

Acemoğlu, D. and Autor, D. 2011. Skills, tasks, and technologies: Implications for employment and earnings. In D. Card & O. Ashenfelter, *Handbook of Labor Economics* (No. 16082; Vol. 4, pp. 1043–1171). Amsterdam, Netherlands: Elsevier. https://doi.org/10.1016/S0169-7218(11)02410-5.

Acemoğlu, D. and Restrepo, P. 2018. The race between man and machine: Implications of technology for growth, factor shares, and employment. *American Economic Review*, 108(6): 1488–1542.

Acemoğlu, D. and Restrepo, P. 2020. Robot and jobs: Evidence from US labor markets. *Journal of Political Economy*, 128(6): 2188–2244. https://novafrica.org/wp-content/uploads/2017/06/Daron-Acemoğlu.pdf.

Acosta Henríquez, G. 2018. Incorporación de la tecnología de impresión 3D a las carreras de Ingeniería y Arquitectura de la Universidad Católica de El Salvador [Incorporation of 3D printing technology to the Engineering and Architecture careers of the Catholic University of El Salvador]. *Anuario de Investigación*, 7: 293–310.

Acosta, M., Yagual Velastegui, A., and Coronel Pérez, V. 2018. Perspectivas de la economía digital en Latinoamérica: Caso de Ecuador [Perspectives of the digital economy in Latin America: Case of Ecuador]. *3C Empresa: Investigación y Pensamiento Crítico*, 7(3): 29–43.

Ahmad, N. and Schreyer, P. 2016. Are GDP and Productivity Up to the Challenges of the Digital Economy? *International Productivity Monitor*, 30: 4–27.

Alcácer, V. and Cruz-Machado, V. 2019. Scanning the Industry 4.0: A literature review on technologies for manufacturing systems. *Engineering Science and Technology, an International Journal*, 22(3): 899–919.

Alvarez-Aros, E. L. and Bernal-Torres, C. A. 2021. Technological competitiveness and emerging technologies in Industry 4.0 and Industry 5.0. *Anais Da Academia Brasileira de Ciencias*, 93(1).

Álvarez Medina, M. de L. and Negrete Martínez, M. V. 2019. La Industria 4.0 en México y el apoyo de los clústeres automotrices, A.C, para su desarrollo [Industry 4.0 in Mexico and the support of automotive clusters, A.C, for its development]. *XXIV Congreso Internacional de Contaduría, Administración e Informática*. http://congreso.investiga.fca.unam.mx/docs/xxiv/docs/8.06.pdf.

Amsden, A. H. 1992. *Asia's next giant: South Korea and Late Industrialization*. Oxford University Press on Demand.

Arechavala Vargas, R. 2013. *Las universidades públicas mexicanas: los retos de las transformaciones institucionales hacia la investigación y la transferencia de conocimiento [Mexican Public Universities: The Challenges of Institutional Transformations Towards Research nd Knowledge Transfer].* Porto: XV Latin Ibero-American Conference on Management of Technology.

Asato, J., Galván, P., Daniela, G., Godoy, J., and Ortega, C. 2018. Desarrollo de competencias profesionales ante los retos tecnológicos de la Industria 4.0 en México [Development of professional skills in the face of the technological challenges of Industry 4.0 in Mexico]. *Pistas Educativas*, 40(130): 2057–2071.

Ascúa, R. A. 2021. Industry 4.0 in manufacturing SMEs of Argentina and Brazil. *Journal of the International Council for Small Business*, 2(3): 203–222.

Autor, D. H. 2015. Why are there still so many jobs? The history and future of workplace automation. *Journal of Economic Perspectives*, 29(3): 3–30. https://doi.org/10.1257/jep.29.3.3.

Belli, L. and Cavalli, O. 2019. *Internet Governance and Regulations in Latin America: Analysis of Infrastructure, Privacy, Cybersecurity and Technological Developments in Honor of the Tenth Anniversary of the South School on Internet Governance.* Río de Janeiro: FGV Direito Rio. https://www.gobernanzainternet.org/book/book_en.pdf.

Benzell, S. G., Kotlikoff, L. J., LaGarda, G., and Sachs, J. D. 2015. *Robots Are Us: Some Economics of Human Replacement* (No. 20941). National Bureau of Economic Research.

Bitar, S. 2016. Why and how Latin America should think about the future. Washington, D.C.: *The Dialogue Leadership for the Americas* (second edition). https://globaltrends.thedialogue.org/wp-content/uploads/2016/12/Global-Trends-Report-Revised-PDF-for-web-posting.pdf.

Blackhurst, J., Craighead, C. W., Elkins, D., and Handfield, R. B. 2005. An empirically derived agenda of critical research issues for managing supply-chain disruptions. *International Journal of Production Research*, 43(19): 4067–4081.

Burke, R. J. and Ng, E. 2006. The changing nature of work and organizations: Implications for human resource management. *Human Resource Management Review*, 16(2), 86–94.

Castro Márquez, D. E., Camargo Barbosa, J. A., and Castro Silva, H. F. 2018. La transformación y disrupción de las tecnologías de la información y las políticas económicas de colombia como parte de la globalización empresarial [The transformation and disruption of information technologies and economic policies in Colombia as part of business globalization]. *Revista Colombiana de Tecnologías de Avanzada*, 1(31): 66–71.

Christensen, C. M. 1997. *The Innovator's Dilemma: When New Technologies Cause Great Firms to Fail.* Harvard Business Review Press.

Cruz Sánchez, O. M. 2017. *Innovación disruptiva: Aportes conceptuales para organizaciones en Latinoamérica [Disruptive innovation: Conceptual contributions for organizations in Latin America].*

Dalle, D., Fossati, V., and Lavopa, F. 2013. Política industrial: ¿el eslabón perdido en el debate de las Cadenas Globales de Valor? [Industrial policy: The missing link in the debate on Global Value Chains?]. *Revista Argentina de Economía Internacional*, 2: 3–16.

Danneels, E. 2004. Disruptive technology reconsidered: A critique and research agenda. *Journal of Product Innovation Management*, 21(1): 246–258

Dedehayir, O., Ortt, J. R., and Seppänen, M. 2017. Disruptive change and the reconfiguration of innovation ecosystems. *Journal of Technology Management and Innovation*, 12(3): 9–21.

Feliciano-Cestero, M. M., Ameen, N., Kotabe, M., Paul, J., and Signoret, M. 2023. Is digital transformation threatened? A systematic literature review of the factors influencing firms' digital transformation and internationalization. *Journal of Business Research*, 157.

Finnegan, D. and Kona, P. 2020, May 28. Rapidly Onboard and Prep Your Data for Machine Learning [Webinar]. In *InfoWorks Webinars Series*. https://go.infoworks.io/machine-learning-webinar.

Gallipoli, G. and Makridis, C. A. 2018. Structural transformation and the rise of information technology. *Journal of Monetary Economics*, 97: 91–110. www.rcfea.org.

Gutiérrez Arenas, A. and Quintero Arango, L. F. 2019. La innovación como activo estratégico para la productividad en la era tecnológica [Innovation as a strategic asset for productivity in the technological era]. *Science of Human*, 4(2): 308–330.

Hult, G., Tomas M., Gonzalez-Perez, M. A., and Lagerström, K. 2020. The theoretical evolution and use of the Uppsala Model of Internationalization in the international business ecosystem. *Journal of International Business Studies*, 51(1): 38–49.

Ibarra, N. 2019. Reinventando la auditoría: El impacto de las tecnologías disruptivas en la auditoría interna [Reinventing auditing: The impact of disruptive technologies on internal audit]. *Revista Académica Gente Clave*, 3(2): 146–153.

International Monetary Fund [IMF]. 2020. *Regional Economic Outlook: Sub-Saharan Africa. COVID-19: An Unprecedented Threat To Development.* Washington, D.C.: International Monetary Fund, Publication Services. https://library.unccd.int/Details/fullCatalogue/1560.

Jacobs, J. and Webber-Youngman, R. C. W. 2017. A technology map to facilitate the process of mine modernization throughout the mining cycle. *Journal of the Southern African Institute of Mining and Metallurgy*, 117(7): 637–648.

Joyanes Aguilar, L. 2017. Ciberseguridad la colaboración público-privada en la era de la cuarta revolución industrial (Industria 4.0 versus ciberseguridad 4.0) [Cybersecurity public-private collaboration in the era of the fourth industrial revolution (Industry 4.0 versus cybersecurity 4.0)]. *Cuadernos de estrategia*, 185: 19–64.

Li, M., Porter, A. L., and Suominen, A. 2018. Insights into relationships between disruptive technology/innovation and emerging technology: A bibliometric perspective. *Technological Forecasting and Social Change*, 129: 285–296.

Martínez-Tejada, V., Mejía, S., Jaramillo-Isaza, F., and Álvarez-Lainez, M. 2014. Nanotecnología para Colombia: Una mirada histórica, pasando por el contexto global, latinoamericano y las regiones [Nanotechnology for Colombia: A historical look, going through the global, Latin American context and regions]. *Revista Nano Ciencia y Tecnología*, 2(1): 49–64.

Mejía Huidobro, M. A., Camacho Vera, A. D., and Marcelino Aranda, M. 2020. Estrategias del sector público y privado para la implementación de la Industria 4.0 en México [Public and private sector strategies for the implementation of Industry 4.0 in Mexico]. *Revista UPIICSA Investigación Interdisciplinaria*, 6(1): 13–31.

Nahavandi, S. 2019. Industry 5.0-a human-centric solution. *Sustainability*, 11(16): 4371.

Paap, J. and Katz, R. 2004. Predicting the "unpredictable": Anticipating disruptive innovation. *Research Technology Management*, 47: 13–22.

Peres-Núñez, W. 1993. ¿Dónde estamos en la política industrial? [Where are we in industrial policy?]. *Revista de La CEPAL*, 51: 37–49.

Pietrobelli, C. and Staritz, C. 2017. Cadenas Globales de Valor y Políticas de Desarrollo [Global Value Chains and Development Policies]. *Desarrollo Económico*, 56(220): 371–391. http://www.jstor.org/stable/44736001.

Ríos Navarro, D. 2017. La accesibilidad de las TIC en Costa Rica: Un cambio disruptivo en la mente de la sociedad costarricense [ICT accessibility in Costa Rica: A disruptive change in the mind of Costa Rican society]. *Revista Latinoamericana de Derechos Humanos*, 28(1): 177–198.

Rosales, O. 1994. Política industrial y fomento de la competitividad [Industrial policy and promoting competitiveness]. *Revista de La CEPAL*, 53: 59–79.

Rotolo, D., Hicks, D., and Martin, B. R. 2015. What is an emerging technology? *Research Policy*, 44(10): 1827–1843.

Schwab, K. 2018. *The Global Competitiveness Report 2018*. www.weforum.org/gcr.

Song, C. S. and Kim, Y. K. 2022. The role of the human-robot interaction in consumers' acceptance of humanoid retail service robots. *Journal of Business Research*, *146*: 489–503.

Suzigan, W. and Furtado, J. 2006. Política Industrial e Desenvolvimento [Industrial Policy and Development]. *Brazilian Journal of Political Economy*, 26(102): 163–185.

Trullén, J. 2006. La nueva política industrial española: Innovación, economías externas y productividad [The new Spanish industrial policy: Innovation, external economies and productivity]. *Economía Industrial*, 393: 17–31.

Vidal Ledo, M. J., Carnota Lauzán, O., and Rodríguez Díaz, A. 2019. Tecnologías e innovaciones disruptivas [Disruptive technologies and innovations]. *Revista Cubana de Educacion Médica Superior*, 33(1): 1–13.

World Bank. 2020. Trading for development in the age of global value chains: World development report.

World Intellectual Property Organization (WIPO). 2022. In S. Dutta, B. Lanvin, L. Rivera León, and S. Wunsch-Vincent (eds.), *Global Innovation Index 2022: What is the future of Innovation-Driven Growth?* (Volume 200). World Intellectual Property Organization.

Ynzunza, C., Izar, J. and Bocarando, J. 2017. El entorno de la industria 4.0: Implicaciones y Perspectivas Futuras [The Industry 4.0 environment: Implications and Future Perspectives]. *ConCiencia Tecnológica*, 54: 33–45.

Zemtsov, S. 2020. New technologies, potential unemployment, and 'nescience economy' during and after the 2020 economic crisis. *Regional Science Policy and Practice*, 12(4): 723–743.

Chapter 12

Analyzing the Digital Entrepreneurial Ecosystem: Evidence from the Information Technology-Related Small and Medium Enterprises in an Emerging Economy

Md Noor Un Nabi, S. M. Misbauddin, Farzana Akter, Mohammad Awal Hossen, and Fatema Tuj Zohora

Abstract

In emerging economies, firms, especially Small and Medium Enterprises (SMEs), have attempted to bolster their competitive positions by incorporating digital technologies, which sees them operate in a broader Digital Entrepreneurial Ecosystem (DEE). The DEE includes varied actors and technologies facilitating digital infrastructure, the Internet, broadband communications, operating systems, and the cloud. However, when it comes to developing economies, knowledge on the nature and components of DEE is limited. Therefore, to fill this research gap, this chapter seeks to accomplish two objectives: (1) identify the different parameters of DEE and (2) determine how these parameters perform according to the perceptions among the ecosystem actors/stakeholders. For this, Bangladesh has been chosen as the empirical ground. Based on the DEE frameworks provided by Sussan and Acs (2017) and Song (2019), data were collected through case studies and face-to-face personal interviews with the entrepreneurs of 10 information and communication technology firms. By delineating the components of the DEE from a developing country, this chapter contributes to the extant literature on digital entrepreneurship and the digital entrepreneurial ecosystem. In addition, this chapter bears practical implications for the ecosystem partners and digital entrepreneurs to leverage the DEE components in improving firm performance.

Keywords: Digital entrepreneurship, digital entrepreneurial ecosystem, entrepreneurial ecosystem, Small and Medium Enterprises (SMEs), digital citizenship, stakeholders

Introduction

The COVID-19 pandemic created an atmosphere of widespread uncertainty that pushed businesses to adopt transformative business models by embracing digital platforms. Literature shows that the adoption of digital technologies can facilitate Small and Medium Enterprises (SMEs) in attaining increased performance and strategic competitiveness (Chan *et al.*, 2019; Kimuli *et al.*, 2021; Kraft *et al.*, 2022). This explains why SMEs are encouraged by experts to adopt digital entrepreneurship to counter the consequences of the pandemic. More digital platform-based SMEs are emerging that establish themselves through leveraging mobile and collaborative technologies, Internet of Things (IoT), advanced telecommunication infrastructure, big data, artificial intelligence (AI), cloud computing, blockchain technology, and many other technologies (Feng *et al.*, 2021; Loonam and O'Regan, 2022; Purbasari *et al.*, 2021). Therefore, firms and governments have emphasized building an entrepreneurial ecosystem to support enterprises (Acs *et al.*, 2017). Entrepreneurial ecosystems imply collaboration where the individual firm partners with other group actors to develop the products or services (Adner and Kapoor, 2010; Iansiti and Levien, 2004; Williamson and De Meyer, 2012). Entrepreneurial ecosystem denotes the stakeholders that require an alignment for a product or service to operationalize in a market (Adner, 2017). With the proliferation of technologies and AI, more tech-based start-ups like Facebook, Snapchat, Twitter, Uber, and AirBnB are emerging. The basic proposition of these digital enterprises is their ability to connect customers worldwide and decrease transaction costs. Such global firms have grown due to the revolution of information and communication technologies (ICT) and a robust and healthy digital entrepreneurial eco-system (DEE). Seen from this lens, the digital entrepreneurial ecosystem is a rising research issue among researchers. However, the extant litera-ture on the digital entrepreneurial ecosystem needs to be explored (Sussan and Acs, 2017). The concept of the digital entrepreneurial ecosystem was given a structural framework by Acs *et al.* (2017), who averred that it is a stable system comprising different digital entities and their interactions to increase the system's functioning, information sharing, and collaborative innovation to successfully launch digital apps, products, or services to create customer value in the digital marketplace.

We find a dearth in the literature regarding the framework and con-ceptualization of DEE, especially in the context of emerging countries. Sussan and Acs (2017) proposed an integrative framework that brings together the digital and entrepreneurial ecosystems. Song (2019) reconfig-ured the DEE concept by critically evaluating and modifying the DEE framework of Sussan and Acs (2017). Nambisan (2017) discussed the implication of digital technologies on entrepreneurship and contributed to digital entrepreneurship. Therefore, the DEE domain needs more research to identify its components and how the stakeholders perceive DEE from their perspectives. This chapter aims to fill the research gap by investigat-ing DEE elements in an emerging country context. It seeks to identify the different parameters of a DEE and how these parameters are performing according to the perceptions of the ecosystem actors.

For the empirical context of the research, Bangladesh has been selected. As a developing country in Southeast Asia, Bangladesh has been emphasizing the need to build a vibrant entrepreneurial ecosystem for digital start-ups so that information technology can be harnessed to offer products or services with high demands at home and abroad. Therefore, Bangladesh needs a robust digital entrepreneurial ecosystem. To achieve a digital Bangladesh, the government has made efforts to create SMEs based on digital platforms to face the era of the digital industry. The gov-ernment anticipates SMEs to be vital in promoting connectivity on digital platforms. Technology dependence will ensure SMEs' survival in the aftermath of the COVID-19 pandemic. Thus, developing the digital entre-preneurial ecosystem is crucial and expected to grow in the post-pandemic period (EY Analysis, 2021).

As such, this chapter will analyze Bangladesh's existing digital entre-preneurial ecosystem, demonstrating the actual scenario of each element of the entrepreneurial ecosystem. Its findings are expected to enrich the literature on digital entrepreneurship and the digital entrepreneurial eco-system, particularly in the COVID-19 pandemic era, and offer policy recommendations to the government in developing DEE for SMEs. In addition, the research also has implications for SMEs in emerging econo-mies to leverage the DEE components in attaining more excellent perfor-mance results.

Literature Review

Defining digital entrepreneurship

Digital entrepreneurship entails embracing traditional methods by empha-sizing new technologies, the opportunities created by these technologies, and new business forms (Kollmann *et al.*, 2022; Sahut *et al.*, 2021). It is therefore broadly defined as creating new ventures and transforming existing businesses by developing or using novel digital technologies (Nedumaran and Saroja, 2020). Many countries, including developing countries, have viewed digital entrepreneurship as a critical pillar for eco-nomic growth, job creation, and innovation. However, a detailed charac-terization of technology entrepreneurship is needed to work out plans for a smoother transition of conventional businesses into digital platforms (Giones and Brem, 2017). Digital entrepreneurship is much nearer to the data systems' idea of artifacts, platforms, and information infrastructure (Naudé and Liebregts, 2020). Digital entrepreneurs often do not care about the precise technology behind their business plan; they focus on the services supported by the technologies.

Conceptualizing the entrepreneurial ecosystem

The concept of an entrepreneurial ecosystem consists of two terms. The first term, "entrepreneurial," is often understood as a driver of innovation and productivity and an engine for sustainable economic growth (Emembolu *et al.*, 2022; Song *et al.*, 2021). In the classic sense, entrepre-neurs start businesses, hire labor, mobilize resources, and maintain their operational business. Entrepreneurs are venture owners who create new values by exploiting new products, services, and markets and expanding their economic activities (Mason and Brown, 2014).

In natural science, the concept of an "ecosystem" denotes a system consisting of interrelated elements characterized by the interaction within the community or cohort members (Adner, 2017). In line with the biological systems, the entrepreneurial ecosystem also comprises components such as people, groups, institutions, stakeholders, and organizations that interconnect through continuous interaction. Like the biological ecosystem affected by environmental determinants, the entrepreneurial ecosystem is also influenced by different laws, policies, or cultural norms. Furthermore, these ecosystems are facilitated by entrepreneurship patronage programs (Duan *et al.*, 2020). Hence, designing the supporting interventions requires carefully analyzing the ecosystem's intricacies (Brown and Mason, 2017; Mas and Gómez, 2021). The entrepreneurial ecosystem is the environment in which entrepreneurs exert their activities to develop new products/services (Ratten, 2020). In the context of developed countries, the ecosystem components are congenial for business success, whereas, in the case of developing countries, the elements are weak in supporting entrepreneurs.

The elements of an entrepreneurial ecosystem

Isenberg (2011) asserts that the entrepreneurial ecosystem consists of six domains, as follows:

(1) **Culture:** Culture denotes the social norms, values, and beliefs in a specific geographic area where visible business success, risk tolerance, business failure, innovation, value creation, and ambition are highly correlated with entrepreneurship indicators (Beugelsdijk *et al.*, 2017; Ferraro and Briody, 2017).
(2) **Policies and leadership:** Institutional support mechanisms, financial assistance, regulatory conventions, incentives, incubators, research organizations, business-oriented legislation, and contract enforcement procedures are combined to enrich the entrepreneurial ecosystem (Leithwood, 2001).
(3) **Access to finance:** Favorable financial policies facilitate new venture creation from different socioeconomic and environmental contexts. Financial capital measures include microloans, seed capital, public capital markets, shares, and debentures.

(4) **Human capital:** The existence of workforce, higher education, and pragmatic entrepreneurship training programs affect entrepreneurship. Therefore, human capital is necessary for the business ecosystem (Salamzadeh and Ramadani, 2021).

(5) **Markets:** Markets require potential consumers, robust distribution networks, a prompt customer feedback system, and rapid consumer adoption to enrich entrepreneurship. Besides, a strong market connection motivates entrepreneurs.

(6) **Supports:** Support mechanisms are needed to make all other components function. Government institutions can support entrepreneurship by offering telecommunication, transportation, and energy infrastructures. Non-governmental organizations can provide support by organizing business plan contests, business workshops, conferences, and entrepreneur-specific associations.

Defining the digital entrepreneurial ecosystem

A digital system implies a self-organized way of comprising heterogeneous digital entities and their interrelations to extend system utility, gain edges, promote information sharing, inner and inter cooperation, and system innovation. The digital system is applied in business, data management, service, social networks, and education (Cearra and Saiz, 2021; Li *et al.*, 2012). A DEE is a way in which digital entrepreneurship emerges and develops. A digital entrepreneurial ecosystem is necessary for the success of digital entrepreneurship (Spigel, 2016; Zahra *et al.*, 2022). Suppose we treat a digital venture as characterized by individualism. In that case, we will then observe a DEE in which numerous resources and parts are often integrated to facilitate the operation of digital entrepreneurship as a kind of collectivism (Corallo *et al.*, 2007; Smirnov *et al.*, 2020). The DEE is the ICT infrastructure supporting cooperation, knowledge sharing, and digital entrepreneurship schemes. The DEE includes varied technologies that power the digital infrastructure, powerful chips, the Internet, the World Wide Web, broadband communications, programming languages, operating systems, and the cloud (Cetindamar *et al.*, 2020; Song, 2019). The nature of the Internet provides open access and standards that allow anyone to develop and share applications on the Internet. DEE also includes different types of users and co-creators of the system and governance issues. The technology comes from the research carried out by corporations, universities, and governments.

The elements of the digital entrepreneurial ecosystem

Based on the studies of Sussan and Acs (2017) and Song (2019), the components of DEE are depicted in Table 1.

Materials and Methods

Research approach

The primary purpose of this chapter is to explore the components of the digital entrepreneurial ecosystem in Bangladesh. It has been operationalized by analyzing the natural environment of the digital ecosystem. This study is qualitative in nature. Qualitative research is particularly appropriate for exploring objective information and data about the perceptions of a specific population (Hammarberg *et al.*, 2016). The data were collected through face-to-face personal interviews with the entrepreneurs of digital entrepreneurial firms. The justification behind using interviews is that it is a medium for extracting detailed perceptions and experiences among respondents (Yin, 2013). Considering the qualitative nature of the data, semi-structured interviews have been adopted (Saunders *et al.*, 2009). Open-ended questions facilitated the interviews. Audio recording of the interviews was done. The duration of the interviews was between 45 and 75 minutes. The contents of the interview have been reproduced as transcripts for analysis. To analyze the factors, the entire transcript has been grouped to generate the findings. Next, the findings were compared with preselected parameters.

Empirical setting of the research

Bangladesh has been chosen as the empirical ground to understand the intricacies of DEE from an emerging country context. Technology-based SMEs have flourished in Bangladesh in the last few years (Masroor *et al.*, 2020). These digital-platform-based SMEs, software firms, and freelancing companies created employment, fostered an entrepreneurial culture, and acted as catalysts to build a cohesive entrepreneurial ecosystem. The current research has been conducted through the interview method on ten (10) information and communication technology firms, which comprised two (02) software development firms, two (02) payment gateway companies, one (01) online travel agency, three (03) online shops,

Table 1.   Elements of DEE.

i. Motivation	ii. Financing	iii. Training	iv. Internet	v. Fixed Broadband
– Motivation is the driving force behind an entrepreneur's actions. – The government's role is important in creating motivation for starting digital entrepreneurship.	– This is a prime concern during the early stage of start-ups. – The government's focus on financing can promote a strong DEE (Frimanslund, 2022).	– Lack of training and unskilled employees can lead to venture terminations in the DEE (Ozkeser, 2019).	– This is a core element in the DEE. – Promotion of the Internet by both the government and the private sector strengthens the ecosystem.	– Fixed broadband technologies including optical fiber, wireless, and satellites contribute to the DEE by providing high-speed data transmission.

vi. Mobile Telecommunication	vii. Satellite Communication	viii. User Device	ix. Digital Commerce	x. Digital Law
– It enables wireless communication and enhances convenience and efficiency.	– It utilizes satellite technology to enable long-distance communication. – It plays a role in the DEE by providing communication capabilities.	– User devices like laptops, smartphones, tablets, security cameras, and routers are crucial for the DEE. – These devices serve as enablers for digital business activities (Schulte-Althoff et al., 2020).	– Government support in promoting digital e-commerce is vital for the DEE (Jungcharoensukying et al., 2020).	– Digital laws govern the legal rights and restrictions related to technology use (Elia et al., 2020). – Digital laws address issues of digital accountability, such as illegal file sharing, software piracy, hacking, identity theft, and copyright infringement.

xi. Digital Security	xii. Digital Access	xiii. Digital Citizenship	xiv. Digital Marketplace
– Digital security protects online identities, assets, and technology from criminals.	– Digital access encompasses the necessary hardware, software, and technical support for engaging with ICT-based practices (Tandon *et al.*, 2020). – It also includes the social and technical skills required to effectively use ICT-based practices.	– Digital citizenship refers to individuals' abilities and knowledge to effectively use the Internet and digital technologies. – Digital citizenship enables responsible participation in social and civic activities in the DEE.	– It is a platform for the public and private sector to access and purchase IT commodities and services. – The digital marketplace can leverage cloud computing to deliver cost-effective services in the DEE.

one (01) studio, and one (01) fiber optics network infrastructure company. The interviews were conducted face to face. The convenience sampling method was used for selecting the samples. Table 2 shows the list of interviewees with company names, positions held by the interviewees, date of interviews, and interview duration.

Findings of the Study

This segment provides the scenario of the DEE by exploring each element of DEE from the perspective of each of the sample firms.

Motivation for starting digital entrepreneurship

It is conspicuous that most firms believe there is a climate for being motivated to pursue entrepreneurship (Table 3). However, they were either unable or did not try to connect with the government. The entrepreneur of the IT firm Apps Master got motivated by the government because he was studying at Chittagong University of Engineering and Technology (CUET) in Bangladesh. He opined that entrepreneurs can be motivated if they obtain an education at a governmental institution. The employee of Nagad stated that Nagad is a wing of governmental business that motivates them. Conversely, a senior employee of Summit Communication said that the government had taken a project to increase the broadband connection to all divisions and thanas. As a result, they were motivated by the government.

Financial sources analysis

To analyze financial sources, we have identified the sources of financing, whether the entrepreneurs have asked for loan or not, the rejection of loans, and the comments about the financing climate.

Table 4 shows that eight IT firms asked for loans from financial institutions whereas four firms were rejected, resulting in a rejection of loan rate at 50%. Moreover, out of 10 IT firms, seven managed financing with their own personal fund. An entrepreneur, Mr. Abir Hasan of Apps Master, opined that the probability of getting loan increases if the applicant can prove that the start-up has a good future and products with higher public demands. Mr. Bashar Al Sunny from Studio Firefly mentioned in his

Table 2.   Description of the interview partners.

Serial No.	Name of the Company	Business Type	Interviewee Position	Date of the Interview	Duration of the Interview
1	Pix smite	Software development	CEO	05/10/2022	55 minutes
2	Apps master	Software development	CEO	12/09/2022	68 minutes
3	Wallet Mix	Payment gateway company	Personal Assistant of CEO	03/11/2022	73 minutes
4	Nagad	Payment gateway company	Territory Officer, Barisal Zone	07/09/2022	70 minutes
5	Avijatrik	Online travel agency	CEO	05/10/2022	56 minutes
6	Khulna E-shop	Online shop	CEO	03/10/2022	65 minutes
7	Ali Express Community Bangladesh	Online shop	CEO	18/09/2022	52 minutes
8	Bahari Gohona	Online shop	CEO	24/10/2022	73 minutes
9	Firefly Studio	Studio	CEO	28/10/2022	50 minutes
10	Summit Communications	Fiber optics network infrastructure company	Deputy registrar	11/10/2022	60 minutes

Table 3.   Motivation for starting digital entrepreneurship.

Serial No.	Name of the Company	Sources of Motivation	Climate of Motivation
1	Pix Smite	Personal	Exists
2	Apps Master	Governmental	Strongly exists
3	Walletmix	Personal	No comments
4	Nagad	Governmental	Exists
5	Avijatrik	Personal	Doesn't exist
6	Khulna E-shop	Personal	Doesn't exist
7	Ali Express Community Bangladesh	Personal	Exists
8	Bahari Gohona	Personal	Exists
9	Studio Firefly	Personal	Exists
10	Summit Communication	Governmental	Strongly exists

Table 4.   Financial sources analysis.

Serial No.	Name of the Company	Sources of Financing	Asking for Loan	Rejection of Loan	Climate of Financing
1	Pix Smite	Personal	Yes	Yes	Exists
2	Apps Master	Governmental	Yes	No	Exists
3	Walletmix	Other Business	Yes	No	Exists
4	Nagad	Governmental	No comments	No comments	Exists
5	Avijatrik	Personal	Yes	Yes	Doesn't exist
6	Khulna E-shop	Personal and bank	Yes	Yes	Doesn't exist
7	Ali Express Community Bangladesh	Personal and bank	Yes	No	Exists
8	Bahari Gohona	Personal	No	No	Doesn't exist
9	Studio Firefly	Personal	Yes	Yes	Doesn't exist
10	Summit Communication	Personal, bank, and governmental	Yes	No	Strongly exists

interview that he approached a governmental project to get financing but, unfortunately, he was unable to get it because of high competition. In this regard, Mr. Nehar Sarwar Ayon, the entrepreneur of Avijatrik, said that financial institutions require collateral for business loans.

Table 5.   Analyzing the sources of training.

Serial No.	Name of the Company	Sources of Training	Media of Training	Climate of Training
1	Pix Smite	Online	YouTube	Exists
2	Apps Master	Governmental project	University	Strongly exists
3	Walletmix	Foreign	On the job	Doesn't exist
4	Nagad	Private	On the job	Exists
5	Avijatrik	Personal	On the job	Doesn't exist
6	Khulna E-shop	Personal	On the job	Doesn't exist
7	Ali Express Community Bangladesh	Personal	On the job	Exists
8	Bahari Gohona	Personal	On the job	Exists
9	Studio Firefly	Personal	Private institution	Exists
10	Summit Communication	Foreign and private	On the job	Doesn't exist

Sources of training

The interviews provided us with the actual sources of training, the media of training, and the training climate (see Table 5). The IT firm Apps Master received training from the government, whereas other firms got training from individual sources. In the case of Mr. Abir Hasan, the founder of Apps Master, it was easy for him to attend the training projects conducted by the government. The Walletmix informed us that their business concept is very novel in the Bangladesh context, so their training is unavailable there. As such, they brought in their training from abroad. Summit Communication mentioned that their technical training was very practical, which was not available in Bangladesh. So, they hired skilled employees from abroad. Other IT firms took training either from personal experience or online courses on YouTube or other sites. It can therefore be averred that the training climate of the DEE needs to be strengthened if businesses are to prosper.

Scope of the internet

The interviewees held opinions about the specification of the Internet and the government's control over it. Table 6 depicts the overall satisfactory

Table 6.   Analyzing the scope of Internet.

Serial No.	Name of the Company	Speed of Internet	Cost of Internet	Government Control Over Internet
1	Pix Smite	Moderate	High cost	Very satisfied
2	Apps Master	Moderate	Costly	Very satisfied
3	Walletmix	Moderate	Costly	Very satisfied
4	Nagad	Moderate	Costly	Very satisfied
5	Avijatrik	Moderate	Moderate	Satisfied
6	Khulna E-shop	Moderate	Cheap	Average
7	Ali Express Community Bangladesh	Moderate	Costly	No comments
8	Bahari Gohona	Moderate	Cheap	Good
9	Studio Firefly	Moderate	Moderate	Satisfied
10	Summit Communication	Very good	Cheap	Very satisfied

state of the Internet in Bangladesh and the firms' perception that Internet speed needs improvement. Most firms concur that the Internet price is still costly. Another critical point is that the government is trying to enhance Internet connectivity in Bangladesh. In this connection, the executive of Summit Communication stated that the government had taken IT projects to facilitate the Internet at union and upazilla levels. For this reason, the government is considering providing 5G licenses in Bangladesh. Nevertheless, it is a matter of concern that the Internet quality in Bangladesh is still in a moderate position compared with that of the developed countries.

Characteristics of fixed broadband connection

It is conspicuous that IT firms depend on broadband connections (see Table 7). Moreover, it is also evident that this connection has a massive public demand. Still, it has a high cost, slow speed, and line drop out problems. The entrepreneurs in this case suggest that the broadband connection and Internet can be improved through effective measures adopted by the government.

Table 7. Analyzing the fixed broadband connection.

Serial No.	Company Name	Limitations of Fixed Broadband Connections	Strengths	Comments
1	Pix Smite	• Higher price • Lower coverage • Line drop • Lack of governmental control	• Fast speed • Low installation costs	Moderate
2	Apps Master	• Broadband increases piracy • Lower coverage	• High speed with FTP server	Very good
3	Walletmix	• Speed is not accurate according to package • Lower coverage	• The entire IT industry depends on broadband connections	Moderate
4	Nagad	• Lower coverage • Higher price • Speed is not accurate	• No comments	Better than moderate but not very good
5	Avijatrik	• Remote areas are not connected	• Service is moderate • All divisional cities are connected	Moderate
6	Khulna E-shop	• Line drop • Server down	• Unlimited Internet • Higher speed • Low cost	Moderate
7	Ali Express Community Bangladesh	• Remote areas are not connected	• Speed is better	Moderate
8	Bahari Gohona	• Remote areas are not connected	• Higher speed • Low cost	Moderate
9	Studio Firefly	• Lower coverage • Lower speed	• Cheap	Moderate
10	Summit Communication	• Lower coverage	• High speed • Low cost • Secure	Very Good

Contribution of mobile telecommunication

Mobile telecommunication plays a vital role in the growing digital entrepreneurship ecosystem. According to the interview findings, mobile telecommunication entails higher telephone and Internet charges. Moreover, mobile operators only serve GSM and 3G networks in remote areas, which is why many people need high-speed Internet, a big obstacle for IT business. Furthermore, the service of customer care, the package of Internet, and the call rate all serve to confuse the entrepreneur because there is severe competition in the mobile telecommunication market. By contrast, mobile operators do corporate social responsibility activities to promote entrepreneurship. The findings in Table 8 suggest the government needs to intervene and optimize the mobile telecommunications sector.

Availability of user device

While IT firms believe that the availability of user devices in Bangladesh helps promote their business, some claim that the quality of devices could be better than that of developed countries because most of the devices are imported from China (Table 9). Moreover, some entrepreneurs complain that the generation or technology of the devices in Bangladesh is one or two years behind. So, if anyone wants to buy an updated device, they must either pay a high price for the product or pay more tax to import it. Besides, few international brands have offices in Bangladesh.

Assessing digital citizenship rate

The interviewed IT firms have claimed that digital citizenship has rocketed in the last five years, which is a lucrative opportunity for their business (Table 10). Summit Communication, Bahari Gohona, Ali Express Community Bangladesh, Avijatrik, and Nagad have noticed that 80% of their average customers are strongly digitalized. They can order their product through mobile phones and can make payments online. In addition, they keep technical knowledge about the Internet and smart devices. Most firms believe that there is a robust ecosystem for being digital. It is a very positive factor in this regard. The availability of user devices can be attributed as a significant reason behind the increasing rate of digital citizenship.

Table 8. Analyzing the contribution of mobile telecommunication.

Serial No.	Company Name	Advantages and Disadvantages of Mobile Telecommunication	Inspiration for Entrepreneurs from Telecommunication Companies	Comments
1	Pix Smite	• Eco-friendly • Higher call rate • Competitive	No	Moderate
2	Apps Master	• 3G, 4G • High call rate • High speed internet	Yes: Teletalk "Agami" SIM	Very good
3	Walletmix	• Lack of government control	Yes. They are providing offers like changing an operator but keeping the same number	Moderate
4	Nagad	• Higher cost of internet • High speed	No comments	Better than moderate but not very good
5	Avijatrik	• They are providing good service • Providing very average 4G Internet	Yes	Moderate
6	Khulna E-shop	• Low charge in call and Internet • Weak Internet coverage in remote areas	No	Moderate
7	Ali Express Community Bangladesh	• Strong network • High call rate	No comments	Moderate
8	Bahari Gohona	• Lack of commitment • High call rate	No	Moderate
9	Studio Firefly	• Good network coverage • High competition	Yes. Grameen Phone is offering a digital entrepreneurial workshop	Moderate
10	Summit Communication	• High coverage of GSM network • Satisfactory speed	Yes	Very good

Table 9.   Availability of user device.

Serial No.	Name of the Company	Strength for the Entrepreneur	Weakness for the Entrepreneur	Comments
1	Pix Smite	• Lower price compared to developed countries • Devices are imported from China	• Unreliable devices • Lack of high configured device • No official showroom of Apple	Average
2	Apps Master	• Getting digital device at cheap price	• Behind in advanced technology	Average
3	Walletmix	• They are advanced according to their needs	• They are backward in adoption of technology	No comments
4	Nagad	• There is no limitation	• Devices are updated late • They have to pay a lot for devices	Average
5	Avijatrik	• Android system phones are available	• No weakness	Very good
6	Khulna E-shop	• Lower cost	• Quality of device varies among countries	Good
7	Ali Express Community Bangladesh	• Easily available • Lower price	• Sometimes required to pay taxes	Average
8	Bahari Gohona	• Lower price	• Lower quality	Average
9	Studio Firefly	• Easily available • Lower price	• Lower quality	Average
10	Summit Communication	• Helps to reduce manpower • Available advanced technology	• Lack of after sales service	Very good

Analyzing digital law

One of the most critical elements of the digital entrepreneurial ecosystem is digital law in Bangladesh, which entrepreneurs need to be better informed about (Table 11). Moreover, the implementation of the law is sub-standard. The process for implementing legislation on digital technology is very long, in some cases, taking over six months. Once implemented, the local authorities on occasion do not accept complaints and do not implement them effectively, which can be a source of frustration.

Table 10. Digital citizenship rate.

Serial No.	Name of the Company	Rate of Digital Citizenship of Business	Opportunity for Being Digital	Comments
1	Pix Smite	20% to 30%	yes	Rate is increasing
2	Apps Master	50%	yes	No comments
3	Walletmix	60%	yes	Better than before
4	Nagad	70%	yes	Enough digital
5	Avijatrik	90%	yes	Older generations need to embrace digitalization
6	Khulna E-shop	70%	yes	No comments
7	Ali Express Community Bangladesh	90%	yes	Enough
8	Bahari Gohona	60%	yes	Almost enough
9	Studio Firefly	Average	yes	Younger generation is more digital
10	Summit Communication	100%	yes	Customer has enough knowledge

Scope of digital access

Digital access in Bangladesh for IT business is considered by entrepreneurs to be in a good position (Table 12). Most explain that they and their customers can gain full digital access, such as the fact that they can pay or receive through online or mobile banking in Bangladesh. However, a few entrepreneurs expressed that they face access problems during international payment or receipt.

Analyzing digital commerce and marketplace

In this segment, the primary concern is to identify the credibility of e-commerce products and the safety of the e-commerce payment (Table 13). The e-commerce sector has been enriched hugely over the last five years. Currently, the e-commerce of Bangladesh and its markets are regarded by entrepreneurs to be in a stable position, creating lucrative demand. Moreover, the payment method is becoming safe, too. This means that e-commerce and its marketplace will be boosted in the near

Table 11.   Analyzing digital law.

Serial No.	Name of the Company	Knowledge about Digital Law	Implementation of Digital Law	Comments
1	Pix Smite	No idea at all	No idea	No comments
2	Apps Master	Yes	No	Police is not helpful in this case
3	Walletmix	Yes	No	No comments
4	Nagad	Yes	No	No comments
5	Avijatrik	Yes	No	Implementing some nowadays
6	Khulna E-shop	No	No comments	No comments
7	Ali Express Community Bangladesh	Yes	No	Nobody is concerned about this
8	Bahari Gohona	Yes	Yes	Only for registered businesses
9	Studio Firefly	Yes	No	Takes a long time
10	Summit Communication	Yes	No	Need to improve more

future. Nevertheless, irregular delivery schedules among some larger e-commerce companies have created challenges in maintaining customer trust. In this case, they will require appropriate policies and monitoring to ensure governance in the digital commerce sector.

Discussion and Conclusion

The main objective of this research is to explore the elements of the digital entrepreneurial ecosystem in Bangladesh. The study identified the bottom lines of the digital entrepreneurial ecosystem and how entrepreneurs perceive DEE elements. In this research, ten (10) components of the digital entrepreneurial ecosystem have been investigated: motivation, financing, training source, the scope of the Internet, fixed broadband, mobile telecommunication, user device, digital citizenship, digital law, digital access, digital commerce, and marketplace. In the case of motivation, it has been observed that the government is trying to motivate digital entrepreneurs by communicating with students at public universities, colleges, or other

Table 12. Scope of digital access.

Serial No.	Name of the Company	Facing Problem in Digital Access	Sector of Facing Digital Access Problem	Comments
1	Pix Smite	Yes	International payment method	Average
2	Apps Master	Yes	International payment method	Average
3	Walletmix	No	No comments	Good
4	Nagad	No	No comments	Good
5	Avijatrik	No	No comments	Good enough
6	Khulna E-shop	Yes	Local and international payment system	Average
7	Ali Express Community Bangladesh	No	No comments	Average
8	Bahari Gohona	No	No comments	Good
9	Studio Firefly	Yes	Local and international payment system	Average
10	Summit Communication	No	No comments	Good

public and private institutions. However, the government's intervention is limited to promoting digital entrepreneurship through business incubators and financing options. In such an environment, personal inspiration and hard work remain the primary motivators for starting up a digital firm. The government can take steps to address this through IT workshops and programs through which young students can be motivated to become future entrepreneurs.

The most challenging path for digital entrepreneurs is financing. The findings from the interviews suggest a 50% chance of loan rejection either from private banks or governmental institutions. Entrepreneurs must therefore come forward to a digital business with their own funds. They can get the finance if they can deposit equivalent collateral to financial institutions. Moreover, some private financial institutions offer business loans that are also complex for entrepreneurs because the banks require

Table 13.   **Digital commerce and marketplace.**

Serial No.	Name of the Company	Credibility of E-commerce Goods and Service	Safety of E-commerce Payment	Comments
1	Pix Smite	Credible	Moderate	Average
2	Apps Master	Highly credible	Safe	Very good
3	Walletmix	Credible	Safe	No comments
4	Nagad	Credible	Safe	It should be improved more
5	Avijatrik	Credible	Safe	Average
6	Khulna E-shop	Credible	Safe	Average
7	Ali Express Community Bangladesh	Credible	Moderately safe	Average
8	Bahari Gohona	Credible	Safe	Good
9	Studio Firefly	Credible	Safe	Average
10	Summit Communication	Credible	Safe	Average

the IT firms to show a profit for a specific period, which makes it tough to get finance in Bangladesh for digital entrepreneurs.

Moreover, the training facilities for digital entrepreneurs are not widely available. Most entrepreneurs train by themselves online, even though some institutions provide training in exchange for funding. Still, the high cost of the Internet makes it difficult for remote and rural customers to access high-speed Internet. Bangladesh's mobile telecommunication sector has significantly improved due to the concerted efforts of the government and telecommunication companies. For example, Grameenphone, the leading telecom operator in Bangladesh, has been conducting ICT workshops to develop the ICT platform. In addition, Banglalink has taken on ICT incubator projects. Moreover, they are preparing to launch a 5G network, which is another step forward in enhancing the digital ecosystem. Mobile telecommunication in Bangladesh is now bringing benefits to digital entrepreneurs. Another significant effort in Bangladesh will be satellite communication. The Bangabandhu Satellite-1 is the first Bangladeshi geostationary communications and broadcasting satellite, which has brought revolutionary changes to Bangladesh's communication arena. Moreover, the user device availability and the digital citizenship of Bangladesh have a positive correlation. The more devices that are upgraded, the more the citizens become digitalized. So, it is an excellent opportunity for ecosystem participants and digital entrepreneurs to access the untapped market.

Lastly, implementing digital law has not been satisfactory. The long processing times, unwillingness to deal with complaints by the police, and bribes all disrupt the ecosystem. Furthermore, digital access is still limited when compared to developed countries. As one of the most entrepreneurial challenges is to build up a thriving e-commerce marketplace, the government must implement digital security laws and appropriate regulations to control e-commerce companies. Proper regulatory measures and private sector interventions can ensure discipline in the e-commerce sector and bolster the digital entrepreneurial ecosystem.

In conclusion, this chapter's main purpose was to provide a structured analysis on the state of the components within the digital entrepreneurial ecosystem. To accomplish this objective, the research interviewed 10 digital entrepreneurial firms to investigate their perceptions and opinions. The study discerned from them the strong as well as weak standpoints of the ecosystem. Factors like the Internet, devices, mobile networks, digital citizenship, digital access, and e-commerce are considered by them to be vital, which benefit firms and the overall ecosystem. By contrast, the downside of the ecosystem is the implementation of digital laws, which are ineffective in the ecosystem. Proper governance of the ecosystem and control measures for e-commerce companies will demand more attention from the various stakeholders. Moreover, managing finance is another significant challenge that requires financial institutions and governments to secure more funding for start-ups. Ultimately, the digital entrepreneurial ecosystem is a relatively novel concept, particularly for emerging countries, which needs exploration and development from academicians and practitioners.

Implications of the Research

This chapter holds both theoretical and practical significance. Considering that the concept of DEE is still nascent, our research findings contribute to this burgeoning literature. They identify the components of the ecosystem from a developing country context while solidifying the extant literature by providing empirical evidence of DEE. Finally, the results from Bangladesh shed new light on the elements that make up DEE.

The study also bears practical implications. The ecosystem for digital firms has developed special significance due to the growth of Web 2.0 as well as the challenges brought on by the COVID-19 pandemic, which has led the firms to go digital even as more tech start-ups have emerged. This situation led to DEE becoming more relevant. The context of Bangladesh presents different strengths and weaknesses related to the components of the DEE. This is particularly important for policymakers and governments to take congenial measures to strengthen the ecosystem. Notably, the research in this chapter sheds light on increasing digital citizenship and improving digital laws to ensure governance in the ecosystem. Furthermore, the ecosystem participants and digital entrepreneurs can interpret directions on leveraging the ecosystem to achieve better firm performance indicators.

Future Research Directions

This chapter has pinpointed the components of the ecosystem, which are expected to arouse further research from those interested in the ecosystem. The elements of DEE identified in our study can be tested empirically in both developing and developed country contexts through longitudinal studies. Besides, further research may be based on quantitative methods on how the DEE concepts can be combined with institutional support to improve a firm's performance. Finally, the components of DEE require empirical investigation regarding how the elements can predict and influence the firm performance indicators.

References

Acs, Z. J., Stam, E., Audretsch, D. B., and O'Connor, A. 2017. The lineages of the entrepreneurial ecosystem approach. *Small Business Economics*, 49(1): 1–10.

Adner, R. 2017. Ecosystem as structure: An actionable construct for strategy. *Journal of Management*, 43(1): 39–58.

Adner, R. and Kapoor, R. 2010. Value creation in innovation ecosystems: How the structure of technological interdependence affects firm performance in new technology generations. *Strategic Management Journal*, 31(3): 306–333.

Beugelsdijk, S., Kostova, T., and Roth, K. 2017. An overview of Hofstede-inspired country-level culture research in international business since 2006. *Journal of International Business Studies*, 48: 30–47.

Brown, R. and Mason, C. 2017. Looking inside the spiky bits: A critical review and conceptualisation of entrepreneurial ecosystems. *Small Business Economics*, 49(1): 11–30.

Cearra, J. and Saiz, M. 2021. Experimenting a methodology to improve the entrepreneurial ecosystem through collaboration and digitalization. *Journal of Small Business Strategy*, 31(1): 51–65.

Cetindamar, D., Lammers, T., and Sick, N. 2020. Digital technologies, competitiveness & policies: An integrative city-based policy roadmap for entrepreneurial ecosystems. In R. Tiwari and S. Buse (Eds.), *Managing Innovation in a Global and Digital World* (pp. 49–62). Springer Gabler, Wiesbaden.

Chan, C. M., Teoh, S. Y., Yeow, A., and Pan, G. 2019. Agility in responding to disruptive digital innovation: Case study of an SME. *Information Systems Journal*, 29(2): 436–455.

Corallo, A., Passiante, G., and Prencipe, A. 2007. *The Digital Business Ecosystem*. Edward Elgar Publishing.

Duan, C., Kotey, B., and Sandhu, K. 2020. Transnational immigrant entrepreneurship: Effects of home-country entrepreneurial ecosystem factors. *International Journal of Entrepreneurial Behavior & Research*, 27(3): 711–729.

Elia, G., Margherita, A., and Passiante, G. 2020. Digital entrepreneurship ecosystem: How digital technologies and collective intelligence are reshaping the entrepreneurial process. *Technological Forecasting and Social Change*, 150: 119791.

Emembolu, I., Emembolu, C., Aderinwale, O., and Lobijo, E. 2022. Digital entrepreneurship in Africa: Case studies of Nigeria and South Sudan. In O. Adeola, J. N. Edeh, R. E. Hinson, and F. Netswera (Eds.), *Digital Service Delivery in Africa* (pp. 135–162). Palgrave Macmillan, Cham.

EY Analysis. 2021. https://www.ey.com/en_gl/alliances/what-business-ecosystem-means-and-why-it-matters. Accessed October 10, 2022.

Feng, N., Xue, J., Zhao, R., and Yang, S. 2021. Exploring SMEs' behavioral intentions of participating in platform-based innovation ecosystems. *Industrial Management & Data Systems*, 121(11): 2254–2275.

Ferraro, G. P. and Briody, E. K. 2017. *The Cultural Dimension of Global Business*. London: Taylor & Francis.

Frimanslund, T. 2022. Financial entrepreneurial ecosystems: An analysis of urban and rural regions of Norway. *International Journal of Global Business and Competitiveness*, 17(1): 24–39.

Giones, F. and Brem, A. 2017. Digital technology entrepreneurship: A definition and research agenda. *Technology Innovation Management Review*, 7(5): 44–51.

Hammarberg, K., Kirkman, M., and de Lacey, S. 2016. Qualitative research methods: When to use them and how to judge them. *Human Reproduction*, 31(3): 498–501.

Iansiti, M. and Levien, R. 2004. *The Keystone Advantage: What the New Dynamics of Business Ecosystems Mean for Strategy, Innovation, and Sustainability*. Boston: Harvard Business Press.

Isenberg, D. 2011. The entrepreneurship ecosystem strategy as a new paradigm for economic policy: Principles for cultivating entrepreneurship. Paper Presented at the *Institute of International and European Affairs* (pp. 1–13).

Jungcharoensukying, E., Feller, J., O'Flaherty, B., and Treacy, S. 2020. An exploratory conceptual model for digital entrepreneurs within entrepreneurial ecosystems. Paper presented in *ECIE 2020: 15th European Conference on Innovation and Entrepreneurship*. Academic Conferences International Limited (pp. 789–797).

Kimuli, S. N. L., Sendawula, K., and Nagujja, S. 2021. Digital technologies in micro and small enterprise: Evidence from Uganda's informal sector during the COVID-19 pandemic. *World Journal of Science, Technology and Sustainable Development*, 18(2): 93–108.

Kollmann, T., Kleine-Stegemann, L., de Cruppe, K., and Then-Bergh, C. 2022. Eras of digital entrepreneurship. *Business & Information Systems Engineering*, 64(1): 15–31.

Kraft, C., Lindeque, J. P., and Peter, M. K. 2022. The digital transformation of Swiss small and medium-sized enterprises: Insights from digital tool adoption. *Journal of Strategy and Management*, 15(3): 468–494.

Leithwood, K. 2001. School leadership in the context of accountability policies. *International Journal of Leadership in Education*, 4(3): 217–235.

Li, W., Badr, Y., and Biennier, F. 2012. Digital ecosystems: Challenges and prospects. In *Proceedings of the International Conference on Management of Emergent Digital EcoSystems* (pp. 117–122).

Loonam, J. and O'Regan, N. 2022. Global value chains and digital platforms: Implications for strategy. *Strategic Change*, 31(1): 161–177.

Mas, J. M. and Gómez, A. 2021. Social partners in the digital ecosystem: Will business organizations, trade unions and government organizations survive the digital revolution? *Technological Forecasting and Social Change*, 162: 120349.

Mason, C. and Brown, R. 2014. *Entrepreneurial Ecosystems and Growth-oriented Entrepreneurship*. Final report to OECD, 30(1): 77–102.

Masroor, I., Alam, M. N., Hossain, S. M. A., and Misbauddin, S. M. 2020. Moderating effect of uncertainty on the relationship between effectuation and internationalisation speed: A study on small and medium software firms of Bangladesh. *International Journal of Export Marketing*, 3(3): 261–286.

Nambisan, S. 2017. Digital entrepreneurship: Toward a digital technology perspective of entrepreneurship. *Entrepreneurship Theory and Practice*, 41(6): 1029–1055.

Naudé, W. and Liebregts, W. 2020. Digital entrepreneurship research: A concise introduction. IZA Discussion Paper No. 13667. SSRN: https://ssrn.com/abstract=3691380. Accessed November 25, 2022.

Nedumaran, G. and Saroja, R. 2020. A study on support digital entrepreneurship. *Dogo Rangsang Research Journal*, 10(6): 261–272.

Ozkeser, B. 2019. Impact of training on employee motivation in human resources management. *Procedia Computer Science*, 158: 802–810.

Purbasari, R., Muttaqin, Z., and Sari, D. S. 2021. Digital entrepreneurship in pandemic Covid 19 Era: The digital entrepreneurial ecosystem framework. *Review of Integrative Business and Economics Research*, 10: 114–135.

Ratten, V. 2020. Coronavirus and international business: An entrepreneurial ecosystem perspective. *Thunderbird International Business Review*, 62(5): 629–634.

Sahut, J. M., Iandoli, L., and Teulon, F. 2021. The age of digital entrepreneurship. *Small Business Economics*, 56(3): 1159–1169.

Salamzadeh, A. and Ramadani, V. 2021. Entrepreneurial ecosystem and female digital entrepreneurship–Lessons to learn from an Iranian case study. In S. Rezaei, J. Li, S. Ashourizadeh, V. Ramadani, and S. Gërguri-Rashiti (Eds.), *The Emerald Handbook of Women and Entrepreneurship in Developing Economies* (pp. 317–334). Bingley: Emerald Publishing Limited.

Saunders, M., Lewis, P., and Thornhill, A. 2009. *Research Methods for Business Students*. London: Pearson Education.

Schulte-Althoff, M., Schewina, K., Lee, G. M., and Fürstenau, D. 2020. On the heterogeneity of digital infrastructure in entrepreneurial ecosystems. Paper presented at *HICSS* (pp. 1–10).

Smirnov, V., Semenov, V., Zakharova, A. and Dulina, G. 2020. Analysis of the potential of digital youth entrepreneurship development in Russia. Paper presented in *Ecological-Socio-Economic Systems: Models of Competition and Cooperation (ESES 2019)* (pp. 16–20). Atlantis Press.

Song, A. K. 2019. The digital entrepreneurial ecosystem—A critique and reconfiguration. *Small Business Economics*, 53(3): 569–590.

Song, Y., Dana, L. P., and Berger, R. 2021. The entrepreneurial process and online social networks: Forecasting survival rate. *Small Business Economics*, 56(3): 1171–1190.

Spigel, B. 2016. Developing and governing entrepreneurial ecosystems: The structure of entrepreneurial support programs in Edinburgh, Scotland. *International Journal of Innovation and Regional Development*, 7(2): 141–160.

Sussan, F. and Acs, Z. J. 2017. The digital entrepreneurial ecosystem. *Small Business Economics*, 49(1): 55–73.

Tandon, A., Gupta, A., Goel, P., and Singh, V. K. 2020. Impact of digitisation on entrepreneurial ecosystems: An Indian perspective. *International Journal of Business and Globalisation*, 25(2): 154–169.

Williamson, P. J. and De Meyer, A. 2012. Ecosystem advantage: How to successfully harness the power of partners. *California Management Review*, 55(1): 24–46.

Yin, R. K. 2013. Validity and generalization in future case study evaluations. *Evaluation*, 19(3): 321–332.

Zahra, S. A., Liu, W., and Si, S. 2022. How digital technology promotes entrepreneurship in ecosystems. *Technovation*, 119: 102457.

Chapter 13

The Role of MNEs in Industry 4.0 Transformation in ASEAN

Maria Cecilia Salta-Macesar

Abstract

Industry 4.0 can play a significant role in unlocking the manufacturing potential, increasing efficiency, and enhancing the industrial competitiveness of Association of Southeast Asian Nations (ASEAN). Foreign Multinational Enterprises (MNEs) are increasingly playing an important role in the development of the Industry 4.0 ecosystem in the ASEAN region, involving a wide spectrum of technology applications (from automation, additive manufacturing (AM) to Industrial Internet of Things and smart factories). Many MNEs are also investing in the region to build digital infrastructure, manufacture industrial automation (IA) hardware, and operate close to clients in the region's vibrant manufacturing industry. This chapter analyses Foreign Direct Investment (FDI) and MNEs in Industry 4.0 in ASEAN. In particular, it examines the role of MNEs in Industry 4.0 transformation through adoption and provision of technology solutions. In conclusion, this chapter highlights the significance of improving the investment environment by establishing relevant policies to incentivize the adoption of advanced manufacturing technologies for Industry 4.0 transformation.

Keywords: Industry 4.0, foreign direct investment (FDI), multinational enterprises (MNEs), Association of Southeast Asian Nations (ASEAN), digital infrastructure

Introduction

Industry 4.0 is playing a significant role in unlocking manufacturing potential, increasing efficiency, and enhancing industrial competitiveness in the Association of Southeast Asian Nations (ASEAN). Its potential for a new industrial revolution has pushed them to adopt Industry 4.0 transformation plans to attract investment and foreign technologies through favorable regulatory frameworks, investment incentives, and other facilitation measures.

ASEAN countries are cooperating on Industry 4.0 transformation with the adoption of several related agreements including the ASEAN Declaration on Industrial Transformation to Industry 4.0, the ASEAN Digital Master Plan 2025, the implementation of the ASEAN Consolidated Strategy on the Fourth Industrial Revolution for ASEAN, and the ongoing establishment of the ASEAN Smart Cities Network.

Foreign Direct Investment (FDI) and Multinational Enterprises (MNEs) play key roles in the development of the Industry 4.0 ecosystem in ASEAN, including in manufacturing hardware and supplying technology solutions, ranging from automation, additive manufacturing (AM) to Industrial Internet of Things (IIoT) and smart factories. Investors from around the world are upgrading facilities with Industry 4.0 technologies, establishing smart factories, training centers, and centers of excellence. They invest in the region to build the digital infrastructure and data centers to support the industrial transformation and the rapid growth of the digital economy (PWC, 2016).

This chapter analyses the roles of FDI and MNEs in the development of Industry 4.0 in ASEAN as investors, suppliers, and adopters of advanced technology solutions. The analysis covers Industry 4.0 value chains, from industrial automation, AM, and IIoT to smart factories development.[1]

FDI in Industry 4.0 in ASEAN

MNEs contribute to Industry 4.0 transformation in ASEAN through various channels:

---

[1]This chapter is an expansion (with new cases) of the findings contained in ASEAN Secretariat and UNCTAD (2020, 2021).

 (i) Establishing digital infrastructure (5G networks and data centers).
 (ii) Upgrading facilities with industrial automation (IA) and digital technologies, application of IIoTs, and establishment of smart factories.
(iii) Manufacturing IA products, parts, and equipment.
(iv) Supplying advanced and smart manufacturing technology solutions (e.g., automation, robots, AM, and IIoTs) to more customers.
 (v) Establishing Industry 4.0 research and development (R&D) facilities, technology hubs, and centers of excellence, including skills development and training centers.

The manufacturing industry is a major recipient of FDI in ASEAN, rising from \$29 billion in 2010 to \$45 billion in 2021. FDI in manufacturing accounted for more than one-quarter of total FDI flows to the region.

FDI inflows to manufacturing in ASEAN has steadily increased since the 2000s. Although FDI flows declined sharply in 2020 due to the COVID-19 global pandemic, it strongly rebounded in 2021 at \$45 billion, increasing by 134% from 2020. Strong investment in electronics (semiconductors) and electrical equipment (including batteries for electric vehicles) pushed up FDI in manufacturing in 2021. Announced investments in electronics and electrical equipment quadrupled to \$32.9 billion in 2021, increasing the share of these categories in the total value of greenfield investment to about 52%, from 12.4% in 2020. Expansion and technology upgrades to cope with supply chain challenges and growing Industry 4.0 technologies demand, with government policy support, underpinned the strong FDI inflows (UNCTAD, 2020).

The vibrant regional manufacturing hub provides a growing pool of customers for Industry 4.0 technologies. Industry 4.0 adoption by MNEs, local companies, and SMEs increases industrial efficiency and transforms the region into a more competitive global manufacturing hub, further increasing the attractiveness of ASEAN for FDI, particularly in such value chain sectors.

Factors influencing MNEs' Industry 4.0 activities in ASEAN

This section provides insights on what factors influence and drive MNEs' investment activities in the region.

Drivers and motivations

MNE activities in Industry 4.0 and the digital economy have led to a robust level of FDI. Rapid industrial growth, regional integration, and industrial linkages as well as improving investment environment in ASEAN are all key drivers. MNEs invest in ASEAN for various reasons: (1) growing market for industry 4.0 hardware and technology solutions, (2) proximity of Industry 4.0 technologies' suppliers/providers to markets, (3) strengthening production capacity, capability, and efficiency (Digital News Asia, 2013); and (4) regional integration and improving investment environment with countries taking measures to actively attract Industry 4.0 projects (see Table A.1).

MNE subsidiaries continued to invest in industrial automation during the period 2020–2021 to address both pandemic-related challenges (e.g., decreasing manpower due to lockdowns) and post-pandemic issues (McKinsey, 2021). The aim was to increase efficiency and implement corporate-wide Industry 4.0 transformation. Cypress Manufacturing, a subsidiary of Infineon Technologies (US), in the Philippines upgraded its technology in 2020–2021. Other MNEs in the Philippines such as: Schneider Electric (France) allocated 5% of annual revenues for investments in Industry 4.0 technologies; Amkor Technology (US) spent 10% to 20% of its annual budget for manufacturing technology upgrade and expansion. Continental (Germany) in Malaysia, Philippines, and Thailand continued investments in production technology and capacity expansion.

Regional and national policies

Another important driver is the improving regulatory environment as ASEAN Member States adopt national plans for industrial transformation, with policies and measures to attract FDI in Industry 4.0. For example, Malaysia launched the National Policy on Industry 4.0 or Industry4WRD in October 2018. The policy aims to increase industrial productivity by 30% by 2030. Industry4WRD provides a comprehensive transformation agenda for manufacturing and related services and encourages companies to adopt smart technologies and to promote Malaysia as a high-tech destination and a total solution provider (Wong *et al.*, 2021). Under Industry4WRD, the Government through the Malaysia Development Bank established the RM2 billion Industry Digitalization Transformation Fund, with a 2% interest subsidy. The fund is aimed to help accelerate the adoption of Industry 4.0 technologies. To further incentivize automation and modernization of the manufacturing industry, the Industry4WRD Intervention Fund provides SMEs with up to 70% of the amount that is financed and guaranteed.

Singapore enacted policies that established specific facilities and institutional arrangements to accelerate Industry 4.0 transformation, including building a vibrant research and innovation ecosystem and purpose-designed industrial facilities. The Economic Development Board (EDB) lists 17 priority business activities and industries that the Government aims to attract (e.g., advanced manufacturing, innovation, information and communications technology [ICT]). It offers investors corporate tax exemption under the Pioneer Certificate or a concessionary tax rate of 5% or 10% on income derived from qualifying activities for 5 years under the Development and Expansion Certificate. Specific grants and schemes are provided such as Tech@SG Programme for companies to establish their core teams in Singapore; Research and Innovation Scheme for Companies (RISC) in technology development and innovation activities, Training Grant for Companies (TGC) in manpower capability development in new technologies and industrial skills. Several programs were established to support companies in research on emerging technologies and encourage Industry 4.0 adoption. These include the National Robotics Program, the National Additive Manufacturing Innovation Cluster for applying 3D printing research into commercial applications, the Singapore Smart Industry Readiness Index to help companies evaluate their readiness for Industry 4.0 adoption and design their transformation roadmaps, the SkillsFuture Series for Advanced Manufacturing for new industry-relevant skills training programs, and the Advanced Remanufacturing and Technology Centre (ARTC) for public–private partnerships on advanced manufacturing research and its industrial applications, and capacity building in Aerospace, fast moving consumer goods, e-commerce, energy, land transport, and medical technology. In 2021, Singapore announced Manufacturing 2030, a 10-year roadmap to increase manufacturing value-added by 50% by 2030 and for the city-state to become a global business, innovation, and talent hub for Advanced Manufacturing.

Thailand launched Thailand 4.0 in 2016, a 20-year national development plan to transition the country into an innovation-driven economy, identifying science, technology, innovation, value addition, and R&D as important areas in this regard. New industries promoted under Thailand

4.0 included robotics and automation, aviation and logistics, biofuels and biochemicals, smart electronics, next-generation automotive, agriculture and biotechnology, and industries for a medical hub. In 2017, Thailand launched the Eastern Economic Corridor, which consisted of the Digital Park Thailand and sought to boost digital transformation efforts. The Board of Investment (BOI) targeted 12 sectors for investment, including smart electronics, robotics, and the digital economy. Qualified investors in these sectors are offered (1) corporate income tax exemption (for core technologies and R&D projects) and a tax holiday for new technologies as well as a high-impact investment matching grant for R&D, training, and innovation; (2) exemption from import duties on machinery and on raw materials imported for use in production for export and for R&D; (3) a 50% reduction of corporate income tax; (4) an investment tax allowance of up to 70% of the invested capital on net profit derived within 10 years; (5) 100% foreign ownership (no local requirements, no export requirements, no restriction on foreign currency), and (6) land ownership rights. The BOI provides additional tax deductions for companies installing automation systems (machinery and software) or undertaking advanced technology training activities in 2019 and a 3-year 50% reduction in corporate income tax for technology upgrades of manufacturing facilities and production efficiency improvements in 2021. To speed-up Industry 4.0 transformation, the Thai BOI approved a 3-year corporate income tax exemption covering 100% of the investment in Industry 4.0 upgrade and is aimed toward Industry 4.0 projects requiring higher investments.

ASEAN member states have cooperated at the regional level through agreements, action plans, and declarations, and efforts to promote the digital economy, Industry 4.0 transformation, cybersecurity, e-commerce, smart cities development, and manpower development to support Industry 4.0 transformation. The major agreements (ASEAN Secretariat website) are as follows:

- The ASEAN Agreement on Electronic Commerce signed in November 2018 has provisions to facilitate cross-border e-commerce by creating an environment of trust and confidence. It also seeks to deepen regional cooperation to develop and intensify the use of e-commerce.
- ASEAN Smart Cities Network signed in November 2018 facilitates cooperation on developing smart cities with private sector participation. It involves 26 ASEAN cities applying smart technologies

(e.g., urbanization, the IIoT, and big data) to improve efficiency and support rapid adoption of Industry 4.0.

- The ASEAN Declaration on Industrial Transformation to Industry 4.0 signed in November 2019 seeks to advance regional cooperation by promoting the adoption of Industry 4.0. The major elements include, facilitating ASEAN's industrial transformation to achieve sustainable development, fostering industrial collaboration among member states, and creating a prosperous and equitable ASEAN community by embracing innovation and digital technologies in Industry 4.0.
- The ASEAN Declaration on Human Resources Development for the Changing World of Work signed in June 2020 seeks to prepare ASEAN's human resources with competencies for Industry 4.0 as well as potentially negative impact of disruptive technologies.
- The ASEAN Digital Masterplan 2025 signed in January 2021 provides a guide toward achieving a digital community and economic bloc, and is powered by secure and transformative digital services, technologies, and ecosystems. Major activities include, promoting investment in new technologies, removing regulatory barriers to digital market operations, supporting social measures for digital inclusion and digital skills, and ensuring digital safety of the end users.
- The Consolidated Strategy on the Fourth Industrial Revolution for ASEAN signed in October 2021 is designed to provide policy guidance in building the ASEAN Digital Community across the three official pillars: the ASEAN Political-Security Community, the ASEAN Economic Community, and the ASEAN Socio-Cultural Community.

Characteristics of Industry 4.0 technologies players

Industry 4.0 technologies include: industrial automation (IA)/robotic technologies, IIoT, big data, artificial intelligence, AM, smart factory development, and digital twin application. Each kind of technology has its own set of players with their distinct features and characteristics (i.e., players' nationality, type of corporate structure, and motivations), which in turn influences the MNEs investment activities and location choices in the region (see Figure 1).

MNEs headquartered in the European Union (specifically Belgium, France, Germany, Netherlands, Switzerland, and the United Kingdom), Japan, Republic of Korea, Taiwan (China), and the US are the most active in IA/robotic technology, IIoT, AM, and other advance manufacturing

Industry 4.0 Technology	Nationality of FDI	Main Activities (2020–2022)	ASEAN Location Motivations	MNES
Industrial Automation (IA)/ Cobots	European Union, Japan, United States	Centers of Excellence, Customers Service Centers, Partnerships with public and private sectors to support Industry 4.0 adoption, develop new technologies, conduct skills training, expansion, greenfield new manufacturing facilities and new client projects	• Indonesia, Malaysia, Viet Nam, Singapore, Thailand • Growing market, supportive policies, regional integration, proximity to clients	Siemens (Germany), ABB (Switzerland), Emerson (United States), Schneider Electric (France), Rockwell Automation (United States), Mitsubishi Electric (Japan), Yokogawa Electric (Japan), Omron (Japan), Ametek EIG (United States), Phoenix Contact (Germany), Fanuc (Japan)
Industrial Internet of Things (IoT) providers	United States, European Union, Japan, Republic of Korea	Pursuit of partnerships (ie. Government agencies, other 4IR technology providers, with customers) to develop product offerings and new solutions and to start new engagements	• Indonesia, Malaysia, Philippines, Singapore, Thailand, Viet Nam • Growing market, development of smart cities and digital infrastructures, supportive policies	Amazon Web Services, C3 IoT, IBM, Microsoft States, PTC Inc, Cisco Systems (all United States), Ericsson (Sweden), NXP Semiconductors (Netherlands), Samsung Electronics (Republic of Korea), Mitsubishi Electric Asia (Japan), Yokogawa Electric (Japan), Advantech (Taiwan Province of China)
Additive Manufacturing (AM)	European Union (Germany mostly), Japan, United States, Taiwan Province of China	Advanced Manufacturing facilities, Centres of Excellence, R&D, Technology Centres, Regional HQ, partnerships with public and private institutions for new AM materials and solutions (other sectors)	• Singapore (majority), Thailand • Growing market for advanced manufacturing, proximity to market/clients, presence of Industry 4.0 ecosystem, supportive policies	Thyssenkrup (Germany), Yamazaki Mazak (Japan), Materialise (Belgium), New Kinpoo Group (Taiwan Province of China), HP (United States), Siemens Additive (Germany), Sodick (Japan)

Figure 1.   Characteristics of FDI in key Industry 4.0 technologies

Source: ASEAN Investment Report 2022 Research

technologies. In IA, most MNEs are large entities and/or part of a group of companies with a long history in industrial manufacturing. They have multiple presence in the region (two or three manufacturing facilities, regional headquarters, centers of excellence, and sales offices in ASEAN member states).

Two types of foreign companies provide IIoT hardware and solutions. The first are MNEs with IA technologies and IIoT (hardware and software). Examples are ABB (Switzerland–Sweden), Samsung (Republic of Korea), Yokogawa (Japan) (Business Wire, 2019), Bosch (Germany) (Manufacturing Tomorrow, 2020). The second are MNEs that are "stand alone" and highly specialized in technology software solutions. They offer cloud services, data centers, colocation spaces, and IIoT solutions. The majority of these are in the US, such as IBM, Amazon Web Services, Microsoft, Cisco Systems, PCT Inc., and Texas Instruments.

MNEs providing AM technologies are involved in manufacturing of industrial machines.

Role of FDI and MNEs in Industry 4.0 Transformation

This section highlights key roles and cases of MNEs contributing toward Industry 4.0 development in ASEAN. The cases cover MNEs as investors, suppliers, users, developers of hardware and software solutions, and providers of Industry 4.0 skills development.

Investment in Industry 4.0 technologies

Upgrading Industry 4.0 technologies by MNEs and local companies in ASEAN encourage hardware and technology solution suppliers to be present or expand in the region. Hardware manufacturers (e.g., of sensors, semiconductors, automation machines, and robots) upgrade their production facilities with advanced IA systems (*The Nation*, 2018) (see Table A.2).

Industries with volume production and in manufacturing locations with limited labor supply or high costs tend to automate more. Foreign subsidiaries are more receptive to IA technologies due to stronger financial capabilities, larger exposure to IA, and influences from their headquarters. IA/robotic technology ensures consistency of product quality and production predictability. Subsidiaries of MNEs such as BMW and Continental (Germany), Procter and Gamble and Motorola (US), Tetra Pak (Switzerland), and Toyota, Mitsubishi, Honda, Suzuki, Tanaka Precision, Denso, Sharp, and Sumitomo Electric (all Japan) have adopted IA for their factories in ASEAN.

The ongoing adoption of Industry 4.0 technologies in ASEAN varies and depends on the level and maturity of industrialization in member states. Foreign and local firms are relatively less active in emerging manufacturing locations (i.e., Cambodia, Lao PDR, and Myanmar). Electronics and automotive are key sectors utilizing Industry 4.0 technologies (UNDP, 2020). Others like metal and machinery, food and beverage are also witnessing the deployment of automation and the application of advanced digital technology solutions (e.g., IIoT).

AM is being adopted in the aerospace, maritime, and healthcare industries in ASEAN, particularly in Malaysia, Singapore, and Thailand, with demand shifting from prototyping to industrial 3D printing of parts (Thyssenkrupp, 2019). The adoption of AM technology by other industries widens the coverage of ASEAN's Industry 4.0 transformation.

Spillover effect and technology adoption by local companies

The positive experience of foreign MNEs in advanced manufacturing technologies encourages domestic companies to embark on a similar transformation process. The Dexa Group, an Indonesian pharmaceutical company, deployed the Alibaba Cloud IoT solution to scale up operation to meet demand, control costs, and maintain data security. Shera, a Thai manufacturer and distributor of fiber cement products, adopted Microsoft digital solutions and platforms, including the IoT, to increase productivity. Tan Boon Ming, a one-stop appliance store in Malaysia, deployed Microsoft digital and IoT solutions enabling the company to obtain real-time data on the company's warehouse, logistics, inventory, and sales situation. Other examples of local linkages in Industry 4.0 and technologies supplied by foreign MNEs are as follows:

- *Davao Union Cement Corporation* (Philippines) installed automation equipment and solutions systems as well as digitalized its main production and secondary processes. All were supplied by Siemens (Germany).

- *DHL* (Germany) *Indonesia* employed Huawei (China) smart workplace solutions to digitalize all its operations by using real-time big data management. DHL Indonesia's supply chain operations improved procurement, labeling, and delivery performance, reducing customer complaints and work hours.
- *Proton* (Malaysia) contracted Accenture in 2010 to expand and improve its SAP-based enterprise resource planning system.
- *PT Indolakto* (Indonesia), a dairy producer, worked with Koerber (Germany) to implement a system with automated storage technology in its distribution center thereby increasing capacity by 25%. ABB (Switzerland) also supplied a robotic technology solution to PT Indolakto (BeritaJatim, 2019).
- *PT JVC Electronic Indonesia*, an electronic manufacturer, adopted robotic technology used in the production of audio–visual and navigation devices for cars. Technology was supplied by Universal Robots (Denmark).
- *Sanwa Group* (Singapore), a plastics manufacturer, adopted Schneider Electric's (France) smart manufacturing and automation solutions to support remote monitoring of energy consumption, temperature, humidity, and pressure, with a centralized command station to manage operations and access real-time data (Schneider Electric, 2023). The automated facilities (i) relieve staff to perform and upskill for more valuable tasks, (ii) double production output, (iii) enable faster and better diagnostics, (iv) reduce energy consumption and associated costs, and (v) result in near zero defective production.
- *Siam City Cement* (Thailand) adopted Fujitsu's (Japan) smart manufacturing solutions in 2017, including robot-assisted inspections, data analytics for predictive maintenance, machine learning, and a remote operation center. It recorded a 2% improvement in annual efficiency and a 10% decrease in maintenance costs (Fujitsu, 2023). These smart manufacturing solutions enabled preventive maintenance that results in avoiding unplanned downtime and increasing productivity.
- *PT Nusantara Parkerizing* (Indonesia) established an automated warehouse with support from Daifuku (Japan) to improve efficiency in controlling raw material supply and facilitate production plans effectively.
- *Tan Thang* (Viet Nam) cement plant in 2018 got ABB (Sweden–Switzerland) to install an integrated digital automation and electrical

equipment solution, which stabilized production and enabled efficient use of raw materials and energy, increasing its production by up to 2 million tons per year.

- *Vinacomin Motor Industry*, a subsidiary of State-owned Vinacomin Group (Viet Nam), in 2018 obtained support from Universal Robots (Denmark) for some automation aspects of its plant by deploying collaborative robots, thereby increasing productivity three-fold and increasing orders by up to 60%. The company expected to reach a return to investment in less than 6 years and planned to add three to five more collaborative robots.
- Vinfast (Viet Nam), car manufacturer, contracted Siemens (Germany) to install complete automation equipment for all production lines including press to paint, body, sub-assembly, and engine.
- Dairy products manufacturer, Vinamilk (Viet Nam), had Tetra Pak install an automation system to control the entire plant. All production equipment are connected, with individual units communicating with one another.

Close business relationships allow major MNEs to push local suppliers (including SMEs) to adopt Industry 4.0 technologies. For instance, Motorola in Malaysia undertakes joint product development and encourages manufacturing transformation and industrial automation with local SME suppliers (i.e., Qdos Flexicircuits Sdn Bhd, Suiwah Corp Bhd, NationGate Technology Sdn Bhd, and Dufu Technology Corp Bhd). As such, these local SME suppliers have upgraded production facilities through advanced manufacturing technologies to maintain Motorola's product standards and meet increasing order volumes. PT. Toyota Motor Manufacturing Indonesia has more than 130 companies in its supply chain, many of them having automated facilities and moving toward Industry 4.0 with adoption of advanced industrial and digital connectivity. These suppliers include PT. Astra Otoparts (Hong Kong, China), PT Asmo, and Denso (Japan).

Investments of related MNEs and diversity of Industry 4.0 ecosystem

The presence of diverse MNEs operating in different technologies enriches the digital ecosystems; allowing companies (both foreign and local) to procure the relevant technologies and solutions for their Industry 4.0 transformation. Some domestic MNEs and many SMEs prefer segmented and customized solutions to be installed on a phase-by-phase basis due to cost considerations. The presence of more MNEs operating in the Industry 4.0 ecosystem provides a wider selection menu for a staged transformation process.

MNEs set-up multiple business functions, i.e., R&D, centers of excellence, sales and regional offices, digital and cloud hubs, manufacturing facilities, in more than four countries (Singapore, Malaysia, Indonesia, Thailand, and Viet Nam), enlarging ASEAN's Industry 4.0 ecosystem. See Table A.1 for other examples.

AM MNEs have established mini advanced manufacturing facilities to showcase this technology and offer clients to engage in smaller scale advanced technology manufacturing. Examples of AM MNEs are GE Additive, (US), Yamazaki Mazak (Japan), and Voestalpine (Austria).

Foreign MNEs facilitate the participation of local Industry 4.0 players in the ecosystem and create roles for them in the value chain. In IA and IIoT, many local players/SMEs have evolved from distributors for foreign MNEs to become systems integrators as they learn about technologies and solutions, with some becoming regional companies. For example: Singapore-based Astech in Malaysia and Thailand (through a joint venture with Thai-based Sumipol); Pumas Automation and Robotics in Malaysia, the Philippines, and Viet Nam; Servo Dynamics in Malaysia, Thailand, and Viet Nam; TDS Technology in Indonesia, Malaysia, and Thailand; Lin Wah Engineering Works in Indonesia and Viet Nam; Factronics Systems Engineering in Malaysia and Thailand. Other types of partnerships in AM include, 3DMaker (Vietnam) partnering with Misumi Corporation and TSK (both Japan) for technology solutions and equipment support. 3D Matters (Singapore) used 3D printing software solutions from Rhinoceros 5, Autodesk (both US), DS Solidworks (France), and QuantAM (United Kingdom). CMTI (Malaysia) is using Stratasys' (US) 3D printing technology solutions. Ecomaylene 3D (Singapore) is on the e-commerce platforms of Amazon (US) and Lazada (China) for marketing.

Production networks, collaboration, and regional linkages

MNEs adopt advance technologies and digital solutions to form stronger production networks. For instance, Continental (Germany) installed smart glasses and greater interconnectivity (IIot) for database sharing and remote monitoring to link its manufacturing facilities in the region with each other and with their headquarters. Schneider Electric (France) fully installed end-to-end visibility control tower to operate and monitor the flow of products to and from various SE manufacturing facilities in the region and abroad.

Industry 4.0 MNEs, with and without manufacturing facilities, form business linkages and networks of authorized local distributors as a modality for deeper penetration into the ASEAN market. Rockwell Automation has a network of authorized distributors in Indonesia, Malaysia, the Philippines, Singapore, Thailand, and Viet Nam; Bosch has local sales and service partners in Indonesia, Malaysia, the Philippines, Singapore, Thailand, and Viet Nam. Universal Robots formed a partnership with Asia Integrated Machine (Philippines) to support the increasing use of robots in the electronics, automotive, and food and beverage industries in the Philippines, and B&R Industrial Automation has a network of local dealers in many ASEAN countries. In Malaysia, Comau Robotics & Automation (Italy) partnered with DNC Automation, a local distributor. AM MNE Formlabs (US) has an office in Singapore and a network of resellers in other ASEAN countries. Other AM MNEs partnerships are: Markforge (US) with Chemtron (Singapore) for Indonesia, Malaysia, and Singapore; ORLaser (Germany) with Eye-2-Eye Communications (Singapore) for Indonesia, Malaysia, the Philippines, Singapore, and Viet Nam; Voxel Jet (Germany) with Cad Cast (Thailand) for the ASEAN market.

There are partnerships that seek to create international collaborations and linkages between the region and the global Industry 4.0 ecosystem. An example includes Stratasys (US) and SIA Engineering (Singapore) to use Stratasys' additive-manufactured aerospace parts and solutions for SIA's clients of more than 80 international airlines and aerospace equipment manufacturers. In another case, a consortium was formed under a Joint Industry Program of the Singapore Shipping Association and the National Additive Manufacturing Innovation Cluster to develop innovative AM technologies for 10 types of marine parts for various vessel types (Maritime and Port Authority of Singapore, 2020). Members of this consortium include DNV-GL (Norway), Kawasaki Heavy Industry (Japan), Hamworthy Pumps (Norway), Wartsila (Finland), Thyssenkrupp (Germany), Tytus3D (US), Wilhelmsen Ship Management (Norway), OSM Maritime Group (Norway), Executive Ship Management

(Singapore), Thome Ship Management (Singapore), Berge Bulk (Singapore), Carnival Maritime (Germany), and Ivaldi Group (US). Furthermore, Autodesk (US) and MIMOS (Malaysia's national applied research and development center) have established 3D printing facilities in Malaysia, while Harn Engineering (Thailand) is a domestic distributor for Materialise (Belgium) and its Mimics Innovation Suite software that creates 3D-printed models of medical devices.

Centers of excellence and technical skills

MNEs' centers of excellence and R&D collaborate with government agencies, research institutions, and industry associations among others to develop new advanced manufacturing technology solutions. For example, AM MNEs' collaborations are focused on developing new AM machinery and platforms for industrial applications (i.e., maritime, aerospace, health, manufacturing) and in conducting research on new AM materials and products (i.e., 3D-printed magnets and electromagnetic components and 3D-printed bio-tissues). AM MNEs provide technology while research institutions facilitate the involvement of local experts, skilled workers, industry access, and site-testing. Examples of such partnerships include, PTT Chemical Group (Thailand) and Nanyang Technological University (Singapore) to develop materials for 3D printing of automotive parts (3D Printing Industry, 2017), Structo (Singapore) with pro3dure (Germany) for access to a range of dental 3D-printing materials (Structo, 2020), Renishaw (United Kingdom) with Singapore Polytechnic for AM skills development and with 3D Metalforge (Singapore–US) for specific requirements to support 3D Metalforge's clients, Thyssenkrup (Germany) with Wilhemsen (Norway) and the Singapore government to jointly develop AM for the maritime industry, TUV SUD (Germany) with National University of Singapore Centre for Additive Manufacturing to introduce 3D printing implants for people.

Some MNEs are establishing centers of excellence with training functions and training centers to help clients with Industry 4.0 transition. Some have partnered with local universities and institutions for courses and training modules and contributed to skills development. For example, Delta Electronics (Taiwan Province of China) supported developments of industrial automation skills in Thailand through collaboration with local institutions and established the Delta Automation Academy, which offers industrial automation courses for undergraduates and Delta Industrial

Automation Laboratories in three local universities. Siemens (Germany) partnered with educational institutions and governments in some ASEAN member states to provide training and student access to its technology software and hardware. It also partnered with the Singapore Institute of Technology and the Department of Technical and Vocational Education and Training in Yangon, Myanmar. Bosch (Germany) is one of the initial partners in MDEC's Digital Transformation Acceleration Programme to help the Malaysian Government promote Industry 4.0. In addition, it partnered with a local skills and management development center in Kedah for the latter to use Bosch's educational tools to train students and workers to be Industry 4.0 ready and hosted masterclasses for SMEs to introduce Industry 4.0 solutions (Disruptive Tech ASEAN, 2020). Huawei (China) announced in 2018 an investment of $81 million to build OpenLabs, which will cultivate ICT talent in Southeast Asia. Denso Ten (Japan) transferred technologies to local suppliers through its Lean Automation System Integrators program by using its engineers, mostly from Japan, as master trainers. It partnered with the Department of Industry Promotion under the Ministry of Industry, universities (i.e., Sirindhorn International Institute of Technology under Thammasat University), to develop personnel who can implement lean automation in robotics and the IoT.

Smart Factories Development

An increasing number of foreign and local MNEs are establishing or transforming their facilities into smart factories (McKinsey, 2018). The integration of automation, connectivity, data and advanced digital technologies, and "machine communicating with machine" or the IIoT is essential to attain digitalization of manufacturing and "smart factories" (McKinsey, 2020). When more manufacturing companies adopt advanced manufacturing technologies, the industry becomes more competitive and efficient, ready for Industry 4.0 and conducive to FDI (see Figure 2).

The number of foreign and local MNEs that are establishing smart factories is growing. They are contracting MNEs to supply equipment, technology solutions, and installations to build smart factories. Such production facilities feature interconnection and interoperability of advanced digital technologies (e.g., IA, AI-enabled robotic, sensors, machine learning, IIoTs, and cloud). Smart factories in the region tend to be in countries that are major manufacturing hubs and provide more efficient digital ecosystems.

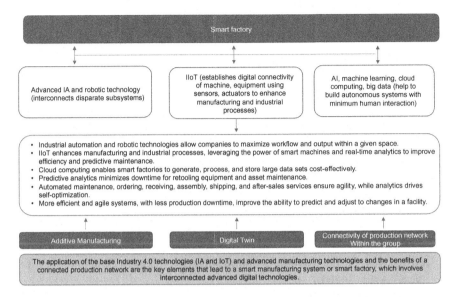

Figure 2. Smart Factory foundation: Industry 4.0 technologies

Source: ASEAN Investment Report 2020–2021.

The following are some MNEs with smart factories in ASEAN. They include (i) manufacturers of Industry 4.0 technology hardware, such as automation machines and equipment, sensors, and semiconductors; and (ii) manufacturing companies that operate in the automotive, electronic, food and beverage industries, and biotechnology.

- *Acecook* (Japan) has an advanced food manufacturing facility in Viet Nam. Its production operation is fully automated, connected, and self-contained. All processes from raw materials to finished products to packaging are controlled. It has installed a supply chain management system that can connect information between the plant and the warehouse (Coursehero, 2018).
- *Amgen* (US) established a smart manufacturing plant in Singapore that enabled the company to carry out data analytics across products and sites to predict overall performance, quality, and the likelihood of successfully manufacturing additional batches without extending production schedules. The system nearly halved the volume of process monitoring documentation, saving the company 1,200 working hours.
- *Amkor* (US) is one of the world's largest providers of outsourced (OSAT) semiconductor packaging, design, and test services with

production facilities in the Philippines, Malaysia, and Viet Nam. It is constructing a smart manufacturing facility in Bac Ninh, Viet Nam. Its factory in the Philippines employs Industry 4.0 technologies for economies of scale. Industrial automation, robotization, big data, IoT, and remote monitoring have been installed and utilized by Amkor's manufacturing facilities (Amkor News Release, 2021).

- *Afton* (US), a chemical manufacturer, opened a plant in Singapore in 2016 with a high level of automation and connectivity, using advanced distributed control systems to manage plant processes and utilities systems, ensuring safety, and boosting productivity. It has installed a remote machine–human interface, which reduces manual communications and human error (Global Business Reports, 2016).

- *Bosch Rexroth* (Germany) opened a smart factory in Thailand in 2017. The factory relies heavily on highly automated manufacturing to serve customers in the growing automobile production industry (Digital News Asia, 2017).

- *Continental AG* (Germany) has manufacturing facilities in Malaysia, Philippines, and Thailand. Its ASEAN-based facilities are transitioning to almost 100% smart factory by utilizing many Industry 4.0 key technologies (i.e., cobots, robots, high automation, predictive maintenance, big data, and artificial intelligence). The facilities are inter-connected, including an integrated and unified database with its headquarters. Remote monitoring can be performed in these facilities (ASEAN Secretariat and UNCTAD, 2022).

- *Dyson* (United Kingdom), an electronics manufacturer, opened a new global headquarters in Singapore in 2022, hosting an expanded R&D center with next-generation motor technology, connectivity, and material science (*The Straits Times*, 2022). Its facilities have advanced manufacturing technologies including IA, robotic technologies, IIoT, machine learning, AI, and predictive maintenance among others. Dyson also has an advanced manufacturing facility in the Philippines (*The Straits Times*, 2020).

- *Infineon* (Germany) (ARC Advisory Group, 2016), a semiconductor MNE with a significant presence in ASEAN, has invested more than $80 million in Singapore. The factory uses data analytics, advanced automation, and IIoT, which has helped to reduce direct labor costs by 30% and improve capital efficiency by 15%. Infineon, with a $27 million investment in 2020, has embedded AI technology in every job function in its operations.

- *Micron Technology* (US) has transformed its computer memory and data storage business in Singapore from a simple environment using statistical analysis of production processes to a sophisticated system involving deep learning and AI to draw insights from factory operations. It uses sensors and IIoTs (e.g., cameras and acoustic equipment) to collect and analyze data for making real-time decisions. The digital transformation in manufacturing reduced scrap and product downgrades by 22%. The application of advanced analytics reduced the time to ramp up new products by 50%. Deep-learning optical-defect detection improved yields by 2%, and the integrated deviation management platform reduced the time required to resolve quality issues by 50% (Micron Technology Press Release, 2020; World Economic Forum website).
- *Nidec's* (Japan) Philippine subsidiary started its Industry 4.0 transformation in 2015 by installing key technologies from Nidec Japan on a phase-by-phase basis and has fully automated its production lines (with robotic/cobot technologies) by 2022. Its technology is characterized with machine-to-machine talk, remote monitoring, IoT and connectivity, and predictive analysis (ASEAN Secretariat and UNCTAD, 2022).
- *Pegatron* (Taiwan, China), an electronic manufacturer and one of Apple's leading parts suppliers, has built an advanced manufacturing facility in Indonesia in 2019. The facility adheres to its corporate wide policy of production process automation and application of AI. It employs a smart production approach through system integration and establishment of information network. The facility is producing IoT products and other electronics. Pegatron has allocated $1.5 billion investment in stages for its Indonesian facility (KR-Asia, 2019).
- *Schneider Electric* (France) (Industrial Automation Asia website) is a supplier of smart factory solutions to manufacturing clients based in ASEAN from its three smart manufacturing facilities in Batam (1) and the Philippines (2). The smart factories showcase the benefits of digital transformation for making informed, data-driven decisions to achieve operational efficiency by using a wide range of IIoT technologies, including smart sensors, alarm prediction management, site benchmarking, and augmented reality. It tracks operation performance in real time, enabling better visibility of machine performance and preventive maintenance needs. The Batam smart factory has reduced hours spent on maintenance by 17%, waste material by 46%, and machine downtime by 44% 1 year after its establishment. It is also a testbed for

machine learning, AI, predictive and digital maintenance, and connected machines and processes.

- *Sumitomo Chemical* (Japan) started a global IIoT project in Singapore in 2016 with Accenture which includes support from EDB. The company has incorporated advanced technologies, including digitalizing plant-related operations, and visualizing and upgrading global supply chain information. Such expertise in Singapore will be rolled out to the group's other global plants.

Some ASEAN MNEs have begun their Industry 4.0 transformation process or have achieved almost 100% smart factory transformation with support from other MNEs. Examples include Chandra Asri, Kimia Farma, PT Bogasari, PT Garuda Food, PT Indolakto, and Sritex, all of which are in Indonesia. Nationgate, Pentamaster, and Vitrox in Malaysia and Davao Union Cement in the Philippines. PLC Industries and Kulicke & Sofa in Singapore alongside Thai Beverage Group, Siam City Cement, Somboon Advance Technology, Utac Thai Group in Thailand. Finally, there is VinFast, Vinacomin, Vinamilk in Viet Nam (Vu, 2021).

Conclusion

FDI across Industry 4.0-related sectors in ASEAN has been increasing rapidly since the 2010s. They include FDI or MNE activities in digital infrastructure such as data centers, industrial automation, AM, industrial Internet of Things, and other technology applications. Increasing demand by local and foreign firms in ASEAN to adopt advanced manufacturing technologies and build smart factories have been the key drivers. The large and expanding pool of manufacturing firms and underlying future business prospects have continued to help attract FDI in Industry 4.0 across ASEAN countries.

MNEs are playing an active role in the transformation process (i) by upgrading their plants with advanced technologies and (ii) as investors and suppliers of equipment and technology solutions. They invest in ASEAN to improve manufacturing efficiency, including through smart factories. As investors, they operate in the region to manufacture and supply equipment, develop technology solutions, and establish centers of excellence, technology hubs, R&D facilities, and digital infrastructure (e.g., data centers) — all of which contribute to a more vibrant manufacturing industry and a more competitive Industry 4.0 ecosystem. MNEs play a key role in MNE–SME linkages whereby the former supports local and foreign manufacturing SMEs upgrade facilities and increase efficiency. In many cases, SMEs are not just clients to MNEs but also suppliers, and SMEs are coached in providing quality parts and components and services. Some MNEs are influencing their SME vendors to upgrade technology to improve efficiency, align with production goals, and serve MNE partners effectively. Some MNEs support the digital transformation of SMEs in ASEAN when (i) MNE-technology suppliers are present and create demonstration effects, and (ii) MNEs with Industry 4.0 technology packages adapt them for application to the SME's environment.

The improving investment environment and the policy push toward Industry 4.0 transformation by the ASEAN member states has played a major role in encouraging FDI. Specific investment incentives and Industry 4.0 policies has encouraged MNEs to invest in the region. For example, the Malaysian Investment Development Authority (MIDA) offers pioneer status with a 5-year income tax exemption of 100% of the statutory income to high technology projects, including manufacturing of Industry 4.0 hardware, advanced electronics, and semiconductors. Thai's BOI provides a 3-year corporate income tax exemption covering 100% of the investments to companies upgrading their manufacturing facilities with Industry 4.0 technologies. In this regard, policy decisions matter when attracting Industry 4.0 FDI. Strengthening regional cooperation in Industry 4.0, development of smart city networks, and the rapid growth of the digital economy as well as regional integration are further impetus helping the region attract more MNEs to invest or expand operations in ASEAN. MNE activities and Industry 4.0 transformation will further increase the attractiveness of ASEAN as a global manufacturing hub.

Industry 4.0 development across ASEAN is uneven. Most development and Industry 4.0 related FDI are concentrated in those countries with a more mature manufacturing base. Such concentration could widen the gap between the more developed ASEAN economies and the emerging ones (PWC, 2019). There is a need to promote widespread adoption across the region and regional cooperation as well as policies that can promote regional production networks. Such an approach could help to address the challenge of uneven growth.

In supporting further Industry 4.0 transformation, ASEAN governments could consider adopting policies incentivizing local companies to hasten the adoption of related technologies to increase the manufacturing efficiency. There is a need for major stakeholders (i.e., relevant government ministries, foreign and domestic MNEs, domestic R&D, and technology institutions) to collaborate and establish partnerships, at both the regional and national levels. This will contribute toward building a stronger ecosystem. A joint committee, that meets regularly, could also be considered. It could discuss and develop concrete actions and adopt specific measures to promote adoption and attraction of FDI in Industry 4.0 that could then be implemented across ASEAN. A major challenge in Industry 4.0 transformation is skills development and availability of skilled human resources. Building national productive capacities through training and skills development is imperative to move forward. This could be done through public–private partnership in Industry 4.0 skills development at both the national and regional levels, and attract FDI to establish training centers and technology hubs.

While this chapter has analyzed the roles of MNEs in Industry 4.0 transformation, it is limited by the scope of analyses. In particular, future research should focus on providing a close examination of the role of MNEs in strengthening the capacity of SMEs (as vendors and investors) in Industry 4.0 transformation. Future studies could also focus on examining the connection between key Industry 4.0 actors in facilitating further growth of regional production networks.

References

3D Printing Industry. 2017. Petrochemical company PTTGC developing 3D printing materials for automotive industry with NTU Singapore. https://3dprintingindustry.com/news/petrochemical-company-pttgc-developing-3d-printing-materials-automotive-industry-ntu-singapore-116549. Accessed July 17, 2023.

ASEAN Secretariat and UNCTAD. 2021. *ASEAN Investment Report 2020–2021. Investing in Industry 4.0.* Jakarta and Geneva: ASEAN Secretariat and UNCTAD.

ASEAN Secretariat and UNCTAD. 2022. ASEAN Investment Report 2022. Jakarta and Geneva: ASEAN Secretariat and UNCTAD.

Amkor News Release. 2021. Amkor Technology Announces Plans to Expand Advanced Packaging Technology Capacity with New Factory in Bac Ninh, Vietnam. https://c44f5d406df450f4a66b-1b94a87d576253d9446df0a9ca62e

142.ssl.cf2.rackcdn.com/2021/11/AMKR-Press-Release-VietnamFactory Expansion_EN.pdf.

BeritaJatim. 2019. ABB shows robotic technology for Mamin.

Business Wire. 2019. Yokogawa to start offering ERP solutions to industrial customers in Southeast Asia.

Coursehero. 2018. Valuable Capabalities: Acecook Viet Nam. https://www. coursehero.com/file/p3fm315/Valuable-capabilities-Acecook-Vietnam-applies-the-layout-of-production/. Accessed July 17, 2023.

Digital News Asia. 2013. NXP boosts Singapore presence to strengthen Asian "footprint." https://www.digitalnewsasia.com/enterprise/nxp-boosts-singapore-presence-to-strengthen-asian-footprint. Accessed July 17, 2023.

Disruptive Tech ASEAN. 2020. Bosch's journey from a 'things' company to an IoT company. https://disruptivetechnews.com/big_news/boschs-journey-from-a-thing-company-to-an-iot-company/. Accessed July 17, 2023.

Fujitsu. 2023. Smart factory ready for wider adoption, promising to transform manufacturing business. https://www.fujitsu.com/th/en/themes/enabling-digital/asia/smart-factory/articles/smart-factory-productivity-in-thailand. html. Accessed July 20, 2023.

Global Business Reports. 2016. Special Report on Singapore. https://www. gbreports.com/wp-content/uploads/2016/09/CW-Singapore-2016-v7-medres. pdf. Digital News Asia. 2017. Bosch opens first smart factory in Thailand.

Industrial Automation Asia Website. https://www.iaasiaonline.com. Accessed July 20, 2023.

KR-Asia. 2019. Pegatron opened its first Southeast Asia factory line in Indonesia, but its not for Apple products. https://kr-asia.com/pegatron-opened-its-first-southeast-asia-factory-line-in-indonesia-but-its-not-for-apple-products. Accessed July 17, 2023.

Manufacturing Tomorrow. 2020. Bosch Rexroth introduces a new world of automation.

Maritime and Port Authority of Singapore. 2020. 11 joint industry projects awarded S\$1.625 million to drive maritime innovation. https://www. marineinsight.com/shipping-news/11-joint-industry-projects-awarded-s1-625-million-to-drive-maritime-innovation/. Accessed July 17, 2023.

McKinsey. 2018. Industry 4.0: Reinvigorating ASEAN manufacturing for the future. Digital Capability Centre, Singapore. https://www.mckinsey.com/ business-functions/operations/our-insights/industry-4-0-reinvigorating-asean-manufacturing-for-the-future. Accessed July 17, 2023.

McKinsey. 2020. Industry 4.0: Reimagining manufacturing operations after COVID-19. https://www.mckinsey.com/business-functions/operations/our-insights/industry-40-reimagining-manufacturing-operations-after-covid-19. Accessed July 17, 2023.

McKinsey. 2021. Covid-19: An inflection point for Industry 4.0. https://www.mckinsey.com/business-functions/operations/our-insights/covid-19-an-inflection-point-for-industry-40. Accessed July 17, 2023.

Micron Technology. 2020. Micron joins the WEF Global Lighthouse Network. 2020. https://www.micron.com/about/blog/2020/february/micron-joins-the-wef-global-lighthouse-network. Accessed July 17, 2023.

PWC. 2016. Industry 4.0: Building the Digital Enterprise. https://www.pwc.com/gx/en/industries/industries-4.0/landing-page/industry-4.0-building-your-digital-enterprise-april-2016.pdf.

PWC Strategy + Business. 2019. Sustaining Southeast Asia's Momentum. https://www.strategy-business.com/article/Sustaining-Southeast-Asias-Momentum. Accessed July 17, 2023.

Schneider Electric. 2023. Sanwa Group customer story. https://www.se.com/ww/en/work/campaign/life-is-on/case-study/sanwa-group.jsp. Accessed July 20, 2023.

Structo. 2020. Structo announces partnership with German 3D printing materials manufacturer, pro3dure. Extending range of applications in the Velox ecosystem. https://www.structo3d.com/blogs/press-releases/structo-announces-partnership-with-german-3d-printing-materials-manufacturer-pro3dure-extending-range-of-applications-in-the-velox-ecosystem. Accessed July 17, 2023.

The Nation. 2018. GE 'optimising' its regional plants. https://www.nationthailand.com/business/30360585. Accessed July 17, 2023.

The Straits Times. 2020. Dyson to set up new advanced manufacturing hub in Singapore, in $4.9b investment across 3 countries. https://www.straitstimes.com/business/dyson-to-set-up-new-advanced-manufacturing-hub-in-spore-in-ps275b-investment-across-3. ARC Advisory Group. 2016. Sounding out an IIoT application in Asia. Accessed July 17, 2023.

The Straits Times. 2022. First look inside Dyson's new global HQ in Singapore. https://www.youtube.com/watch?v=zeV792nUT7o. Accessed July 17, 2023.

Thyssenkrupp. 2019. "Additive manufacturing: Adding up growth opportunities for ASEAN", https://www.slideshare.net/singhal.abhinav/additive-manufacturing-am-adding-up-growth-opportunities-for-asean. Accessed July 17, 2023.

United Nations Conference on Trade and Development (UNCTAD). 2020. Investment Policy Monitor, Special Issue, No. 4, May 2020.

United Nations Development Programme (UNDP). 2020. Adaptation and Adoption of Industry 4.0 in Cambodia. https://www.undp.org/cambodia/publications/adaptation-and-adoption-industry-40-cambodia.

Vu, K. M. 2021. Industry 4.0 transformation in Viet Nam's manufacturing sector: The current state and policy issues, country paper prepared for ASEAN Investment Report 2020–2021.

Wong, C-Y, VGR Chandran and Ng B-K. 2021. FDI in Industry 4.0: The case of Malaysia, country paper prepared for ASEAN Investment Report 2020–2021.

World Economic Forum. WEF global lighthouse network : Micron Technology Singapore. https://initiatives.weforum.org/global-lighthouse-network/light houses/micron---singapore/aJY68000000Kz0mGAC#. Accessed July 17, 2023.

Appendix

Table A.1.   FDI location choices and motivations in Industry 4.0 in ASEAN (selected cases).

MNE	Nationality	Industry 4.0 Technologies	Presence	Motivation
ABB	Switzerland	IA, IIoT	Regional robotics digital operation center (Malaysia)	Harness and educate potential markets for various Industry 4.0 technologies, proximity to clients.
Advantech	Taiwan Province of China	IIoT	Offices (Indonesia, Malaysia, Singapore, Thailand, Vietnam)	Increasing market-related activities in the region (i.e., Indonesia, Malaysia, Thailand).
Amazon Web Services (AWS)	US	IoT and other technology solutions	Indonesia and Singapore (region Location); Malaysia (2 Edge Network Locations (smaller Data Centers that cache content to end users), Philippines (1), Singapore (4) (AWS Edge Network Location) Offices (Indonesia, Malaysia, Philippines, Thailand, Viet Nam) Regional HQ (Singapore)	Market opportunities (whether by country, by customer segment, by vertical, or by solutions), with Southeast Asia as a growing region. There is large demand for AWS.
Bosch	Germany	IA, IIoT	3 smart factories for mobility solutions in Thailand	Growing market; offer solutions to clients in the region through IIoT solutions hub and software and engineering R&D center in Viet Nam.
Cisco	US	IIoT	Offices (Indonesia, Malaysia, Myanmar, Philippines, Singapore, Thailand, Vietnam)	ASEAN market is ready for digitalization; proximity to clients.

Continental AG	Germany	IA, advanced manufacturing technologies	Advanced manufacturing facilities (Malaysia, Philippines, Thailand)	Manufacturing efficiency, global corporate policy, pandemic challenges.
Denso	Japan	IA, IIoT	Operations (Philippines)	Prepare production capabilities and capacity for the increasing demand for smart vehicles.
Eaton Corporation	Ireland	IA	Facility in Singapore	Market expansion, favorable investment environment, strategic regional hub.
Emerson	US	IA, advanced manufacturing technologies	Automation solutions center, a pervasive sensing center of excellence, an analytical manufacturing and integration center, and an additive manufacturing center (Singapore)	Harness and educate market on Industry 4.0 technologies, proximity to clients.
Ericsson	Sweden	IIoT, connectivity solutions	Offices (Brunei Darussalam, Cambodia, Indonesia, Malaysia, Philippines, Singapore, Thailand, Viet Nam) Regional HQ (Singapore)	—
GE	US	IIoT, advanced manufacturing solutions	Indonesia (Plant Facilities and Offices); Malaysia (ASEAN Headquarters); Singapore (complex manufacturing, engineering services, research and customer applications development, leadership development and regional commercial operations; Asia Digital Operations Centre)	Growing market.
Huawei	China	IoT and other software solutions	Offices (Indonesia, Malaysia, Philippines, Thailand, and Viet Nam) Regional HQ (Singapore)	

(Continued)

Table A.1.   (*Continued*)

MNE	Nationality	Industry 4.0 Technologies	Presence	Motivation
Honeywell	US	IA, IIoT, advanced manufacturing solutions	Offices (Indonesia, Philippines, Thailand, Viet Nam) A new regional headquarters (Malaysia) First Asian Industrial Cyber Security Centre (Singapore) Manufacturing facility (Thailand)	Growing market, harness growing markets in the region.
Intel	US	IIoT hardware (semiconductor chips)	Manufacturing facilities (assembly and test in Malaysia and Viet Nam)	Supportive government policies, growing market, production hub for the region and other areas outside.
Micron Technology	US	IIoT hardware (semiconductor chips)	Manufacturing facilities (Malaysia, Singapore) Global operations HQ (Singapore) NAND Centre of Excellence (Singapore)	Supportive government policies, growing market, production hub for the region and other areas outside.
Mitsubishi Electric	Japan	IA, advanced manufacturing technologies	Operations in several ASEAN countries	Regional integration, rapid industrial growth, market opportunities, proximity to market and clients.
Omron	Japan	IA	2 facilities with IA, showroom, automation center (Indonesia)	Growing market for electronic components.
PTC Inc.	US	IoT	Offices in Malaysia, Singapore, Thailand, and Viet Nam	Growing market, proximity to market and clients.
Rockwell Automation	US	IA, IIoT and advanced manufacturing solutions	Office (Indonesia, Malaysia, Philippines, Thailand, Viet Nam) Manufacturing, Regional HQ (Singapore)	Growing and strategic market, increased operations in the region, support clients in the region with industrial digital transformation through the company's connected services experience center in Singapore.

SAP	Germany	IIoT	Offices (Indonesia, Malaysia, Philippines, Singapore, Thailand, Vietnam) Singapore (Asia Pacific HQ and Innovation Lab)	Growing market.
Schneider Electric	France	IA, advanced manufacturing technologies and solutions	Manufacturing and logistics (Malaysia, Thailand, and Viet Nam) Regional HQ, innovation hub, regional logistics center, small and advanced manufacturing facility (Singapore) Smart factories (Indonesia, Philippines)	Regional integration, growing regional market, increasing new generation of firms capable of adopting digital technologies.
Siemens Industrial Automation	Germany	IA, advanced manufacturing technologies	Offices (Cambodia, Indonesia, Malaysia, Myanmar, Philippines, Singapore, Thailand, Vietnam) Malaysia (Siemens Innovative Resources & Technology Centre, Siemens Customer Experience Centre) Singapore (Asia Pacific HQ; Advance Manufacturing Transformation Centre, including Digital Enterprise Experience Center, Additive Manufacturing Experience Center)	Growing market and manufacturing industry, pandemic challenges.
TMEIC	Japan	IA	Operations in Singapore	Growing regional market.
Yamazaki Mazak	Japan	IA, IIoT, advanced manufacturing technologies	Singapore (Southeast Asia base, advanced manufacturing, and R&D facility) Technology/Technical Centres (Indonesia, Malaysia, Thailand, and Viet Nam)	Growing market. Strong regional presence and a smart factory in Singapore to showcase and support existing and potential clients.
Yokogawa	Japan	IA, IIoT, advanced manufacturing solutions	Sales and Installation Services (Indonesia, Malaysia, Philippines, Thailand, Viet Nam) Regional HQ, Manufacturing facility (Singapore)	Growing demand.

Sources: ASEAN Investment Report 2020–2021, ASEAN Investment Report 2022, company websites, press, and media release.

Table A.2.   MNEs upgrading own factories with Industry 4.0 technologies (selected cases).

Company	Nationality	Facility/Location	Activity
Amkor Technology	US	Malaysia, Philippines, Viet Nam	• Amkor Philippines invests about $70 million annually (10–20% of its annual budget) for manufacturing technology upgrade and expansion. • Invested in Industry 4.0 technologies such as industrial automation, island robotization (as there is still manual assistance in terms of loading and unloading of materials), big data, IoT, and remote monitoring system.
Bosch	Germany	Malaysia, Singapore, Thailand, Viet Nam	• Invested $368 million during 2011–2018 to upgrade its facilities in Viet Nam, which includes manufacturing, a software development center, and an automotive engineering center.

Continental	Germany	Manufacturing subsidiaries (Malaysia, Philippines, Thailand); Singapore (R&D supporting the operations in Asia, excluding China). It is also expanding in Viet Nam	• Global corporate policy.
			• Operated a smart factory embedding many aspects of Industry 4.0 technologies (i.e., cobots, robots, high automation, predictive maintenance, big data, and artificial intelligence).
			• Upgraded and expanded the ASEAN factories during the pandemic:
			  - Integrated database for all the facilities and its headquarters in Germany.
			  - Remote monitoring technology where headquarters could discuss and monitor production processes.

			• Philippine subsidiary installed additive manufacturing (3D printing), smart glass devices, remote support, handheld computers, cobots, Manufacturing Execution System (MES), and Traceability System.
Delta Electronics	Taiwan Province of China	Manufacturing facility, Thailand	Transformed its facility using advanced manufacturing solutions: • 70 four-axis selective-compliance assembly. • Robot arms developed by the parent company for the Thai plant. • Smart machines using vision systems and sensors to automatically detect product defects
Emerson	US	Thailand	• Automated its manufacturing facilities. • Invested $10 million in 2017 to upgrade compressor plant in Rayong by adopting additional automation technologies and other industrial technologies from third parties. • Continued to upgrade its air-conditioning manufacturing in Thailand with automation to support the company's business expansion in Asia.
General Electric	US	Singapore (digital operations) Singapore, Viet Nam (smart factories)	• Opened an Asia digital operations center in Singapore in 2017 to support GE's global information technology services and to deliver IT and digitalization technology to companies across the group. • GE's two smart factories in ASEAN use advanced manufacturing technologies, digitization, and data analytics to enhance productivity and quality.

(Continued)

Table A.2. (*Continued*)

Company	Nationality	Facility/Location	Activity
Honda	Japan	Manufacturing facilities (Indonesia, Philippines, and Thailand)	• GE's regional expansion centers on upgrading IA technologies across its factories in the region instead of building new plants. • Honda Parts Mfg. Philippines has been installing Industry 4.0 technologies before the pandemic to increase efficiency. • Fully automated production for die casting to produce parts for both ICE and EV battery-powered automotives. Robotic technology is used.
Hitachi Industrial Solutions	Japan	Smart factory hub for Southeast Asia (Lumada Center), Thailand	Established center to market factory solutions using IoT throughout Southeast Asia.
Mitsubishi Electric	Japan	A new company (MELCO Factory Automation Philippines)	Established company to expand and upgrade its factory automation business.
		Singapore-based Akribis Systems	Acquired equity stake in Akribis to strengthen Mitsubishi's IA businesses by incorporating Akribis's linear servo systems into the technology portfolio and Mitsubishi's e-factory facilities.
		New Factory Automation Centre in Malaysia	Started operations to strengthen servicing and support and facilitate expansion for its factory automation systems business.

Company	Country of origin	Operations	Description
Nidec	Japan	Cambodia, Philippines, Thailand, Viet Nam	• Nidec Philippines (NCF) started Industry 4.0 transformation in 2015. • NCF has invested $20+ million in technology upgrade; employed key Industry 4.0 technologies on a phase-by-phase basis to optimize the production process. • NCF has automated its production lines (with robotic/cobot technologies) and installed IoT enabling machine communicating with machine, remote monitoring, and predictive analysis. • Industry 4.0 technologies and equipment are supplied by Nidec Japan.
Schneider Electric	France	Indonesia, Philippines, Singapore, Thailand, and Viet Nam	• Continued upgrade of Batam factory. • Partnered with Aveva (United Kingdom) to further digitalize the manufacturing process. Batam facility operated as a smart factory from 2018. • Cikarang–Jakarta factory became automated and connected in 2019.
Techman Robot	Taiwan Province of China	Techman Electronics' Thailand factory	Introduced Techman robots, cobots, and advanced software solutions to improve assembly and increase production efficiency.
Yokogawa Electric	Japan	Singapore and Thailand operations	Introduced new business unit focused on enterprise resource planning solutions.
		All ASEAN countries	Introduced new sensors for wireless IIoT solution.

Sources: Media and press releases, Company websites, ASEAN Investment Reports 2020–2021 and 2022.

Appendix

Factor and Sub-factor Rankings

In this section, rankings are determined by calculating scores based on the eight factors: Factor Conditions, Demand Conditions, Related Industries, Business Context, Workers, Policymakers and Administrators, Entrepreneurs, and Professionals. Each factor consists of two sub-factors, resulting in a total of 16 sub-factors. To ensure fairness, equal weights were assigned to the two sub-factors within each factor. These scores were derived from the base data used in our research. For detailed statistical tables at the criteria level, please refer to the website (ipsncr.org).

	1. Factor conditions			1.1. Natural resources			1.2. Processed resources	
Rank	Country/Region	Index	Rank	Country/Region	Index	Rank	Country/Region	Index
1	Australia	42.78	1	Australia	49.04	1	Australia	36.51
2	Canada	35.69	2	Canada	41.82	2	New Zealand	31.02
3	Kuwait	31.23	3	Kuwait	32.78	3	Kuwait	29.69
4	New Zealand	28.60	4	Russia	29.57	4	Canada	29.57
5	UAE	27.34	5	UAE	29.50	5	Oman	26.41
6	Russia	25.71	6	New Zealand	26.18	6	UAE	25.18
7	Oman	18.26	7	Saudi Arabia	18.15	7	Finland	22.03
8	Saudi Arabia	17.30	8	Peru	16.23	8	Russia	21.85
9	Finland	15.33	9	Chile	15.26	9	Sweden	19.25
10	Sweden	13.11	10	Colombia	13.17	10	Saudi Arabia	16.45
11	United States	10.45	11	Oman	10.11	11	Austria	13.51
12	Chile	10.04	12	Brazil	9.81	12	United States	13.13
13	Peru	8.88	13	Panama	9.68	13	Czechia	8.70
14	Austria	7.88	14	Finland	8.63	14	Slovenia	7.16
15	Colombia	7.86	15	United States	7.78	15	Malaysia	6.96
16	Malaysia	6.74	16	Sweden	6.97	16	Netherlands	6.69
17	Brazil	5.80	17	Malaysia	6.53	17	Denmark	5.90
18	Slovenia	5.36	18	Argentina	6.04	18	Poland	5.90
19	Czechia	5.25	19	Ukraine	4.56	19	Germany	5.19
20	Panama	5.02	20	Slovenia	3.57	20	South Africa	4.98
21	Argentina	4.94	21	Croatia	3.49	21	Chile	4.83

22	Poland	4.65	22	Poland	3.41	22	Croatia	4.43
23	Ukraine	3.97	23	Indonesia	3.15	23	China	4.35
24	Croatia	3.96	24	Greece	3.09	24	Belgium	4.23
25	Netherlands	3.83	25	Cambodia	2.66	25	Argentina	3.84
26	Germany	3.64	26	Austria	2.24	26	Slovak Republic	3.81
27	South Africa	3.56	27	Guatemala	2.15	27	Ukraine	3.37
28	Denmark	3.43	28	South Africa	2.14	28	Indonesia	3.28
29	Indonesia	3.21	29	Germany	2.08	29	United Kingdom	3.10
30	China	2.90	30	Mexico	1.97	30	France	3.01
31	Slovak Republic	2.74	31	Czechia	1.80	31	Türkiye	2.79
32	Greece	2.41	32	Türkiye	1.79	32	Thailand	2.64
33	Belgium	2.33	33	Hungary	1.78	33	Israel	2.60
34	Türkiye	2.29	34	Slovak Republic	1.67	34	Colombia	2.55
35	France	2.16	35	Nigeria	1.57	35	Switzerland	2.49
36	Hungary	2.13	36	Vietnam	1.57	36	Hungary	2.49
37	Thailand	2.03	37	Switzerland	1.53	37	Brazil	1.79
38	Switzerland	2.01	38	China	1.45	38	Egypt	1.73
39	United Kingdom	2.00	39	Thailand	1.42	39	Greece	1.73
40	Mexico	1.73	40	Spain	1.39	40	Peru	1.53
41	Israel	1.68	41	Philippines	1.36	41	Mexico	1.50
42	Vietnam	1.51	42	France	1.30	42	Vietnam	1.45
43	Egypt	1.46	43	Egypt	1.18	43	Italy	1.21
44	Cambodia	1.37	44	Italy	1.13	44	Dominican Republic	1.20

(Continued)

(*Continued*)

	1. Factor conditions			1.1. Natural resources			1.2. Processed resources	
Rank	Country/Region	Index	Rank	Country/Region	Index	Rank	Country/Region	Index
45	Nigeria	1.30	45	Japan	1.08	45	Spain	1.18
46	Spain	1.29	46	Morocco	1.01	46	Nigeria	1.03
47	Guatemala	1.20	47	Netherlands	0.98	47	Japan	0.96
48	Italy	1.17	48	Denmark	0.95	48	Korea, Republic of	0.89
49	Dominican Republic	1.03	49	United Kingdom	0.91	49	India	0.85
50	Japan	1.02	50	Dominican Republic	0.86	50	Philippines	0.51
51	Philippines	0.94	51	Kenya	0.82	51	Pakistan	0.50
52	India	0.78	52	Sri Lanka	0.82	52	Bangladesh	0.44
53	Korea, Republic of	0.74	53	Israel	0.76	53	Panama	0.35
54	Morocco	0.65	54	India	0.71	54	Singapore	0.30
55	Sri Lanka	0.55	55	Jordan	0.61	55	Sri Lanka	0.29
56	Kenya	0.52	56	Korea, Republic of	0.58	56	Morocco	0.28
57	Pakistan	0.46	57	Belgium	0.44	57	Guatemala	0.26
58	Bangladesh	0.34	58	Pakistan	0.41	58	Kenya	0.23
59	Jordan	0.34	59	Taiwan, China	0.32	59	Taiwan, China	0.19
60	Taiwan, China	0.26	60	Bangladesh	0.24	60	Jordan	0.08
61	Singapore	0.16	61	Singapore	0.03	61	Cambodia	0.07
62	Hong Kong SAR	0.03	62	Hong Kong SAR	0.00	62	Hong Kong SAR	0.05

Notes: Factor Conditions comprise two sub-factors: *Natural Resources* and *Processed Resources*. Overall, Australia, Canada, Kuwait, New Zealand, and UAE demonstrated high competitiveness in both sub-factors, highlighting their strengths. The sub-factor *Natural Resources* is eva uated based on per capita reserves of resources such as oil, natural gas, and coal. Additionally, measurements include land area and freshwater resources to assess the overall *Natural Resources* factor. The sub-factor *Processed Resources* is evaluated based on the per capita volume of processed energy resources, including oil, natural gas, coal, wood, and meat. This measurement provides insights into the competitiveness of countries in utilizing and processing these resources.

2. Demand conditions			2.1. Demand size			2.2. Demand quality		
Rank	Country/Region	Index	Rank	Country/Region	Index	Rank	Country/Region	Index
1	United States	79.97	1	United States	89.44	1	Finland	93.05
2	China	62.96	2	China	66.86	2	Denmark	85.58
3	Switzerland	56.72	3	Germany	46.64	3	Switzerland	79.92
4	Germany	54.71	4	Switzerland	33.52	4	Sweden	78.21
5	Finland	54.59	5	Japan	31.93	5	Canada	73.79
6	Denmark	53.47	6	United Kingdom	29.64	6	Taiwan, China	72.72
7	United Kingdom	49.40	7	Singapore	29.39	7	Korea, Republic of	71.57
8	Sweden	49.21	8	France	28.49	8	Austria	71.26
9	Japan	49.17	9	Netherlands	28.19	9	United States	70.50
10	Canada	49.11	10	Hong Kong SAR	24.78	10	Belgium	70.30
11	Singapore	47.81	11	Canada	24.42	11	Australia	69.74
12	France	47.54	12	Australia	22.33	12	United Kingdom	69.17
13	Hong Kong SAR	46.93	13	Korea, Republic of	21.49	13	Hong Kong SAR	69.08
14	Korea, Republic of	46.53	14	Belgium	21.44	14	France	66.59
15	Australia	46.03	15	Italy	21.39	15	Japan	66.41
16	Belgium	45.87	16	Denmark	21.36	16	Singapore	66.23
17	Netherlands	45.76	17	Sweden	20.21	17	UAE	66.16
18	Austria	44.97	18	Austria	18.69	18	Italy	64.77
19	Taiwan, China	44.35	19	UAE	17.41	19	Netherlands	63.33
20	Italy	43.08	20	Spain	16.74	20	Germany	62.78

(Continued)

(Continued)

2. Demand conditions			2.1. Demand size			2.2. Demand quality		
Rank	Country/Region	Index	Rank	Country/Region	Index	Rank	Country/Region	Index
21	UAE	41.78	21	Finland	16.14	21	Colombia	61.90
22	New Zealand	37.54	22	Taiwan, China	15.99	22	New Zealand	61.59
23	Saudi Arabia	33.69	23	Israel	15.50	23	Peru	60.11
24	Poland	33.52	24	New Zealand	13.48	24	China	59.07
25	Spain	33.38	25	India	13.07	25	Croatia	58.60
26	Kuwait	32.73	26	Mexico	11.53	26	Thailand	57.44
27	India	32.64	27	Russia	11.30	27	Nigeria	57.30
28	Colombia	32.13	28	Saudi Arabia	10.34	28	Saudi Arabia	57.04
29	Thailand	32.08	29	Poland	10.32	29	Vietnam	57.01
30	Israel	31.92	30	Czechia	9.77	30	Poland	56.73
31	Croatia	31.55	31	Kuwait	8.85	31	Kuwait	56.61
32	Vietnam	31.39	32	Brazil	8.02	32	Indonesia	55.95
33	Mexico	31.30	33	Slovenia	7.97	33	Panama	55.72
34	Peru	31.24	34	Türkiye	7.00	34	Philippines	55.57
35	Indonesia	30.61	35	Slovak Republic	6.96	35	Greece	53.92
36	Greece	30.19	36	Hungary	6.76	36	Türkiye	53.11
37	Türkiye	30.06	37	Thailand	6.71	37	India	52.20
38	Panama	29.86	38	Malaysia	6.59	38	Chile	51.38
39	Nigeria	29.32	39	Greece	6.47	39	Dominican Republic	51.31
40	Philippines	29.16	40	Vietnam	5.77	40	Mexico	51.06
41	Chile	28.36	41	Oman	5.41	41	Spain	50.01
42	Slovenia	27.06	42	Chile	5.33	42	Argentina	48.93

Rank	Country	Value	Rank	Country	Value	Rank	Country	Value
43	Czechia	27.02	43	Indonesia	5.27	43	Israel	48.33
44	Malaysia	26.72	44	Croatia	4.50	44	Guatemala	48.31
45	Dominican Republic	26.71	45	Panama	4.00	45	Egypt	46.94
46	Argentina	26.38	46	Argentina	3.83	46	Malaysia	46.85
47	Brazil	26.28	47	South Africa	3.36	47	Slovenia	46.15
48	Guatemala	24.71	48	Philippines	2.74	48	Sri Lanka	45.97
49	Egypt	24.35	49	Peru	2.37	49	Bangladesh	45.48
50	Hungary	23.88	50	Colombia	2.35	50	Brazil	44.53
51	South Africa	23.47	51	Dominican Republic	2.10	51	Czechia	44.26
52	Sri Lanka	23.44	52	Ukraine	1.89	52	South Africa	43.57
53	Bangladesh	23.40	53	Egypt	1.77	53	Ukraine	42.70
54	Ukraine	22.30	54	Nigeria	1.35	54	Hungary	40.99
55	Jordan	20.60	55	Bangladesh	1.33	55	Jordan	40.33
56	Slovak Republic	20.02	56	Morocco	1.30	56	Cambodia	36.24
57	Oman	18.94	57	Guatemala	1.11	57	Kenya	34.52
58	Russia	18.93	58	Sri Lanka	0.91	58	Slovak Republic	33.09
59	Cambodia	18.18	59	Jordan	0.87	59	Oman	32.46
60	Kenya	17.41	60	Pakistan	0.85	60	Pakistan	28.53
61	Pakistan	14.69	61	Kenya	0.29	61	Russia	26.55
62	Morocco	13.60	62	Cambodia	0.12	62	Morocco	25.89

Notes: The countries showing strong competitiveness for *Demand Conditions* are the United States (US), China, Switzerland, Germany, and Finland. Particularly, the US demonstrated a robust performance in this factor, primarily due to its superior advantage in *Demand Size*. Despite its small domestic market size, Switzerland ranks among the top five for *Demand Conditions*. This achievement is driven by high ratings in purchasing power, degree of openness, and market sophistication. The sub-factor, *Demand Size*, is measured by GDP, GDP per capita, and exports and imports of goods and services. It is important to note that this sub-factor is not solely determined by the domestic market size but also by the degree of openness to international trade, financial, and investment flows. *Demand Quality* is measured by surveys among customers on their sensitivity to quality, design, health and environment, intellectual property rights, and new technology. Countries with strength in this sub-factor boast sophisticated and discerning consumers, motivating firms to continuously innovate and enhance the competitiveness of their products and services.

3. Related infrastructure

Rank	Country/Region	Index
1	Finland	62.71
2	Denmark	62.31
3	Austria	62.07
4	Switzerland	61.14
5	Sweden	60.24
6	Taiwan, China	59.72
7	Singapore	59.70
8	Netherlands	58.42
9	Belgium	58.17
10	United States	58.15
11	Czechia	57.28
12	Korea, Republic of	56.47
13	Hong Kong SAR	56.13
14	New Zealand	55.59
15	Australia	55.45
16	France	54.76
17	UAE	54.40
18	Germany	54.02
19	Japan	53.75
20	Israel	53.48
21	Slovenia	52.68

3.1. Industrial infrastructure

Rank	Country/Region	Index
1	United States	60.16
2	Singapore	53.11
3	Austria	51.92
4	Switzerland	49.69
5	Hong Kong SAR	49.68
6	Korea, Republic of	49.65
7	Denmark	48.92
8	Hungary	46.98
9	Israel	46.90
10	Sweden	46.22
11	Finland	45.85
12	Czechia	45.55
13	UAE	45.50
14	Australia	43.63
15	France	43.28
16	Japan	42.93
17	New Zealand	42.72
18	Netherlands	42.59
19	Belgium	42.35
20	Germany	42.24
21	Taiwan, China	41.79

3.2. Living infrastructure

Rank	Country/Region	Index
1	Finland	79.57
2	Taiwan, China	77.65
3	Denmark	75.69
4	Sweden	74.26
5	Netherlands	74.24
6	Belgium	73.99
7	Switzerland	72.60
8	Austria	72.22
9	Czechia	69.02
10	New Zealand	68.47
11	Australia	67.28
12	Slovenia	67.26
13	Spain	66.69
14	Singapore	66.30
15	France	66.23
16	Germany	65.81
17	United Kingdom	65.37
18	Japan	64.58
19	UAE	63.30
20	Korea, Republic of	63.29
21	Hong Kong SAR	62.58

Rank	Country	Score
22	United Kingdom	52.01
23	Spain	51.82
24	Hungary	51.24
25	Canada	49.98
26	Italy	49.93
27	Greece	48.78
28	Croatia	46.93
29	Kuwait	46.35
30	Poland	45.95
31	Saudi Arabia	45.65
32	Slovak Republic	44.91
33	China	43.13
34	Thailand	42.72
35	Malaysia	42.36
36	Oman	39.37
37	Chile	39.22
38	Panama	37.87
39	Ukraine	37.50
40	Russia	37.07
41	Dominican Republic	37.06
42	Colombia	36.14
43	Vietnam	36.09
44	Peru	35.33

Rank	Country	Score
22	Canada	41.33
23	Italy	40.99
24	United Kingdom	38.65
25	Slovenia	38.10
26	Kuwait	38.01
27	Saudi Arabia	37.89
28	Malaysia	37.87
29	Greece	37.12
30	Spain	36.95
31	Croatia	35.84
32	Russia	33.62
33	China	33.39
34	Poland	33.21
35	Oman	33.20
36	Slovak Republic	32.79
37	Thailand	32.72
38	Panama	31.57
39	South Africa	28.01
40	Mexico	27.68
41	Colombia	26.95
42	Dominican Republic	26.59
43	Chile	26.44
44	Brazil	25.87

Rank	Country	Score
22	Greece	60.45
23	Israel	60.06
24	Italy	58.86
25	Poland	58.68
26	Canada	58.63
27	Croatia	58.03
28	Slovak Republic	57.03
29	United States	56.14
30	Hungary	55.50
31	Kuwait	54.70
32	Ukraine	53.94
33	Saudi Arabia	53.41
34	China	52.87
35	Thailand	52.71
36	Chile	52.00
37	Argentina	51.72
38	Türkiye	49.01
39	Dominican Republic	47.53
40	Peru	47.04
41	Malaysia	46.85
42	Vietnam	46.54
43	Oman	45.55
44	Colombia	45.33

(*Continued*)

(Continued)

Rank	3. Related infrastructure Country/Region	Index	Rank	3.1. Industrial infrastructure Country/Region	Index	Rank	3.2. Living infrastructure Country/Region	Index
45	Argentina	35.26	45	Vietnam	25.64	45	Jordan	45.19
46	Mexico	34.92	46	Peru	23.63	46	Indonesia	44.99
47	Indonesia	34.12	47	Indonesia	23.26	47	Sri Lanka	44.89
48	Jordan	33.82	48	Morocco	22.73	48	Panama	44.17
49	Brazil	33.41	49	Jordan	22.45	49	Philippines	42.99
50	Türkiye	33.37	50	India	21.38	50	India	42.46
51	South Africa	32.70	51	Ukraine	21.06	51	Mexico	42.17
52	India	31.92	52	Guatemala	19.59	52	Brazil	40.95
53	Philippines	30.83	53	Kenya	19.49	53	Russia	40.51
54	Sri Lanka	30.35	54	Egypt	18.99	54	Egypt	40.37
55	Egypt	29.68	55	Argentina	18.80	55	South Africa	37.39
56	Morocco	27.55	56	Philippines	18.68	56	Guatemala	34.51
57	Guatemala	27.05	57	Bangladesh	18.58	57	Morocco	32.36
58	Nigeria	24.11	58	Cambodia	18.04	58	Nigeria	31.48
59	Bangladesh	23.16	59	Türkiye	17.74	59	Pakistan	28.37
60	Kenya	23.00	60	Nigeria	16.75	60	Bangladesh	27.74
61	Pakistan	21.25	61	Sri Lanka	15.82	61	Kenya	26.52
62	Cambodia	20.30	62	Pakistan	14.13	62	Cambodia	22.56

Notes: The countries that showed a strong performance in *Related Industries* include Finland, Denmark, Austria, Switzerland, and Sweden. The measurement of *Related Industries* encompasses various aspects of infrastructure, including transportation (such as motor vehicles, civil aviation, maritime transport, and international travel), communication (such as the number of mobile phone subscribers and Internet users), finance (capital value and capital accessibility), and science and technology (the number of scientists and engineers, the quality of scientific research institutions, research and development expenditure, and international patents granted). *Living Infrastructure* consists of indices related to education, social security, and quality of life. Education is evaluated based on public spending on education, student-to-teacher ratio, secondary and tertiary enrollment rates, and international student mobility. Quality of life is measured using indicators such as the Gini index, the Human Development Index, CO_2 emissions, and the availability of leisure, sports, and cultural facilities.

4. Business context			4.1. Structure			4.2. Rivalry		
Rank	Country/Region	Index	Rank	Country/Region	Index	Rank	Country/Region	Index
1	Singapore	71.72	1	Finland	90.58	1	Hong Kong SAR	76.52
2	Hong Kong SAR	68.36	2	Denmark	83.89	2	Singapore	73.41
3	Netherlands	60.76	3	Netherlands	83.30	3	UAE	39.59
4	Finland	58.92	4	Canada	83.09	4	Netherlands	38.23
5	Denmark	58.70	5	Sweden	81.79	5	Belgium	36.19
6	Belgium	55.65	6	Switzerland	78.03	6	Denmark	33.51
7	Sweden	54.94	7	Belgium	75.11	7	Switzerland	29.32
8	Switzerland	53.67	8	New Zealand	74.71	8	Vietnam	28.56
9	UAE	53.01	9	Australia	71.87	9	Sweden	28.09
10	Canada	52.39	10	United States	71.05	10	Finland	27.27
11	Austria	47.37	11	Singapore	70.03	11	Cambodia	25.95
12	Germany	45.85	12	Austria	69.75	12	Slovenia	25.60
13	New Zealand	45.19	13	Germany	69.24	13	Hungary	25.20
14	United Kingdom	44.43	14	UAE	66.44	14	Slovak Republic	25.00
15	Australia	44.17	15	Italy	65.20	15	Austria	25.00
16	Taiwan, China	44.11	16	Taiwan, China	65.10	16	United Kingdom	23.80
17	Vietnam	43.48	17	United Kingdom	65.07	17	Taiwan, China	23.12
18	United States	42.98	18	Korea, Republic of	64.64	18	Germany	22.47
19	Italy	41.14	19	Hong Kong SAR	60.19	19	France	22.36
20	Korea, Republic of	40.99	20	Vietnam	58.39	20	Czechia	22.28
21	France	40.20	21	Indonesia	58.12	21	Canada	21.69

(Continued)

(Continued)

4. Business context			4.1. Structure			4.2. Rivalry		
Rank	Country/Region	Index	Rank	Country/Region	Index	Rank	Country/Region	Index
22	Czechia	38.94	22	France	58.04	22	Oman	21.57
23	Slovenia	37.01	23	India	56.55	23	Malaysia	21.36
24	Malaysia	36.78	24	China	56.07	24	Thailand	19.58
25	Greece	36.64	25	Czechia	55.60	25	Greece	19.45
26	Panama	36.12	26	Peru	55.45	26	Spain	18.87
27	Thailand	35.42	27	Philippines	54.94	27	Croatia	18.67
28	Chile	34.90	28	Colombia	54.92	28	Poland	18.40
29	Spain	34.69	29	Panama	54.07	29	Kuwait	18.23
30	Philippines	34.33	30	Greece	53.83	30	Panama	18.17
31	Indonesia	34.19	31	Chile	53.04	31	Israel	17.49
32	Poland	34.11	32	Malaysia	52.21	32	Korea, Republic of	17.33
33	Kuwait	34.00	33	Thailand	51.26	33	Italy	17.09
34	Peru	33.85	34	Nigeria	51.04	34	Chile	16.77
35	India	33.79	35	Japan	50.58	35	Australia	16.46
36	Colombia	33.43	36	Spain	50.51	36	Ukraine	16.26
37	Japan	33.26	37	Poland	49.82	37	Japan	15.95
38	China	32.98	38	Kuwait	49.78	38	Saudi Arabia	15.76
39	Israel	32.85	39	Argentina	49.27	39	New Zealand	15.66
40	Hungary	32.84	40	Slovenia	48.43	40	Jordan	15.55
41	Jordan	31.81	41	Israel	48.22	41	South Africa	15.26
42	Saudi Arabia	31.29	42	Jordan	48.07	42	Mexico	14.97

43	Dominican Republic	30.29
44	Nigeria	30.02
45	Argentina	29.60
46	South Africa	29.21
47	Türkiye	29.03
48	Cambodia	28.94
49	Mexico	28.89
50	Croatia	28.85
51	Brazil	27.98
52	Slovak Republic	27.27
53	Egypt	26.88
54	Guatemala	26.37
55	Oman	25.10
56	Ukraine	24.71
57	Sri Lanka	23.91
58	Pakistan	23.71
59	Kenya	22.45
60	Bangladesh	22.04
61	Russia	21.16
62	Morocco	14.82

43	Dominican Republic	47.98
44	Saudi Arabia	46.81
45	Türkiye	46.02
46	Brazil	45.08
47	South Africa	43.16
48	Egypt	42.92
49	Mexico	42.81
50	Guatemala	41.84
51	Hungary	40.48
52	Pakistan	39.05
53	Croatia	39.02
54	Sri Lanka	36.61
55	Bangladesh	35.77
56	Ukraine	33.16
57	Kenya	33.15
58	Cambodia	31.93
59	Russia	30.03
60	Slovak Republic	29.53
61	Oman	28.63
62	Morocco	14.94

43	United States	14.90
44	Morocco	14.70
45	Philippines	13.71
46	Dominican Republic	12.59
47	Russia	12.29
48	Peru	12.25
49	Türkiye	12.04
50	Colombia	11.94
51	Kenya	11.75
52	Sri Lanka	11.22
53	India	11.03
54	Guatemala	10.90
55	Brazil	10.88
56	Egypt	10.85
57	Indonesia	10.26
58	Argentina	9.92
59	China	9.88
60	Nigeria	9.01
61	Pakistan	8.38
62	Bangladesh	8.32

Notes: The countries/regions that revealed strengths in the factor of *Business Context* are Singapore, Hong Kong SAR, Netherlands, Finland, and Denmark. The sub-factor *Structure* evaluates the efficiency of business governance and ethical practices within firms. Survey data, including aspects like a firm's decision-making process, the development of unique brands, and equal treatment of domestic and foreign firms, were used to measure these components. Business morality encompasses indices such as social value, ethical practices, health and safety performance, and environmental concerns. *Rivalry* focuses on market openness concerning foreign direct investment, financial portfolio, and trade. Countries with strengths in this sub-factor are more likely to have a higher degree of both domestic and international competition, making them attractive destinations for multinational companies to conduct international business.

	5. (Unskilled) workers			5.1. Quantity of workers			5.2. Quality of workers	
Rank	Country/Region	Index	Rank	Country/Region	Index	Rank	Country/Region	Index
1	China	72.60	1	China	92.61	1	Denmark	86.73
2	Philippines	63.35	2	India	69.91	2	Netherlands	85.58
3	India	63.13	3	Cambodia	68.29	3	Canada	83.43
4	Singapore	62.35	4	Pakistan	67.63	4	Sweden	79.91
5	Mexico	62.30	5	Thailand	64.75	5	Switzerland	79.85
6	Thailand	61.65	6	Mexico	63.83	6	Singapore	77.84
7	Denmark	60.98	7	Guatemala	62.74	7	Taiwan, China	74.49
8	Kuwait	59.91	8	Malaysia	60.80	8	Kuwait	74.28
9	Vietnam	59.83	9	Philippines	60.78	9	Belgium	73.34
10	Poland	59.58	10	Egypt	59.42	10	Australia	72.44
11	Taiwan, China	59.31	11	Ukraine	56.64	11	Italy	67.83
12	Malaysia	59.15	12	Vietnam	56.16	12	New Zealand	67.82
13	Canada	58.88	13	Dominican Republic	54.36	13	Spain	66.71
14	Netherlands	58.16	14	Saudi Arabia	54.08	14	Poland	66.35
15	Panama	57.93	15	Argentina	53.84	15	Philippines	65.92
16	Guatemala	57.76	16	Panama	53.23	16	Austria	65.73
17	Indonesia	56.30	17	Poland	52.81	17	United Kingdom	65.71
18	Switzerland	56.15	18	Indonesia	52.39	18	United States	64.56
19	Sweden	55.58	19	Chile	50.78	19	Germany	64.42
20	Argentina	55.33	20	Brazil	50.49	20	Colombia	63.69
21	Belgium	54.79	21	Jordan	50.24	21	Czechia	63.61

Rank	Country	Value	Rank	Country	Value	Rank	Country	Value
22	Italy	54.12	22	Russia	47.04	22	Nigeria	63.59
23	Korea, Republic of	53.95	23	Singapore	46.86	23	Vietnam	63.49
24	New Zealand	53.69	24	Bangladesh	46.63	24	Panama	62.63
25	United States	53.28	25	Korea, Republic of	46.50	25	Korea, Republic of	61.40
26	Brazil	53.06	26	Oman	46.37	26	Hong Kong SAR	61.37
27	Peru	52.42	27	UAE	46.12	27	Mexico	60.78
28	Hong Kong SAR	52.21	28	Japan	46.02	28	Indonesia	60.20
29	UAE	51.96	29	Kuwait	45.55	29	Peru	59.60
30	Japan	51.91	30	Peru	45.25	30	Israel	59.20
31	United Kingdom	51.62	31	Taiwan, China	44.14	31	Thailand	58.56
32	Chile	51.46	32	Israel	43.56	32	UAE	57.80
33	Israel	51.38	33	Greece	43.15	33	Japan	57.79
34	Nigeria	51.31	34	Hong Kong SAR	43.06	34	Malaysia	57.51
35	Dominican Republic	51.27	35	Slovenia	42.91	35	Türkiye	57.00
36	Australia	51.19	36	Kenya	42.90	36	Argentina	56.82
37	Germany	50.94	37	Sri Lanka	42.43	37	India	56.34
38	Czechia	50.92	38	United States	41.99	38	Greece	56.29
39	Saudi Arabia	50.83	39	Italy	40.41	39	Brazil	55.63
40	Spain	49.91	40	New Zealand	39.56	40	Guatemala	52.78
41	Greece	49.72	41	Nigeria	39.03	41	China	52.60
42	Cambodia	49.16	42	Hungary	38.32	42	Chile	52.14
43	Ukraine	48.29	43	Czechia	38.23	43	Slovenia	51.82
44	Austria	48.16	44	Croatia	38.18	44	Croatia	50.52

(Continued)

(Continued)

| | 5. (Unskilled) workers | | | 5.1. Quantity of workers | | | 5.2. Quality of workers | |
Rank	Country/Region	Index	Rank	Country/Region	Index	Rank	Country/Region	Index
45	Jordan	47.79	45	United Kingdom	37.53	45	France	50.39
46	Slovenia	47.37	46	Germany	37.46	46	Dominican Republic	48.18
47	Pakistan	47.17	47	Finland	37.28	47	Saudi Arabia	47.58
48	Colombia	47.06	48	Belgium	36.24	48	Kenya	47.58
49	Oman	46.28	49	Denmark	35.22	49	Oman	46.19
50	Kenya	45.24	50	Canada	34.34	50	Jordan	45.34
51	Egypt	44.92	51	Slovak Republic	33.52	51	Sri Lanka	43.77
52	Croatia	44.35	52	Morocco	33.46	52	Hungary	40.40
53	Sri Lanka	43.10	53	France	33.46	53	Ukraine	39.93
54	Türkiye	42.21	54	Spain	33.11	54	Bangladesh	34.55
55	France	41.92	55	Switzerland	32.46	55	South Africa	34.03
56	Bangladesh	40.59	56	Sweden	31.25	56	Finland	33.97
57	Russia	39.86	57	Netherlands	30.75	57	Russia	32.68
58	Hungary	39.36	58	Austria	30.60	58	Egypt	30.41
59	Finland	35.62	59	Colombia	30.42	59	Cambodia	30.02
60	Morocco	29.65	60	Australia	29.93	60	Pakistan	26.71
61	Slovak Republic	27.10	61	Türkiye	27.42	61	Morocco	25.85
62	South Africa	17.72	62	South Africa	1.40	62	Slovak Republic	20.68

Notes: China, the Philippines, India, Singapore, and Mexico showed a strong performance in (*Unskilled*) *Workers*. They all demonstrated strong competitiveness in this factor due to their advantage in either the *Quantity of Workers* and *Quality of Workers*, or both. The sub-factor *Quantity of Workers* is evaluated based on factors such as the size of the labor force, employment rate, working hours, and monthly compensation for manufacturing workers. *Quality of Workers* is measured by indicators including literacy rate, attitude and motivation, education, the openness of the labor market, and the relationship between managers and workers. Countries with strengths in this sub-factor are considered to have a relatively favorable attitude among workers and conducive working conditions. Overall, these countries demonstrate strong competitiveness in (*Unskilled*) *Workers*, benefiting from either a large and productive labor force or a high-quality workforce.

6. Policymakers and administrators			6.1. Policymakers			6.2. Administrators		
Rank	Country/Region	Index	Rank	Country/Region	Index	Rank	Country/Region	Index
1	Singapore	92.15	1	Singapore	88.38	1	Singapore	95.91
2	Denmark	88.01	2	Denmark	87.85	2	Switzerland	88.50
3	Switzerland	86.22	3	Switzerland	83.94	3	Denmark	88.17
4	Netherlands	85.91	4	Netherlands	83.68	4	Netherlands	88.15
5	Sweden	83.38	5	Canada	83.23	5	Finland	85.18
6	Finland	81.80	6	Sweden	83.13	6	Hong Kong SAR	83.84
7	Canada	81.60	7	Finland	78.43	7	Sweden	83.64
8	Australia	78.60	8	UAE	78.33	8	Australia	81.45
9	New Zealand	78.47	9	New Zealand	75.76	9	New Zealand	81.18
10	UAE	76.38	10	Australia	75.75	10	Canada	79.97
11	Austria	73.68	11	Austria	74.07	11	Japan	77.16
12	Belgium	71.26	12	Belgium	70.53	12	UAE	74.43
13	Germany	71.08	13	Germany	69.08	13	United States	73.69
14	United States	70.72	14	China	68.96	14	Austria	73.29
15	United Kingdom	69.92	15	United States	67.76	15	Taiwan, China	73.13
16	Taiwan, China	68.88	16	United Kingdom	66.97	16	Germany	73.09
17	Hong Kong SAR	67.29	17	Vietnam	65.80	17	United Kingdom	72.87
18	Japan	67.15	18	Taiwan, China	64.64	18	Belgium	71.99
19	France	66.62	19	France	63.49	19	France	69.75
20	Korea, Republic of	65.53	20	Korea, Republic of	63.05	20	Korea, Republic of	68.01
21	Israel	60.20	21	Saudi Arabia	60.55	21	Israel	63.78

(Continued)

(Continued)

6. Policymakers and administrators			6.1. Policymakers			6.2. Administrators		
Rank	Country/Region	Index	Rank	Country/Region	Index	Rank	Country/Region	Index
22	China	59.55	22	Japan	57.13	22	Chile	60.53
23	Saudi Arabia	58.09	23	Israel	56.63	23	Czechia	55.96
24	Chile	57.61	24	Egypt	55.77	24	Saudi Arabia	55.63
25	Vietnam	54.78	25	India	55.37	25	Slovenia	54.32
26	Czechia	53.32	26	Kuwait	54.89	26	Malaysia	51.76
27	Italy	52.06	27	Chile	54.69	27	Spain	51.38
28	Kuwait	51.40	28	Jordan	52.96	28	Italy	51.32
29	Greece	51.17	29	Italy	52.80	29	Greece	50.36
30	India	50.02	30	Greece	51.99	30	China	50.14
31	Malaysia	49.37	31	Panama	51.61	31	Poland	49.97
32	Panama	48.23	32	Hong Kong SAR	50.74	32	Kuwait	47.91
33	Jordan	47.89	33	Czechia	50.67	33	Panama	44.86
34	Poland	46.84	34	Indonesia	49.87	34	Philippines	44.84
35	Spain	46.67	35	Russia	49.09	35	India	44.68
36	Slovenia	46.49	36	Malaysia	46.98	36	Vietnam	43.76
37	Philippines	45.88	37	Oman	46.91	37	Oman	43.12
38	Indonesia	45.14	38	Philippines	46.91	38	Jordan	42.81
39	Oman	45.02	39	Cambodia	46.84	39	Colombia	42.21
40	Colombia	43.93	40	Colombia	45.65	40	Indonesia	40.41
41	Egypt	43.01	41	Bangladesh	44.89	41	Hungary	39.65
42	Russia	40.24	42	Poland	43.71	42	Slovak Republic	38.95

#			#			#		
43	Hungary	37.56	43	Spain	41.97	43	Croatia	36.60
44	Argentina	37.33	44	Argentina	39.52	44	Thailand	35.84
45	Thailand	36.42	45	Slovenia	38.67	45	Argentina	35.15
46	Dominican Republic	35.67	46	Nigeria	38.31	46	Dominican Republic	34.94
47	Cambodia	35.26	47	Pakistan	38.22	47	Türkiye	34.72
48	Türkiye	35.08	48	Thailand	37.00	48	Brazil	32.10
49	Bangladesh	33.85	49	Dominican Republic	36.40	49	Russia	31.40
50	Peru	31.78	50	Hungary	35.47	50	Peru	31.16
51	Pakistan	31.49	51	Türkiye	35.45	51	Egypt	30.25
52	Brazil	30.84	52	Mexico	32.85	52	Kenya	27.44
53	Nigeria	30.67	53	Morocco	32.84	53	Morocco	26.55
54	Slovak Republic	30.59	54	Ukraine	32.65	54	South Africa	26.52
55	Morocco	29.70	55	Peru	32.41	55	Ukraine	25.51
56	Croatia	29.26	56	Kenya	30.66	56	Pakistan	24.76
57	Ukraine	29.08	57	Guatemala	29.67	57	Sri Lanka	24.48
58	Kenya	29.05	58	Brazil	29.59	58	Mexico	24.38
59	Mexico	28.62	59	Slovak Republic	22.23	59	Cambodia	23.69
60	Guatemala	25.67	60	Croatia	21.93	60	Nigeria	23.04
61	South Africa	24.01	61	South Africa	21.50	61	Bangladesh	22.81
62	Sri Lanka	19.28	62	Sri Lanka	14.08	62	Guatemala	21.66

Notes: The countries that showed strengths in the factor of *Policymakers & Administrators* are Singapore, Denmark, Switzerland, Netherlands, and Sweden. *Policymakers* are evaluated based on five criteria, which include (1) the effectiveness of parliament/congress processes, (2) legislative outcomes, (3) ethics, (4) education level, and (5) the international experience of policymakers. Similarly, *Administrators* are measured using five criteria, which encompass (1) the efficiency of policy implementation processes, (2) the effectiveness of policy outcomes, (3) ethics, (4) education level, and (5) the international experience of bureaucrats. Economies that exhibit strengths in both sub-factors are recognized for their high competitiveness in terms of ethical standards, international experience, quality regulations, and efficient policy implementation capabilities.

	7. Entrepreneurs			7.1. Personal competence			7.2. Social context	
Rank	Country/Region	Index	Rank	Country/Region	Index	Rank	Country/Region	Index
1	United States	80.76	1	United States	80.86	1	Netherlands	89.13
2	Netherlands	80.05	2	Denmark	76.51	2	Denmark	83.32
3	Denmark	79.91	3	Canada	75.40	3	United States	80.67
4	Canada	76.82	4	New Zealand	72.92	4	Sweden	80.25
5	Sweden	75.91	5	Switzerland	72.29	5	Singapore	79.58
6	Singapore	74.48	6	Belgium	72.21	6	UAE	79.30
7	Switzerland	73.53	7	Finland	72.09	7	Canada	78.24
8	Finland	71.76	8	Sweden	71.58	8	United Kingdom	76.98
9	UAE	70.64	9	Netherlands	70.96	9	Switzerland	74.77
10	United Kingdom	70.59	10	Singapore	69.37	10	Finland	71.43
11	New Zealand	70.26	11	Hong Kong SAR	67.93	11	Australia	71.09
12	Hong Kong SAR	68.15	12	Czechia	65.76	12	Hong Kong SAR	68.37
13	Belgium	67.84	13	Australia	64.34	13	New Zealand	67.61
14	Australia	67.71	14	United Kingdom	64.19	14	Taiwan, China	66.15
15	Germany	62.63	15	Colombia	62.90	15	Germany	65.36
16	Austria	61.95	16	Austria	62.55	16	Belgium	63.48
17	Czechia	59.13	17	UAE	61.98	17	China	61.36
18	Taiwan, China	58.63	18	Germany	59.90	18	Austria	61.36
19	Israel	58.48	19	Israel	57.15	19	Korea, Republic of	60.43
20	Chile	57.07	20	Chile	56.58	20	Israel	59.82
21	China	56.41	21	France	56.45	21	Poland	57.68

22	France	55.58	22	Saudi Arabia	55.38	22	Chile	57.56
23	Colombia	55.06	23	India	54.23	23	France	54.72
24	Korea, Republic of	53.35	24	China	51.47	24	Vietnam	52.93
25	Saudi Arabia	52.94	25	Mexico	51.44	25	Czechia	52.49
26	India	51.40	26	Taiwan, China	51.11	26	Slovenia	52.44
27	Indonesia	50.48	27	Indonesia	50.64	27	Saudi Arabia	50.50
28	Slovenia	50.29	28	Italy	48.75	28	Indonesia	50.32
29	Poland	49.86	29	Croatia	48.75	29	Italy	49.90
30	Italy	49.33	30	Malaysia	48.49	30	India	48.56
31	Malaysia	48.06	31	Slovenia	48.15	31	Malaysia	47.62
32	Mexico	47.27	32	Dominican Republic	46.90	32	Colombia	47.22
33	Dominican Republic	46.92	33	Korea, Republic of	46.28	33	Kuwait	47.21
34	Panama	45.41	34	Slovak Republic	44.98	34	Dominican Republic	46.93
35	Kuwait	45.04	35	Jordan	44.63	35	Thailand	46.91
36	Spain	43.23	36	Panama	44.10	36	Panama	46.71
37	Jordan	43.14	37	Oman	43.25	37	Türkiye	46.26
38	Türkiye	41.47	38	Spain	43.17	38	Japan	44.71
39	Oman	40.70	39	Kuwait	42.86	39	Spain	43.30
40	Thailand	40.30	40	Poland	42.03	40	Mexico	43.10
41	Slovak Republic	39.98	41	Hungary	41.17	41	Peru	42.54
42	Croatia	38.61	42	South Africa	40.65	42	Philippines	41.97
43	Hungary	38.26	43	Nigeria	39.09	43	Jordan	41.65
44	Japan	38.16	44	Guatemala	38.98	44	Egypt	41.49

(Continued)

(Continued)

7. Entrepreneurs			7.1. Personal competence			7.2. Social context		
Rank	Country/Region	Index	Rank	Country/Region	Index	Rank	Country/Region	Index
45	Peru	37.49	45	Greece	37.13	45	Oman	38.15
46	Philippines	37.33	46	Türkiye	36.68	46	Kenya	38.12
47	Greece	37.07	47	Brazil	35.16	47	Morocco	37.28
48	Egypt	37.06	48	Thailand	33.70	48	Greece	37.01
49	South Africa	36.93	49	Pakistan	33.35	49	Russia	35.98
50	Nigeria	35.42	50	Philippines	32.69	50	Hungary	35.36
51	Vietnam	34.95	51	Egypt	32.63	51	Slovak Republic	34.99
52	Guatemala	34.31	52	Peru	32.44	52	South Africa	33.22
53	Morocco	33.12	53	Japan	31.61	53	Argentina	33.13
54	Brazil	32.10	54	Morocco	28.96	54	Nigeria	31.74
55	Kenya	31.94	55	Kenya	25.77	55	Ukraine	31.36
56	Pakistan	31.58	56	Bangladesh	25.52	56	Pakistan	29.80
57	Argentina	27.80	57	Sri Lanka	24.89	57	Guatemala	29.65
58	Russia	25.68	58	Argentina	22.47	58	Cambodia	29.09
59	Bangladesh	24.97	59	Cambodia	17.21	59	Brazil	29.03
60	Cambodia	23.15	60	Vietnam	16.98	60	Croatia	28.47
61	Sri Lanka	21.82	61	Russia	15.39	61	Bangladesh	24.41
62	Ukraine	20.77	62	Ukraine	10.18	62	Sri Lanka	18.76

Notes: The countries that showed strong performance in the factor of *Entrepreneurs* include the US, Netherlands, Denmark, Canada, and Sweden. The sub-factor, *Personal Competence*, is evaluated based on criteria such as the decision-making process, core competencies of entrepreneurs, education level, and international experience. These factors contribute to the overall competence and capability of entrepreneurs. *Social Context* consists of criteria such as the availability of entrepreneurs, support from the social system, openness to foreign entrepreneurs, new business development, and the social status of entrepreneurs. These factors assess the broader social environment in which entrepreneurship thrives. Overall, these countries exhibit strong competitiveness in the *Entrepreneurs* factor, leveraging the personal competence of entrepreneurs and the supportive social contexts for entrepreneurial endeavors.

	8. Professionals			8.1. Personal competence			8.2. Social context	
Rank	Country/Region	Index	Rank	Country/Region	Index	Rank	Country/Region	Index
1	Netherlands	83.96	1	Netherlands	81.82	1	Netherlands	86.11
2	Singapore	82.10	2	Singapore	81.77	2	Denmark	83.29
3	UAE	79.80	3	Finland	80.10	3	Switzerland	82.65
4	Denmark	79.29	4	UAE	77.48	4	Singapore	82.43
5	Switzerland	77.40	5	Denmark	75.28	5	UAE	82.11
6	United States	74.35	6	United States	73.39	6	Canada	76.93
7	Canada	73.26	7	Switzerland	72.14	7	United States	75.32
8	Sweden	71.52	8	Canada	69.60	8	Belgium	75.05
9	Finland	70.46	9	Taiwan, China	69.58	9	Sweden	74.15
10	Belgium	69.50	10	Sweden	68.89	10	Australia	71.62
11	United Kingdom	67.90	11	Vietnam	67.65	11	United Kingdom	69.55
12	Taiwan, China	67.11	12	United Kingdom	66.26	12	New Zealand	65.90
13	Australia	65.96	13	Indonesia	64.82	13	Hong Kong SAR	65.16
14	Vietnam	65.66	14	Hong Kong SAR	64.41	14	Indonesia	65.10
15	Indonesia	64.96	15	Belgium	63.94	15	Taiwan, China	64.65
16	Hong Kong SAR	64.78	16	Korea, Republic of	63.48	16	Germany	64.56
17	Korea, Republic of	64.01	17	Austria	63.40	17	Korea, Republic of	64.54
18	Austria	62.31	18	India	61.30	18	Vietnam	63.67
19	New Zealand	61.96	19	China	60.83	19	India	61.72
20	Germany	61.59	20	Philippines	60.37	20	Austria	61.22
21	India	61.51	21	Nigeria	60.31	21	Finland	60.82

(*Continued*)

(Continued)

	8. Professionals			8.1. Personal competence			8.2. Social context	
Rank	Country/Region	Index	Rank	Country/Region	Index	Rank	Country/Region	Index
22	China	59.93	22	Australia	60.30	22	Kuwait	59.72
23	Czechia	58.81	23	Czechia	58.84	23	China	59.03
24	Philippines	58.57	24	Saudi Arabia	58.70	24	Czechia	58.78
25	Saudi Arabia	56.53	25	Germany	58.63	25	Dominican Republic	58.72
26	Kuwait	56.03	26	Greece	58.34	26	Italy	58.24
27	Poland	54.94	27	New Zealand	58.01	27	Philippines	56.77
28	Italy	54.91	28	Panama	55.99	28	Poland	55.37
29	Panama	54.44	29	Poland	54.50	29	Chile	55.19
30	Dominican Republic	54.07	30	Israel	52.43	30	Saudi Arabia	54.37
31	Israel	52.53	31	Kuwait	52.34	31	Malaysia	53.42
32	Nigeria	51.75	32	Colombia	52.34	32	Panama	52.89
33	Greece	51.71	33	Italy	51.58	33	Israel	52.64
34	Thailand	51.21	34	Thailand	51.36	34	Slovenia	52.51
35	Colombia	50.96	35	Argentina	50.60	35	Peru	52.11
36	Malaysia	50.04	36	Cambodia	50.40	36	Thailand	51.06
37	Cambodia	49.97	37	Dominican Republic	49.43	37	Colombia	49.59
38	Chile	49.95	38	Türkiye	48.57	38	Cambodia	49.53
39	Argentina	49.40	39	Croatia	47.57	39	Japan	48.73
40	Slovenia	48.25	40	Hungary	47.39	40	South Africa	48.52
41	Peru	48.10	41	Jordan	47.38	41	Argentina	48.20
42	Japan	47.86	42	Japan	46.99	42	France	47.72
43	Jordan	46.61	43	Malaysia	46.67	43	Egypt	46.81

44	Türkiye	46.35	44	Mexico	46.62	44	Jordan	45.84
45	Spain	45.53	45	Spain	45.66	45	Spain	45.39
46	Hungary	45.40	46	Chile	44.71	46	Greece	45.07
47	France	45.34	47	Peru	44.09	47	Bangladesh	44.55
48	Mexico	44.93	48	Slovenia	43.99	48	Türkiye	44.13
49	South Africa	44.70	49	France	42.95	49	Kenya	43.57
50	Croatia	44.02	50	Bangladesh	41.04	50	Hungary	43.41
51	Bangladesh	42.80	51	South Africa	40.88	51	Mexico	43.25
52	Egypt	42.56	52	Brazil	39.31	52	Nigeria	43.19
53	Brazil	41.13	53	Pakistan	38.31	53	Brazil	42.96
54	Kenya	40.73	54	Egypt	38.31	54	Croatia	40.46
55	Pakistan	39.10	55	Kenya	37.89	55	Pakistan	39.88
56	Ukraine	38.55	56	Ukraine	37.23	56	Ukraine	39.88
57	Sri Lanka	33.84	57	Sri Lanka	34.97	57	Morocco	39.00
58	Slovak Republic	31.40	58	Guatemala	30.19	58	Slovak Republic	33.89
59	Morocco	31.27	59	Slovak Republic	28.92	59	Sri Lanka	32.72
60	Russia	29.09	60	Oman	28.47	60	Russia	30.98
61	Oman	28.36	61	Russia	27.20	61	Oman	28.24
62	Guatemala	27.71	62	Morocco	23.54	62	Guatemala	25.22

Notes: The competitive countries for the factor of *Professionals* are Netherlands, Singapore, UAE, Denmark, and Finland. The sub-factor *Personal Competence* of Professionals is evaluated based on five survey criteria, which include (1) decision-making abilities among professionals, (2) opportunity management skills, (3) core competencies of professionals, (4) education level, and (5) international experiences. These criteria gauge the overall competence and capabilities of professionals. *Social Context* is measured using five survey data points, including (1) availability of professionals, (2) mobility within the professional field, (3) compensation levels, (4) social status of professionals, and (5) market openness to foreign professionals. These factors provide insights into the supportive social environment and opportunities available for professionals. Overall, these countries excel in the factor *Professionals* due to their competent professionals and favorable social contexts that facilitate professional development and attract talent from around the world.

Index

business concept, 285
business ecosystem, 278

C
Canada, 78
Carr, N., 142
causal loop diagrams (CLDs),
222–224, 226, 228–232, 238
central knowledge districts (CKDs),
135
ChatGPT, 1–4, 16, 18, 34, 55, 103,
109, 114
Chile, 90
China, 57, 66, 75, 85
citizen-centered, 151
class reference experimentation,
143
cloud computing, 102, 109
cluster-based growth strategies, 145
CNC systems, 140
co-creative approaches, 151
cohesion, 146
communitarian, 148
competitive advantages, 181
competitiveness, 144–145, 160,
220–222, 233
complex adaptive innovation
ecosystems, 138
computer *Watson*, 108
conceptual, analytical clarification,
143
convenience sampling method, 282
cooperative strategies, 221
core–periphery pattern of FDI, 165
Cortivision, 177
CosmoEye, 178
cost strategy (CS), 36–37, 43, 59
cost strategy index (CSI), 35
COVID-19 pandemic, 274
cryptocurrencies, 118
Current Competitiveness Index
(CCI), 29

cyber-security, 103, 180
Czech Republic, 87

D
decentralized autonomous
organizations (DAOs), 119
decision-making algorithms, 143
DEE concepts, 296
DEE elements, 275
DEE framework, 273, 275
Deep Blue, 108
deep learning, 115, 139, 143
Denmark, 78
depopulation, 160
destructive creation, 129
developing country context, 295
development strategies, 189–192,
207, 212
differentiation strategy (DS), 36–37,
43, 59
digital citizenship, 288, 296
digital entrepreneurial ecosystem,
273, 276
digital entrepreneurial firms,
295
digital entrepreneurship, 274, 276
digital entrepreneurship ecosystem,
288
digital entrepreneurship scheme,
278
digital infrastructure, 303, 320
digital law, 290
digital platforms, 113, 274
digital technologies, 103–104, 303,
307
digital transformation, 306, 319
Digital Transformation Acceleration
Programme, 316
digital venture, 278
digitization, 105, 118
disruptive innovation, 141
disruptive urban AI regime, 132

spatial clusters, 149
STEM subjects, 136
sustainability, 143, 146
sustainable economic growth, 276
Sweden, 80
Switzerland, 79
systems thinking, 222–223, 232–233

T
Taiwan, China, 85
Tanzania, 188–192, 194–210,
    212–213
Tech City, 137
technical knowledge, 288
technical training, 285
technological culture, 259
technological gentrification, 132, 142
technology adoption, 159
technology-based SMEs, 279
technopoles, 131
term-priority matrix, 38, 41, 64, 66, 73
*The Competitive Advantage of
    Nations*, 5
Three Vs, 106
TIME magazine, 115
training climate, 285

U
UAE, 80
United Kingdom, 84

United Nations Sustainable
    Development Goals, 144
United States, 57, 75, 79
unmanned aviation industry, 178
untapped market, 295
urban AI regime, 129
urban development, 141
urban entrepreneurship, 145
urban technopoles, 135
utopian pragmatist policy, 146

V
value creation, 277
Vietnam, 91
virtual reality, 180
Virtuar, 180
vulnerability, uncertainty, complexity,
    and ambiguity (VUCA), 160

W
Web 2.0, 296
welfare statism, 147
wireless local area network (WLAN),
    105
World Economic Forum (WEF),
    28–30, 43, 103
World Wide Web, 104

Z
Zuboff, S., 142

Printed in the United States
by Baker & Taylor Publisher Services